LIGHT AND TRUTH;

COLLECTED FROM

THE BIBLE AND ANCIENT AND MODERN HISTORY,

CONTAINING THE

UNIVERSAL HISTORY

OF THE

COLORED AND THE INDIAN RACE,

FROM THE CREATION OF THE WORLD
TO THE PRESENT TIME.

BY R. B. LEWIS,

A COLORED MAN.

Search this work with care and candor;
Every line and page you read
Will brighten all the truths of Scripture,
Proved by history — plain indeed.

BOSTON:

PUBLISHED BY A COMMITTEE OF COLORED GENTLEMEN.

BENJAMIN F. ROBERTS, PRINTER.

1844.

Must Have Books
503 Deerfield Place
Victoria, BC
V9B 6G5
Canada

ISBN: 9781773236957

Copyright 2021 – Must Have Books

INTRODUCTION.

WE publish this volume of collections from sacred and profane history, with a determination that a correct knowledge of the Colored and Indian people, ancient and modern, may be extended freely, unbiassed by any prejudicial effects from descent or station. In this country, where the former are subjected to the deepest degradation — where every variety of persecution is measured out to this unfortunate race, it is highly expedient that "Light and Truth" should be promulgated, in order that oppressors shall not consider it an indispensable duty to trample upon the weak and defenceless. In a large portion of this country, men, women and children, belonging to this race, are held as articles of merchandize by the whites; the iron heart of gain hath forgotten every sacred and social relation, while, at its expense, millions have perished on the cursed rack. The history of this class is well known in many states in this country. But in some countries a mighty contrast is visible; colored men enjoy every inherent attainment, free from human interference.

The Indians in this country are also an abused people. The lofty hills the verdant plains, and the beautiful vallies that the poor Indian, only three centuries since, could proudly call his own, are now possessed by a foreign people. Here and there we see a wanderer; they have been driven from their homes to inhabit the wilderness west of the Rocky Mountains. In other countries this class are more happily situated.

The author of this compilation has been some years in gathering this information. He is a descendant of the two races he so ably vindicates. His manuscripts have been inspected by several learned gentlemen, who recommend them in the highest terms. Among his subscriptions, we find persons in every situation in society. Quite a number of clergymen of the different denominations, lawyers, doctors, &c., &c., comprise a majority of the subscribers.

We, the undersigned, in consideration of the valuable information contained in this work, and in behalf of the welfare of the Colored and Indian race, submit the same to a candid perusal.

THOMAS DALTON,
CHARLES H. ROBERTS,
ANDRESS V. LEWIS,
JAMES SCOTT,
} *Publishing Committee.*

Boston, January 25, 1844.

CONTENTS.

CHAPTER I.— THE HISTORY OF MAN.

Primitive Man — The Land of Ethiopia, . . 9
The fall of Man — His Location, . . . 10
The Sons of Adam, ... 10
The Generation of Adam, ... 11
The Sons of Noah, ... 13
The Generations of Ham, ... 15
The Generations of Japhet, . . . 18
The Blessings and Generations of Abraham, . . 19
The Two Nations of Isaac, ... 23
The Generations of Esau — The Red People, . 24
The People of Ethiopia, ... 25
The Descendants of Egypt, ... 26
The Generations of Jacob, ... 30

CHAPTER II.— ANCIENT CITIES AND KINGDOMS.

Cities of Ethiopia, ... 40
The Kingdom of Assyria, ... 43
The Kingdom of Ethiopia, ... 46
The Kingdom of Egypt, ... 48
The Cities of Egypt, ... 50
The Land of Canaan, ... 63
The Towns and Cities of Jordan, . . . 73
The Cities of Judea, ... 79
The Cities of Galilee, ... 89
The Cities of Asia Minor, ... 91
The Cities of Persia and Media, . . . 96
The Kingdom and Cities of Syria, . . . 98
Cities of Africa, ... 103

Cities of Arabia, ... 107
The Cities of Edom, ... 110
The Amalekites, ... 111
The Cities of Moab, ... 112
The Grecian Cities, ... 114
The Roman Empire, ... 115
The Kingdom of Macedonia, . . . 117
The Islands of the Mediterranean, . . 119
African Islands, ... 122

Chapter III.

Antiquity of America, ... 124

Chapter IV.—Ancient Kings and Wars.

Abraham the Prince, a Conqueror of Kings, . . 128
The Ethiopian Kings of Egypt, . . . 129
The Character of Julius Cæsar, . . . 137
A Comparison of Cæsar with Cato, . . . 138
The Character of Cato, ... 139
The Egyptians rise against Persia supported by the Athenians, 140
The Ancient Kings, ... 142
Darius's Conquest of India, &c., . . . 152
Alexander, ... 153
The Overthrow of the Persian Empire, . . 154
The History of Xerxes, ... 154
Arabian Kings, ... 163
The Ethiopian Kings of Babylon and Assyria, . . 164
The Kings of Abyssinia, ... 169
The Kings of the Hebrews, ... 170
The Kings of Judah, ... 172
The Kings of Israel, ... 177
The Governors of Judea, ... 180
The Kings of Syria, ... 182
The Governors of Syria, ... 185
The Kings of Rome, ... 185
The List of Judges and Term of Service, . . 188
The Judges of Israel, ... 189

Chapter V.— Colored Generals and Soldiers.

Hanno, ... 193
Hamilcar, ... 193
Imilcon, ... 194
Hannibal, ... 194
Scipio Africanus, ... 195
Pompey, ... 197
Cimon, ... 199
Belisarius, ... 200
Col. Henry Diaz, ... 201
Colored Soldiers, ... 206
The last American War with Great Britain, . . 207
Proclamation to the Free People of Color, . . 209

Chapter VI.—Destruction of Jerusalem.

The Great City of Jerusalem, ... 210
The Upper City, ... 211
The Lower City, ... 211
A Description of Solomon's Temple, . . 212
The Destruction of Jerusalem, ... 217
Destruction of the Jews, ... 243

Chapter VII.— The Present State of Judah and Israel.

The Hebrews or Israelites, the Jews, . . . 246
The Indian Tribes in America, . . . 249
The True Christians in this Land are Indians, . . 273

Chapter VIII.—The Arts and Sciences.

Early Discoveries, Inventions, &c. . . . 280
Astronomy, ... 287
Rhetoric, ... 289
Architecture, ... 289
The Lake of Mœris, ... 298
Temples of Egypt, ... 301
The Explanation of Five Grand Virtues, . . 302

The Grecian Philosophers, ... 303
The Roman Philosophers, ... 303

Chapter IX.

Modern Eminent Colored Men, ... 304

Chapter X.— The Great Historical Ages.

Ancient Historians, ... 309
Ancient Poets, ... 311
A Short View of Augustine's City of God, . . 315
Modern Historians, ... 326
Female Writers, ... 330
Burning of the Libraries, ... 334

Chapter XI.— The Ancient Arabians.

The Arabic Language, ... 337
The Word Negro, ... 339
The Hair of Men's Heads, ... 343
The Rock of Gibraltar, ... 343
The Moorish Castle, ... 343

Chapter XII.— History of the Prophets.

History of the Prophets, ... 347
Shepherds of Antiquity, ... 360
The Generation of Jesus Christ, . . . 362
The Birth of Jesus Christ, ... 367

Chapter XIII.— Periods, &c.

Periods, ... 369
Chronological Table, from A. D. 826 to 1791, . 370

Chapter XIV.—St. Domingo or Hayti.

Hayti, ... 385
Extracts from the Letter of the Abbe Gregoire, . 396
Colored Republics of Guiana, . . . 398
Scale of Complexion, ... 400

LIGHT AND TRUTH.

CHAPTER I.

THE HISTORY OF MAN.

PRIMITIVE MAN — THE LAND OF ETHIOPIA.

THE CREATION took place 4004 years before the Christian era, according to the Jewish computation. In the sixth day of the creation, God created man, in his own image. "In the Image of God created He him; male and female created He them."—(Gen. i. 27.) "And the Lord God formed man of the dust of the ground, and breathed into his nostrils the breath of life, and man became a living soul."—(Gen. ii. 7.) [The scriptures evidently distinguish between the spirit and soul.—(1 Thess. v. 23: Heb. iv. 12.) The word which we call soul is used to denote mere animal life, the seat of sensations, appetites and passions.—(Gen. 1: 20.) Here the word translated *life* is the same with that which is elsewhere translated *soul*. Hence we have our bodies and animal life in common with brutes; but the spirit, which was created in the likeness or image of God, and which raises man above the brutes that perish, makes him a rational and accountable being.]—(Gen. i. 26, 27: ii. 7.)

Adam, the first person, was created of the dust of the earth; and the Lord God formed the dust into an inanimate figure, and made a *man*. Eve, the second person, was formed of a rib taken out of man's side, and called a *woman*. "And the Lord God took the man, and put

2

him into the Garden of Eden, to dress it and to keep it."
— (Gen. ii. 15.) The location of this garden was eastward from Canaan, and north from the river Gihon, the
land of Ethiopia. — (Gen. ii. 13.) The soil of Eden
was very rich, and *black;* it produced the richest fruit
and trees of all the earth.

THE FALL OF MAN — HIS LOCATION.

THE transgression of Adam and Eve, commonly called
the fall of man, took place, probably, soon after the creation, and has been most awful in its consequences. For
their transgression, Adam and his companion were driv-
en out of the garden, to till the ground of Ethiopia, it
needing cultivation in consequence of the curse.—(Gen.
iii. 17.) Adam and his posterity settled on the river Gihon, that went out of the Garden of Eden, and compassed the whole land (or country) of Ethiopia; and they
tilled the ground, from which Adam was taken. — (Gen.
ii. 13: iii. 23.)

The word *Adam* is derived as follows: Adam, Adamah,
Adami, Admah — which means *earthy.* The earth is a
rich, dark substance, and from it our first parents were
taken. Now if we admit that Dr. Brown's and other Bible Dictionaries are correct in their explanations of the
meaning of terms, then the deduction must be that Ethiopia (Gen. ii. 13,) was *black,* and the first people were
Ethiopians, or blacks.

THE SONS OF ADAM.

CAIN and Abel were the first offspring of Adam and
Eve. Cain was a tiller of the ground; Abel a keeper of
sheep. In process of time, it came to pass that Cain
brought, of the fruit of the ground, an offering unto the
Lord; and Abel, he also brought of the firstlings of his
flock, and of the fat thereof. And the Lord had respect
unto Abel and to his offering; but unto Cain and to his
offering he had not respect. Hence arose, on the part
of Cain, a disaffection towards his brother, which resulted in the death of Abel, about thirty years after the cre-

ation. This was the first instance of death (temporal) in our world; and of death by the hands of a fellow man — a brother.

Adam's third son, Seth, was born A. M. 130.

The foundation of the first antediluvian empire was laid by the sons and sons' sons of Adam; and lasted the space of 1656 years. This was the empire of Ethiopia.

Cain went out from the presence of the Lord, and dwelt in the land of Nod, *on the east of Eden*, (now Persia.) "And Cain knew his wife; and she conceived, and bare Enoch; and he builded a city, and called it after the name of his son, Enoch." — (Gen. iv. 16, 17.)

THE GENERATION OF ADAM.

ADAM was a man formed of the earth, reddish in color. — (Josephus; Genesis, ch. 1, 2, 4 and 5.)

Adam begat Seth, and died at the age of 930 years.

Seth begat Enos, and died at the age of 912 years.

Enos begat Cainan, and died at the age of 905 years.

Cainan begat Mahalaleel, and died at the age of 910 years.

Mahalaleel begat Jared, and died at the age of 895 years.

Jared begat Enoch, and died at the age of 962 years.

Enoch begat Methuselah, and, at the age 365, " was not, for God took him."

Methuselah begat Lamech, and died at the age of 969 years.

Lamech begat Noah, and died at the age of 777 years.

And Noah was 500 years old; and Noah begat Shem, Ham and Japhet.

Lamech, the fifth in descent from Cainan, was the father of Jabal, who first lived in tents, and owned cattle — and of Jubal, "the father of all such as handle the harp and the organ" — and of Tubalcain, "an instructor of every artificer in brass and iron." Thus early did the necessities of man establish the right of property, and originate the mechanical arts; and the patriarchal government which existed in the antediluvian ages—the knowledge and experience acquired in a life of many

centuries — must have been favorable to a high degree
of perfection in these arts, and the science of music.

In the six hundredth year of Noah, and 2348 years
before Christ, "the flood of waters was upon the earth."
The prediction of the deluge to Noah was of the nature
of a warning to him, in order that he might prepare himself against it.   A knowledge of the deluge was communicated to him 120 years before the event took place.
It entirely covered the earth; and destroyed all the inhabitants, with the exception of the eight individuals who
composed Noah's family, and a pair of each species of
animals — all of whom were preserved in the ark.   The
ark was built in expectation of the flood; it was a structure 480 feet or more in length, 81 in breath, and 41 in
height.   It was sufficiently capacious to answer the purpose for which it was designed; and was three stories
high, containing many small compartments for the suitable accommodation of its intended occupants.

At the appointed time, the family of Noah — and all
kinds of beasts, birds and reptiles, by pairs — went into
the ark.   "And God blessed righteous Noah and his
family; and the Lord shut him in, in the six hundredth
year of Noah's life, in the second month, the seventeenth
day of the month."

This period embraces 1656 years from the creation.*

Noah and his companions came out of the ark 2347
years before Christ, to till and replenish the earth.   And
Noah builded an altar unto the Lord, and took of every
clean beast and of every clean fowl, and offered burnt
offerings upon the altar.   And Noah and his family soon
journeyed from Mount Ararat eastward to Armenia; and
the whole earth was of one language and of one speech.
And it came to pass, as they journeyed from the east,
that they found a plain in the land of Shinar, (Chaldea,)
and they dwelt there.   And they said one to another, Go
to, let us make brick, and burn them thoroughly.   And
they had brick for stone, and slime had they for mortar.
And they said, Go to, let us build a city, and a tower,

_____

* According to the time used in scripture, Noah and his companions continued in the ark one year and ten days.   The ark floated on the waters 150
days, and then rested on one of the summits of Mt. Ararat; but it was several months before the waters entirely subsided.

whose top may reach unto heaven; and let us make us a name, lest we be scattered abroad upon the face of the whole earth. And the Lord came down to see the city and the tower, which the children of men builded. And the Lord said, Behold, the people is one, and they have all one language, and this they begin to do; and now nothing will be restrained from them which they have imagined to do. Go to, let us go down, and there confound their language, that they may not understand each other's speech. So the Lord scattered them abroad from thence upon the face of all the earth. This important event, recorded in Gen. xi., occurred about 2160 years before Christ, and was the origin of the division of the human family into distinct nations.

THE SONS OF NOAH.

The sons of Noah who went forth out of the ark, were Shem, Ham and Japhet — and of them was the whole earth peopled.

To the descendants of Ham, I have generally given the name of *Ethiopians* — blacks with frizzled or curly hair. The descendants of Shem were denominated *Assyrians* and *Syrians* — blacks with long straight hair.

Shem had five sons — Elam, Ashur, Arphaxad, Aram and Laud — who inhabited the land from the Euphrates to the Indian Ocean and Abyssinia.

Elam left a posterity called Elamites — the ancestors of the Persians.

Ashur lived at the city of Nineveh, and named his subjects Assyrians, who became the most fortunate nation.

Arphaxad named the Arphaxadites, now called the Chaldeans.

From Aram sprang the Aramites, whom the Greeks call Syrians.

Laud founded the Ladites, who are now called the Lydians.

Aram had four sons — Uz, Ul, Gather and Mesa.

Uz founded Trachonitis and Damascus — between Palestine and Celosyria.

Ul founded Armenia; and from Gather sprang the Bactrians.

Mesa was the progenitor of the Mesaneans, whose country is now called Chaax Spaani.

Sala was the son of Arphaxad, and Heber was the son of Sala. From Heber the Jews received the name of Hebrews; he was among their progenitors, according to Josephus. Heber begat Jactan, and Phaleg, who was thus called, because he was born at the dispersion of the nations. Phaleg's sons were Elmodad, Saleph, Asermoth, Jerah, Adoram, Aizel, Decla, Eba, Abimael, Sabeus, Ophir, Euilat and Jobab. — These settled on the Cophen, an Indian river, and in a part of Asia near it.

The son of Shem was Arphaxad.

The son of Arphaxad was Salah.

The son of Salah was Eber.

The son of Eber was Peleg.

The son of Peleg was Reu.

The son of Reu was Serug.

The son of Serug was Nahor.

The son of Nahor was Terah.

The son of Terah was Abram, afterwards called Abraham.

The sons of Abraham were Ishmael and Isaac.

Ishmael grew up, and married a wife, by birth an Egyptian, from whence his own mother herself was originally derived. By this wife were born to Ishmael twelve sons—Nabaiath, Keder, Abdeel, Mabsam, Idumas, Masmaos, Mason, Chodaa, Theman, Jetur, Naphesus and Kadmud. These inhabited all the country from the Euphrates to the Red Sea, and called it Nabatene. They are an Arabian nation, and name their tribes from these, both because of their own virtue, and because of the dignity of Abraham, their father. — (Josephus.)

The sons of Abraham, by Keturah, were Zimran, Jokshan, Medam, Midian, Ishbak and Shua.

The sons of Jokshan were Saba and Dedan.

The sons of Dedan were Asshurim, Letushim and Leummim.

The sons of Midian were Ephah, Epher, Hanoch, Abidah and Eldaah. All these were the offspring of Keturah, the Canaanitish woman. — (Gen. xxv.)

The sons of Esau were Eliphaz, Reuel or Jethro, Jeush, Jaalam and Korah.

THE HISTORY OF MAN.

The sons of Eliphaz were Teman, Omar, Zephi, Gatam, Kenaz, Timna and Amalek.

The sons of Reuel were Nahath, Zerah, Shammah and Mizzah—the sons of Esau by the daughter of Ishmael.—(Gen. xxxvi. Chron. i.)

These were the generations of Shem, after their families and tongues, in their countries and nation; they are called blacks by a Grecian historian—being a people with long, straight hair.

THE GENERATIONS OF HAM.

THE meaning or signification of the following words is found in Dr. Brown's Dictionary of the Bible: "Ethiopia"—blackness; "Ethiopians"—black; "Cush"—Ethiopians—black; "Cushen," "Cushi," "Cuth," "Cuthah"—Ethiopia, blackness.

That portion of the earth which was first peopled, after Adam and Eve had left Paradise, was the land of Ethiopia, by the Ethiopians, on the river Gihon, that went out of the Garden of Eden, "which compasseth the whole land (or country) of Ethiopia," 4003 years before Christ.—(Gen. ii. 13.) The children of Ethiopia were from Adam to Noah, through the lineage of Seth.—(Gen. v.)

The generations of Ham, the son of Noah, an Ethiopian, were Cush, Miriam, Phut and Canaan.—(Gen. x. 1: chap. i.; 2218 years before Christ.) They possessed the land from Syria and Amanus, and the mountains of Libanus, and all its seacoast, and as far as the ocean —holding it as their own.

The Cushites were the descendants of Cush. Calmet believes that a colony of Cushites settled in the northern part of Assyria, on the Araxes—the present Aras or Araxis—a river which rises near the Euphrates, and falls into the Caspian Sea. Calmet's Dictionary of the Bible renders Cush the province of Cuthah. Brown thinks that the Cuthahites, who emigrated into Samaria, were descendants of Cush. —(2 Kings xvii. 24.)

Misraim (Mesraites,) founded Egypt; the country was called Mestre, and the inhabitants Mestreans.

Phut possessed himself of Lybia, and gave the name

of Phutites to its inhabitants. In the country of the Moors, there is a river of this name.

Canaan, the fourth son of Ham, inhabited the land now called Judea; and following the customs of the times, named it from himself, Canaan.

The sons of Cush were Seba, Habilah, Sabtah, Raamah, Sabtechah and Nimrod. — (Gen. x.)

Sheba, or Seba. There were several of this name:— 1. The son of Cush, who gave his name to a country in Arabia. — (Gen. x. 7: Ps. lxxii. 10.) 2. The grandson of Cush. — (Gen. x. 7.) 3. The son of Joktan.— (Gen. x. 29: Gen. xviii.) 4. The grandson of Abraham. — (Gen. xxv. 3.) All these seem to have taken up their residence in Arabia, or Abyssinia in Africa, and perhaps most of them in the south part of Arabia and Ethiopia, near the Red Sea. One or more of these Shebas gave name to the country whose queen came to visit Solomon, bringing him large presents of gold, spices and precious stones. This is also the name of a famous well, sometimes called Sheba, and sometimes Beersheba. — (Gen. xxvi. 33.)

Havilah (Evilas,) was the father of the Evileans, who are called Getuti, and inhabited Arabia, near the Red Sea.

Sabtah (Sabathes,) was the founder of the Sabathens, a nation now called by the Greeks, Astaborans, who settled in Arabia, near the Persian Gulf.

The Sabactens, descendants of Sabtechah, (Sabactas,) settled likewise in Arabia, upon the borders of the Red Sea; and the Ragmeans, the descendants of Raaman (Ragmus,) settled in Ethiopia.

Nimrod, the son of Cush, an Ethiopian, was a mighty one upon the earth. He built Babel, Erech, and Accad Calneh, and founded the Babylonian Empire, building Babylon, his capital, in the land of Shinar, or Chaldea, also known as the Land of Nimrod. — (Gen. x.: Micah v. 6.)

Raamah had two sons; one of whom, Judasas, settled the Judadeans, a western nation of Ethiopians.

The sons of Misraim, eight in number, possessed the country from Gaza to Egypt, which took its name from Philestim, one of them. A part of that country was called Palestine by the Greeks.

Misraim's sons were Ludiem, Enemim, Labim, Nedim, Pethrosim, Chesloim, Cophthorim and Philestim. In consequence of the devastations of the Ethiopic war, we are acquainted with the names only of these — if we except Philestim, previously mentioned, and Labim, who settled and gave his name to Lybia.

The Canaanites, called by the Greeks Phœnicians and Ethiopians, were the descendants of Canaan, the fourth son of Ham, and grandson of Noah; and inhabited the land of Canaan — the country now called Judea. The border of the Canaanites was from Sidon, as thou comest from Gaza, unto Gagar; as thou goest unto Sodom, and Gomorrah, and Admah, and Zeboim, even unto La-sha. The sons of Canaan were Sidon, Heth, the Jebu-site, the Amorite, the Girgashite, the Hivite and the Ar-kite, the Sinite, the Arvadite, the Zemarite, and the Ha-mathite. — (Gen. x.)

The Sidonians built Sidon in the province of Phœnicia.

The children of Heth built the city of Hebron, in the land of Canaan. Abraham was a mighty prince among them, and buried Sarah, his wife, in the field of the sons of Heth. — (Gen. xxiii.)

Heshbon was a city of the Amorites.

Hamath and Ashina, built by the Hamathites, border on Tyre and Sidon.

Amathus settled in Amathine, which is even now call-ed Amathe by the inhabitants; although the Macedonians named it Ethiopia, from one of his posterity. Amathus is the name of a city on the island of Cyprus. Arudeus possessed the island of Libanus.

The Amalekites were the descendants of Amalek, of the family of Ham; they inhabited the southern part of Canaan, and were the first of the nations. — (Numbers, xxiv. 20.)

The Anakines were also the offspring of Ham, and were a powerful people; their cities were walled, and very great.

The men of Cuth made (or built,) Nergal. — (2 Kings, xvii. 30.) *Cushi* came with tidings unto King David of the death of Absalom, his son from the army. — (2 Sam. xviii.) All the princes sent Jehudi, the son of Nathani-ah, the son of Shelamiah, the son of *Cushi.*—(Jer. xxxvi.

14.)   *Cushi*, the son of Jedediah, the son of Amariah, the son of Hizkiah. — (Zephaniah i. 1.)   The tents of *Cushen*. — (Habakkuk iii. 7.)

And it shall come to pass in that day, that the Lord shall set his hand again the second time to recover the *remnant* of his people, which shall be left from Assyria, and from Egypt, and from Pathran, and from *Cush*, and from Elam, and from Shinar (or Chaldea,) and from Hamath, and from the islands of the sea. Then shall the *Ethiopians*, the *despised, oppressed and outcast of Israel*, be gathered together as one, from the four quarters of the earth, unto God. — (Is. xi. 11, 12.)

These were the descendants of Ham, who were denominated blacks by the Grecian historian. Their hair was frizzly or curly. — (Herodotus, &c. &c.)

The Phœnicians — the Canaanites of sacred history — were among the most early civilized nations of the earth. We, the Christian and civilized people of the present day, are indebted to them for our knowledge of navigation. The *fragments of Sanchoniatho* are the most ancient monuments of writing, after the books of Moses. Greece was indebted to the Phœnicians and Egyptians for the first principles of civilization — the founders of that kingdom being the ancient Phœnicians.

THE GENERATIONS OF JAPHET.

JAPHET had seven sons. Their settlements began at the mountains of Taurus and Amanus; they extended them in Asia as far as the river Tanais, and in Europe to Cadiz. Settling themselves upon the land which was previously unoccupied, they founded nations called by their own names; for Gomer founded those whom the Greeks now call Galatians, (Gauls,) but were then called Gomerites.

Magog founded those, that from him, were called Magogites — but by the Greeks, Scythians.

Madai founded the Medeans, who are called Medes by the Greeks, and from Javan, Jouia.

Thobel founded the Thobelites, who are now called Iberas.

Mosoch founded the Mosachem; now they are called Cappadocians.

The three sons of Gomer were Aschanaz, Riphath, and Thrugramma.

Aschanaz founded the Aschanasians, who are now called, by the Greeks Rheginians.

Rephath founded the Ripheans, now called Paphlagonians.

Thrugramma founded the Thrugrammeans, who, as the Greeks resolved, were named Phrygians.

The three sons of Javan were Elisa, Tharsus, and Cethimus.

Elisa gave name to the Elisians, who were his subjects; they are now the Æolians.

The Cilicians were anciently called Tharsians, from Tharsus; their metropolis also is Tarsus.

Cethimus possessed the island of Cethima; it is now called Cyprus.

These were the generations of Japhet, after their families and tongues, in their countries and nations; who were also denominated colored people by the Grecian historian.

THE BLESSING AND GENERATIONS OF ABRAHAM.

NAHOR, (Gen. xi. 23,) or Nachor, (Josh. xxiv. 2,) was the name of Abraham's grandfather, and also the name of one of Abraham's brothers, (Gen. xi. 26,) who married Milcah, the daughter of Haran, (Gen. xi. 19.) He lived at Haren, which is thence called the city of Nahor, (Gen. xxiv. 10.)

Abram was the son of Terah; and Sarai, Abram's wife, his daughter-in-law. Abram was born in Chaldea, in the city of Ur, (Gen. xi. 31,) but forsook the place of his birth and connections, to settle in Canaan. And the Lord made a covenant with Abram, saying, Unto thy seed I have given this land, from the river of Egypt unto the great river Euphrates. And the Lord said unto him, I am the Lord, that brought thee out of Ur of the Chaldees, to give thee this land to inherit it. And Abram and family went down into Egypt, to sojourn during a greivous famine in Canaan; but returned and dwelt in the land of Canaan. Now Sarai, Abram's wife, was barren; and she gave her handmaid, an Egyptian or Ethiopian, named Hagar, to Abram to wife. And of Hagar, Ishmael was born to Abram, when he was eighty-six years old.—(Gen. xvi., xvii.)

And when Abram was ninety years old and nine, the Lord appeared unto Abram, and said unto him, I am the Almighty God: walk before me, and be thou perfect. And I will make my covenant between me and thee, and will multiply thee exceedingly. And Abram fell on his face before the Lord, and God talked with him, saying, As for me, behold my covenant is with thee, and thou shalt be the father of many nations. Neither shall thy name any more be called Abram, but thy name shall be Abraham—for a father of many nations have I made thee. And I will make thee exceedingly fruitful, and I will make nations of thee, and kings shall come out of thee. And I will establish my covenant between me and thee, and thy seed after thee in their generations, for an everlasting covenant, to be a God unto thee, and to thy seed after thee.

And Abraham said unto God, O that Ishmael might live before thee! And God said, As for Ishmael, I have heard thee. Behold, I have blessed him, and will make him fruitful, and will multiply him exceedingly; twelve princes shall he beget, and I will make him a great nation.—(Gen. xvii. 20: xxv. 16.) Abraham's circumcision of every male child, at eight days old, was established as a token of the covenant between him and God. And Abraham was ninety years old and nine when he was circumcised in the flesh of his foreskin. And Ishmael, his son, was thirteen years old, when he was circumcised in the flesh of his foreskin. In the self same day was Abraham circumcised, and Ishmael his son.—(Gen. xvii. 26.)

And Ishmael dwelt in the wilderness of Paran; and his mother took him a wife out of the land of Egypt.—(Gen. xxi. 21.

And these are the names of the sons of Ishmael, the son of Abraham:—Nebajoth, Kedar, and Abdeel; and Mibsam, Misnona, and Dumah; Massa, Hadar, and Temah; and Jetur, Naphish, and Kedemah — twelve princes, towns and castles, according to their nations. And they dwelt from Havilah unto Shur, that is before Egypt, as thou goest toward Assyria. — (Gen. xxv.)

Ishmael peopled Arabia, and a part of Asia. The Moors were his descendants.

And God said unto Abraham, As for Sarai, thy wife, thou shalt not call her name Sarai, but Sarah shall be her name; and I will bless her, and give thee a son also of her: yea, I will bless her, and she shall be a mother of nations; kings of people shall be of her. — (Gen. xvii.)

Sarah conceived, and bare Abraham a son in his old age; at the set time of which God had spoken unto him: and Abraham called his name Isaac; and circumcised him when he was eight days old, as God had commanded him: and Abraham was a hundred years old when Isaac was born. And there was a famine in the land, beside the first famine that was in the days of Abraham. And Isaac went to Gerer; and the Lord appeared unto him, and said, Go not down into Egypt; dwell in the land which I shall tell thee of; sojourn in this land, and I will be with thee, and will bless thee; for unto thee, and unto thy seed, I will give all these countries, and I will perform the oath which I sware unto Abraham thy father; and I will make thy seed to multiply as the stars of heaven, and I will give unto thy seed all these countries; and in thy seed shall all the nations of the earth be blessed. — (Gen. xx, xxvi.)

Isaac had now arrived at mature age, and Abraham called one of his servants, probably Eliezer, (Gen. xv. 2,) and made him swear that he would obtain a wife for Isaac; not among the Canaanites, (where they then dwelt, and who were to be cut off, according to the revealed purpose of God,) but in Abraham's native country, and from among his own kindred. This enterprise terminated successfully, and every desire of the patriarch respecting Isaac's marriage was answered.

ABRAHAM removed his tent to Egypt; and having become very rich in servants, men and women, cattle, silver and gold, he returned from Egypt to Canaan. Lot, his nephew, had been with him, and shared his prosperity;

and it happened that his servants fell into some strife
with the servants of Abraham.   As it was evident that
their property was too great for them to dwell together,
Abraham, though in every respect entitled to deference,
generously proposed to his nephew to avoid controversy
by an amicable separation.   He offered Lot his choice
of the territory, on the right or left as it pleased him.   A
rare illustration of meekness and condescension.   Lot
chose to remove to the eastward, and occupy that part of
the fertile plain of Jordan where Sodom and Gomorrah
stood.

After the death of Sarah, Abraham's wife, he took a
second wife, named Keturah, a Canaanite woman.   The
nation of the Troglodytes were derived from Abraham
by Keturah, by whom he had six sons, men of courage
and possessed with sagacious minds — Zambran, Jazar,
Madan, Madian, Josabak and Sous.   The sons of Sous
were Sabathan and Dadan.   The sons of Dadan were
Latusim, Assur and Luam.   The sons of Madian were
Ephas, Ophren, Anoch, Ebidas and Eldas.   For all
these sons and grandsons, Abraham contrived to settle
them in colonies: and they took possession of Troglodytes, and the country of Arabia the Happy, as far as it
reaches to the Red Sea.   It is related of this Ophren,
that he made war against Libya, and took it, and that
his grandchildren, when they inhabited it, called it from
his name, Africa; and, indeed, Alexander Polyhistor
gives his attestation to what I here assert.   He says:
"Oleodemus, the prophet, who was also called Malchus,
who wrote a history of the Jews in agreement with the
history of Moses, their legislator, relates, that there
were many sons born to Abraham by Keturah; nay, he
names three of them — Apher, Surim and Japhran; that
from Surim was the land of Assyria denominated; and
that from the other two, Apher and Japhran, the country of Africa took its name, because these men were
auxiliary to Hercules, when he fought against Libya and
Antaeus; and that Hercules married Aphra's daughter,
and of her begat Diodorus; and that Sophanx was his
son, from whom the people called Sophacians were thus
denominated."   Thus we find that Abraham was the father of many nations: Through Ishmael, he was the

progenitor of the nations of Arabia; through the sons of Keturah, of the inhabitants of the Troglodytes or Africa; through Isaac, he possessed Canaan. And the whole testimony of history proves these nations *colored*.

THE TWO NATIONS OF ISAAC.

ISAAC, the son of Abraham, was forty years old, when he took Rebekah to wife, the daughter of Bethuel the Syrian, Nahor's son, one of Abraham's brothers, (Gen. xi. 26, xxiv. 47,) and the sister to Laban the Syrian, of Padanaram. The *Syrians* were blacks, with long, straight hair.—(Herodotus, &c. &c. Gen. xxv.)

And Isaac entreated the Lord for his wife, because she was barren; and the Lord was entreated of him, and Rebekah his wife conceived. And the children struggled together within her; and she said, If it be so, why am I thus? And she went to inquire of the Lord. And the Lord said unto her, Two nations are in thy womb, and two manner of people shall be separated from thy bowels. And when her days to be delivered were fulfilled, behold there were twins in her womb; and the firstborn was red all over, like a hairy garment, and they called his name Esau.—(Gen. xxv. 23, 24, 25.) His brother's name was Jacob, who was afterwards called Israel. [The first clothing worn by the ancients, were *hairy garments.*—"The Lord God made coats of skins, and clothed them."—(Gen. iii. 21.) "And they wandered about in sheep-skins and goat-skins," ram-skins and badger-skins, dyed red.—(Ex. xxv. 5.) Ram-skins dyed red, were used in the construction of the tabernacle. Dr. Clarke has proved, from Homer, Pliny, and modern travellers, that there are rams whose natural color is red. From this fact, it may be deduced that Esau was red all over, like a hairy garment.] Esau became a cunning hunter, a man of the field; and was loved of Isaac. But he depsised his birthright, and sold it to Jacob for a mess of red pottage.—(Gen. xxv. 30.) Isaac, however, blessed Esau his son, and said unto him, Behold, thy dwelling shall be the fatness of the earth, and of the dew of heaven from above; and by thy sword

thou shalt live.—(Gen. xxvii. 39, 40.) A hunter or
archer, (Gen. xxi. 20,) one who is skillful in the use of
the bow and arrows, as Esau was. The weapons of war
formerly used, were the sword, spear, bow and arrow,
sling, javelin, &c. Esau, the Edomite or Indian, went
into the field, or wilderness, with his bow and quiver, to
hunt for venison; and he came in from his hunting, and
brought wild meat unto Isaac, his father.—(Gen. xxvii.)

THE GENERATIONS OF ESAU—THE RED PEOPLE.

Esau, who is Edom, which signifies red. The red
people.—(Gen. xxv. 30; Josephus.)

The wives of Esau were Judith, the daughter of Beeri the Hittite, and Bashemath, and Adah, the daughters
of Elon the Hittite, and Aholibamah, the daughter of
Anah, the daughter of Zibeon the Hivite; and Mahaleth,
and Bashemath, Ishmael's daughters, Abraham's son,
sister of Nebajoth. And Adah bare to Esau, Eliphaz;
and Bashemath bare Reuel; and Aholibamah bare Jeush, and Jalaam, and Hora; these are the sons of Esau
which were born unto him in the land of Canaan. And
Esau took his wives, and his sons, and his daughters,
and all the persons of his house, and his cattle, and all
his beasts, and all his substance which he had got in the
land of Canaan, and went into the country from the face
of his brother, Jacob; for their riches were more than
that they might dwell together. Thus dwelt Esau in
Mount Seir.—(Gen. xxxvi.)

The sons of Eliphaz were Teman, Omar, Zephi, Gatam and Kenaz; and Timna, sister of Lotan, bare to E-
liphaz, Amalek.

The sons of Reuel were Nahath, Zerah, Shammah,
and Mizzah.

The son of Zerah was Jebob, king of Edom.—(1 Chr.
i. 44.)

These were the descendants of Esau, the father of the
Edomites, and were dukes of Edom.—Duke, (Gen.
xxxvi. 15,) means only a chief, or leader, answering to
the chiefs of tribes of Indians, in America.

These are the sons of Mount Seir the Horite, who in-

THE HISTORY OF MAN.

habited the land: Lotan, and Shobal, Zibeon, and Anah who was king, and Dishon, Ezer, and Dishan; these are the dukes of the Horites, the children of Seir in the land of Edom.

The children of Lotan were Hori and Heman.

The children of Shabal were Alvan, Manahath, Ebal, Shepho, and Anam.

Ajah and Anah were the sons of Zibeon.

The children of Anah were Dishon, and Aholibamah, the wife of Esau.

The children of Dishon were Hemdan, and Eshban, Ithran and Cheran.

Bilhan, Zaavan and Akan were the children of Dishan.

THE PEOPLE OF ETHIOPIA.

WERE not the Ethiopians and Lubims a huge host, [or a great army,] with very many chariots and horsemen? (2 Chron. xvi. 8.)

Come up, ye horses, and rage ye chariots, and let the mighty men come forth; the Ethiopians and Lybians that handle the shield, and the Lydians that handle and bend the bow.— (Jer. xlvi. 9.)

Candace, queen of the Ethiopians of Sheba, came with a very great company to Jerusalem.— (2 Chron. ix.: Matt. xii. 42: Acts viii. 27.)

Tirhakah, king of Ethiopia.— (2 Kings, xii. 9: Isa. xxxvii. 9.)

Ahasuerus, the king, reigned even unto Ethiopia.— Esther i. 1.)

Thus saith the Lord, the king of Assyria shall lead away the Egyptians prisoners, and the Ethiopian captives, young and old, naked and barefoot. — (Isa. xx. 4.) [Even as they are led away at this day, naked and barefoot, by Americans.]

Ethiopia shall soon stretch out her hand unto God.— (Psalm lxviii. 31.)

Repentance and return of Israel unto God, our Savior, from beyond the river of Ethiopia.—(Zeph. iii. 9, 10.

Are ye not as the children of the Ethiopians unto me, O children of Israel, saith the Lord. —(Amos ix. 7.)

3

Thus saith the Lord, the labor of Egypt and merchandize of Ethiopia. — (Isa. xlv. 14.)

Persia, Ethiopia, and Libya, with shields and helmets. Eze. xxxviii. 5.)

Ethiopia and Egypt were her strength.—(Nah. iii. 9.)

The land of Ethiopia. — (Gen. ii. 13.)

The Ethiopians. — (2 Chron. ii. 16.)

Zerah, the Ethiopian, with an host of a thousand thousand, and three hundred chariots. — (2 Chr. xiv. 9.)

Ethiopia—this man was born there.—(Ps. lxxxvii. 4.)

Ethiopia — their expectation. — (Isa. xx. 5.)

The river of Ethiopia.— (Isa. xviii. 1.)

Ethiopia—for thee. — (Isa. xliii. 3.)

The Ethiopian. — (Jer. xiii. 23.)

Ebedmelech, the Ethiopian eunuch, who took up Jeremiah the prophet, out of the pit or dungeon. — (Jer. xxxviii., xxxix.)

The border of Ethiopia. — (Ezek. xxix. 10.)

Ethiopia, Libya and Lydia, and all the mingled people. — (Eze. xxx. 5.)

Behold, a man of Ethiopia, an eunuch of great authority. — (Acts viii. 27.)

Herodotus, the great father of history, pronounces the Ethiopians the most majestic and beautiful of men.

The Kenites, or Ethiopians, that came out of the city of Hemath, (1 Chron. ii. 55; Num. xxiv. 21,) were the descendants of Hobab, Raguel or Jethro, the priest of Midian, and the father of Heber the Kenite, and Zipporah the Ethiopian woman, Moses' wife. The children of the Kenites went up out of their city, with the children of Judah, into the wilderness of Judah, and dwelt among the people. — (Exodus ii. 18, 21; iii. 1, 4, 18; Num. x. 18, 21; xii. 1; Judges iv. 11.)

THE DESCENDANTS OF EGYPT.

ISHMAEL. (Gen. xvi. 11.) The son of Abraham, by Hagar. The wife of Ishmael was an Egyptian woman, for his mother took him a wife out of the land of Egypt. (Gen. xxi. 21.) The names of the sons of Ishmael have been heretofore given.

ISHMAELITES. (Gen. xxxvii. 25.) The descendants of Ishmael. The company of Ishmaelites to whom Joseph was sold are elsewhere called Midianites.— (Gen. xxxvii. 28.) Probably they were Ishmaelites who dwelt in Midian. It is evident, however, that the two names were sometimes applied to the same people, (Judges viii. 22, 24,) though we know the descendants of Midian were not Ishmaelites, [for Midian was a son of Abraham by Keturah.]

HAGAR. (Gen. xvi. 1.) An Egyptian woman, who lived in the family of Abraham, as a servant or bond woman. Sarah being childless, she proposed to Abraham that he should receive Hagar as his wife; and the fruit of this connection was Ishmael. Previous to his birth, his mother, being ill-treated by Sarah, fled from the house, and while in the wilderness, was informed by an angel what would be the character of her child, and that his posterity would be innumerable. The birth of Ishmael was in A. M. 2094; and as Abraham supposed that the promises of God respecting his seed were to be fulfilled in Ishmael, he nurtured him with much care.— (Gen. xvii. 18.)

AGAR, or HAGAR. This Agar is Mount Sinai, in Arabia, and answereth to Jerusalem which now is, and is in bondage with her children.— (Gal. iv. 25.)

HAGARENES, (Ps. lxxxiii. 6,) or HAGARITES, (1 Chron. v. 10, 20,) are the descendants of Hagar, and are of course the same with the Ishmaelites or Midianites.

PHARAOH was a king of Egypt, who gave his wife's sister in marriage to Hadad. His queen was Tahpenes, by whom he had Genubath.

HADAD. (1 Kings, xi. 14.) A descendant of the royal family of Edom. When David conquered that country, (2 Sam. viii. 14,) and cut off its male population, certain of the king's household escaped the general massacre, and fled, taking with them Hadad, then a little child. After a time, they went into Egypt, and young Hadad was presented to the king, and probably his royal descent was made known. The king received him with great favor, and in process of time he married the queen's sister, and the families were afterwards on terms of the closest intimacy. After David's death, Hadad request-

ed Pharaoh to let him return to Edom. And this he
probably did, as we find him mentioned as Hadad the
Edomite, and the adversary of Solomon.—(1 Kings, xi.
14—22.)

ALEXANDRIANS. A class of Jews, natives of Alexandria, a city of Egypt in Africa, and speaking that language. They were very numerous at Jerusalem.—(Acts
vi. 9.)

BERNICE, (Acts xxv. 13, 23,) or BERENICE, as the name
is sometimes spelled, was the daughter of Agrippa, surnamed the Great, and sister to the younger Agrippa,
king of the Jews. She was first betrothed to Mark, son
of Alexander, governor of the Jews at Alexandria. She
however married her own uncle, Herod, king of Chal-
cis. After his death, she married Polemon, king of
Pontus, but abandoned him, and, returning to Agrippa,
her brother, lived with him in incest. They sat with
pomp to hear Paul preach. (Acts xxv.)

JOSEPH, (Gen. xxx. 24,) son of Jacob and Rachel, was
born in Mesopotamia, A. M. 2256, and married the
daughter of one of the priests or princes of Egypt, and
had two children, Manasseh and Ephraim.

MANASSEH. (Gen. xli. 51.) The first-born of Joseph.
When he and his brother Ephraim were boys, and Jacob, their grandfather, was about to die, Joseph took
them into the patriarch's presence, to receive his blessing. On this occasion, he adopted them into his own
family, as his own children, and in a most significant
and interesting manner, predicted the superiority of
Ephraim over Manasseh, as it respected numbers, &c.
(Gen. xlviii. 5—20. Comp. Num. i. 32, 33, 35: ii. 18,
20: Ps. lxxx. 2.)

EPHRAIM. 1. A person. (Gen. xli. 52.) The second
son of Joseph. Though younger than Manasseh, he
was the object of peculiar favor; and the prediction of
their grandfather Jacob was literally fulfilled. (Comp.
Gen. xlviii. 8—20: Num. ii. 18, 21.)

EPHRAIM. 2. Tribe of—occupied one of the most eli-
gible sections of the Land of Promise. The Mediterranean was on the west, and the river Jordan on the east,
a portion of Manasseh on the north, and parts of Dan
and Benjamin on the south. The city of Shiloh was

within the bounds of Ephraim; and after the revolt of
the ten tribes, the capital of their kingdom was always
within the bounds of Ephraim; and hence the whole
kingdom is sometimes called Ephraim.—(Jer. xxxi. 9,
18, 20.)

EPHRAIM. 3. City of—(2 Sam. xiii. 23.) A considerable town, situated about eight miles north of Jerusalem, on the way to Jericho, and within the bounds of the
tribe of Benjamin. It was to this place, that our Savior
retired after the raising of Lazarus, (John xi. 54,) and it is
not improbable the same place is intended in 2 Chr. xiii. 19.

ZEPHANIAH, (Jer. xxix. 25,) the son of Maasseiah, who
is called the *second priest*, was put to death by Nebuchadnezzar, at Riblah.—(2 Kings xxv. 18—21.)

SAMUEL, an eminent prophet, born at Ramah, in the
tribe of Ephraim, and from his birth dedicated by his
mother to God's service.—(1 Sam. iii. 1.)

JARHA married the daughter of Sheshan. [And Sheshan had a servant, an Egyptian, whose name was Jarha. And Sheshan gave his daughter to Jarha his servant to wife; and she bare him Attai. And Attai begat
Nathan, and Nathan begat Zabad, and Zabad begat
Ephlal, and Ephlal begat Obed, and Obed begat Jehu,
and Jehu begat Azariah, and Azariah begat Helez, and
Helez begat Eleasah, and Eleasah begat Sisamai, and
Sisamai begat Shallum, and Shallum begat Jekamiah,
and Jekamiah begat Elishama.]—(1 Chron. ii. 35—41.)

SOLOMON, the king, was building his own house thirteen
years; and he finished all his house for Pharaoh's daughter, whom he had taken to wife. Pharaoh, king of
Egypt, went up and took the city of Gezer from the Canaanites, and gave it for a present unto his daughter,
Solomon's wife. Ahimaaz was in Napthali; he took
Basmath, the daughter of Solomon, to wife. The son of
Abinadab, in all the region of Dor; which had Taphath,
the daughter of Solomon, to wife.—(1 Kings, chap. 4, 7, 9.)

TAHPENES, the queen, was the wife of Pharaoh; and
the sister of Tahpenes was the wife of Hadad, to whom
she bare Genubath; and Genubath was in Pharaoh's
household, among the sons of Pharaoh.—(1 Kings xi. 14.)

DAVID — king of Israel — whose sister was Abigail,
the wife of Jether the Ishmaelite; and she bare Amasa.
(1 Chron. ii. 17.)

THE GENERATIONS OF JACOB.

JACOB, the second son of Isaac, and founder of the Jewish nation, was born, A. M. 2167. Jacob's wives were Rachel and Leah, the daughters of Laban, (Gen. xxviii. 2,) the brother of Rebekah. And the Lord said unto Jacob, Return unto the land of thy fathers, and to thy kindred, and I will be with thee. And Jacob sent and called Rachel and Leah to the field, unto his flock, and said unto them, I see your father's countenance, that it is not towards me as before; but the God of my father hath been with me. And Rachel and Leah answered and said unto him, Is there yet any portion or inheritance for us in our father's house? Are we not counted of him strangers? For he hath sold us, and hath quite devoured also our money. For all the riches that God hath taken from our father, that is ours, and our children's; now then, whatsoever God hath said unto thee, do. Then Jacob rose up, and set his sons and his wives upon camels; and he carried away all his cattle, and all his goods which he had gotten, the cattle of his getting, which he had gotten in Padan-aram, for to go to Isaac his father, in the land of Canaan.

The sons of Jacob were Reuben, Simeon, Levi, Judah, Issachar, Zebulon, Benjamin, Dan, Naphtali, Gad, Asher and Joseph ; all these were the sons of Jacob, or Israel, that came with Jacob, their father, out of the land of Canaan into Egypt, except Joseph, who was already there. The Canaanites, were called by the Greeks, Phœnicians and Ethiopians!

And the children of Israel increased abundantly, and waxed exceedingly mighty; they married the daughters of Egypt, Ethiopia, &c.—(Genesis; Exodus, i. and xii.)

The sons of Reuben and their families were Hanoch, of whom cometh the Hanochites ; Pallu, of whom cometh the Palluites ; Hesron, of whom cometh the Hesronites; Carmi, of whom cometh the Carmites. These are the families of the Reubenites, and the number of them was forty-three thousand seven hundred and thirty souls. —(Gen. xlvi.; Numbers xxvi)

Simeon, the second son of Jacob, was born in the year 2247. The sons of Simeon, by a Canaanitish or Ethio-

pian woman, and their families, were Jemuel or Nemuel,
of whom cometh the Nemuelites; Jemin, of whom cometh the Jeminites; Jachin, of whom cometh the Jachin-
ites; Ohad, or Zerah, of whom cometh the Zerhites;
and Shaul, of whom cometh the Shaulites. These are
the families of the Simeonites, and the number of them
was twenty-two thousand and two hundred souls.—(Gen.
xlvi. Num. xxvi.)

Levi, (Gen. xxix. 34.) third son of Jacob and Leah.
He was concerned in a bloody affair with the Shechemites, which occasioned the denunciatory and prophetic
language of his father respecting him, (Gen. xlix. 5—7,)
and which was fully verified in the history of his posterity. The opposition of his descendants to the idol-wor-
ship, which was practised by the others, was the occasion
of the mitigation of their curse.—(Ex. xxvi. 29.) His
descendants are called Levites. The sons of Levi, by a
Canaanitish woman, and their families, were Gershon,
of whom cometh the Gershonites; Kohath, of whom
cometh the Kohathites; and Merari, of whom cometh the
Merarites.

The sons of Gershon, and their families, were Libni,
of whom cometh the Libnites; and Shimei, of whom
cometh the Shimeites.

The sons of Kohath, and their families, were Amram,
[the father of Moses, Aaron and Miriam,] of whom cometh the Amramites; Izchar, of whom cometh the Izchar-
ites; Hebron, of whom cometh the Hebronites; and
Uzziel, of whom cometh the Uzzielites.

The sons of Mahari were Mahli, of whom cometh the
Mahlites; and Mushi, of whom cometh the Mushites.

The sons of Judah, by the daughter of Shuah, a Canaanitish or Ethiopian woman, the grand-daughter of
Abraham and Keturah, were Er, Onan and Shelah. Er,
and Onan the husband of Tamar, and after their death,
Shelah their brother, were promised by Judah to Tamar,
his daughter in-law. Through Tamar's seed came the
Messiah. [Gen. xxv. 28; 1Chron. ii. 2; 1749 years B. C.]
The sons of Judah by Tamar were Zerah, [the Ethiopian,] of whom cometh the Zarhites; and Pharez, his
brother, of whom cometh the Pharezites. These were
the families of Judah, and the number of them was

seventy-six thousand five hundred souls.—(Gen. xxxviii; Num. xxvi.; 1 Chron. ii.; 2 Chron. xiv. 9.)

Issachar, (Gen. xxx. 18,) was the fifth son of Jacob and Leah. The prophetical description of him uttered by his father, (Gen. xlix. 14, 15,) was fulfilled in the fact that the posterity of Issachar were a laborious people, and addicted to rural employments; hardy and patient to bear the burdens both of labor and war. The sons of Issachar, and their families, were Tola, of whom cometh the Tolaites; Pua, of whom cometh the Punites ; Jashub, of whom cometh the Jashubites; Shimron, of whom cometh the Shimronites. These were the families of Issachar, and the number of them was sixty-four thousand three hundred souls.—(Gen. xlvi.; Num. xxvi.)

Zebulun, or Zabulon, the sixth son of Jacob by Leah, born about A. M. 2256, from whom sprang one of the tribes of Israel. When this tribe came out of Egypt, their fighting men amounted to 57,400, commanded by Eliab, the son of Elon. They increased 3100 in the wilderness. They had their inheritance between the Sea of Galilee and the Mediterranean, and enriched themselves by fisheries, commerce, and the manufacture of glass. The sons of Zebulon, and their families, were Sered, of whom cometh the Sardites; Elon, of whom cometh the Elonites: Jahleel, of whom cometh the Jahleelites. These were the families of Zebulonites, and the whole number of them was sixty thousand five hundred souls.—(Gen. xlvi. 14.; Num. xxvi.)

Benjamin, (Gen. xxxv. 18,) was the youngest son of Jacob and Rachel. His mother died immediately after his birth, which took place near Bethlehem, when the family were on their journey from Padan-aram to Canaan. With her dying breath, she called him Benoni, [the son of my sorrow,] but his father gave him the name of Benjamin, [the son of my right hand.] The sons of Benjamin, and their families, [1732 B. C.] were Belah, or Bela, of whom cometh the Belaites; Ashbel of whom cometh the Ashbelites; Becher, Gera, Ehi, Rosh; Ahiram, of whom cometh the Ahiramites; Muppim or Shupham, of whom cometh the Shuphamites; Huppim or Hupham, of whom cometh the Huphamites. The sons of Bela, and their families, were Ard, of whom cometh

the Ardites; and Naaman, of whom cometh the Naa-
manites.   These were the families of Benjamin, and the
number of them was forty-five thousand six hundred souls.
—(Gen. xlvi.; Numbers xxvi.)

Dan, (Gen. xxx. 6,) was the fifth son of Jacob. The
prediction uttered by Jacob, respecting Dan, (Gen. xlix.
16, 17.) is variously interpreted. It is probable that the
elevation of his tribe to an equal rank with the others,
notwithstanding he was born of a concubine, was foretold in Gen. v. 16; and the residue of the prediction may
allude to the subtle and crafty disposition of his descendants.   Indeed, we know that Samson, [who was among
the most noted of them,] was remarkably successful in
stratagem, (Judg. xiv. 15,) and perhaps the same trait
was characteristic of their tribe.—(Judg. xviii. 26, 27.)
The son of Dan was Hushim or Shuham, of whom cometh the Shuhamites. The mother of Hiram, an Ethiopian king of Tyre, was a daughter of Dan.—(Num. xxvi.
2 Chron. ii. 14.)

Naphtali, (Gen. xxx. 8,) or Nephthalim, (Matt. iv. 15,)
was a son of Jacob, by Bilhah. The sons of Naphtali,
and their families, were Jahzeel, of whom cometh the
Jahzeelites; Guni, of whom cometh the Gunites; Jezer,
of whom cometh the Jezerites; Shillem, of whom cometh the Shillemites ; Huram, or Hiram, was an Ethiopian king of Tyre, of the tribe of Naphtali. These were
the families of Naphtali, and the number of them
was forty-five thousand four hundred souls.—(Gen. xlvi.;
Num. xxvi.; 1 Kings vii. 14.)

Gad, (Gen. xxx. 9—11 ; Num. i. 25,) was the son of
Jacob, by Zilpah, Leah's handmaid. The sons of Gad,
and their families, were Ziphion, or Zephon, of whom
cometh the Zephonites ; Haggi,* of whom cometh the
Haggites ; Shuni, of whom cometh the Shunites ; Ez-
bon, or Ozni, of whom cometh the Oznites ; Eri, of
whom cometh the Erites; Arod, of whom cometh the
Arodites; Arela, of whom cometh the Arelites. These
were the families of Gad, and the number of them was
forty thousand five hundred souls.—(Gen. xlvi. Num.
xxvi.)

* Haggai, the prophet of God.—(Ezra v. 1.)

The sons of Asher, and their families, were Jimnah, or Jimna, of whom cometh the Jimnaites; Ishuah or Jesui, of whom cometh the Jesuites ; Beriah, of whom cometh the Beriites ; and Sarah, their sister. The sons of Beriah were Heber, of whom cometh the Heberites; Malchiel, of whom cometh the Malchielites. These were the families of Asher, and the number of them was fifty-three thousand four hundred souls.—(Gen. xlvi.; Num. xxvi.)

The sons of Joseph, and their families, [1745 years B. C.] by Asenath, the daughter of Potipherah, Priest of On, an Egyptian [Ethiopian] woman. [Pharaoh, the king, called Joseph's name Zaphnath-paaneah, and made him ruler over all the land of Egypt, and gave him to wife Asenath.] The sons of Joseph were Manasseh, of whom cometh the Manassehites ; Ephraim, of whom cometh the Ephraimites. The son of Manasseh, by an Egyptian woman, was Machir, of whom cometh the Machirites. The son of Machir, by the daughter of an Egyptian, was Gilead, of whom cometh the Gileadites. The sons of Gilead were Jeezer, of whom cometh the Jeezerites ; Helek, of whom cometh the Helekites ; Asriel, of whom cometh the Asrielites; Shechem, of whom cometh the Shechemites ; Shemida, of whom cometh the Shemidaites ; Hepher, of whom cometh the Hepherites. The son of Hepher was Zelophehad. Zelophehad had no sons, but daughters, whose names were Mahlah, Noah, Hoglah, Milcah and Tirzah. These were the families of Manasseh, [Egyptians or Ethiopians,] and the number of them was fifty-two thousand seven hundred souls. (Gen. & Num.)

According to the Book of Mormon, [written by Joseph Smith, Jr.] the people of Nephi, and the remnant of the house of Israel, were the descendants of Joseph and Ishmael. Thus we discover the account of Lehi, the prophet, to be of the genealogy of Joseph, a Caananite, and Asenath, an Egyptian woman, [blacks]. The sons of Lehi, by Sariah, were four—Laman, Lemuel, Sam and Nephi ; and they took the daughters of Ishmael for wives, [dark red people].

The sons of Ephraim, and their families, by an Egyptian woman, were Shuthelah, of whom cometh the Shu-

thalites ; Becher of whom cometh the Bachrites ; Ta-
han, of whom cometh the Tahanites. The son of Shuthelah was Eran of whom cometh the Eranites ; the men
of Ephraim and Mt. Ephraim ; Samuel the prophet was
the son of Elkanah ; Elkanah was the son of Jeroham,
the son of Eli, the son of Tohu, the son of Zuph, an
Ephrathite. These were the families of Ephraim, of
Egypt, and the number of them was thirty-two thousand
five hundred souls.—(Gen. xlvi.; Num. xxvi.; 1 Sam. i.)

The sons of Amram, and their families, by Jochebad,
the daughter of Levi, his father's sister, a Canaanitish
woman, borne to him in Egypt, were Aaron and Moses,
and his daughter was Miriam, their sister. — (Ex. vi. 20.)

The sons of Aaron, and their families, by Elisheba,
the daughter of Amminadab, sister of Naashon, a Canaanitish woman, were Nadab, Abihu, Eleazer and Ithamar. The son of Eleazer, by one of the daughters of
Putiel, was Phinehas. These were the families of Aaron, and the number of them was twenty-three thousand
males.—(Ex. vi.; Num. iii, 26.)

The sons of Moses, the man of God, and their families by Zipporah, the daughter of Reuel, Jethro or Raguel, an Ethiopian woman, were Gershom, and Eliezer,
who was of the tribe of Levi. — (1 Chron. xxiii.; Ex. iii.
18; Num. x. 29; xii. 9.) The sons of Gershom, whose
wife was an Egyptian woman, were Shebuel, Libni, Shimei, Jeahath, Zimmah, Joah, Iddo,* Zerah and Jeaterai.
Shebuel was the chief ruler of the treasure of the house
of God, in Jerusalem. (1 Chron. vi. 23 — 25.) The
sons of Shimei, an Ethiopian, were Jahath, Zina, Jeush
and Beriah ; Jahath was the chief. (1 Chron. xxiii.)—
And of the sons of Eliezer, Rehabiah was the chief.
The sons of Rehabiah were Isshiah, Jeshaiah, Joram
Zichri and Shelomith ; and his brethren were over
all the treasures of the dedicated things in the house of
the Lord at Jerusalem. — (1 Chron. xxvi.) These were
the sons and grandsons of Moses, and Zipporah, an Ethiopian woman.

---

*Iddo, the prophet of God, and Zechariah his son, who prophesied un-
to the Jews that were in Judah and Jerusalem, in the name of the God
Israel. — (2 Chron. xii. 15; Ezra v. 1; Zechariah.)

The sons of Jethro, the priest of Midian, Moses' father
in-law, an Ethiopian, were Nahath, Zerah, Shammah,
Mizzah and Habab the Great, who was as eyes to Moses
in the wilderness ; and he also had seven daughters.—
(Ex. ii. 16, 18 ; Num. x. 29 ; 1 Chron. i. 37.)

The sons of Zerah, the son of Judah, were Zimri,
Ethan, Heman, Calcal, Dara and Zabdi. The son of
Ethan was Azariah.—(Josh. vii. 1 ; Chron, ii. 6.)

The sons of Heman the Great, were Bukkiah, Matha-
nia, Uzziel, Sherbuel, Jerimoth, Hananiah, Hanani,
Eliathah, Giddalli, Ramamti, Jeshbekashah, Mallathi,
Hathir and Mahaziath. God gave unto Heman, the
king's seer, fourteen sons and three daughters. All
these were under the hand of their father for singers in
the house of the Lord, with harps, cornets, flutes, sack-
buts, dulcimers, cymbals, psalteries, and all kinds of
music. — (Dan. iii.; 1 Chron. xxv.) The number of
singers in the house of God, was two hundred and eighty-
eight souls.—(1 Chron. xxv. 7.)

The son of Zabdi was Carmi. The son of Carmi was
Achan, of the tribe of Judah; he was stoned to death
for concealing a part of the spoil taken at Jericho.—
(Josh. vii. 5, 25.)

Pethahiah, the son of Meshozabeel, of the children of
Zerah, [the son of Judah,] was at the king's hand in
all matters concerning the people.—(Nehemiah xi. 23.)
Zerah, of the tribe of Judah, (Josh. vii. 1,) of Zerah
cometh the families of the Zarhites.— (Num. xxvi. 20.)
The sons of Zerah, Jeuel, and their brethren were six
hundred and ninety able men of Israel.—(1 Chron. ix.)

The sons of Phares, the twin brother of Zerah, the
Ethiopian, were Hezron, or Esrom, and Humul, and
among their descendants was Joseph, the husband of
Mary, unto whom was born *Jesus*, who is called *Christ
the Lord*.—(Matt. i. 2.)

The sons of Hezron, or Esrom, were Jerahmeel, Ram
and Chelubai.—(1 Chron. ii.; Matt. i.) The son of Ram,
or Aram, was Amminadab, or Aminabab. The son of
Amminadab was Nahshan, or Naassan. The son of Nahshan was Salmon. The son of Salmon was Boaz, by
Rachab. Hemath, the father of the house of Rechab.
The men of Rachab.—(1 Chron. ii. 55; iv. 11, 12;

Matt. i. 5.) Hamath was built and inhabited by the
Hamathites, Canaanites, Ethiopians, &c.—[Herodotus.]

The son of Boaz was Obed, by Ruth, the Moabitish
woman—the daughter of Pharaoh, a woman of the Moabites, Ammonites, Edomites, Zidonians and Hittites—
a colored people.—(1 Kings, xi. 1; Matt. i. 5.)

The son of Obed was Jesse, an Ephrathite. The son
of Jesse was David, the king of nations, whose sister's
name was Abigail, the descendant of Egypt by Ephraim,
of the tribe of Joseph.—(Gen. xli. 46: xx; 1 Sam. xvii.
12; Matt. i.)

Abigail, David's sister, married Jether the Ishmaelite,
the descendant of Ishmael, an Egyptian.—(Gen. xxi. 25;
1 Chr. ii. 17.)

The son of David, by Bath-shua, or Bath-sheba, the
daughter of Ammiel, or Eliam, was Solomon, of her that
had been the wife of Uriah the Hittite.—(2 Sam. xi. 3,
12, 24: 1 Chron. iii. 5.) The Hittites are Canaanites—
Ethiopians.—[See Grecian historian.]

Solomon, king of Israel. In his reign there were a
great number of kings in Africa and Arabia. "Twelve
kings reigned over the twelve districts called Nomes, in
Egypt. Solomon had seven hundred wives, princesses;
daughters of the kings of the Moabites, Ammonites,
Edomites, Zidonians or Sidonians, and Hittites—Ethiopian women. "The queen of Ethiopia, or of the
South, bare Solomon a son;" and his concubines were
three hundred women, [nobility,] of the Ethiopians and
Moors.

The son of Solomon, the Hittite, was Raboam, by
Naamah, an Ammonitish woman.

King Solomon married the daughter of Pharaoh, king
of Egypt; and he gave as a present unto his daughter,
Solomon's wife, the city of Gezer. And Solomon was
thirteen years in building his own house for the daughter of Pharaoh, his wife; and he finished it, and she
came up out of the city of David, unto her house which
Solomon had built for her, into Jerusalem, the upper
city; a woman of the Moabites, Ammonites, Edomites,
Sodinians and Hittites—an Ethiopian woman.—(1 Kings
iii. 1, 7; i. 8, 9; xvi. 24; xi; 2 Chron. xii. 13; Matt. i.
7; Herodotus, &c.)

Raboam, the son of Solomon, begat Abia, and Abia begat Asa, and Asa begat Josaphat, and Josaphat begat Joram, and Joram begat Ozias, and Ozias begat Joathim, and Joathim begat Achaz, and Achaz begat Ezekias, and Ezekias begat Hezekiah, and Hezekiah begat Manasses, and Manasses begat Amon, and Amon begat Josias, and Josias begat Jechonias, and Jechonias begat Salathiel, and Salathiel begat Zorobabel, and Zorobabel begat Abiud, and Abiud begat Eliakim, and Eliakim begat Azor, and Azor begat Sadoc, and Sadoc begat Achim, and Achim begat Eliud, and Eliud begat Eleazer, and Eleazer begat Matthan, and Matthan begat Jacob, and Jacob begat Joseph the husband of Mary, of whom was born *Jesus* who is called *Christ the Lord.*

The sons of Joseph were James, Joses, Simon or Salome, and Judas.—(Matt. xiii. 55; Mark vi. 3; xv. 40.)

These were the descendants of ancient Jacob or Israel, who was willing to give his daughters unto the sons of the Hivites and all the Ethiopian nations of the country, at their request, and to take unto themselves their daughters in exchange, providing every male of them would be circumcised, that they might become one people under the covenant of grace and works made by God unto Israel.—(Gen. xxxiv. 21, 22.)

The cities of Tyre and Sidon were founded by blacks, who were the same with the Canaanites, and spoke the Hebrew language.—(Matt. xv. 21-28.) [Then Jesus went thence, and departed into the coasts of Tyre and Sidon. And behold a woman of Canaan came out of the same coasts, and cried unto him, saying, Have mercy on me, O Lord, thou son of David; my daughter is grievously vexed with a devil. But he answered her not a word. And his disciples came and besought him, saying, Send her away, for she crieth after us. But he answered and said, I am not sent but unto the lost sheep of the house of Israel. Then came she and worshipped him, saying, Lord, help me. But he answered and said, It is not meet to take the children's bread, and to cast it to dogs. And she said, Truth, Lord; yet the dogs eat of the crumbs which fall from their master's table. Then Jesus answered and said unto her, O woman, great is thy faith; be it unto thee even as thou wilt. And her daughter was made whole from that very hour.]

Sarepta was a city of Sidon. [Thus saith the Lord, I tell you of a truth, Many widows were in Israel in the days of Elias, when the heaven was shut up three years and six months, when great famine was throughout all the land; but unto none of them was Elias sent, save unto Sarepta, a city of Sidon, unto a woman that was a widow.]—(Luke iv. 25, 26.)

The Queen of the South, or Sheba, daughter of Jokshan, and grand-daughter of Abraham by Keturah, (Gen. xxv. 2, 3; 1 Kings, x. 2; Chron. ix; Matt. xii. 42; Acts viii. 27;) came from Ethiopia—or, in the language of Scripture, from the uttermost parts of the earth—to Jerusalem, with a very great company, to hear and see all the wisdom of Solomon. She desired to try him in allegories or parables, in which he had been instructed by Nathan. The annals of Abyssinia say that she was a pagan when she left Sheba or Azab, but being filled with admiration at the sight of Solomon's works, she became a proselyte to Judaism, while at Jerusalem. She likewise bore Solomon a son, whom she called Menilek, and carried him with her in her return to Sheba. After the lapse of a few years, Menilek was sent back to Solomon, for education; nor did his father neglect his charge, but had him thoroughly instructed in the Jewish religion. Menilek was crowned king of Ethiopia, in the temple at Jerusalem.

It is certain that circumcision, the observance of the seventh day, and a number of other Jewish rites, are practised by the Ethiopians to this very day; and it is indisputable that their kings are descended in a direct line from Solomon. It is probable that this powerful nation—the Ethiopians of Abyssinia—were conquered by Shishak, about the time of the civil wars in Egypt.

The celebrated Joash, the king of Israel, reigned forty years in Jerusalem. His mother's name was Zibiah, of Beer-sheba, or Sheba, a city or country of the Sabeans. —(Gen. x. 7; 2 Chron. xxiv.)

LIGHT AND TRUTH.

CHAPTER II.

ANCIENT CITIES AND KINGDOMS.

CITIES OF ETHIOPIA.

ETHIOPIAN is a name derived from the "Land of Ethiopia," the first settled country before the flood. "The second river that went out of Eden, to water the garden, or earth, was Gihon; the same that encompasseth the whole land, or country, of *Ethiopia*."— (Gen. ii. 13.) Here Adam and his posterity built their tents, and tilled the ground.—(Gen. iii. 23, 24.)

The first city was Enoch, built before the flood, in the land of Nod, on the east of Eden—a country now called Arabia. Cain, the son of Adam, went out of Eden, and dwelt in the land of Nod. We suppose, according to an ancient custom, he married his sister; and she bare Enoch. And Cain built a city, and called the name of the city after the name of his son, Enoch. (Gen. iv. 16, 17.) We know there must have been more than Cain and his son Enoch in the land of Nod, to build a city, but who were they ? * * * * [Malcom's Bible Dictionary.]

The first great city described in ancient and sacred history was built by the Cushites, or Ethiopians. They surrounded it with walls, which, according to Rollin, were 87 feet in thickness, 350 feet in height, and 480 furlongs in circumference. And even this stupendous work they shortly after eclipsed by another, of which

Diodorus says, "Never did any city come up to the greatness and magnificence of this."

It is a fact well attested by history, that the Ethiopians once bore sway, not only in all Africa, but over almost all Asia; and it is said that even two continents could not afford field enough for the expansion of their energies. "They found their way into Europe, and built a city on the western coast of Spain, called by them Iberian Ethiopia." "And," says a distinguished writer, "wherever they went, they were rewarded for their *wisdom*."

THE TOWER OF BABEL.—Nimrod, the son of Cush, an Ethiopian, attempted to build the Tower of Babel.—(Gen. x. 8–10; xi. 4–9.) One hundred and two years after the flood, in the land of Shinar—an extensive and fertile plain, lying between Mesopotamia on the west, and Persia on the east, and watered by the Euphrates—mankind being all of one language, one color, and one religion—they agreed to erect a tower of prodigious extent and height. Their design was not to secure themselves against a second deluge, or they would have built their tower on a high mountain; but to get themselves a famous character, and to prevent their dispersion by the erection of a monument which should be visible from a great distance. No quarries being found in that alluvial soil, they made bricks for stone, and used slime for mortar. Their haughty and rebellious attempt displeased the Lord; and after they had worked, it is said, twenty-two years, he confounded their language. This effectually stopped the building, procured it the name of *Babel*, or *Confusion*, and obliged some of the offspring of Noah to disperse themselves and replenish the world. The tower of Babel was in sight from the great city of Babylon. Nimrod was a hunter and monarch of vast ambition. When he rose to be king of Babylon, he re-peopled Babel, which had been desolate since the confusion of tongues; but did not dare to attempt the finishing of the tower. The Scriptures inform us, he became "mighty upon earth;" but the extent of his conquests is not known.—[Malcom's Bible Dictionary.]

The private houses, in most of the ancient cities, were simple in external appearance; but exhibited in

the interior all the splendor and elegance of refined
luxury. The floors were of marble; alabaster and gild-
ing were displayed on every side. In every great house
there were several fountains, playing in magnificent
basins. The smallest house had three pipes—one for
the kitchen, another for the garden, and a third for
washing. The same magnificence was displayed in the
mosques, churches and coffee houses. The environs
presented, at all seasons of the year, a pleasing verdure,
and contained extensive series of gardens and villas.

THE GREAT AND SPLENDID CITY OF BABYLON.—This
city was founded by Nimrod, about 2247 years B. C., in
the land of Shinar, or Chaldea, and made the capital of
his kingdom. It was probably an inconsiderable place,
until it was enlarged and embellished by Semiramis; it
then became the most magnificent city in the world,
surpassing even Nineveh in glory. The circumference
of both these cities was the same; but the walls which
surrounded Babylon were twice as broad as the walls of
Nineveh, and having 100 brass gates. The city of Babylon stood on the river Euphrates, by which it was
divided into two parts, eastern and western; and these
were connected by a cedar bridge of wonderful construction, uniting the two divisions. Quays of beautiful marble adorned the banks of the river; and on one bank
stood the magnificent Temple of Belus, and on the other
the Queen's Palace. These two edifices were connected
by a passage under the bed of the river. This city was
at least 45 miles in circumference; and would of course
include eight cities as large as London and its append-
ages. It was laid out in 625 squares, formed by the
intersection of 25 streets at right angles. The walls,
which were of brick, were 350 feet high, and 87 feet
broad. A trench surrounded the city, the sides of
which were lined with brick and water-proof cement.
This city was famous for its hanging gardens, constructed by one of its kings, to please his queen. She
was a Persian, and was desirous of seeing meadows
on mountains, as in her own country. She prevailed
on him to raise artificial gardens, adorned with meadows and trees. For this purpose, vaulted arches were
raised from the ground, one above another, to an almost

inconceivable height, and of a magnitude and strength sufficient to support the vast weight of the whole garden. Babylon was a great commercial city, and traded to all parts of the earth then known, in all kinds of merchandize; and she likewise traded in slaves, and the souls of men. For her sins she has been blotted from existence — even her location is a matter of supposition. Great was Babylon of old; in merchandize did she trade, and in souls. For her sins she thus became blotted from the sight of men.

THE KINGDOM OF ASSYRIA.

THE foundation of the Assyrian Empire was laid by Asshur, the second son of Shem, and the grandson of Noah, about 2229 years B. C. Its name was derived from that of its founder.

Mr. Rollin, and other writers, state that Nimrod, the son of Cush, or Belue of the ancients, was placed over Assyria, and afterwards made himself master of the country. By the moderation of his government, he became very popular among his new subjects. He built several cities. Belue, according to the statements of some writers, was the same with Nimrod, the great grandson of Noah. Belue was succeeded by Ninus, in honor of whom Nineveh had received its name. And he, in gratitude to his father, obliged his subjects to pay divine honors to the memory of Belue, who was probably the first king that the people deified, on account of his great actions. Ninus appears to have been the first prince who united the spirit of conquest with political science. He divided the Assyrian Empire into provinces; and instituted three councils and three tribunals, by which the government was administered and justice distributed.

Ninus, the successor of Asshur, is said to have united the kingdoms of Assyria and Babylon. He made war upon many of the nations, for the sake of extending his empire. He reduced the greater part of Asia, and totally subdued the northern province of Persia, now known by the name of Corassan. After this, he rebuilt

Nineveh, and married Semiramis, a female conqueror and able sovereign, who could assemble 200,000 men; and by her had a son, named Ninyas. Semiramis assumed the sovereign power during the minority of her son. She swayed the sceptre with great dignity, for the space of forty years. She enlarged her empire, and visited every part of her vast domains. She built cities in various districts of the Assyrian kingdom, and cut roads through mountains, in order to make the intercourse between the provinces easy. — [Assyrian Chronology.]

The early history of Assyria is involved in obscurity. We know from the sacred history that it was a powerful nation. (Num. xxiv. 22.) And its capital was one of the most renowned of the eastern world. — [See NINEVEH.] It fell into the hands of the Medes; the monarchy was divided between them and the Babylonians, and the very name of Assyria was thenceforth forgotten.— [See GEOGRAPHY OF THE BIBLE, page 24.]

ACCAD. (Gen. x. 10.) A city in Shinar, built by Nimrod. Modern travellers have intimated the probability that the ruins of this ancient city are to be seen about six miles from the present Bagdad.

The present city of BAGDAD stands upon the site of Seleucia. It was founded A. D. 762, by the Saracens, and continued to be the seat of their Caliphs for 500 years. It then experienced various changes, till A. D. 1638, when it fell into the hands of the Turks, who still retain it. Though greatly reduced from the splendor and size it had when under the Saracens, it still enjoys a great trade, especially to Persia; and has a population of 20,000 inhabitants.

The great city of HAMATH was founded by the descendants of Ham. [Pass ye unto Calneh, and see; and from thence go ye to Hamath, the great.]—(Gen. xi. 18; Amos v. 2; 2 Kings xvii. 24; 2 Chron. viii. 4.)

The city of RIBLAH, in the land of Hamath, where Nebuchadnezzar, king of Babylon, gave judgment against Zedekiah, king of Judah, and slew Zedekiah's sons before his eyes. Also the king of Babylon slew all the nobles of Judah in Riblah, and bound Zedekiah with chains, and carried him to Babylon. — (Jer. xxxix. 5-7.)

CALNEH, (Gen. x. 10; Amos vi. 2.) One of the cities

of Babylonia, built by Nimrod, and supposed to be the same with Calno, (Isa. x. 9,) Canneh, (Ezek. xxvii. 23,) and the Ctesiphon of more modern times. It was situated on the east bank of the Tigris, opposite to Babylon, and was a place of commercial importance.

CARCHEMISH. (2 Chron. xxxv. 20.) A town on the eastern bank of the Euphrates, the Chebar, or Khaboor, falls into it. It is now known as Kirkisia. It was taken from the Assyrians by the king of Egypt, (2 Kings xxiii. 29,) who left it in charge of a garrison. Nebuchadnezzar, king of Babylon, afterwards took it from the Egyptians, with great slaughter, in fulfilment of the remarkable prophecy of Jeremiah.—(Jer. xlvi. 1–12.)

ERECH. (Gen. x. 10.) A city of Chaldea, built by Nimrod, on the Tigris. It was called Erecca and Aracca, by the Greeks and Romans. Some have supposed there were two places of this name; and others, that Erech was the same with Edessa, [now Orfah,] in northern Mesopotamia.

HALAH. (2 Kings xvii. 6; xviii. 11.) A province of Assyria, supposed by some, to be the same with Calah, (Gen. x. 12,) and with Holwan, or Cholwan, of the modern Arabs.

HARAN. A town standing on a small river of the same name, which flowed into the Euphrates through the northwestern part of Mesopotamia. It was called after the eldest brother of Abraham. Near this town occurred the celebrated defeat, by the Parthians, of the Roman army under Crassus, who was slain, with 20,000 of his men, B. C. 53. The place still retains its ancient name, and is peopled by a few Arabs.

The city of NINEVEH, (Jonah iii. 6,) the capital of Assyria, (2 Kings xix. 36,) and rival of Babylon, was situated on the Tigris, north-east of Babylon, probably near the modern village of Nania, opposite to Mosul. It signifies *the dwelling of Ninus*, and therefore we may presume was founded by Nimrod, also called Ninus, after his son, though some regard Asshur as the founder. According to Diodorus Siculus, Nineveh became one of the largest cities in the world. It was 19 miles in length, and 11 in breadth, and from 48 to 50 miles in circumference, [as may be inferred from Jonah's account, (Jonah

iii. 3,) confirmed by that of Strabo,] and contained a population of 600,000. — (Jonah iv. 11.) It was surrounded by a wall 100 feet high, and wide enough for three carriages to go abreast; it was fortified by 1500 towers, of 200 feet in height. For its luxury and wickedness, the judgments of God fell upon it. — (Nahum iii. 1; Zeph. ii: 13–15.) In the twenty-ninth year of the reign of Josiah, king of Judah, Nineveh was utterly destroyed by the Medes. It was afterwards partially rebuilt, but never became considerable, and was finally destroyed by the Saracens, in the seventh century. It is now called Mosul, and is only famous for being the residence of the patriarch of the Nestorians.

REZEPH. (2 Kings xix. 12.) Probably it stood where Arsoffa now is, from 20 to 30 miles west of the Euphrates. Rabshakeh mentions it among the cities conquered by the Assyrians. — (Isa. xxxvii. 12.)

The city of SELEUCIA was situated 45 miles southward, on the banks of the Tigris. It was sometimes called New Babylon. It became the capital of Babylonia, and in time utterly supplanted the old city.

SEPHARVAIM, or SEPHARVITES. They seem to have originally dwelt north of Media, or about Siphora, on the river Euphrates. Sennacherib, king of Assyria, ravaged the country about the days of Hezekiah, and after destroying great numbers, colonized most of the remainder in Canaan, where they at length became a tribe of Samaritans.

TIGRIS was founded by Ninus, the son of Nimrod, who began his reign, according to Usher, A. M. 2737.

TELABIB—a city or district between the rivers Chebar and Saocoras. — (Ezek. iii. 15.)

UR—an ancient city of Chaldea, or Mesopotamia, where Terah and Abraham dwelt. — (Gen. xv. 7.)

THE KINGDOM OF ETHIOPIA.

ETHIOPIA. (Acts viii. 27.) The Hebrew word Cush, which is here and elsewhere translated Ethiopia, seems to have been applied to at least three distinct countries.

The Cushites were the descendants of Cush. Calmet

believes that a colony of Cushites settled in the northern
part of Assyria on the Araxes — the present Aras or
Araxis — a river which rises near the Euphrates and falls
into the Caspian sea. Gihon, (Gen. ii. 13,) one of the
rivers of Eden, was supposed by some to be the Araxes,
which empties into the Caspian sea. Gihon signifies *im-
petuous;* and this is the course of the Araxes.

In Zeph. iii. 10, where the prophet speaks of Judah's
return from captivity, it refers probably to the country
east of the Tigris, the principal seat of the captivity,
which is called Cuthah. — (2 Kings xvii. 24. Comp. Ps.
lxviii. 31 and Isa. xviii.) Profane writers call this country Ethiopia, or Cush, from which the modern name
Khusistan is derived.

In Num. xii. 1, the word Ethiopia is applied to a country
of southern Arabia, lying along the Red Sea, elsewhere
called Cushan, (Hab. iii. 7,) in which last passage allusion
is made to the portion of history recorded in Num. xxxi.

Ethiopia, (Isa. xi. 11,) a country in Arabia Petrea,
bordering on Egypt, of which Zipporah, the wife of Moses, was a native.

ETHIOPIAN EMPIRE. South of Egypt there was once
a very large empire, consisting of 45 kingdoms, according to Pliny. The region is very mountainous. In it
were two noted cities, Axuma and Meroe, which could
furnish at least 250,000 soldiers, and 400,000 who were
artificers, manufacturers and forgers. Some of these
mountains abound in salt, others in iron, copper, gold,
&c. The chief river of Ethiopia is the Nile; it receives
most of the inferior streams of that region, and is greatly swollen by the immoderate showers that fall in Ethiopia, in the months of June and July. The middle portion of Ethiopia, called Lower Ethiopia, was very little
known to the Europeans; it was computed to contain
1,200,000 square miles. Abyssinia, or Upper Ethiopia,
is about 900 miles in length, and 800 in breadth.

The northern part of Ethiopia was called by the Hebrews, Seba, (Isa. xliii. 3,) after the eldest son of Cush,
(Gen. x. 7,) and by the Romans, Meroe. The inhabitants are said to have been men of stature, (Isa. xlv. 14,)
and this is confirmed by an eminent Greek historian,
who says they are "the tallest of men."

The Ethiopian queen Candace [which, as profane historians say, was the common name of the queens of that country,] reigned in Seba. Her treasurer was baptized by Philip, (Acts viii. 27.) There is a version of the scriptures in the Ethiopian tongue.

The Kingdom of ABYSSINIA, INDIA, or ETHIOPIA. In the days of Ahasuerus, the king, it was called India; (Esther i. 1,) for Ahasuerus reigned from India even unto Ethiopia, or from Abyssinia, [see map of AFRICA,] over an hundred and seven and twenty provinces, [countries.]

SABA was a royal city of Ethiopia, which Cambyses afterwards named Meroe, from his own sister. This city was encircled by the rivers Nile and Astrapus, and enclosed by strong walls. [Strabo.]

GONDAR was a city of Abyssinia, situated on a very high hill, surrounded by a high wall and deep valley. Population 50,000.

Diodorus Siculus, an ancient historian, informs us, that "the Ethiopians consider the Egyptians as one of their colonies."

THE KINGDOM OF EGYPT.

EGYPT, HER CITIES, AND THE DESCENDANTS OF HAM. — HAM, (Gen. ix. 22,) the son of Noah. He had four sons, one of whom was the ancestor of the Canaanites. The empires of Assyria and Egypt were founded by the descendants of Ham; and the republics of Tyre, Zidon and Carthage were for ages the monuments of their commercial enterprise and prosperity. Africa, in general, and Egypt in particular, are called the land of Ham, (Ps. lxxviii. 51; cv. 23; cvi. 22.) A place east of the Jordan, called Ham, is mentioned, in Gen. xiv. 5.

Egypt (Ex. i. 1,) was one of the most ancient and interesting countries on the face of the earth. The foundation of the kingdom of Egypt is ascribed to Menes, 2183 years B. C. In the Old Testament, the Hebrew word translated Egypt is Mizraim, which was the name of one of the sons of Ham, (Gen. x. 6,) the founder of the nation. It is sometimes called Ham, (Ps. lxxviii.

51; cv. 23, 27; cvi. 22,) and also Rahab. (Ps. lxxxvii. 4; lxxxix. 10; Isa. li. 9.) The Arabs now call it Mizr.

Misraim, the grandson of Ham, led colonies into Egypt, from Babylon, which lasted 1663 years. Menes, who was a descendant from Ham, united several independent principalities, which thenceforth became one monarchy under him. The States he united were Thebes, Thin, Memphis and Tanaris. Under his government, Egypt made rapid progress in civilization and the arts and sciences.

The inhabitants of Lower Egypt were colonies from Syria and Arabia — men of various tribes — originally shepherds and fishermen — who were gradually consolidated into one nation.

Egypt is bounded on the east by the Red Sea and the Isthmus of Suez; on the south by Ethiopia; on the west by Lybia; and on the north by the Mediterranean Sea. (Ezek. xxix. 10; xxx. 6.) It anciently comprehended an incredible number of cities, and was remarkably populous.

The Nile runs from south to north, through the whole country, about 200 leagues; and the country is enclosed by ridges of mountains on each side.

The greatest breadth of Egypt is from Alexandria to Damietta — being about 50 leagues.

Ancient Egypt may be divided into three principal parts: Upper Egypt, otherwise called Thebais, which was the most southern part; Middle Egypt, or Heptanomis, so called from its seven names; and Lower Egypt, which included what the Greeks called Delta, and all the country as far as the Red Sea, and along the Mediterranean to Rhinocolura, or Mt. Casius. Strabo stated that, under Sesostris, all Egypt became one kingdom, and was divided into 36 governments, or Nomi: 10 in Thebais, 10 in Delta, and 16 in the intermediate country. The cities of Syene and Elephantina divided Egypt from Ethiopia.

The Egyptians extended their reputation by other means than conquest. Egypt loved peace, because it loved justice; and maintained soldiers only for its security. She became known by her sending colonies into all parts of the world, and with them laws and civilization. She triumphed by the wisdom of her councils, and the superiority of her knowledge; and this empire of the mind appeared more noble and glorious to them than that which is achieved by arms and conquest. But nevertheless Egypt has given birth to illustrious conquerors.

A portion of the Egyptians seem to have been the descendants of Abraham, by Hagar; and of Esau, by Bashemath, the daughter of Ishmael.

THE CITIES OF EGYPT.

ALEXANDRIA. A celebrated city in Lower Egypt, situated between Lake Mareotis and the western branch of the Nile, near its mouth, 125 miles north-west of Grand Cairo. It was founded by Alexander the Great, from whom it had its name, B. C. 331. It vied almost in magnificence with the ancient cities of Egypt, and for a long time was the seat of learning and commerce. Among the monuments of its ancient grandeur are Pompey's Pillar, 75 feet high, two obelisks, and the Catacombs. In the height of its splendor it is said to have contained 600,000 inhabitants. — [Rollin.]

Its commerce extended to every part of the then known world. The Ptolemies made it their royal residence; and each successive monarch labored to embellish it. When the Romans, at the death of Cleopatra, B. C. 26, annexed Egypt to their empire, they respected and preserved the beauties of this city and it continued to flourish. In a ship belonging to Alexandria, Paul sailed for Rome, (Acts xxvii. 6.) Christianity was early planted in this place. Mark is said to have founded the church here, A. D. 60, and was here martyred, A. D. 68. Here Apollos was born, (Acts xviii. 24.) Numerous Jews resided here, engaged in trade and commerce, 50,000 of whom were murdered under the Emperor Nero. Clemens Alexandrinus, Origen, Athanasius, and other eminent ministers flourished here. Under the Saracens, who conquered it A. D. 646, it soon began to decay. They stupidly burnt its famous library of 700,000 volumes. The famous version of the Old Testament, called the Septuagint, was made here nearly 300 years B. C. It then contained 4000 baths and 400 theatres. It is now dwindled to a village, with nothing remarkable but the ruins of its ancient grandeur. — [Malcom's Bible Dictionary.]

Modern Alexandria is built of the ruins of the ancient city, and contains a population of 15,000.

The city of ABYDOS, or the Buried City, was so called by the Arabs, from its being beneath the surface of the ground. The traveller enters it by an excavation made for the especial purpose, assisted by his guide, and descending, finds himself within the ruins of a large city, with broad streets, temples of worship, and dwellings excavated in the solid rock. The extent of Abydos is supposed to be three or four miles; but it has never been thoroughly explored by travellers. The question has been started, whether this city was originally built above ground, and sunk by some great convulsion of nature, or built originally beneath the surface, as it appears at the present time. Mr. Buckingham thought it could hardly have been sunk, as the walls of the buildings retain their firmness and perpendicularity. He therefore thought that it was originally built where it now stands. Neither did he think it had been buried by a whirlwind from the desert, as some had supposed, because the soil which covered it was not of sand, but of clay. He thought it probable that it had been built as an appendage to the great Labyrinth, to assist in initiating the priests into the rites and mysteries of their calling, and furnishing them with the means of rehearsing, in an uninhabited city, the parts which they would be called upon to enact in public.

The ancient cities of BUBASTIS [or city of Isis,] and HELIOPOLIS [or city of Osiris, or the Sun,] where the mythological rites of the Egyptians were performed, were remarkable for being seats of religious ceremonies. The resemblance between the mythology of Egypt and that of India were very striking. The festivals were very similar — particularly the illuminations, for which Bubastis was celebrated. This city, in the magnificence of its illuminations, surpassed all the other Egyptian cities. There was also an annual festival of lamps in Hindostan — when all classes sent forth on the Ganges their lamps of various kinds, according to their different stations and means, which were carried down into the distant ocean. When illuminated with many thousands of lamps, some of which were of the most costly kind, and variegated, the Ganges presented a most brilliant, picturesque and interesting spectacle.

GRAND CAIRO. Cairo is the great metropolitan city of Egypt. It is situated about 120 miles from the sea, 20 miles south of the Delta, and three miles from the bank of the Nile. It is about ten miles in circumference, and compactly built, of an irregular form, having many sides, and streets, lanes and alleys running in every direction, and marvellously crooked. The population is variously estimated, but cannot be certainly determined, as a strong prejudice exists among the Mahometans, against numbering the people, originating in their gloomy doctrines of fatality. It probably contains, however, about 600,000 inhabitants; although some travellers estimate its population at a million. The citadel is a large fort, situated on a high rock; admirably chosen for strength, and might have been considered impregnable before the discovery of gunpowder. In the citadel is the palace of Mehemet Ali, the present Pacha of Egypt, and his beautiful gardens and public squares. In the outskirts of the city is the "Place of Ezebekeeah," a large open space, which is used as a promenade by the inhabitants, where sometimes 10,000 of them are seen enjoying themselves in various amusements. During the inundation of the Nile, this Place of Ezabekeeah is overflowed by means of a canal, the flood gates of which are opened; and on the following day the lake is covered with hundreds of highly ornamented boats and gondolas, which are filled with the citizens of Cairo, presenting a brilliant spectacle, enlivened with a variety of melodious music.

Grand Cairo, which seems to have succeeded Memphis, was built on the other side of the river. The castle of Cairo is one of the greatest curiosities in Egypt. It stands on a hill without the city, has a rock for its foundation, and is surrounded with walls of a vast height and solidity. You go up to the castle by a way hewn out of the rock, and which is so easy of ascent that loaded horses and camels get up without difficulty. The greatest rarity in this castle is Joseph's well, so called, either because the Egyptians are pleased with ascribing their most remarkable works to that great man, or because there is really such a tradition in the country. This is a proof, at least, that the work in question is very ancient; and it is certainly worthy the magnificence of the most powerful kings of Egypt. This well has, as it were, two stories, cut out of the rock to a prodigious depth. One descends to the reservoir of water, between the two wells, by a stair-case seven or eight feet broad, consisting of 220 steps, and so contrived that the oxen employed to throw up the water go down with all imaginable ease, the descent being scarce perceptible. The well is supplied from a spring, which is almost the only one in the whole country. — [Rollin.]

NOMES was the city of Sais, the residence of the celebrated King Amasis. This city was ornamented with magnificent buildings, temples and monuments, by order of Amasis; but this sovereign was ambitious of erecting a monument of an unique character, far surpassing in grandeur of conception and execution anything which had yet been done. He therefore caused a Monolith of colossal size, *a Temple carved out of a single block of stone*, to be constructed and placed in the city. This Monolith was wrought at Sienna, at the celebrated quarries where the beautiful and compact Sienite granite was found, at the distance of several hundred miles above Canopus. This temple, formed from the solid rock, was 21 cubits in length, 14 in breadth, and 8 in height — and the Egyptian cubit was supposed to be about four English feet. This enormous mass of stone was conveyed to the capital of Amasis by the waters of the Nile, and employed 2000 men for three years. Mr. Buckingham supposed that by mechanical powers it was first conveyed to the edge of the river, and then placed on an enormous raft, and when the inundation, or annual tide of the Nile took place, it was floated a certain distance, until the river subsided, when the raft grounded, and remained immovable till the next inundation. Three years thus passed away before this wonderful Monolith was conveyed to the city of Sais. This was one of the most extraordinary among the antiquities of Egypt — and it must be evident that the Egyptians were possessed of great mechanical power, to be able to place such huge masses of stone in their proper positions, and to erect obelisks of stupendous size. It was related by Herodotus that one of the kings of Egypt, when his workmen were about erecting a huge obelisk, caused his son to be lashed to the top of it, and when the machinery was set in motion, he bade them at their peril be particularly careful that the monument was not injured, as the life of his son would in that case be endangered. Sais, like Canopus, is now in ruins; and the remarkable Monolith had been buried in the soil for ages, until it was disinterred by some Europeans, and found to be perfect.

The city of Ox, (Gen. xli. 45,) or AVEN, (Ezek. xxx. 17,) is the same with Bethshemesh, or *house of the sun*, (Jer. xliii. 13,) and was called by the Greeks, Heliopolis, or *city of the sun.* These names are given to the place, because it was the principal seat of the Egyptian worship of the sun. It was one of the oldest cities in the world, and was situated in the land of Goshen, on the east of the Nile, about five miles above modern Cairo. Eighteen centuries ago, this city was in ruins, when visited by Strabo. Herodotus says the inhabitants were "the wisest of the Egyptians." The father-in-law of Joseph was high priest of On. This was the city of Moses, according to Berosus, and accounts for his being "learned in all the wisdom of the Egyptians," (Acts vii. 22.) Heliopolis was the Greek translation of Bethshemesh, "the house or city of the sun," and is called (Jer. xliii. 13,) "Bethshemesh in the land of Egypt," to distinguish it from a place of the same name in Canaan. — (Josh. xix. 38.)

According to Josephus, this city was given to the family of Jacob, when they first came to sojourn in Egypt; and we know that it was a daughter of the priest of the temple situated here who was given in marriage to Joseph. Here also, in the time of Ptolemy Philadelphus, Onias, a Jew, obtained leave to erect a temple similar to the one at Jerusalem, which was for a long time frequented by the Hellenist Jews. There is an apparent reference to it by several of the prophets. [See passages above cited.]

The ruins of this ancient city lie near the modern village Materia, about six miles from Cairo, towards the north-east. Nothing now remains but immense dikes and mounds, full of pieces of marble, granite and pottery; some remnants of a sphynx, and an obelisk, still erect, of a single block of granite, 58 feet above ground, and covered with hieroglyphics.

PATHROS, a city or canton of Egypt. It is probably the Phaturis of Pliny. It had its name from Pathrusim, the fifth son of Mizraim, who built or peopled it. — (Gen. x. 14; Isa. xi. 11. Comp. Jer. xliv. 1, 15, and Ezek. xxix. 14, xxx, 14.) This is the Thebais of the Greeks, and Said of the Arabs, the same with Upper or Southern Egypt. Some of the Jews, had withdrawn to this region, and there given themselves up to idolatry; but Jeremiah forewarns them of the tremendous judgments which awaited them.

PITHOM and RAMESES were the two cities for the building of which the Hebrews made brick. — (Ex. i. 11.) The situation of them is now unknown. Herodotus mentions a city called Pathumos, situated on the canal made to join the Red Sea and the river Nile. Pithom, (Ex. i. 11,) was one of Pharaoh's treasure cities, public granaries, or places for the storage of grain. It is supposed, from its relative situation, to be the Patoumos of the Greeks; inasmuch as the facilities of access to it and transportation from it would lead to its selection for this purpose. Raamses or Rameses, (Gen. xlvii. 11; Ex. xii. 37; Num. xxxiii. 3,) was also one of Pharaoh's treasure cities or public granaries, probably fortified for the security of the stores.

ROSETTA was located on the west bank of one of the branches of the Nile, near the Mediterranean, and was the city of Haroun el Raschid, a name celebrated in the Arabian Nights. Rosetta was a truly oriental city, the buildings being nearly all of Saracenic architecture, which differs from the light Gothic only in substituting minarets for towers, and in surrounding them with majestic domes. It contained about 12,000 inhabitants, principally Mahometans; and was picturesquely situated among groves of palm trees; and in approaching it, the minarets and towers presented a beautiful appearance, peering above the trees.

Syene, (Ezek. xxix. 10,) was a very ancient city, on
the southern frontier of Egypt, near the ruins of which
is the modern city of Assooar or Aswan.   The site of
Syene shows some granite columns, and a confused mixture of monuments. "Here," says a celebrated modern geographer, "the Pharaohs and the Ptolemies raised
the temples and the palaces which are found half buried
under the drifting sand.   Here are the quarries from
which the obelisks and colossal statues of the Egyptian
temples were dug.   And on the polished surface of some
of the native rocks are found hieroglyphic sculptured representations of Egyptian deities."

Tahapanes, the same as Tehaphenes, was a large city
in the north of Egypt, called by Herodotus the Pelusiac
Daphne. — (Jer. ii. 16; Exek. xxx. 18.)   Hither many
Jews emigrated after the ruin of their country, and took
Jeremiah with them. — (Jer. xliii. 7–9.)

The city of the Crocodiles is much dilapidated—many
of the stones and building materials having been taken
away, to assist in constructing other cities.

Canopus was situated on the western bank of the
western branch of the seven-fold Nile.   It extended
along the bank for five or six miles, and was about the
same extent in width, being of a semi-circular form.
One of its greatest peculiarities was the magnificence of
all its buildings, showing that, like Palmyra, it was inhabited only by persons of great wealth.   This city derived its importance, not from trade, like Alexandria,
but owed its prosperity to another and more potent cause
—a cause which, if existing in this country at the present time, would raise up a magnificent city with even
greater rapidity than was ever the case in former times.
This charm, which attracted crowds of people from the
east and from the west, the north and the south, consisted in its *fountains*, which possessed, or had the reputation
of possessing, the remarkable property of restoring to
elderly ladies all the health and beauty with which they
had been blessed in the morning of life.   They bathed
themselves in the waters of the fountains, and the pleasing transformation was supposed to take place.   These
wonderful baths drew vast numbers to the city of Canopus, and these being almost entirely persons of opulence,

would account for the absence of humbler dwellings, and
for the gorgeous architecture, the beautiful sculpture,
and the splendid palaces with which Canopus abounded.
But when the delusion vanished, and the people no longer believed in the virtues of the fountains, it is probable
the desertion of the city was as sudden as its rise and
prosperity had been rapid. This delusion, it has been
humorously said by a distinguished traveller, was no
greater than actually exists in the 19th century, in England and America. It is true, people do not believe in
fountains of youth; but they believe that *pills* and *lotions*
will produce an effect as marvellous as that ascribed to
the baths of Canopus. Any one may be convinced of this
fact by reading the newspaper advertisements of the day,
from which it will appear that if people become sick it is
their own fault; and if they die they have no one but
themselves to blame.

DAMIETTA is situated on the eastern bank of a different branch of the Nile, and is remarkable for having been
the city which was the residence of the Crusaders. The
architecture of the buildings and the appearance and customs of the inhabitants, approach nearer to those of the
cities of Europe than any other eastern city. The inhabitants are cheerful, and possess a spark of vivacity
uncommon with the Turks, and such as is seldom met
with in other cities of the East. Its population is about
20,000.

GOSHEN. 1. (Gen. xlv. 10.) A fertile section of pasture land in the north-eastern division of Egypt, between
the Red Sea and the River Nile, upon the southern border of Canaan, allotted by Joseph to his father and his
brethren, where they dwelt for upwards of two hundred
years. It was, for grazing purposes, the best of the
land. — (Gen. xlvii. 6, 11.) Mr. Smith, an American
missionary, passed, with a caravan, through the northern
district of ancient Goshen, in 1827; and he describes it
as an immense sandy desert, drifted with sand banks;
and presenting here and there, in small patches, a few
shrubs of evergreen, like our whortleberry bushes, on
which the Bedouins pasture their flocks. Rameses and
Pithon are mentioned as cities of Goshen, and the supposed ruins of them are described by modern travellers.

The Pacha of Egypt has lately established a colony of
500 Syrians in the ancient land of Goshen, for the purpose of cultivating the mulberry and rearing silk-worms.

2. (Josh. xv. 51.) A city in the territory of Judah,
which gave the name of the land of Goshen to the country around it.

HEPTANOMIS was so called from the seven Nomi or
districts it contained—Lower Egypt, which included what
the Greeks call Delta, and all the country as far as the
Red Sea, and along the Mediterranean to Rhinocolura,
or Mt. Casius.

HERMOPOLIS is in ruins, but its streets, squares, palaces, and some of its private dwellings remain; and while
walking through its desolate streets, and standing beneath the gorgeous temples, the traveller cannot but feel
lost in admiration at their beauty and splendor.

HELIOPOLIS. At this city, in its palmy days, was a college of great celebrity, where Greeks and Romans, and
citizens of other places in Europe, used to resort to acquire knowledge. It was there that the doctrine of the
metempsychosis, or transmigration of souls, was taught,
and which, by Pythagoras the Samian and other philosophers, was carried over into other countries. Those
who entertained a belief in this doctrine supposed that
there was a time when every soul was independent of a
body; that when a body was afterwards created, a soul
entered into it, and there continued till the natural term
of its existence had expired; and if, during this state of
probation, it conducted with rectitude and propriety, ful-
filling all the duties prescribed by the moral law, the
soul would afterwards pass into the body of a being of a
higher grade than the one it had left, and at the close of
every term of its existence, it would go on improving, if
it continued to conduct in a blameless manner — at length
getting advanced in the scale of improvement beyond human perfection, it would constitute the essence of an angel, or some superior being, and still improving, would
finally become incorporated with Deity itself. This
was the system of rewards. The system of punishment
was of a corresponding nature. If a person conducted
ill, the soul, at his death, would enter into the body of
an inferior human being, or perhaps an animal— and if

his conduct had been exceedingly vicious and depraved, it would enter into the body of an animal of the most degraded and detested class.

MEMPHIS. This city was built by Uchoreus, king of Egypt, on the west side of the Nile, and was the capital of Middle Egypt, or Heptanomis. It was 150 furlongs, or more than 7 leagues, in circumference, and stood at the point of the Delta, in that part where the Nile divides itself into several branches or streams. Southward from the city, the king raised a vast and high mole; on the right and left, he dug deep moats to receive the river. These were faced with stone, and raised, near the city, by a strong causeway — the whole designed to secure the city from the inundations of the Nile and the incursions of enemies. A city so advantageously situated, and so strongly fortified that it was almost the key of the Nile, and by this means commanded the whole country, soon became the usual residence of the Egyptian kings. Here were many stately temples, the god Apis, pyramids, &c. — (Rollin.)

NOPH, (Isa. xix. 13; Jer. ii. 16; Ezek. xxx. 13, 16,) was probably the ancient Memphis, in Middle Egypt, on the Nile, 15 miles south of old Cairo. It was the residence of the earlier kings of Egypt, and is said to have been about 20 miles in circumference. In the seventh century it fell into the hands of the Saracens; and the predicted judgments of God, on account of its idolatry and general corruption, gradually effaced every trace of its ancient magnificence. In the time of Strabo, there were many splendid remains, among which he describes a temple of Vulcan, of great magnificence; another of Venus; and a third of Osiris, where the Apis or sacred ox was worshipped. He also mentions a large circus; but he remarks, that many of the palaces were in ruins, and describes an immense colossus which lay prostrate in front of the city; and among a number of sphinxes, some were buried in sand up to the middle of the body, while of others only the heads were visible above the sand. Some monuments were to be seen 600 years after the time of Strabo's visit, when the Saracens had possession of the country; but at present there is scarcely a vestige of its former grandeur to be found. This has led

some to conjecture that its site was overflowed by the
Nile; but it is much more probable that it has been covered by the continual encroachment of the sands, which,
we see, were advancing in the time of Strabo. And it
cannot be doubted but that a large part of ancient Egypt
has already been completely buried by the sands from the
wilderness.

No, (Jer. xlvi. 25; Ezek. xxx. 14,) is generally supposed to be the famous city of Thebes, in Upper Egypt,
extending itself on both sides of the Nile. — (Nah. iii. 8.)
The fact is so uncertain, however, that we should not
feel justified in introducing an article upon Thebes. Instead of No, in Jer. xlvi. 25, it should be rendered *Ammon of No*, or the seat or dwelling of the god, Ammon.
It was probably applied to two or three places. A distinction was sometimes made between the No spoken of
in Nahum iii. 8 — 10, and the No mentioned by Jeremiah and Ezekiel. The destruction of the former [sup-
posed to be Thebes,] is described in detail, as already
past, while the doom of the other [which is supposed to
have been in Lower Egypt,] is predicted by Jeremiah
and Ezekiel as a future event. No, was the chief seat of
the worship of Jupiter Ammon. Its ruins are the wonder and delight of all travellers. — (Jer. xlvi. 25.)

The city of THEBES. The foundation of the kingdom
of Thebes was laid by the celebrated Cadmus, a Phœnician or Ethiopian. The city of Thebes, in Upper
Egypt, was one of the most splendid cities in the world,
and was built by Busiris, king of Egypt, now called Said.
Temples and palaces have been discovered, which are
still almost entire, adorned with innumerable columns
and statues. Travellers give us accounts of one palace
in particular, whose remains seem to have existed sole-
ly to eclipse the glory of the most magnificent edifices
of ancient or modern times. Four walks, extending farther than the eye can see, and bounded on each side with
sphinxes composed of materials as rare and extraordinary as their size is remarkable, serve for avenues to
four porticoes, whose height is amazing to behold. Besides, those who describe this wonderful edifice had not
time to explore it thoroughly, and suppose they saw no
more than half its extent. A hill, which in appearance

stood in the middle of this stately palace, was supported by 120 pillars, each of which was six fathoms in circumference, and of proportionable height, intermixed with obelisks which so many ages have not been able to demolish. Painting had displayed all her art and magnificence in this edifice. The colors themselves, which soonest feel the injury of time, still remain amidst the ruins of this wonderful structure, and preserve their beauty and lustre. So happily could the Egyptians imprint a character of immortality on all their works.—[Lib. 17, p. 805.] Strabo, who was on the spot, describes a temple he saw in Egypt very much resembling that of which we have been speaking.

The ruins of Thebes, lie on both sides the Nile, for a space of nearly nine miles along the river, and reaching far inland. The modern names of Luxor, Carnac and Kourna are given only to parts of the same city, whose ancient circuit was 27 miles, the whole of which space is now full of fallen columns, colossal statues and obelisks. It is reported to have had an hundred gates, out of each of which it could send 20,000 soldiers and 200 chariots. The palace of Memnon, with its vast porticoes, colossal statues, and almost endless rows of columns, shows that the kings who once reigned here were very rich, and that the artists by whom the edifices were erected were able and intelligent men, although they were built so long ago that history can tell us very little about them.

THEBAIS, derives its name from Thebes, which with its hundred palaces and hundred gates, might vie with the noblest cities of the world. It was celebrated by Homer, an Ethiopian, whose description is generally familiar. It acquired the surname of Hecatompylos, to distinguish it from the other Thebes, in Bœotia. It was equally large and populous, and according to history it could send out at once 200 chariots and 10,000 fighting men at each of its gates. The Greeks and Romans have celebrated its magnificence and grandeur, though they saw only its ruins, so august were its remains.— [Strabo and Rollin.]

The Thebans, says Diodorus, considered themselves as the most ancient people of the East, and asserted that philosophy and astronomy originated with them.

THEBES, what a glory on thy temples sate,
  When monarchs hardly less than gods were thine,
Though mystery and darkness shroud thy fate,
  The glimpse imagination gives us is divine.

Through the long vista, as we gaze, half hid,
  Distinct though distant, graceful, though austere,
Palace and pillar, fane and pyramid,
  In awful grandeur and repose appear.

Nations, since born, have wept o'er thy decay;
  Science and Art have flourish'd and have died;
And glory, like a dream, has pass'd away—
  Yet thine imperishable fame shall aye abide.

The native spirit yet may wake and live,
  (Freedom and Culture, what hast thou not done,)
And Ethiopia kindle and revive,
  Like her own table when it felt the sun.

The city of SIN,) Ezek. xxx. 15, 16,) is the Pelusium of the Greeks, and is called *the strength of Egypt*, because of its position as a bulwark. The ruins of it are supposed to have been discovered by the French army in the invasion of Egypt under Bonaparte.

ZOAN, (Num. xiii. 22,) by the Greeks called Tanis, and by the Arabs, San, was one of the oldest cities of the world, founded only seven years later than Hebron, and situated on the Tanitic arm of the Nile. It was evidently the residence of a line of princes, (Isa. xix. 11 — 13; xxx. 4,) and probably the place where Moses wrought the Egyptian miracles.—(Ps. lxxviii. 12, 43.) Ezekiel prophesied against it, (Ezek. xxx. 14,) and its ruins are yet visible, and present numerous pillars and obelisks, as evidence of its former magnificence.

The city of ZOAR. Delta was the city of Tanis, the Zoar of the scriptures, alluded to by the Psalmist, situated in the land of Goshen, where the Israelites were held in bondage. The antiquities of this part of Egypt throw much light on scripture history. The labors of the Israelites, it is thought, were confined to the land of Goshen, and it is not probable they were employed in the construction of the pyramids, as some persons have supposed. In Zoar, which is no longer inhabited, may still be seen the remains of brick work, which, we are taught by Holy Writ, was the employment of the Israelites. The walls of this city were of immense size, being

80 feet in thickness at the base, perpendicular at the outside, but sloping internally, the top being 30 feet thick, and sufficiently extensive for three chariots to ride abreast. The interior portion of the walls was made of bricks without straw. Zoar is now desolate — and the waters of the Nile flow over a portion of this once populous and renowned city.

The RIVER OF EGYPT, (Josh. xv. 47,) does not mean the Nile, but the Sihor, or the brook Bezor, which runs into the Mediterranean. That which is called, (Gen. xv. 18,) by way of pre-eminence, the *River*, (Gen. xli. 1; Ex. vii. 17,) and sometimes Sihor, (Isa. xxiii. 3,) or Shihor, (1 Chron. xiii. 5,) is the Nile, a remarkable river, which flows 1200 miles without meeting a tributary stream. Its overflowings inundate the adjoining country, (Amos viii. 8; ix, 5,) and give it its extraordinary fertility. Hence a failure of this periodical overflowing must occasion the utmost distress. —(Isa. xix. 5, 6.)

The Egyptians were celebrated legislators and able politicians, magistrates born for government, men that have excelled in all arts and sciences, philosophers who carried their inquiries as far as was possible in those early ages, and who have left us such maxims of morality as many Christians ought to blush at.

From the history of Herodotus we learn that the ancient Egyptians were black, and that their hair was frizzly or curly.

The inhabitants of ancient Colchis, since called Mingrelia, were originally Egyptians, and colonized that country when Sesostris, king of Egypt, extended his conquests in the north. They had, like the Egyptians, black skins and frizzly hair, and were the ancestors of the warlike Philistines. Samson's wife was the daughter of a Philistine.—(Judges xxiv.; Herodotus.)

THE LAND OF CANAAN.

CANAAN was the Scripture name of what was called Palestine, or the Holy Land. This name was derived from Canaan, the fourth son of Ham, [literally *black*,] whose posterity settled there, and remained for about

700 years. It is now called Judea, and its divisions, at
different times, have been as follows:

Ancient Canaanitish Division.	Israelitish Div.	Roman Div.
Sidonians,	Tribe of Asher, (in Lebanon,)	
Unknown,	Napthali. (Northwest of the lake of Genessaret.)	Upper Galilee.
Perizzites,	Zebulon. (West of Genesaret.)	
Same,	Issachar. (Valley of Esdraelon, and Mt. Tabor.)	Lower Galilee.
Hivites,	Half tribe of Manasseh. (Dor and Cesarea.)	Samaria.
Same,	Ephraim. (Shechem & Samaria.)	
Jebusites,	Benjamin. (Jericho & Jerusalem.)	
Amorites, Hittites,	Judah. (Hebron & Judea proper.)	Judea.
Philistines,	Simeon. (Southwest of Judah, Dan, and Joppa.)	
Moabites,	Reuben. (Gilead and Heshbon.)	
Ammonites, Gilead,	Ammonites. (Gilead.)	Gilead.
Kingdom of Bashan,	Half tribe of Manasseh. (Golan Bashan.)*	

The boundaries of Canaan, as generally laid down,
are Lebanon on the north, Arabia on the east, Idumea
on the south, and the sea on the west.

At the time when Abraham came into the land of Canaan, there were already in existence numerous towns,
which are mentioned in the book of Genesis; Sodom and
Gomorrah, Zeboim, Admah, Bela, Hebron and Damascus. This last is truly venerable, as it is beyond doubt
the oldest city in the world. The spies who were sent
over Jordan brought back an account of well fortified
cities. In the book of Joshua, we read of no less than
600 towns, of which the Israelites took possession. When
the city of Ai was taken, its inhabitants, who were put
to the sword, amounted to 12,000, (Josh. viii. 16, 25,)
and we are told that Gibeon was a still greater city.—
(Josh. x. 2.)

ASHTAROTH, (Josh. ix, 10,) called Astaroth, (Deut. i.
4,) and Ashteroth Karnaim, (Gen. xiv. 5,) was one of the
chief cities of Bashan, and is supposed to be the same
with the modern Mezaraib, on the route of the pilgrims
from Damascus to Mecca.

* A section of Canaan, extending across from the Jordan to the Mediterranean Sea, and northwardly to the territory of Benjamin and Dan. —
(Josh. xv. 1—63.)

ADAD-RIMMON, a city in the valley of Jezreel, famous for a dreadful battle.—(2 Kings xxiii. 29; Zech. xii. 11.) It was afterward called Maximianopolis, in honor of the emperor Maximian.

ANTIPATRIS, a city of Canaan, situated in a pleasant valley, near the mountains, in the way from Jerusalem to Cæsarea, about 17 miles distant from Joppa, and 42 from Jerusalem.—(Acts xxiii. 31.) It was formerly called Capharsalama, (1 Macc. vii. 31,) but was of little note till enlarged and adorned by Herod, who named it after his father, Antipater.

ADMAH. (Deut. xxix. 23.) The most easterly of the five cities of the plain or vale of Siddim, which were miraculously destroyed by fire, because of their great wickedness. Some infer from Isa. xv. 9, the last clause of which is translated by the Septuagint, *"and upon the remnant of Admah,"* that Admah was not entirely destroyed; but the more probable supposition is, that another city of the same name was afterwards built, near the site of the former.

ARAD. (Judg. i. 16.) A city in the southern border of Judea, whose king opposed the passage of the children of Israel, and even took some of them prisoners, for which they were accursed, and their city destroyed.

ACCHO, a seaport of Canaan, belonging to the tribe of Asher, but not conquered by them.—(Judg. i. 31.) It first became an important city in the reign of Ptolemy Philadelphus, who greatly enlarged and beautified the place, and from whom it was long called Ptolemais. It became famous during the crusades, and was then called St. Jean d'Acre.

AJALON. 1. (Josh. x. 12.) A village of Canaan, situated in the tribe of Dan, between Jerusalem and Ekron. In the vicinity of Ajalon is the valley of the same name, memorable for the miracle of Joshua.

2. A city in the tribe of Asher, also called Aphik, (Judg. i. 31) situated in Lebanon, on the northern border of Canaan, where there is now a village called Aphka. It was here that Benhadad assembled the Syrians, (Josh. xii. 18; xiii. 4; xix. 30; 1 Kings xx. 26,) 37,000 of whom were destroyed by the falling of a wall.

BEER-LAHAI-ROI. (Gen. xvi. 14.) A place in the

southern border of Canaan, near the desert of Shur, which received its name in consequence of the appearance of an angel to Hagar, when she was in exile. The name of the place signifies "the well of him that liveth and seeth me."

BEER-SHEBA. (Gen. xxi. 31.) This was at first the name of a well, near which Abraham long resided, (Gen. xxi. 33,) and Isaac after him, (Gen. xxvi. 32, 33.) It afterwards became a town of considerable note. It was situated about 20 miles south of Hebron, at the southern extremity of the land of Canaan, as Dan was at the northern extremity. Hence the expression, (Judg. xx. 1,) "from Dan to Beer-sheba," denoted the whole length of the land, as also did the expression, "from Beer-sheba to Mt. Ephraim," (2 Chron. xix. 4,) represent the whole length of the kingdom of Judah. The town was within the territory of Judah, and fell finally into Simeon's hands. — (Josh. xv. 28; xix. 2.) At Beer-sheba resided the sons of Samuel, (1 Sam. viii. 2,) and in later times the place was given to idolatry — (Amos v. 5; viii. 14.)

BETHEL, (Gen. xxviii. 19,) was the residence of one of the Canaanite kings; and the Ephraimites, to whom it was assigned in the division of the land, were unable to gain possession of it until they were aided by the treachery of one of the inhabitants. — Judg. i. 22—26.) The tabernacle was stationed a long time in this place. This city was situated east of a line running from Shechem to Jerusalem, and at about an equal distance from each. When Jacob was journeying towards Mesopotamia to avoid the fury of his brother Esau, he lodged at a place near the city of Luz, and was favored with a remarkable vision of the Almighty. For this cause, he named the place, and the adjoining city, Bethel, [house of God.]

BETHSHEAN, a city west of the Jordan, known in ancient geography as Scythopolis, but now called Bysan, and containing only 70 or 80 houses.

BOZRAH was a city situated to the eastward of Bashan.

CANA, of Galilee. (John ii. 1.) A small village about 15 miles north-west of Tiberias, and 6 miles north-east of Nazareth.

CHORASIN. (Matt. xi. 21.) A town on the shore of

the Sea of Tiberias, where Christ wrought miracles; but
its precise location is not known.

DAMASCUS, once a most noble city, and one of the
most ancient on the earth. — (Gen. xiv. 15.) It was
about 50 miles in circumference, situated in a large
plain, and is surrounded by several considerable villages.
The plain is covered with gardens of chestnut, olive, and
fig trees, apricots and vines. According to the best information, Damascus contains about 150,000 souls, about
10,000 of whom are Christians. It is computed that 50,-
000 Mahometan pilgrims annually pass through this city,
from the north, on their way to Mecca.

DOR. (Judg. i. 27.) This is now a small town on the
Mediterranean coast, about nine miles north of Cæsarea.
Its present name is Tortura. It is close upon the beach,
and contains about 500 inhabitants. It was formerly a
royal city, or capital of a district of Canaan, (Josh. xii.
23,) and was assigned to the half tribe of Manasseh.

DEBIR, or Kirjath-Sepher, (Judg. i. 11,) or Kirjath-
Sannah, (Josh. xv. 49.) A stronghold of the sons of
Anak, which was conquered by Joshua, (Josh. x. 38,
39,) and assigned to the tribe of Judah. It was afterwards recaptured by the Canaanites, and again subdued
by the Israelites under Othniel. — (Josh. xv. 15—17.)
It afterwards became a city of the Levites. — (Josh. xxi.
15.) There was another town of this name among the
possessions of Gad, east of the Jordan, (Josh. xiii. 26,)
and a third on the border of Judah and Benjamin. —
(Comp. Josh. viii. 26, and xv. 7.)

EMIMS. (Deut. ii. 10.) A numerous and warlike people of gigantic size, who dwelt on the eastern borders of
Canaan, and who were supplanted by the Moabites.

GEZER. (Josh. xvi. 3.) A town of Ephraim on the
border of Benjamin, north-west of Jerusalem. It remained in the possession of the Canaanites, (Josh. x. 33;
xvi. 10; Judg. i. 29,) till the king of Egypt subdued it,
and gave it to his daughter, the wife of Solomon.

GIRGASITE, (Gen. x. 16,) or Girgashites, (Gen. xv.
21.) A tribe of the Canaanites, who are supposed to
have inhabited a section of the country east of the Sea of
Galilee, from whom the name of the city of Gergesa was
derived.

The city of GILEAD was situated on the river Jabok,
in Canaan. — (Josh. xii. 2.)

HAZOR. (Josh. xi. 10.) A capital city of the Canaan-
ités, where Jabin dwelt, and which was subdued and
burnt by Joshua. —(Josh. xi. 1 — 13.) It was, however, rebuilt and governed by a king of the same name,
whose army was routed by Barak. —(Judg. iv. 2 — 16.)
It was fortified by Solomon, (1 Kings ix. 15,) and in the
general invasion of the country by Tiglath-Pileser, fell
into his hands, (2 Kings xv. 29,) and its inhabitants were
carried into Assyria.

The land of HAVILAH, (Gen. ii. 11,) where the sacred
historian uses the name which afterwards applied to this
land, and which was probably derived from Havilah, the
son of Cush, (Gen. x. 7,) whose descendants peopled it.
It is supposed to be the same with Colchis, between the
Black Sea and the Caspian. Another country of this
name lay between the Euphrates and Tigris, towards the
Persian Gulf, where Chavelæi [or Chavilah,] of later
times is found.   One of these provinces may have been
settled by Havilah, the descendant of Joktan. —(Gen. x.
29.) A third Havilah is supposed to be intended in Gen.
xxv. 18, though that passage may also describe the vast
region last mentioned, between the Persian Gulf on the
east, and Shur by the Red Sea on the west. The phrase
"from Havilah unto Shur," in Gen. xxv. 18, and 1 Sam.
xv. 7, and many other passages seems to be used to designate the opposite extremes of Arabia; in which sense
Havilah may be regarded as the eastern border of the
country inhabited by the Ishmaelites and Amalekites.

HIVITES. (Gen. x. 17.) A horde of the Canaanites
elsewhere called Avims. —(Deut. ii. 23.) They seem to
have been settled in various parts of the land. —(Gen.
xxxiv. 2; Josh. xi. 3, 19.)

HORIMS. (Deut. ii. 1, 22.) A general name for dwell-
ers in caves; and perhaps the same with the Horites.

HORITES. (Gen. xiv. 6.) An ancient and powerful
people, who dwelt in Mt. Seir. — (Gen. xxxvi. 20—30.)

HADAD-RIMMON. (Zech. xii. 11.) From comparing
this passage with 2 Chron. xxxv. 22—25, we infer that
Hadadrimmon was a city or village in the valley of Megiddo.

KISHON.   An ancient river, rising at the foot of Mt.
Tábor.   It is called "the waters of Megiddo," because
Megiddo was built upon its margin.   It is famous for the
battle between Barak and Sisera, and for the destruction
of Baal's prophets.—(1 Kings xviii. 40.)   It is called
"the river before Jokneam."—(Josh. xix. 11.)

JEBUS. (Judg. xix. 10.)   The Jebusite is mentioned
among the descendants of Canaan the son of Ham,
(Gen. x. 16,) and there was a warlike race called Jebusites, inhabiting the mountainous country around Jerusalem, and keeping possession of it, (Josh. xv. 63,) until
it was wrested from them by David, and made the capital of Judea. (1 Chron. xi. 4—8.)   The Jebusites were
probably permitted to remain on the ground after their
conquest.   (2 Sam. xxiv. 16, 24.)   It is supposed they
were dispossessed for a season by Joshua, (Josh. x. 23,
40; xii. 10,) and afterwards regained some districts,
while the Israelites possessed others.—(Comp. Josh. xv.
63; 1 Sam. xvii. 54; 2 Sam. v. 6.)

KENITES. (Gen. xv. 19.)   One of the tribes or nations
who had possession of Canaan in the time of Abraham.
It appears that they were driven from Canaan; and are
afterwards spoken of as dwelling in the highlands near
the Ammonites and Moabites.—(Num. xxiv. 21, 22.)
In the time of Saul, they were found dwelling among or
near the Amalekites.   Jethro, the father-in-law of Moses, was of this nation.

KADMONITES, a tribe of Canaanites east of Jordan,
near Mt. Hermon.—(Gen. xv. 19.)   Cadmus, the famous inventor of the Greek Alphabet, is thought to have
emigrated from this country.

LEBANON, a famous range of mountains in the north of
Canaan.   At the top grew cedars, and at the base excellent vines.   There are two ridges; the eastern, called by the Greeks, Anti-Libanus; and the western, or
Proper Libanus, which runs nearly parallel to the coast
of the Great Sea.   From hence, Solomon's workmen
"brought great stones, costly stones, and hewed stones,
to lay the foundation of the house."—(1 Kings v. 14—
18.)   Mines of iron and copper were worked here.—
(Deut. viii. 9.)   The highest summits, which are probably about 12,000 feet above the level of the ocean, are

always covered with snow, from which descend in summer, sweet and refreshing rivulets on every side. The principal range extends, somewhat in the form of a crescent, from Cilicia to Esdraelon, a distance of 50 leagues. A spur of this mountain next the Holy Land is called Hermon. Another spur to the eastward is Mt. Gilead, where Laban overtook Jacob. — (Gen. xxxi. 25.)

MINNI. (Jer. li. 27.) A province of Armenia, or, more probably, one of the several clans or tribes who were settled on Mt. Taurus, east and south of the Black Sea. The Ashkenites were another of these tribes.

MAKKEDAH. (Josh. x. 10.) One of the principal cities of the Canaanites, which was allotted to Judah, and lay south-west of Jerusalem. There was a remarkable cave here, in which five petty kings concealed themselves, but were discovered by Joshua, and put to an ignominious death.

MIZREPHOTH-MAIM. (Josh. xi. 8.) A place near Sidon, and supposed to be the same with Sarepta.

PERIZZITES, one of the devoted nations of Canaan. They were never fully extirpated. Solomon exacted tribute of them. — (2 Chron. viii. 7.) So late as the days of Ezra we find them intermarried with the Jews. — (Ez. ix. 1.)

SAMARIA. 1. (1 Kings xiii. 32.) The central province or section of the land of Canaan, having Galilee on the north and Judea on the south was called, in the time of Christ, Samaria. It included the possessions of Ephraim and Manasseh, and comprehends the modern districts of Areta and Nablouse; in the former of which are the sites of Cæsarea and Carmel, and in the latter Shechem and the city of Samaria.

2. The city of Samaria, (1 Kings xvi. 24,) from which the above province had its name, was situated about 40 miles north of Jerusalem, and a short distance north-west of Nablouse, [Shechem.] It was founded by Omri, king of Israel, as the capital of Israel, or the ten tribes. — (1 Kings xvi. 29; 2 Kings iii. 1.) The territory was purchased of Shemer, [hence Samaria,] and fortified. — (2 Kings x. 2.) It withstood two unsuccessful sieges by Benhadad, king of Syria, and his powerful allies, (1 Kings 20,) and was finally subdued by Shalmanezer, in

the reign of Hoshea, but not till after a siege of three
years. — (2 Kings xvii. 1—6.) Previous to its fall, it
was given up to every species of sensuality, oppression
and idolatry. It recovered its prosperity, however, and
reached the height of its glory in the time of Herod the
Great, who enlarged and adorned it. The ruins attest
its former magnificence, though it is now but an insignificant village. A modern traveller says, "The situation is extremely beautiful, and strong by nature — more
so than Jerusalem. It stands on a fine large insulated
hill, compassed all round by a broad deep valley; and
when fortified, must have been, according to the ancient
mode of fighting, almost impregnable."

ASHIMA, the god of the Hamathites, who settled in Samaria.

SHECHEM, (Gen. xxxiii. 18,) or Sychem, (Acts vii.
16,) or Sychar, (John iv. 5,) was one of the most ancient cities of Canaan.

SHALEM. Jacob took his women and children, and
flocks and herds, and came to Shalem, a city of Shechem,
which is in the land of Canaan, where he bought a par-
cel of ground of the children of Hamor, for a hundred
pieces of money, and erected there an altar, and called
it El-Elohe-Israel, that is "God, the God of Israel." —
(Gen. xxxiii.) But although Jacob seems to have intended this as his place of permanent residence, yet events
occurred which rendered it expedient for him to remove
to another part of the country.—(Gen. xxxiv.) Jacob was
greatly grieved at the cruel and treacherous conduct of
his sons in the affair of Dinah, and foresaw that it would
render him and his family odious to all the people in the
neighborhood, so as to expose him to be slain with all
his house.

SALEM, (Gen. xv. 18,) has been generally supposed to
be the place which was afterwards called Jerusalem.
(Comp. Ps. lxxvi. 2.) But some think that the place of
which Melchizedec was king was the Shalem of Gen.
xxxiii. 18, or the Salim of the New Testament, [see SA-
LIM,] and that the Salem of the Psalmist is a contraction
of Jerusalem.

SALIM, (John iii. 23,) or Shalem, (Gen. xxxiii. 18,) or
Shalim, (1 Sam. ix. 4,) was south of Bethshean, and west

of Enon. Some suppose it was the same with Shalem or Sychem, but that is not placed near Enon by any
geographers. Probably Melchizedec was king of one of
these places, and not of Jerusalem, as some have maintained.

SODOM, GOMORRAH, ADMAH, ZEBOIM and ZOAR were
five cities of the Canaanites. In the days of Abraham
they had each a king. The Dead Sea now covers the
site of these cities. — (Jude 7.) The Scripture account
of the overthrow of these cities is corroborated by the accounts of Strabo, Diodorus Siculus, Tacitus, Solinus, &c.

SIDON, a great commercial city, and the capital of the
Phœnicians. It was built soon after the flood, by Sidon,
the eldest son of Canaan. Tyre, 25 miles south of it,
was built by a colony from this city. Both cities lay
within the lot of Asher; but that tribe never expelled the
people. Indeed, at one time the Sidonians overcame all
Israel; and in the days of Ahaz they drove a great commerce in exporting the Jews for slaves. — (Joel iii. 4.)
The gospel was at the first proclaimed here, and flourishing churches continued for many ages. After being
lost and won in the crusades, the Saracens finally made
themselves masters of it, A. D. 1289. Some Christians
are yet found here. It now contains 16,000 inhabitants,
and is called Saide.

SAREPTA, (Luke iv. 26,) or Zarephath, (1 Kings xvii.
9.) A Gentile town, lying on the shores of the Mediterranean, between Tyre and Sidon, and belonging to the
latter. Its modern name is Zarpha, or Zarphant. Though
there were many widows in Israel, distressed with the
prevailing famine, Elijah was not sent to them, but to a
Zidonian widow in Sarepta. Messrs. Fisk and King
passed the place in the summer of 1823.

TADMOR, a noble city in the north of Canaan. Its
immediate vicinity was exceedingly fertile, though at a
little distance all was a sandy desert. It was probably
built by Solomon, to facilitate his commerce with the
East. It submitted to Rome, A. D. 130. About 150
years afterward, the Saracens took it. Here lived Lon-
ginus. It is now famous, but only for its ruins. About
30 poor families constitute its population. The modern
name of the town is Palmyra.

Timnath, (Gen. xxxviii. 12,) or Timnah, (2 Chron. xxviii. 18,) situated on the northern border of Judah, was one of the oldest towns of Canaan. In Samson's time it belonged to the Philistines, and he obtained his wife there.

Zemarites, descendants of Canaan, by Zemar, his tenth son. — (Gen. x. 18.)

Zoar. (Gen. xiv. 2.) A small city, originally called Bela, at the southern extremity of the Dead Sea, whose king, with four others, rebelled against Chedorlaomer, and was conquered. It was afterwards threatened with the same destruction as Sodom, but spared at Lot's request, who fled to it for safety from the storm of divine wrath. — (Gen. xix. 20, 22.)

THE TOWNS AND CITIES OF JORDAN.

Abel-meholah. (Judg. vii. 22; 1 Kings xix. 16.) A town in the plain of Jordan, about 10 miles south of Bethshean, and between that and Shechem — distinguished as the birth-place of Elisha, and as the refuge of the Midianites, when pursued by Gideon.

Bethabara. (John i. 28.) A town on the east bank of Jordan, where there was a ford across the river; whence the name, ["house of passage."] At this place John baptized; and here, too, it is supposed, the Israelites crossed the Jordan, under the conduct of Joshua. It lay about 30 miles north-east of Jerusalem, and is probably the same with Beth-barah. — (Judg. vii. 24.)

Enon. (John iii. 23. A town on the west side of Jordan, eight or ten miles south of Bethshean, abounding in water, and distinguished as a place where John baptized.

Nimrim, a city east of Jordan. — (Isa. xv. 6.) It is thought to be the same which St. Jerome calls Nemra.

The wilderness of Paran, (Gen. xxi. 21,) was situated south of Jordan, and extended to the peninsula of Sinai, and from the Dead Sea to the desert of Egypt; so that, in its largest sense, it included the deserts of Kadesh and Zin. It was in this wilderness that Hagar dwelt with Ishmael, and to this place David retired, after the

6

death of Samuel. — (1 Sam. xxv. 1.) Nearly all the
wanderings of the children of Israel were in the great
and terrible wilderness of Paran. (Deut. i. 19. Comp.
Num. x. 12, and xii. 16.) It is now a dreary expanse of
calcareous soil, covered with black flints.

ZARETAN, (Josh. iii. 16,) or Zartanah, (1 Kings iv.
12,) or Zarthan, (1 Kings vii. 46,) or Zereda, (1 Kings
xi. 26,) or Zeredatha, (2 Chron. iv. 17,) or Zererath,
(Judg. vii. 22, are all supposed to denote one and the
same place, viz. a town on the west bank of Jordan, at
the place where the Israelites crossed, when the waters
were gathered into a heap on either side. It was near
Bethshean, and opposite to Succoth.

MIDIAN, (Ex. ii. 15,) or Madian. (Acts vii. 29.) A
country lying around the eastern branch of the Red Sea,
and supposed to have been settled by the posterity of
Midian, fourth son of Abraham and Keturah. Midian
was celebrated for its camels, (Judg. vii. 12,) and the descendants of Ephah, who were the posterity of Midian,
were rich in camels and dromedaries. — (Isa. lx. 6.)
Hither Moses fled, and here he married Zipporah, an
Ethiopian woman, the daughter of Jethro, the priest of
Midian. — (Ex. ii. 21; iii. 1; Num. xii. 1.) Jethro is
also called Raguel, (Numb. x. 29,) and Reuel, (Ex. ii.
18,) and was probably known by either name. It is
highly probable, too, that he was a descendant of Abraham, (Gen. xxv. 2,) but what was the nature of his office as priest, [or prince, as some say it should be rendered,] we know not. — (Num. xii. 1.)

It is supposed that another country called Midian was
situated on the Dead Sea, in Arabia Petrea, adjoining
Moab; but very learned geographers describe but one
land of Midian, and this embraces both sides of the eastern gulf of the Red Sea, extending southwardly near to
Mt. Sinai. Perhaps they might have been distinguished
as Northern and Southern Midian.

There are three distinct countries mentioned in the
Bible, it is believed, peopled by Cush, (Gen. x. 6—8,)
the son of Ham, and father of Nimrod; and one of them
was probably the same with Midian. — (Comp. Ex. ii.
16, 21.)

THE CITIES OF THE PHILISTINES, AND PALESTINE.

THE Philistines and the Caphtorim descended from Casluhim, the son of Mizraim, who peopled Egypt; and their country is perhaps called the isle or country of Caphtor.—(Jer. xlvii. 4.) Their territory was allotted to the Hebrews; but they neglecting to take possession of it, the Philistines were made a severe and lasting scourge to them. — (Josh. xiii. 2, 3; xv. 45—47; Judg. iii. 1—3.) The country lying along the Mediterranean coast, between Joppa and Gaza, was inhabited by the Philistines, and was hence called Palestina; but in Ex. xv. 14, and in Isa. xiv. 29—31, it seems to denote the whole of Judea, as the word Palestine does in its modern acceptation.

ASHDOD, a fortified city of the Philistines, lying in the lot of Judah, and called by the Greeks, and known in the New Testament, by the name of Azotus.—(Acts viii. 40.) It was situated on the Mediterranean, between Askelon and Ekron, 15 or 20 miles north of Gaza. Here was the temple of Dagon, in which the Philistines placed the ark. The city was more than once captured.—(2 Chron. xxvi. 6; Isa. xx. 1.)

APHEK. (1 Sam. iv. 1—11.) A city on the borders of Judah and Benjamin, east of Jerusalem, where the Israelites were defeated by the Philistines, and the ark taken from them. This place is supposed to be the same which is elsewhere called Aphekah. — (Josh. xv. 53.)

ASKELON. (2 Sam. i. 20.) One of the "fenced cities" of the Philistines. It was situated on the eastern shore of the Mediterranean, 12 miles south of Gaza. It was a noble seaport, and was the birth-place of Herod the Great. After the death of Joshua, it fell into the hands of the tribe of Judah. — (Judg. i. 18.) At a short distance to the north is a small village called Scalona, evidently a corruption of the ancient name.

EKRON. (Josh. xv. 45.) A city of the Philistines, lying north west of Gath and north of Ashdod, assigned by Joshua originally to the tribe of Judah, (Judg. i. 18,) but afterwards said to belong to the tribe of Dan. — (Josh. xix. 43.) Neither tribe seems to have been in actual possession of the place. — (Judg. i. 34, 35; 1 Sam.

v. 10; vi. 17; 2 Kings i. 2; Jer. xxv. 20; Amos i. 8; Zeph. ii. 4; Zech. ix. 5, 7.)

GAZA. (Gen. x. 19.) A city, and one of the five principalities of the Philistines. It was situated on the coast of the Mediterranean, at the southern extremity of Canaan, within the tribe of Judah, (Judg. i. 18; 1 Sam. vi. 17,) and about 60 miles south-west of Jerusalem. In the reigns of Jotham and Ahaz it recovered its independence, but was again subdued by Hezekiah. — (2 Kings xviii. 8.) It was afterwards subject to the Persians and Chaldeans, and was captured by Alexander the Great, about 300 B. C. In the time of Eusebius it was a flourishing city, but has been often reduced since that day, and now consists of three small villages, with from 3,000 to 5,000 inhabitants. Messrs. King and Fisk, American missionaries, spent a Sabbath there in 1823. They tell us that the city stands on an elevation; the houses are built of stone. The scenery around is beautiful.

They found several Greeks there, and a Greek priest, who said the church there had been built twelve centuries.

GERAR, (Gen. x. 18,) a capital city of the Philistines, was situated south-west of Gaza, between Kadesh and Shur. — (Gen. xx. 1.) It is remarkable that both Abraham and Isaac retired to this place during the prevalence of a famine, and were both guilty of deceiving Abimelech, the king of the place, respecting their wives. — (Gen. xx. 1; xxvi. 1.) The Valley of Gerar, (Gen. xxvi. 17,) was the residence of Isaac, and probably in the vicinity of the city above described.

GATH. (Josh. xi. 22.) An acient city in the territory of Dan, celebrated as the birth-place of Goliath. — (1 Sam. xvii. 4.) It was situated about 32 miles west from Jerusalem. In the days of David, it was in the possession of the Philistines, and Achish was its king. — (1 Sam. xxi. 10 — 15; xxvii. 1 — 7.) David afterwards captured it. — (2 Sam. xv. 18; 1 Chr. xviii. 1.) It was afterwards subject to frequent revolutions. — (1 Kings ii. 39; 2 Kings xii. 17; xiii. 25; 2 Chron. xi. 8; xxvi. 6.) The inhabitants of Gath are called Gittites, (Josh. xiii. 3,) and the place Gittah-hepher. — (Josh. xix. 13.)

JABNEEL, (Josh. xv. 11,) or Jabneh, (2 Chron. xxvi.

6,) was a city of the Philistines, situated 12 miles south of Joppa. It was called Jamnia by the Greeks and Romans and is now called Gebna or Yebna.

ZIKLAG. (Josh. xix. 5.) A city in the southern extremity of the territory of Judah, though allotted to Simeon. In the time of Saul it was in the hands of the Philistines, and Achish, their king, granted it to David as a temporary residence, when he was flying from the persecution of that wicked monarch.—(1 Sam. xxvii. 6.) During the absence of David and the principal men on a campaign, the Amalekites burned the city, and made the women and children prisoners.

ACCHO, now Acca or Acre, (Judg. i. 31,) or Ptolemais, [so called after the first Ptolemy, king of Egypt, into whose hands it fell about 100 years B. C.) was a sea-port town on the bay of Acre, over against Mt. Carmel, about 30 miles south of Tyre. It was in the territory assigned to the tribe of Asher, and one of the cities from which they were unable to expel the Canaanites; and it is even now considered the strongest place in Palestine. It is mentioned in Acts xxi. 7. Its population is from 10,000 to 15,000, chiefly Jews. The remains of this ancient city are very numerous. Buckingham, who visited it in 1816, found several fragments of buildings, that he had no doubt were constructed in the earliest ages, especially thresholds of doors and pillars for galleries or piazzas.

CÆSAREA. (Acts xxiii. 33.) A considerable town on the coast of the Mediterranean, between Joppa and Tyre, about 62 miles from Jerusalem. Anciently it was a small town, called Stratonice, or the Tower of Strato; it is sometimes called Cæsarea of Palestine, to distinguish it from Cæsarea Philippi, and is supposed by some to be the Hazor of the Old Testament, (Josh. xi. 1.) Herod the Great contributed chiefly to the magnificence of the city, by building some of the most splendid of its edifices, and constructing a fine harbor for it. He called it Cæsarea, in honor of the Emperor Cæsar Augustus. After the destruction of Jerusalem, when Judea became a Roman province, Cæsarea was the chief city of Palestine, (Acts xxvi. 27; xxv. 1, 13,) and was often visited by Paul, (Acts ix. 30; xviii. 22; xxi. 8,) and it was here that he made his eloquent defence before Felix, Festus and Agrippa, (Acts ch. xxiii. xxv. and xxvi.,) and here he suffered two years' imprisonment. Philip the evangelist resided here, (Acts xxi. 8;) and Eusebius the historian was born here. Here Cornelius lived, (Acts x. 1;) here Agrippa was smitten of worms; and here Agabus foretold Paul's imprisonment. — (Acts xxi. 10, 11.) This is the Cæsarea mentioned also in Acts viii. 40; ix. 30; xii. 19; xxi. 8; xxiii. 23, 33; xxv. 4, 13. It is now wholly deserted and desolate; and its ruins have long been resorted to for building materials required at Accho. The present name of the place is Kaisaria.

GAZA. A city between Palestine and Egypt, and about two miles and a half from the Mediterranean Sea. It was anciently a city of the Philistines, but included in the tribe of Judah, which conquered it after the death of Joshua. — (Jud. i. 18.) The Philistines retook it, and kept possession of it till the reign of David. Sampson carried the gates of it to the top of a high hill, on the road towards Hebron; afterwards he was imprisoned and died here. — (Judges xvi.) During the reign of David, it was re-conquered by the Jews, and remained subject to them many years. During the wars of Alexander, it was laid waste; and a new town of the same name being laid out not far distant, it fell into decay, and became desolate, according to the prediction in Zeph. ii. 4. The old town is referred to in Acts viii. 26, as "Gaza which is desert."

ITUREA, a region in the north-east part of Palestine, thought to have derived its name from Jetur, a son of Ishmael. Hauran was one of its cities, whence the province was called Hauranitis by the ancients. Philip was its tetrarch in the days of Christ. — (Luke iii. 1.) The modern name is Houran.

JOPPA. A seaport of Palestine, of very ancient date, though possessing an inferior harbor. Its name is thought to have been derived from Japhet, son of Noah, who founded it. It is now nothing more than a ruinous village of fishermen, called by the natives Jaffa.

THE CITIES OF JUDEA.

JUDEA, or Jewry, is a name now applied to the whole of Canaan, but it was never so called till after the captivity. Sometimes the whole land of Canaan seems in the New Testament to have been called Judea, (Gal. i. 22;) but more properly it was divided into Galilee, Samaria and Judea. Judea, thus taken, contained the original portions of the tribes of Judah, Benjamin, Dan, and Simeon. It consisted of three parts — the plain country, on the west; the hill country, southward of Jerusalem; and the south, towards the borders of the land of Edom. (Matt. iii. 1; Acts ii. 9.)

ADULLAM. (Josh. xv. 35.) An ancient and celebrated city of Judah, 15 or 20 miles south-west of Jerusalem. The king of the place was slain by Joshua. It was fortified by Rehoboam, and probably on account of its strength, was called "the glory of Israel."—Mich. i. 15.) Near this city was a cave, where David secreted himself, when he fled from Achish. The cave, which is supposed to be the same, was visited by Mr. Whiting, an American Missionary, in 1835. He describes it as uneven, intricate, and very capacious; and says it is perfectly plain that 400 men might conceal themselves in the sides of the cave, as David's men did, and escape observation. — (1 Sam. xxii. 1.)

ARIMATHEA. A city of Judea, generally considered to be the same with Ramla, a pleasant town between Jerusalem and Joppa. It is, however, more probably, the city of Ramah, in Mt. Ephraim, called Ramathaim, (1 Sam. i. 1, 19,) and by Josephus, Ramatha.— Matt. xxvii. 57.)

ABEL-BETH-MAACHAH. 2 Kings xv. 29,) a city in the northern district of the tribe of Naphtali, lying southeast of Cæsarea Philippi. To this place Sheba, the son of Bichri, fled and posted himself, when pursued by Joab, general of the army of David. The citizens, however, who feared a siege if they harbored him, cut off his head, at the suggestion of a woman, and threw it over the wall to Joab. (2 Sam. xx. 14—22.) The city was afterwards captured. (1 Kings xv. 20; 2 Kings xv. 29.) Perhaps the phrase, "mother in Israel," (2 Sam. xx.

19,) if it was designed to apply to the place at all, may denote its size and importance. In the days of Christ, it was called Abila.

ANATHOTH. (Josh. xxi. 18.) A city of the tribe of Benjamin, situated a few miles north of Jerusalem. It was the birth-place of Jeremiah, (Jer. i. 1,) and the subject of one of his prophecies, (Jer. xi. 19—22,) as well as of Isaiah's. (Isa. x. 30.) It is also an interesting place in connection with the Jewish history.—(2 Sam. xxiii. 27; 1 Kings ii. 26; Neh. vii. 27.)

ABEL-MEHOLAH. A city west of Jordan, 10 miles south of Bethshan, in the tribe of Manasseh.—(1 Kings iv. 12.) It was the birth-place of Elisha.—(1 Kings xix. 16.) Near this city Gideon defeated the Midianites.

ARCHI. (Josh. xvi. 2.) A town on the southern border of Ephraim, between Bethel and Beth-horon the nether. It is celebrated as the birth-place of Hushai, David's friend.

ARGOB. (Deut. iii. 4.) A district of Bashan, the kingdom of Og, belonging to the half tribe of Manasseh. It lay east of Jordan, near the sea of Galilee, and contained 60 fortified cities. The governor of this place is supposed to be intended in 2 Kings xv. 25.

BETHSAIDA. (Matt. xi. 21.) There were at least two towns of this name in Judea. One was situated on the east bank of the Jordan, near where it falls into the sea of Tiberias. Near this village was the desert or wilderness of Bethsaida.—(Matt. xiv. 15—21; Luke ix. 10.) The other town was called Bethsaida of Galilee, and was situated on the west of Jordan, near the sea of Tiberias. This was the birth-place of Andrew, Peter and Philip. —(Mark xiv. 70; John i. 44.)

BETHANY. (Mark xi. 1.) A village on the south-east side of the Mount of Olives, about two miles from Jerusalem. It was the residence of Lazarus and his sisters. —(John xi. 1.) Christ often resorted thither, especially during the last few days of his ministry; and it was the scene of some of the most interesting events of his life. — (Matt. xxi. 17; xxvi. 6; Mark xi. 11, 12; xiv. 3; John xi. 1—46; xii. 1—3.)

BETHPHAGE. (Matt. xxi. 1.) A small village on the

south-east of Mount Olivet, adjoining Bethany on the
west, nearly two miles east of Jerusalem, belonging to
the priests. Here our Savior obtained the ass for his
lowly triumph.—(Comp. Luke xix. 28—40, with Matt.
xxi. 1—11.)

BETHLEHEM. (Gen. xxxv. 19,) called also Bethlehem
Ephratah, (Micah v. 2,) was so inconsiderable a place
as to be omitted in the general lists of the cities of Judah.—(Josh. xv.; Neh. xi.) It was the birth-place of
David, (Luke ii. 4, 11,) and was still more sacred and
celebrated as the birth-place of the Redeemer.—(Matt.
ii. 1; Luke ii. 4—6.) This city was about six miles
south of Jerusalem. It is called Ephratah and Eph-
rath, and its inhabitants Ephrathites, from its founder.

BEEROTH. (Josh. ix. 17; 2 Sam. iv. 2, 3.) A city of
Benjamin, situated at the foot of the hill on which Gib-
eon was built, a few miles north-east of Jerusalem.—
A place of the same name was also a station of the Is-
raelites, (Deut. x. 6,) and is called Bene-jaakan.—
(Num. xxxiii. 31.)

BEZEK. (Judges i. 4.) A city in the tribe of Judah,
where the Canaanites suffered a severe slaughter, and
their king was taken prisoner. It was at Bezek that
Saul mustered his army, before the attack on Jabesh-gilead. Ancient geographers speak of two towns by
the name of Bezek, situated near each other, about 17
miles from Sichem, on the way to Beth-shan.

The CITIES OF REFUGE, (Deut. xix. 7, 9; Josh. xx.
2, 7, 8,) were six of the Levitical cities, divinely appointed by the Jewish law as asylums, to which those
were commanded to flee, for safety and protection, who
might unintentionally kill a fellow being.

DECAPOLIS, (Matt. iv. 25.) Usually described as a province or canton of Judea, within the half tribe of Manasseh, east of the Jordan; but probably the name is applied to ten detached cities of Persia, which might have
been united in some alliance or confederacy, not extending to the residue of the district within which they were
situated. Geographers generally agree that Scythopolis was the chief of these cities.

ETAM. A city in Judah, built by Rehoboam, (1 Chron.
iv. 32; 2 Chron. xi. 6,) and lying between Bethlehem

and Tekoah. Modern maps place it in the tribe of Simeon, east of Gaza. There was a famous rock of this name, probably near this city.—(Judg. xv. 8, 11.)

The tower of EDAH was the place to which Jacob removed, after the death of Rachel.—(Gen. xxxv. 21.) It is called, also, the "tower of the flocks."—(Micah iv. 8.) It was a place of fine pasturage, about a mile from Bethlehem, supposed to be the very spot on which the Ethiopian shepherds received the announcement of the birth of Christ. It is very remarkable that the Targum of Jonathan calls it "the place where King Messiah shall be revealed in the end of days."

GIBEON. (Josh. x. 2; 1 Chron. xvi. 39.) A great city in Benjamin, five to seven miles northerly of Jerusalem, inhabited by Hivites, who secured the protection and alliance of Joshua by stratagem, (Josh. ix. 4—15,) and were consequently attacked by the five Canaanitish kings, but delivered by the aid of the Israelites.—(Josh. x. 10; Isa. xxviii. 21.) In the close of David's and beginning of Solomon's reign, the sanctuary was there.—(1 Chron. xvi. 39, 40; xxi. 29.)

GIBEAH. (1 Sam. xiii. 2.) A city a few miles north of Jerusalem, called Gibeah of [the children of] Benjamin, (2 Sam. xxiii. 29,) in distinction from one in Judah —(Josh. xv. 57.) It was also called Gibeah of Saul, (2 Sam. xxi. 6,) because it was his birth-place and residence. —(1 Sam x. 26; Isa. x. 29.) Its inhabitants were eminently wicked, as they evinced by their conduct, recorded in Judg. xix. 30, to which Hosea refers as proverbial. —(Hos. ix. 9; x. 9.) The city was terribly destroyed. —(Judg. xx. 46.)

GEBA, (2 Kings xxiii. 8,) called also Geba of Benjamin, (Josh. xxi. 17; 1 Kings xv. 22,) probably to distinguish it from another town of the same name, was one of the most northerly towns of Judea. Hence the expressions in 2 Kings xxiii. 8, and Zech. xiv. 10, denote the length of the land. It was in the vicinity of this place that the Philistines were defeated by David's army. — (2 Sam. v. 25.)

GATH-HEPHER. (2 Kings xiv. 25.) A city in the tribe of Zebulon, and probably in the land of Hepher. —(1

Kings iv. 10.) It is noted as the birth-place of the
prophet Jonah.

GATH-RIMMON. (Josh. xix. 45.) It would seem that
there were at least three cities of this name; one in the
tribe of Dan, (Josh. xxi. 24;) a second in the half tribe
of Manasseh, (Josh. xxi. 25;) and a third in the tribe of
Ephraim. — (1 Chron. vi. 69.)

GILGAL. 1. A city near Jericho, where was an altar.
— (1 Sam xi. 15.) Idols were worshipped here in after
times. (Hos. iv. 15.) 2. A city near Antipatris. —
(Josh. xii. 23.) There remained a village on this spot,
called Galgulis, for several hundred years after Christ.

HEBRON, (Num. xiii. 22,) so called after a son of Caleb, was one of the most ancient cities of Judea, and
was originally called Kirjath-Arba, or the city of Arba,
from its being the residence of a famous giant of that
name. — (Josh. xiv. 15.) Moses calls it Mamre. — (Gen.
xxiii. 19; xxxv. 27.) It was situated on an eminence
from 20 to 30 miles south of Jerusalem, and nearly 100
from Nazareth, (Luke i. 39,) and is still known as the
flourishing town of Habroun, or El-khalil, which means
"the friend," or "the beloved," (2 Chron. xx. 7;) celebrated for the manufacture of glass.

JERUSALEM. (Josh. xviii. 28.) The capital of the
kingdom of Judah. It was probably once called Salem,
(Gen. xiv. 18; Ps. lxxvi. 2; Heb. vii. 1, 2,) and in the
days of Abraham was the abode of Melchizedek, who,
as some suppose, built the city, and was its king. — (Gen.
xiv. 18; Heb. vii.; Ps. xlviii. 2, 13; cxxv. 1, 2.) The
ancient Salem was probably built upon Acra and Moriah,
the eastern and western hills. It stands 42 miles east of
the Mediterranean. When the Jebusites became masters of it, they called it Jebus, (Judg. xix. 10,) or Jebu-
si, (Joshua xviii. 28,) and erected a fortress in the southern quarter of the city, which was afterwards called
Mount Zion, but to which they gave the name of their
ancestor, Jebus. The city was surrounded with a strong
wall, 40 or 50 feet high. Its general form is nearly a
heptagon, or seven sided. The circumference is nearly
three miles. When the Israelites took possession of the
promised land, under Joshua, the children of Benjamin
did not drive out the Jebusites who inhabited Jerusalem;

but continued to dwell with them. [And the children of Israel dwelt among the Canaanites, Hittites, and Amorites, and Perizzites, and Hivites, and Jebusites. And they took their daughters to be their wives, and gave their daughters to their sons, and served their gods.]— (Josh. xviii. 28; Judg. iii. 5, 6.) Although the Israelites took possession of the surrounding territory, the Jebusites still held the castle of Zion, or upper town, until the time of David, who wrested it from them.—(2 Sam. v. 7—9.) [So David took the castle of Zion, which is the city of David. And David dwelt in the castle; therefore they called it the city of David. And he built the city round about, even from Millo round about; and Joab repaired the rest of the city. So David waxed greater and greater, for the Lord of Hosts was with him.]

Jerusalem was the place selected by the Almighty for his dwelling, and here his glory was rendered visible. This was the "perfection of beauty," and the "glory of all lands." Here David sat, and tuned his harp, and sung the praises of Jehovah. Hither the colored tribes came up to worship. Here enraptured prophets saw bright visions of the world above, and received messages from on high for guilty man. Here our Lord and Savior came in the form of a servant, and groaned, and wept, and poured out his soul unto death, to redeem us from sin, and save us from the pains of hell. Here, too, the wrath of an incensed God has been poured out upon his chosen people, and has laid waste his heritage.

JEZREEL. (Josh. xix. 18.) A royal city within the bounds of Manasseh, in the valley of Jezreel, where the tidings of Saul's death, in the battle at Gilboa, were first announced, (2 Sam. iv. 4,) and where his son Ishbosheth reigned after his father's death. —(2 Sam. ii. 9.) It is worthy of remark, that the fountain in Jezreel, where the Israelites encamped before the battle of Gilboa, (1 Sam. xxix. 1,) was the very spot where the crusaders encamped in 1183, when on the eve of a battle with Saladin. Ahab and Joram resided at Jezreel,)1 Kings xviii. 45; 2 Kings ix. 15,) and Jezebel and Joram were slain there, by Jehu.— (2 Kings ix. 24—33.) There was also a city in Judah of this name. —(Josh. xv. 56.)

JERICHO, (Num. xxii. 1,) one of the oldest cities in the

Holy Land, was situated in the tribe of Benjamin, about
20 miles from Jerusalem, and two from the river Jordan.
This city, which was next in size to Jerusalem, was besieged and subdued by the Israelites immediately after
the passage of the Jordan. The siege was conducted
under the divine direction; and, at a given signal, by
the immediate interposition of miraculous power, the
walls fell flat to the earth, probably destroying many
lives, and throwing the citizens into universal conster-
nation. The Israelites marched directly to the heart of
the city, and in obedience to the express command of
God, they put to death every living creature, except Rahab and her family, and the two men sent as spies from
the camp of Israel, (Josh. ii. 1, 2,) whom she had concealed. The city itself was then set on fire; every thing
in it, except the vessels of gold, silver, brass and iron,
which were previously removed, was burnt to ashes, and
the very site of it was cursed. — (Comp. Josh. vi. 26;
1 Kings xvi. 34.)

JABESH, (1 Sam. xi. 5,) or Jabesh-Gilead, (Judg. xxi.
8,) was situated at the foot of Mt. Gilead, within the
territory of Manasseh

JOKNEHAM, (Josh. xii. 22,) was a city of Zebulon. —
(Josh. xxi. 34.) It was situated south of Ptolemais, near
the bay, and is called of Carmel, because it was at the
foot of that mountain.

KABZEEL, (Josh. xv. 21.) or Jekabzeel, (Neh. xi. 25,)
was a city in the northern section of the inheritance of
Judah, just west of the southern extremity of the Dead
Sea. It was the birth-place of Benaiah. — (2 Sam. xxiii.
20.)

KENATH. (Num. xxxii. 42.) A city of Manasseh,
east of Jordan, the supposed ruins of which are called
Kahnat. It is situated on a brook of the same name,
and there are indications of its having been once a splendid city.

KIRJATH, (Josh. xviii 28,) called also Kirjath-jearim,
Kirjath-baal, and Baalah, (Josh. xv. 9, 60; 1 Chron. xiii.
6,) was on or near the boundary line between Judah
and Benjamin, and is therefore mentioned in the above
passages as a city of both tribes; though in Judg. xviii.
12, and 2 Sam. vi. 2, it is called a city of Judah. This

was the native place of Urijah the prophet, (Jer. xxvi.
20,) and it was here that the ark remained many years,
(1 Sam. vii. 1, 2; 2 Sam. vi. 2,) after it had been restored by the Philistines.

LACHISH. (Josh. x. 3.) A city of Judah, lying south
of Jerusalem, and towards the border of Simeon. It was
one of the Canaanitish cities, which was subdued by
Joshua, but it was afterwards rebuilt by Jeroboam, (2
Chron. xi. 9,) and sustained a severe and fruitless siege
by the Assyrians. (2 Kings xviii. 17; xix. 8; 2 Chron.
xxxii. 9; Jer. xxxiv. 7.)

LYDDA. A large village or city, not far from Joppa,
(Acts ix. 38,) eminent for its schools of learned Jews.
It was burnt by Cestius, while its males were gone
to Jerusalem to the feast of tabernacles — God, after
the crucifixion, not taking the care of them at these
times, as he had formerly done. It is now called Dios-
polis.

LIBNAH. (Josh. xxi. 13.) A city in the western part
of Judah, (Josh. xv. 42,) assigned to the priests, and a
city of refuge. — (1 Chron. vi. 57.) Its inhabitants revolted from Joram, (2 Kings viii. 22,) and were defeated
by the Assyrians. (2 Kings xix. 8.) Another Libnah
was situated near Mt. Sinai, (Num. xxxiii. 20,) and a
third in the country of Asher, (Josh. xix. 26,) called
there Shihor-Libnath.

MIZPAH, (1 Kings xv. 22,) or Mizpeh, (Josh. xv. 38.)
This name is given to several places, and implies a post
of observation or a watch-tower. They seem to have been
known as places of convocation on public occasions, religious and civil. 1. (Josh. xv. 38.) A city in the territory of Judah, north of Hebron, and nearly 20 miles
south from Jerusalem. Some geographers place it in the
tribe of Benjamin. — (Josh. xviii. 26.) Samuel dwelt at
Mizpah, (1 Sam. vii. 5, 6,) and Saul was anointed king
there, (1 Sam. x. 17—24;) and hither it is supposed the
Jews often resorted for business and devotion. — (Judg.
xx. 1; 1 Sam. vii. 5—7; x. 17.) It was fortified by Asa,
with the stone and timber which Baasha had been using
for the like purpose at Rama, (1 Kings xv. 22,) and was
the residence of Gedaliah, the governor appointed by
Nebuchadnezzar, after his subjection of the land. — (Jer.

xl. 6.) We find it rebuilt after the return from Babylon
—(Neh. iii. 19.) 2. (Gen. xxxi. 49.) A city in the territory of Gad, where Laban and Jacob entered into a
covenant of friendship, and where Jephthah resided and
mustered his army. — (Judg. xi. 11, 29.)

MARESHAH. (Josh. xv. 44.) A town of Judah, famous as the scene of the battle between Asa, king of
Judah, and Zerah, king of Ethiopia, with his numerous
army. It was also the residence of the prophet Micah.
— (Mic. i. 15.)

MEDEBA. (Josh. xiii. 16.) A city in the eastern part
of the territory of Reuben, which still retains nearly its
ancient name, Madaba. The site of the old town shows
the ruins of a temple, and the excavations of ponds and
reservoirs.

NOB, (1 Sam. xxii. 19,) was a city of the priests in
the territory of Benjamin, and within sight of Jerusalem
on the north. To this place David fled from the fury of
Saul, and obtained from Abimelech, the high priest,
some of the shew-bread, to satisfy his hunger; and also
Goliah's sword for his defence. For this act Saul caused
the city and all that was in it to be destroyed.

OPHNI. (Josh. xviii. 24.) A city of Benjamin, latterly called Gophna, between Shechem and Jerusalem. It
is mentioned by profane historians among the places
through which Vespasian and Titus passed, in their
march of conquest.

RAMA, (Matt. ii. 18,) or Ramah, (1 Sam. i. 19,) was
a small town, situated on an eminence in the territory of
Benjamin, (Josh. xviii. 25,) and about six miles north of
Jerusalem, on the way to Bethel. The name Rama, or
Ramoth, signifies an *eminence*, and hence is a constituent
part of the names of several places, and is sometimes
used generally for any high place. It was here that the
Jews were assembled after the destruction of Jerusalem
by Nebuzaradan, (Jer. xl. 1,) to take their departure
from their beloved country, and to go as captives into a
land of strangers, if not of tyrants. It was this place
that Baasha, king of Israel, once possessed and fortified;
but the king of Judah, by stratagem, wrested it from him.
— (1 Kings xv. 17.) Near to Ramah, Rachel was buried;
and she is represented by the prophet (Jer. xxxi. 15,) as

weeping over the loss of her children, and refusing to be comforted because of their captivity. This, though called Ramathaim-zophim, was also the place of Samuel's birth, residence, death and burial, and where he anointed Saul as king. — (1 Sam. i. 1, 19; ii. 11; vii. 17; viii. 4; xix. 18; xxv. 1,) Ramah, or Ramathaim, or Ramathaim-zophim, of the Old, is the Arimathea of the New Testament, where dwelt Joseph, in whose tomb the body of Christ was buried. — (John xix. 38.) There is now a village on the hill where was the site of Ramah, called Samuele by the Arabs. Jerusalem is easily seen from this height. There was another Rama in Naphthali. — (Josh. xix. 36.)

SIBMAH, (Isa. xvi. 8, 9,) or Shibmah, (Num. xxxii. 38.) A city of Reuben, near by Heshbon, celebrated for the luxuriant growth of the vine. — (Jer. xlviii. 32) It fell into the hands of the Moabites after the captivity of Reuben, Gad and Manasseh, by Tiglath-pileser; and hence the prophets Isaiah and Jeremiah weep for Moab, because the spoiler had broken the vines of Sibmah. Probably the expression in the passage from Jeremiah refers either to the universal reputation of the vines of Sibmah, or it is poetically used to denote the luxuriance of their growth. The "Sea of Jazer" was perhaps 15 or 20 miles from Sibmah.

SHUNEM. (Josh. xix. 18.) A town in the territory of Issachar, and a little south of Nain. It is associated with several important incidents of Jewish history, (1 Sam. xxviii. 4; 1 Kings i. 3; 2 Kings viii. 1—16,) and especially as the place where Elisha tarried on his journeys between Gilgal and Carmel, and where he performed a miracle under circumstances of unusual interest. — (2 Kings iv. 8—37.) The inhabitants were called Shunamites.

SHILOH, (Josh. xviii. 1,) where Samuel began to prophesy, (1 Sam. iii. 21,) and where Abijah lived, 1) Kings xiv. 2,) was a city of Ephraim between Lebanon and Bethel, 10 miles south of Shechem, and about 25 miles north of Jerusalem. Here Joshua fixed the tabernacle of God; and here it continued at least 310 years. Shiloh was one of the names of Jesus Christ — the great Deliverer — he that frees from the law, sin and death.

—(Gen. xlix. 10.) It denotes the Redeemer, the author of our happiness, and our sole peace-maker with God.

TEKOA, a city of Judah, 12 miles south-east of Jerusalem. Around it was an extensive wilderness, or pasture land, and forest. Amos, the prophet, kept a herd here, before his call to the ministry.—(Amos i. 1.)

THEBEZ. (Judg. ix. 50.) A city north-east of Shechem, within the territory of Ephraim, celebrated as the place where Abimelech was slain.

ZORAH, (Josh. xix. 41,) or Zoran. A city belonging originally to Judah, and afterwards to Dan, near the boundary line between them; the birth-place of Samson, (Judg. xiii. 2,) and probably fortified by Rehoboam.— (2 Chron. xi. 10.) It is called Zoreah, (Josh. xv. 33,) and its inhabitants are called Zorites, (1 Chron. ii. 54,) and Jorathites.— (1 Chr. iv. 2.)

ZEMARAIM, a city of Benjamin, not far from Bethel, near which was fought a bloody battle in the days of Jeroboam I. (Josh. xviii. 22.)

The valley of ZEPHATHA, (2 Chron. xiv. 9—13,) was in the south-western section of the territory of Judah, near Mareshah, and is memorable for the battle of the Jews with the Ethiopians. There was also a city of this name, [Zephath,] within the bounds of Simeon. — (Judg. i. 17.)

Judea may be called a mountainous country. The principal mountains mentioned in scripture are Seir, Horeb, Sinai, Hor, Gilboa, Nebo, Tabor, Engedi, Lebanon, Ebal, Amalek, Gerizim, Gilead, Moriah, Paran, Gahash, Olivet, Pisgah, Hermon and Carmel.

THE CITIES OF GALILEE.

GALILEE was the northern part of Canaan, comprehending Issachar, Zebulon, Naphtali and Asher. The upper part was called Galilee of the Gentiles, from its containing many Gentile inhabitants out of the neighboring nations; as the Phœnicians, Syrians, &c. — a mixture of colored population. Peter was detected by his speech, as being a Galilean.— (Mark xiv. 70.) Our Savior and most of the disciples were educated here;

7

and here were most of the miracles wrought. On this account, Jesus and his followers were often called Galileans. — (Luke xxiii. 6; Acts ii. 7.)

CAPERNAUM, a principal city of Galilee. It stood on the western shore of the Sea of Tiberias, in the border of Zebulon and Naphtali, not far from Bethsaida. It received its name from a clear fountain adjacent. Here Christ resided and taught, and here Matthew was called. It is now called Talhume.

NAZARETH. (Matt. xxi. 11.) A town in Galilee, within the territory of Zebulon, from 50 to 70 miles north of Jerusalem, now known as Nassera or Naserah. It was noted for its wickedness. — (John i. 46.) It occupies an elevated site about midway between Mt. Tabor and Cana. Jesus spent much of his time here; and hence the title, Jesus of Nazareth. — (Mark xvi. 6; Luke xxiv. 19; Acts ii. 22.) A precipice of 50 feet, which lies about a mile from the village, is regarded as the place to which the people of the town carried Jesus, with the savage intention of casting him off. — (Luke iv. 29.) There is a Roman Catholic Church here, called the Church of the Annunciation.

NAIN. (Luke vii. 11.) A city of Galilee, south of Mt. Tabor, and but a little distance from Capernaum. It is now a Turkish village, inhabited by Jews, Mohammedans, and a few Christians. The place is distinguished as the scene of one of Christ's most remarkable and affecting miracles. — (Luke vii. 11—15.)

NAIOTH. (1 Sam. xix. 22.) A part of the town of Ramah, [or, as the word signifies, "the meadows of Ramah,"] where a school of the prophets was established.

TIBERIAS, a city of Galilee, built by Agrippa, and so named in honor of the Emperor Tiberias. Hegesippus says it was the same as Cinnereth. In the time of the Jewish wars, this city, then the capital of Galilee, was bravely defended by Josephus the historian; but being taken by Vespasian, it was almost demolished. It was, however, a place of considerable note for many ages after. After the destruction of Jerusalem it flourished greatly, having 13 synagogues and a famous academy, over which a succession of Jewish doctors presided, till the fourth century. Here was held the last session of the Sanhedrim, and here the Talmud was collected. It is still a decent town, and around it are extensive ruins, indicative of its former extent and grandeur. 30 or 40 families of Greek Catholics reside here. The present name of this town is Tabaria.

THE CITIES OF ASIA MINOR.

THE Asia of the Bible is a peninsula, on the western or south-western side of the continent of Asia, which stretches into the Mediterranean or Great Sea, extending east as far as the Euphrates, west to the islands of the sea, north to what is now called the Black sea, and south to the Mediterranean Sea. It includes the provinces of Bithynia, Pontus, Galatia, Cappadocia, Cilicia, Pamphylia, Pisidia, Lycaonia, Phrygia, Mysia, Troas, Lydia, Lysia, and Caria.

ASSYRIA. (2 Kings xv. 19.) A most powerful empire of Asia, the history of which, both in its glory and in its overthrow, is most significantly told by the prophet. — (Ezek. xxxi.) It was founded probably by Nimrod, 120 years after the deluge.

CUTH, or Cutha, (2 Kings xvii. 24, 30,) was evidently, from the connection, a province of Assyria; and Cush is the marginal reading for Ethiopia in Gen. ii. 13, Hab. iii. 7, and elsewhere.

LYDIA. (Ezek. xxx. 5.) There was a celebrated kingdom of Asia Minor known by this name, of which Sardis was the capital. It is supposed to have been settled by the posterity of Lud, a son of Shem. It had Mysia on the north, Phrygia on the east, Caria on the south, and the Ægean Sea on the west. It was once under the dominion of Crœsus, the wealthiest monarch of his age. It was, in the time of the apostles, a province of the Roman empire. The Lydia of the above cited passage is supposed to refer to a place or a people in Africa.

BITHYNIA. (Acts xvi. 7. A province of Asia Minor. It is bounded on the east by Paphlagonia, north by the Black Sea, and south by Phrygia and Galatia. It is directly opposite to Constantinople. The gospel was introduced into this province at an early period. (Comp. Acts ii. 9, and 1 Peter i. 1.) There is a remarkable testimony in ecclesiastical history, to the purity and firmness of the Christians of Bithynia, at the close of the first and the beginning of the second century.

CILICIA. (Acts xxi. 39.) A province in the southeastern district of Asia Minor, lying on the northern coast, at the eastern extremity of the Mediterranean Sea. Its capital city was Tarsus, the birth-place of Paul. The synagogue of "them of Cilicia" (Acts vi. 9,) was a place of Jewish worship at Jerusalem, appropriated to the use of Jews who might be at Jerusalem, from the province of Cilicia. A similar custom in modern times is the fitting up of public houses to accommodate strangers from particular States or countries. Paul, being of this province, was probably a member of this synagogue, and perhaps one of the defeated opposers and controvertists of Stephen. — (Comp. Acts vi. 10, and vii. 58.)

COLOSSE. (Col. i. 2.) A city of Phrygia in Asia Minor, on the river Lycus, [now the Gorduk.] About a year after Paul's epistle was written to the church at this place, it was destroyed by an earthquake. The former site of Colosse is now occupied by the castle and village of Chonos.

CAPPADOCIA. A province in the north-eastern part of Asia Minor, peopled by the descendants of Togarmah, and once forming part of the kingdom of Lydia. It was famous for horses, mules and flocks; and traded in these with the Tyrians. — (Ezek. xxvii. 14.) According to Herodotus, it submitted to the Medes, and then to the Persians, parts of whose worship the inhabitants incorporated with their own idolatry. It afterwards formed a part of the vast Roman empire. Christianity was introduced here in the days of the apostles, (Acts ii. 9,) and continues to this day. At the village of Dacora, in this province, was born Eunomius the Arian. Some of its early pastors were very distinguished for piety and learning.

DERBE. (Acts xiv. 6.) A town of Lycaonia, east of Iconium, whither Paul and Barnabas fled when expelled

from Lystra, and where they preached the gospel with
success. (Acts xiv. 20.) Derbe was the native place
of Gaius. — (Acts xx. 4.)

EPHESUS. (Acts xix. 35.) A celebrated city of Asia
Minor, said to have been built by Ephesus, an Amazon
lady, as early as the days of David. It was situated on
the river Cayster, near its mouth about 30 miles south
of Smyrna, and was the ornament and metropolis of pro-
consular Asia, and celebrated for a magnificent temple
of Diana. This temple was 425 feet in length, 220 in
breadth, and was supported by 100 columns, each 60
feet in height. The building of it occupied 200 years.
When Paul came to the city, A. D. 54, he commenced
preaching in the Jewish synagogue. The blessing of
God attended his ministry.

GALATIA. (Acts xvi. 6.) A province of Asia Minor,
lying east of Phrygia, and called Galatia by the Gauls,
who were the original settlers of it. Christianity was
introduced into this province by the apostle Paul, who
was there once with Silas and Timothy, (Acts xvi. 6,)
about the year 53, and again four or five years afterwards, on his return from Corinth. —(Acts xviii. 23.)

HIERAPOLIS. A city near Colosse, early blessed with
gospel light. —(Col. iv. 13.) It was destroyed by an
earthquake in the time of the apostles. The ruins are
still visible, and the place is called by the Turks, Pam-
buk Kalasi.

ICONIUM. (Acts xiii. 51.) A city of ancient Lycaonia, in
Asia Minor, at the foot of Mt. Taurus, now called Conia,
or Cogni, the capital of Caramania, and residence of a
pacha. It contains at present about 15,000 inhabitants.
It was visited by Paul and Barnabas, who preached the
gospel there, and were so persecuted in consequence of
it, as to be obliged to leave the place. — (Acts xiv. 1 —
6.) Iconium is mentioned by several ancient historians.
Strabo says it was well built, and situated in the richest
part of the province; a place of some consequence, and
strongly fortified by walls four miles in extent. Multitudes were here converted to Christianity, A. D. 45 or
46. — (Acts xvi. 1—3.) The church thus planted may
be traced through eight succeeding centuries.

LYCAONIA. (Acts xvi. 6—11.) A province of Asia

Minor, which the apostle Paul twice visited. It was separated from Phrygia, and created into a Roman province,
by Augustus, and was bounded north by Galatia, east by
Cappadocia, south by Cilicia, and west by Pisidia and
Phrygia. Its chief towns were Iconium, Derbe and
Lystra. It is now a part of Caramania, and subject to
the Turks. The *speech* of this province, (Acts xiv. 11,)
is supposed to have been either the old Assyrian language, or a corruption of the Greek.

MILETUS, or Miletum. A seaport of Caria, in Lesser
Asia, and the capital of both Caria and Ionia. It stood
about 36 miles south-west of Ephesus, and is said to have
been built by Miletus, the son of the god Apollo, whose
temple here was exceedingly magnificent. Here were
four harbors, sufficient to hold all the Persian fleet. Here
Thales and Anaximenes, the philosophers, and Timotheus, the musician, were born.

MESECH, (Ps. cxx. 5,) or Mesech, (Ezek. xxxii. 26.)
A country in the north-eastern angle of Asia Minor, supposed to have been settled by the posterity of Mesech,
the son of Japheth. They had considerable commerce
with Tyre.—(Ezek. xxvii. 13.) Some suppose the Mus-
covites were of this race. The terms Mesech and Kedar, in the above passage from Psalms, is supposed to
denote northern and southern barbarians generally.

MYSIA. (Acts xvi. 7.) A province of Asia Minor,
and at this day a beautiful and fertile country. It has
the sea of Propontis on the north, Lydia on the south,
Bithynia on the east. In the northern section of Mysia
was the province in which the ancient city of Troy was
situated, and not far distant was the Troas mentioned by
Paul.—(Acts xvi. 8; xx. 6; 2 Cor. ii. 12; 2 Tim. iv. 13.)

PHILADELPHIA. (Rev. iii. 7—13.) A city of the province of Lydia, about 70 miles east of Smyrna. Its modern name is Allah-shehr, or Alah-sher, [city of God.]
It contains a population of about 15,000, one twelfth of
whom are nominal Christians. This church was highly
commended; more than any of the seven churches of
Asia, and while her sister cities have fallen into decay,
she still survives, with the remains of her Christian
temples and worship. Her population is said to be the
purest in Asia Minor. Even Gibbon says of her:

"Among the Greek colonies and churches of Asia, Philadelphia is still erect — a column in a scene of ruins."

PISIDIA. (Acts xiii. 14.) A province of Asia Minor, north of Pamphylia. Antioch, though within the province of Phrygia, belonged to Pisidia, and was called Antioch in [or of] Pisidia, to distinguish it from Antioch in Syria. Paul labored in the gospel, not only at Antioch, but throughout the province. — (Acts xiv. 24.)

PONTUS. (1 Pet. i. 1.) The north-eastern province of Asia Minor, lying along the Black Sea, having Colchis on the east, Cappadocia south, and Paphlagonia west. Many Jews resided here in the time of Christ, (Acts ii. 9,) and the gospel was early introduced, and entertained by many, whom Peter addresses in his first epistle. Aquila, Paul's companion, was of this province. —(Acts xviii. 2.) It became a province of Rome in the time of Pompey.

PHRYGIA. (Acts ii. 10.) The largest province of Asia Minor, having Bithynia north, and Lysia south. Its chief towns were Colosse, Laodicea, and Hierapolis. Some of the inhabitants were at Jerusalem, and among the converts on the day of Pentecost. The province was more than once visited by the apostle Paul.

PATARA. (Acts xxi. 1.) A large, rich, seaport town of Lysia, lying over against Rhodes, at the mouth of the Xanthus, called, by Ptolemy Philadelphus, king of Egypt, Arsinoe, in honor of his queen. Here Paul took ship for Phœnicia, when going from Philippi to Jerusalem.

PERGAMOS. The ancient metropolis of Mysia, and the residence of the Attalian kings. It stands on a rich and spacious plain, near the banks of the Caicus, and was famous for its extent and grandeur; for a temple to Esculapius; for a library of 200,000 volumes, which was removed to Egypt by Cleopatra; and for its being the birth place of the celebrated Galen. Parchment was invented here, and received its name from the place.

SARDIS. (Rev. i. 11.) A city of Ancient Lydia, and the site of one of the seven churches of Asia. Its modern name is Sart, and it lies about 30 miles south-east of Thyatira. It is, however, but a miserable village, in-

habited chiefly by shepherds, though it is one of the stop-
ping-places of the Persian caravans. The original city
was plundered by Cyrus, and afterwards desolated by
an earthquake, the ruins of it being still visible a little
distance to the south of the present town.

TELABIB. (Ezek. iii. 15.) A town on the river Chebar, where Ezekiel and many of the Jewish exiles dwelt.
Its site is supposed to be occupied by the modern Thel-
abar.

TROAS. (Acts xvi. 8.) A maritime city of Mysia, on
the Mediterranean, near the mouth of the Hellespont,
four miles from the ancient Troy, and built chiefly with
materials from its ruins. The celebrated siege and capture of Troy occurred, according to Sir Isaac Newton,
about 904 years B. C. or during the reign of Jehosaphat.
Paul visited Troas repeatedly. —(Acts xx. 5—12; 2 Cor.
ii. 12; 2 Tim. iv. 13.)

THE CITIES OF PERSIA AND MEDIA.

PERSIA. (Ezek. xxvii. 10.) An ancient kingdom of
Asia, whose limits have varied considerably at different
periods. The kingdom, as such, was founded by Cyrus,
its inhabitants having been anciently called Elamites,
from their ancestor Elam, the son of Shem, and in later
times Parthians. The thrones of Media and Persia
were united under Cyrus, B. C. 536, (Comp. Dan. vi. 8,
12;) and indeed the whole country, from Egypt to the
Ganges, became incorporated in what was called the
Persian empire.

The celebrated city of PERSEPOLIS. The following
is a correct view of the celebrated ruins of Persepolis,
the ancient capital of Persia, which, in the days of its
prosperity, was one of the wealthiest and most ancient
cities of the world. The magnificent pile of ruins,
which remains after the lapse of so many ages, was the
palace of Darius. This grand and stately structure was
surrounded with a triple wall; the first wall was 16 cubits high, and adorned with many splendid buildings and
lofty towers; the second wall was built in the same manner, but was as high again; the third was drawn like a

quadrant, four square, and 60 cubits high, built of the
hardest marble, and so cemented as almost to defy the
ravages of time. On the four sides were brazen gates,
with curtains or palisades of the same metal, 120 cubits
high, and 410 paces long, for the purpose of giving defence to the city, and striking beholders with terror.
The walls were 600 paces from north to south, and 396
from east to west. The numerous columns, porticoes,
stair-cases, images, &c. are exceedingly magnificent,
even in their ruinous state; and induce the belief that
the Persian empire in all its grandeur, could boast of
nothing more glorious, nor have left anything to posterity more astonishing than the description and ruins of
this once splendid city. The fine plain in which this city
stood was in the eastern part of Persia; it was 20
leagues long and 6 broad, and within this compass there
were more than 1000 villages, adorned with beautiful
gardens.

Alexander the Great, taking Persepolis by storm, put
the unhappy inhabitants to the sword. He likewise
burnt the other cities and villages of that plain. The destroying element rolled onward like an overwhelming
and resistless deluge; and in a little time the dwelling
place of thousands presented nothing but a heap of smok-
ing ruins — one vast picture of desolation. It is supposed that Alexander took 120,000 talents from the city
of Persepolis, and robbed the inhabitants of the plain
of all their valuable property. The spoil was so great
that it required nearly 6,000 camels and mules to carry
it off.

SHUSHAN. (Neh. i. 1; Esth. i. 5.) An ancient extensive, and magnificent city, [called by the Greeks,
Susa, or the city of lilies,] situated on the river Ulai,
[now Kerrah.] It was in the province of Elam, in Persia, now known as Khusistan, and formerly as Susiana.
Shushan was the capital. It is said to have been built
by Memnon, before the Trojan war. It was the winter
residence of the Persian kings from the time of Cyrus,
being sheltered by a high ridge of mountains from the
north-east wind; but in the summer it was so intensely
hot as to be scarcely habitable. Here Daniel had his
vision of the ram and he-goat. — (Daniel viii.)

MEDIA. (Isa. xxi. 2.) This country which probably derives its name from Madai, (Gen. x. 2,) anciently occupied what is now part of the kingdom of Persia, and was bounded north by the Caspian Sea and Armenia, south by Persia proper and west by Assyria. It was a fertile and well cultivated region, and was divided into greater and lesser Media. Ninus, king of Assyria, added this country to his kingdom, and retained it till the time of Sennacherib, when it revolted, and his son became king, B. C. 700. It fell into the hands of Cyrus the Great, about 556 B. C. who perfectly united Media and Persia, forming the Medo-Persian kingdom. Hence, by Esther and Daniel, the laws and chronicles· of the Medes and Persians are always mentioned together. God employed the Medes to punish Babylon, and then sent them the cup of his wrath by Cyrus. — (Isa. xiii. 17, 18; xxi. 2, 3; Jer. xxv. 25.)

ACHMETHA. (Ezra vi. 2.) The Ecbatana of ancient Media, and the place where the records of the kingdom were preserved. The place is occupied, as it is supposed, by the modern city of Hamadan, in Persia. It was surrounded by seven walls, and at one period was considered the strongest and most beautiful city of the east, except Nineveh and Babylon.

PARTHIANS, (Acts ii. 9,) or the inhabitants of Parthia, originally a province of Media, on its eastern side, situated between the Persian Gulf and the Tigris. The Parthians seem to have resembled the Cossacks of our day, and were celebrated for their skill in archery, and especially for shooting as they fled, and were a part of the Scythian horde who so long disputed with Rome for the dominion of the east. Parthia was united to the Persian empire, A. D. 226. The Persian language was spoken there; and indeed in Scripture and other ancient writings, Persia and Parthia are often used as synonymous.

THE KINGDOM AND CITIES OF SYRIA.

SYRIA was formerly a province of Canaan. The inhabitants were Canaanites, called by the Greeks, Phœ-

nicians and Ethiopians. It contained 100 flourishing
cities, towns and villages, and 12,000,000 souls within
the kingdom. Every where one might have seen cultivated fields, frequented roads and crowded inhabitants.
[Josephus and Strabo.]

AMORITES. They occupied the portion of Syria which
afterwards constituted the lots of Reuben, Gad, Manasseh, Dan, Judah, Simeon, and Benjamin. As they were
the most powerful of the devoted tribes, all the Canaanites sometimes went under their name.

ANTIOCH. A city of this name was long the capital
of Syria. It was situated on the banks of the Orontes,
twelve miles from the Mediterranean, built by Seleucus
Nicanor, B. C. 301. It was ranked the third city of the
earth, being scarcely inferior to Alexandria. It was
the royal residence of the kings of Syria. Luke and
Theophilus were born in this place. Here Paul and
Barnabas preached, and here the disciples of Christ
were first called Christians. Chrysostom preached here
in the fourth century with great success. This church
was famous for many hundred years. In A. D. 538,
sixty thousand of its inhabitants perished in an earthquake. In 1188, it was demolished by the Saracens. In
1822, a tremendous earthquake completely destroyed
the remains of this once splendid city; and it is now little else than a heap of ruins. Its present name is An-
takia. There were many other cities called Antioch;
none of which are mentioned in Scripture, but that in
Pisidia, which is now called Ak-sher, and sometimes
Antiochio. — (Acts xiii. 14.)

ALEPPO, a city of Syria, stands on four hills, twenty-
two leagues east of Scanderoon. This city is about
three miles in circuit.

DAMASCUS. (Gen. xv. 2.) The capital of ancient
Syria, for three centuries the residence of the Syrian
kings, and the oldest city which now exists. Its modern
name is El-shams. It is situated on the river Baradi,
about two hundred miles south of Antioch, and a hundred and twenty north-east of Jerusalem. The country
around it, within a circuit of twenty or thirty miles, is
well watered, and exceedingly fertile. The city itself is
about two miles in length, and surrounded by a wall.

The streets are narrow, but well paved; and it is said
that one of them, which runs through the breadth of the
city and suburbs, from two to three miles, is still called
"straight." — (Acts ix. 11.) The adjoining country
is so beautiful in scenery, and so rich in soil, that the
orientals regard it as a paradise on earth — such is
its commanding situation.

GADARA, the capital of Peræa, in Cœlo-Syria, stood
about four miles eastward of the Sea of Tiberias. Great
numbers of swine were kept here, which was directly
contrary to the Mosaic law. When Christ, in healing
two possessed persons, suffered the devils to enter their
herd of swine, and drown them, instead of being humbled by their punishment, they besought the Savior to
leave their country. About forty years after, the city
was burnt by the Romans.

HELBON. (Ezek. xxvii. 18.) A Syrian city of great
opulence and antiquity, celebrated for its wines; and
probably the same with Aleppo, [or, as the Arabs say,
Alep or Halab,] which is now one of the most flourishing cities of Turkey. Its buildings are of hewn stone,
and its streets paved with the same. It was once deeply concerned in the India trade, and is still a place of
commercial intercourse and manufacturing enterprise.

ITUREA. (Luke iii. 1.) A province of Syria, which
derived its name from Jetur, a son of Ishmael, whose
posterity inhabited it. It was south of Trachonitis, beyond Jordan, and probably included Auranitis and Bata-
nea. It was overrun by a party of the Israelites in the
time of Jotham king of Judah, and a vast quantity of
spoil taken. — (1 Chr. v. 19, 22.) It is now called
Djedour.

MESOPOTAMIA, (Deut. xxiii. 4.) or Syria, between the
two rivers, elsewhere called Padan-aram, or the plain of
Syria, was the name of the country lying between the
Tigris and the Euphrates. It was the first abode of men
both before and after the flood, and was bounded north
by Armenia, east by Assyria, south by Arabia, and west
by Syria, and embraced the modern El-jesira of Turkey.
Some suppose that the wise men who visited the infant
Jesus, were from this country. Here were the garden
of Eden and the tower of Babel. It was the original

residence of Abraham, Isaac, Jacob, and all their children save Benjamin. (Gen. xi. 31.) It was astonishingly populous, containing, according to Ptolemy, seventy important cities. Christianity, in a mutilated form, still exists here. The region is still fertile, and is now called Diarbekir.

PHŒNICE. (Acts xxvii. 12.) A winter harbor on the southern shore of Crete.

PHŒNICIA. (Acts xxi. 2.) A province of Syria, and, in the largest extent of the term, embracing a strip of land adjoining the eastern coast of the Mediterranean, eighty miles long and twelve broad. Properly, however, it included only the territories of Tyre and Sidon. The Phœnicians were descendants of the Canaanites, and a Syro-phœnician was a Phœnician of Syria. Phœnicia was also subject to the Greek government in the time of our Savior, and hence Tyre and Sidon might be regarded as Greek cities. (Comp. Matt. xv. 22; Mark vii. 26.) The Jews regarded all the rest of the world as Greeks.

Phœnicia is considered as the birth-place of commerce, if not of letters. The soil is still fertile, producing a rich variety of grains and fruits; but all the enterprise and prosperity of the people is blasted by the despotism of the government. Carthage was established by a colony of Phœnicians; and Cadiz, in Spain, is also supposed to have been settled by the same people about one thousand years before Christ. It is thought the Phœninicians pushed their trade as far as Britain, and they probably had settlements on the Red Sea and Persian Gulf. Sir Isaac Newton thinks that vast numbers of Edomites fled hither in the days of David, and carried their arts along with them. The chief city of this region, and sometimes the region itself, is now called Tripoli.

TOB. (Judg. xi. 3, 5.) A district in the south-east of Syria, whither Jephthah fled, and whence he was called to lead the army of Israel.

THE GREAT AND SPLENDID CITY OF SYRIA — PALMYRA. This city was situated about fifteen miles east from Damascus, and one hundred and twenty from Tarabolas or Tripoli. It was the metropolis of Palmyrene, a fertile province of Syria. Surrounded on all sides by

frightful deserts, this province was noted for its large
and splendid cities; its gardens, palaces, and numerous
temples; and the accomplishment of its inhabitants.
This city was called Palmara by the Greeks, Palmyra by
the Romans; in Scriptures, Tadmor; and by Josephus,
Thadamor. Of its origin little is known; but by some
learned historians, it is supposed to have been founded by
Solomon. It flourished for many years; and was unfortunately the cause of frequent and bloody conflicts between the Romans and Carthaginians. It was destroyed
by Antiochus; and re-built and beautifully adorned by
Aurelian. When, however, that country became subject to the Turks, that barbarous, ignorant and bigoted
people shamefully laid it in ruins. The statements of various travellers describe these ruins as very interesting.
The principal, at present, are temples and porticos of
Grecian architecture. These ruins cover several square
miles; and present a melancholy spectacle. The temple of the sun, or rather its ruins, which attracts particular notice, covers a square of 220 yards. It was
high and massive, and adorned within and without with
pilasters, of which 124 are remaining. The Turks, by
beating down the cornices, have deprived the world of
the most finished work of the kind. In this square are
fifty-eight entire pillars, thirty-seven feet high, with capitals of the finest carving. In the middle of this enclo-
sure, stood the Temple encompassed by another row of
pillars fifty feet in height. It was one of the most splendid edifices in the world.

To the north of the temple, is a stately obelisk fifty
feet high, of wreathed work; the sculpture is considered
extremely fine. To the west of this is a spacious entrance to a noble piazza, which is a quarter of a mile in
length, and forty feet in breadth — formed by two rows
of marble pillars twenty-six feet high and nine in circumference. There were originally five hundred and
sixty of these pillars: only one hundred and twenty-nine
are now standing.

SELEUCIA. (Acts xiii. 4.) A city of Syria, on the
shores of the Mediterranean, west of Antioch, and near
the mouth of the Orontes.

ZAREPHATH, or Sarepta, where Elijah dwelt some time

with a widow, was a seaport of Phœnicia, midway between Tyre and Sidon. (1 Kings xvii. 9, 10; Luke iv. 26.) About A. D. 400, it was still of some note. Its present name is Sarfend.

THE GREAT COMMERCIAL CITY OF TYRUS OR TYRE. It was situated at the entry of the sea, and founded by the celebrated Ethiopian wise men, who built a strong city, and heaped up silver as the dust, and fine gold as mire of the streets, (Zech. ix. 3,) with her kings and princes, merchants and captains, pilots and seamen, ships with fine linen broidered work from Egypt for their sails.—(Ez. xxvii.) This mighty city, which once had the entire control of the trade with India, and into whose lap the treasures of the world were poured, is about five miles distant from the other Tyre, and was the city which Alexander reached by means of a causeway from the main land, and entirely consumed it, in accordance with some of the most interesting prophecies, Zech. ix. 3, 4; Isa. xxiii.; Ezek. xxvi., xxviii.;) and we are told by modern travellers that its desolation is complete. Tyre, which is now called Sur, is only inhabited by a few fishermen, who live in the ruins of its primitive state.

THE COLONIES OF TYRE. Carthage, a city in Africa, was one of the colonies of Tyre. It was founded by the Canaanites — Egyptians — blacks. [Herodotus.]

UTICA. This city was built by the Phœnicians in Africa, a colony from Tyre, about 15 miles from Carthage on the Mediterranean.—[Rollin.]

CITIES OF AFRICA.

CARTHAGE. The foundation of this celebrated city is ascribed to Elissa, a Tyrian princess, better known as Dido; it may therefore be fixed at the year of the world 3158; when Joash was king of Judah; 98 years before the building of Rome, and 846 years before Christ. The king of Tyre, father of the famous Jezebel, called in Scripture Ethbaal, was her great-grandfather. She married her near relation Acerbas, also called Sicharbas, or Sichaeus, an extremely rich prince;

Pygmalion king of Tyre was her brother. Pygmalion
put Sichaeus to death in order that he might have an opportunity to seize his immense treasures; but Dido eluded her brother's cruel avarice, by secretly conveying
away her deceased husband's possessions. With a large
train of followers she left her country, and after wandering sometime, landed on the coast of the Mediterranean, in Africa; and located her settlement at the bottom of the gulf, on a peninsula, near the spot where
Tunis now stands. Many of the neighboring people al-
lured by the prospect of gain, repaired thither to sell to
those foreigners the necessaries of life; and soon became incorporated with them. The people thus gathered from different places soon grew very numerous.
And the citizens of Utica, an African city about fifteen
miles distant, considering them as their countrymen, as
descended from the same common stock, advised them
to build a city where they had settled. The other natives of the country, from their natural esteem and respect for strangers, likewise encouraged them to the
same object. Thus all things conspiring with Dido's
views, she built her city, which was appointed to pay an
annual tribute to the Africans for the ground it stood upon,
and called it Carthage — a name that in the Phœnician
and Hebrew languages, [which have a great affinity,]
signifies the "New City." It is said that in digging the
foundation, a horse's head was found; which was thought
to be a good omen, and a presage of the future warlike
genius of that people. Carthage, had the same language,
and national character as its parent state — Tyre. It
became at length, particularly at the period of the Punic
War, one of the most splendid cities in the world; and
had under its dominion 300 cities bordering upon the
Mediterranean. From the small beginning we have described, Carthage increased till her population numbered 700,000; and the number of her temples and other
public buildings was immense.. Her dominion was not
long confined to Africa. Her ambitious inhabitants extended their conquests into Europe, by invading Sardinia, seizing a great part of Sicily, and subduing almost
all of Spain. Having sent powerful colonies every
where, they enjoyed the empire of the seas for more

than six hundred years; and formed a State which was able to dispute pre-eminence with the greatest empire of the world, by their wealth, their commerce, their numerous armies, their formidable fleets, and above all by the courage and ability of their commanders; and she extended her commerce over every part of the known world. A colony of Phœnicians or Ethiopians, known in scripture as Canaanites, settled in Carthage. The Carthaginians settled in Spain and Portugal. The first inhabitants of Spain were the Celtæ, a people of Gaul; after them the Phœnicians possessed themselves of the most southern parts of the country, and may well be supposed to have been the first civilizers of this kingdom, and the founders of the most ancient cities. After these, followed the Grecians; then the Carthaginians.

Portugal was anciently called Lusitania, and inhabited by tribes of wandering people, till it became subject to the Carthaginians and Phœnicians, who were dispossessed by the Romans 250 years before Christ. [Rollin.]

The Carthaginians were masters of all the coast which lies on the Mediterranean, and all the country as far as the river Iberus. Their dominions, at the time when Hannibal the Great set out for Italy, all the coast of Africa from the Aræ Phileanorum, by the great Syrtis, to the pillars of Hercules was subject to the Carthaginians, who had maintained three great wars against the Romans. But the Romans finally prevailed by carrying the war into Africa, and the last Punic war terminated with the overthrow of Carthage. [Nepos in vita Annibalis. Liv.]

The celebrated Cyrene was a very powerful city, situated on the Mediterranean, towards the greater Syrtis, in Africa, and had been built by Battus, the Lacedemonian. [Rollin.]

CYRENE. (Acts xi. 20.) A province and city of Libya. There was anciently a Phœnician colony called Cyrenaica, or "Libya about Cyrene."—(Acts ii. 10.)

CYRENE. A country west of Egypt, and the birthplace of Callimachus the poet, Eratosthenes the historian, and Simon, who bore the Savior's cross. Many Jews from hence were at the Pentecost, and were converted

8

under Peter's sermon. (Acts ii.) The region is now under the Turkish power, and has become almost a desert. It is now called Cairoan. Some of the Cyrenians were among the earliest Christians, (Acts xi. 20.) and one of them, it is supposed, was a preacher at Antioch. (Acts xiii. 1.) We find also, that among the most violent opposers of Christianity, were the Cyrenians, who had a synagogue at Jerusalem, as had those of many other nations. It is said there were 480 synagogues in Jerusalem.

LYBIA, or Libya, (Acts ii. 10.) was anciently among the Greeks a general name for Africa, but properly it embraced only so much of Africa as lay west of Egypt, on the southern coast of the Mediterranean. Profane geographers call it Libya Cyrenaica, because Cyrene was its capital. It was the country of the Lubims, (2 Chron. xii. 3,) or Lehabims of the Old Testament, from which it is supposed to have derived its name.

The ancient city of Cyrene is now called Cyreune, Cairoan, or Cayran, and lies in the dominion of Tripoli. This district of the earth has lately occasioned much interest among Italian and French geographers. Great numbers of Jews resided here. (Matt. xxvii. 32.)

LIBYA, a part of Africa, bordering on Egypt, famous for its armed chariots and horses. — (2 Chron. xvi. 8.)

OPHIR, the son of Joktan, gave name to a country in Africa, famous for gold, which was renowned even in the time of Job, (Job ch. xxii. 24; xxviii. 16,) and from the time of David to the time of Jehoshaphat, the Hebrews traded with it, and Uzziah revived this trade when he made himself master of Elath, a noted port on the Red Sea. In Solomon's time, the Hebrew fleet took up three years in their voyage to Ophir, and brought home gold, apes, peacocks, spices, ivory, ebony, and almug-trees. — (1 Kings ix. 28; x. 11; xxii. 48; 2 Chr. ix. 10.)

TARSHISH, (Isa. xxiii. 1,) or Tharshish. (1 Kings x. 22.) It is supposed that some place of this name existed on the eastern coast of Africa, or among the southern ports of Asia, with which the ships of Hiram and Solomon traded in gold, and silver, ivory, and apes, and peacocks. (2 Chron. ix. 21.) It is said that once in every three years these ships completed a voyage, and brought home their merchandise. Hence, it is inferred, the place with which they traded must have been distant from Judea.

The vessels given by Hiram to Solomon, and those built by Jehoshaphat, to go to Tarshish, were all launched at Eziongeber, at the northern extremity of the eastern gulf of the Red Sea, now called the gulf of Ahaba. (2 Chron. xx. 36.) The name of Tarshish was from one of the sons of Javan. (Gen. x. 4.)

PHUT, (Gen. x. 6,) or Put, (Nah. iii. 9,) was the third son of Ham; and his descendants, sometimes called Libyans, are supposed to be the Mauritanians, or Moors of modern times. They served the Egyptians and Tyrians as soldiers. (Jer. xlvi. 9; Ezek. xxvii. 10; xxx. 5; xxxviii. 5.)

PUL. A district in Africa, thought by Bochart to be an island in the Nile, not far from Syene. (Isa. lxvi. 19.)

SEBA. (Isa. xliii. 3.) A peninsular district of African Ethiopia, deriving its name from the eldest son of Cush, (Gen. x. 7.) who is supposed to have been the progenitor of the Ethiopians. It is called Seba by the Hebrews.

CITIES OF ARABIA.

ARABIA, a large country of Asia, lying partly on the east, but chiefly southward of Canaan. Its greatest length from east to west is about 1620 miles; and its greatest breadth from north to south about 1350. It has the Indian Ocean on the south, the Red Sea and Isthmus of Suez on the west, Canaan and Syria on the north-west and north, the mountains of Chaldea and the Persian Gulf on the east. It is ordinarily divided into three parts.

ARABIA PETRÆA, or the *rocky*, on the north-west, and which is now called Hejiaz. This division contained the land of Cushan, Barnea, Paran, and Midian. The Edomites and the Amalekites also dwelt here, and a very powerful and independent tribe of Ishmaelites. It was a land of shepherds, and the scene of some of the most interesting events in the history of man. Horeb and Sinai were within its bounds. In the south-western part of it now stand the famed cities of Mecca and Medina, so much visited by Mahometan pilgrims. The people of this part are called "Men of the east." (Gen. xxv. 6; Judg. vi. 3.)

ARABIA DESERTA, which lay eastward of Canaan, and comprehended the land of Uz, of Ammon, Moab, Midian, with the country of the Itureans, Hagarenes, &c. The inhabitants have in all ages dwelt in tents, and led a wandering life. It was an exceedingly fruitful land. They claim their descent from Shem. This was also the country of the Ishmaelites, and is now inhabited by the modern Bedouins.

ARABIA FELIX, or the *happy*, on the south of the two former, between the Persian Gulf and Red Sea. Scarcely any part of Arabia is well watered, but Arabia Felix is the most so, and is famed for its opium, myrrh, and other drugs, as well as for fine spices and fruits.

The Arabians are, in general, the descendants of Ishmael. The descendants of Abraham by Keturah, as well as those of Lot and Esau, dwelt also in this land.

AGAR, or Hagar. (Gal. iv. 25.) The history or condition of Hagar is used allegorically in this passage to illustrate the nature of the dispensation from Mount Sinai. Mount Sinai is called Agar by the Arabians.

DUMAH, a country somewhere near or in Arabia Petræa, so called from a son of Ishmael. (Isa. xxi. 11.

DEDAN. (Jer. xxv. 23; xlix. 8; Ezek. xxv. 13.) A district of Arabia Petræa, south of Idumea, or Edom, settled by the descendants of Dedan, son of Jokshan, son of Abraham and Keturah. (Gen. xxv. 3.)

EZION-GEBER, or GABER. (Num. xxxiii. 35; 1 Kings ix. 26.) A city of Arabia, at the head of the eastern or Elanitic gulf of the Red Sea, adjoining Elath. It was here that Solomon's vessels were built, which were intended to trade with Ophir and Tarshish. It derives its name [Ezion-Geber, *or the back bone of a man*,] from a reef of rocks at the entrance of the harbor resembling that part of the human frame.

KEDAR. (Gen. xxv. 13.) A son of Ishmael, whose descendants settled in the southern part of Arabia.

Probably Kedar's posterity were the most numerous and powerful of the family of Ishmael; whence the whole of that country is sometimes called Kedar, (Isa. xxi. 16, 17; lx. 7; Jer. xlix. 28;) and the Ishmaelites generally are called the men of Kedar. They dwelt ordinarily in tents, but sometimes in villages, and their glory and wealth chiefly consisted in flocks and herds. (Isa. xlii. 11; and xxi. 16, 17.)

NEBAIOTH, (Isa. lx. 7,) or NEBAJOTH. (Gen. xxv. 13.) A son of Ishmael, whose descendants are supposed to have settled in Arabia, and to have been the Nabatheans of Greek and Roman history. They were probably rich in flocks and herds; whence the beautiful figure of the prophet above cited, respecting the gathering of the Gentile nations to the sceptre of the Messiah.

PARAN formed a part of Arabia Petræa. (Deut. xxxiii. 2.)

RAAMAH. (Ezek. xxvii. 22.) A country or district of Arabia, trading with Tyre in spices, stones and gold; and is supposed to have been settled by the descendants of Raamah, grandson of Ham. (Gen. x. 7.)

SINAI, the mountain in Arabia, on which Jehovah appeared to Moses, and gave the law. The Hebrews came to this place in the third month of their pilgrimage. The law was given, it is thought, just fifty days after their exodus from Egypt; and hence the Pentecost was observed on the 50th day after the Passover. This mount stands in Arabia Petræa, and is called by the Arabs, Jibbil Mousa, or the mountain of Moses, and sometimes El Tor, or the Mount. It has two summits, Horeb and Sinai; which last is much higher, and is called the Mount of God. The ascent is very steep, and is effected by steps, which the Empress Helena, the mother of Constantine the Great, caused to be cut in the rock. These are now so much worn and decayed, as to make the ascent tedious and difficult. At the top of Sinai, there is an uneven and rugged place, sufficient to hold 60 persons. Here stands a chapel, and near to it is a fountain of fresh water.

SHEBA, or Seba. There were several of this name. 1. The son of Cush, who gave the name to a country in Arabia. 2. The grandson of Cush. 3. The son of Jok-

tan. 4. The grandson of Abraham. All these seem to
have taken up their residence in Arabia, and perhaps
most of them in the south part of it. 5. The son of
Bichri, a Jew who headed a revolt in the reign of David.
6. The name of a famous well, sometimes called Sheba,
and sometimes Beer-sheba. (Gen. x., xxv., xxvi.)

SHEBA, (1 Kings x. 1.) or the Saba of profane history.
A province in the northern part of Arabia, between the
Red Sea and Indian Ocean. It was probably settled by
Sheba, a descendant of Cush, and the inhabitants are
called Sabeans. (Job i. 15.) The queen of Sheba may
well be supposed to have some traditional knowledge of
true religion; and in the commercial intercourse of her
country with that of the Hebrews, might have heard
much of the wisdom and piety of Solomon, the wisest
man, and one of the greatest kings that ever lived on
the earth. To see and converse with him, she undertook
a journey from what was then regarded as the uttermost parts of the earth. (Matt. xii. 42.) Of this journey the present Ethiopians or Abyssines, who are Christians of the Greek Church, have very ancient traditions.
Among the princely presents she made to Solomon, were
gold, ivory, and spices; and the Sabeans were celebrated, on account of their important commerce in these
very products, among the Greeks. (Ps. lxxii. 10, 15;
Isa. lx. 6; Jer. vi. 20.)

SELA, called by the Jews, Jokteel, is probably the
place called Kerek in Burckhardt's travels. In Greek
authors, it is called Petra, and was the celebrated capital of Arabia Petræa. (2 Kings xiv. 7.)

Uz. (Lam. iv. 21.) A district of Arabia, which was
probably settled by the posterity of Uz, or Huz, a descendant of Shem, and distinguished as the dwelling-
place of Job, whose estate was like that of a modern
Bedouin sheikh. It was probably an extensive district,
and perhaps subject to Idumea.

THE CITIES OF EDOM.

ESAU, (Gen. xxv. 25,) or Edom. (Gen. xxxvi. 1.) Son
of Isaac and Rebecca, and twin brother of Jacob.

The most important events of his life are so intimately
connected with the life of Jacob, that they will be considered under that article. His family settled on mount
Seir, east of Jordan, which was hence called Edom,
and his descendants were the Edomites, one of the most
powerful and formidable nations of that age.

EDOMITES. Descendants of Edom, who was called
Esau, because he was hairy, and his complexion red.
He was born A. M. 2173, and sold his birthright for a
mess of red pottage.

JOKTHEEL. (2 Kings xiv. 7.) The name given by
Amaziah to Selah, or the modern Petra. It was the capital of Idumea, and one of the most magnificent of the
ancient cities. It was situated near the base of mount
Hor, about three day's journey from Jericho, and the
same distance from mount Sinai; and must be regarded
as the most singular spot in all Arabia, perhaps in the
whole eastern world.

The RED SEA is that arm of the Indian Ocean which
runs along the southwest side of Arabia, and the east of
Ethiopia and Egypt, to the length of 1200 miles, now
called the Arabian Gulf. As the Edomites had long the
property and use of it for their shipping, it came to be
called the Sea of Edom, which the Greeks translated
into the Red Sea — Edom signifying red. Hence, originated the mistake, that its water, or its bottom, was reddish.

THE AMALEKITES.

AMALEK. (Gen. xxxvi. 16.) He was the son of Eliphaz, and grandson of Esau. Some have supposed him
to be the father of the Amalekites, but they are mentioned as a powerful people, long before the birth of
Amalek. (Gen. xiv. 7.) The Arabians have a tradition that he was the son of Ham.

AMALEKITES. (1 Sam. xv. 6.) A powerful people,
dwelling between the Red and Dead Seas. This nation
inhabited the southern part of Canaan, and is called
(Num. xxiv. 20) the first of all the nations. About A.
M. 2091, Chedorlaomer ravaged their country, at which

time multitudes left it. It is thought by some, that thes*
poured themselves on Egypt, and were the shepherds
mentioned by Manetho.

THE CITIES OF MOAB.

MOAB. 1. The son of Lot, was born about the same
time as Isaac, in A. M. 2103. 2. The land called by
his name, eastward of the Dead Sea, and about the
river Arnon. The present name of this country is El-
Rabba.

ARNON. (Deut. ii. 24.) The principal river east of
Jordan, and originally the boundary between the Moabites and the Ammonites; then between the Moabites and
Amorites; and finally, between the Moabites and the
tribe of Reuben. It is now called the Modjeb or Mujeb,
and is about fifty miles long, emptying into the Dead Sea.
The current in winter is full and rapid, but in summer
the channel is nearly dry.

ABEL-SHITTIM, a town beyond Jordan, in the plain of
Moab. Here 24,000 Israelites were destroyed in one
day for falling into the sins of Moab. (Numb. xxv.) It
was probably the mourning for this event that gave the
name of Abel to the spot.

BETH-JESHIMOTH. (Josh. xiii. 20.) A city of the
tribe of Reuben on the eastern shore of the Dead Sea.
It was formerly in possession of the Moabites, and after
remaining in the tribe of Reuben until the Assyrian captivity, it fell back into the hands of the Moabites. (Ezek.
xxv. 9.)

DIBON. (Josh. xiii. 17.) A city of Moab, a few miles
north of the Arnon, now called Diban. It was built by
the tribe of Gad, and hence called Dibongad. (Num.
xxxiii. 45.) The same place is called Dimon. (Isa. xv.
9.) At a later day it returned again to Moab. (Isa. xv.
2.) In Neh. xi. 25, a Dibon in Judah is mentioned,
which may be the same with Debir. (Josh. xiii. 26.)
A place called Diban is mentioned by modern travellers
as situated about three miles north of the Arnon, or
Madjeb.

HORONAIM, a city of Moab, perhaps the same as Beth-horon. It is thought to be the city which is called by Ptolemy, Avara, and by Josephus, Orona.

JAHAZ. (Num. xxi. 23.) A city on the northern frontier of the Moabites, in the vicinity of which, Moses defeated the army of Sihon, on his refusal to permit him to pass through it peaceably. (Josh. xiii. 18.) It is called by Ptolemy, Ziza.

LUHITH, a city of Moab. (Isa. xv. 5.) Its name in Josephus and Ptolemy, is Lyssa.

MIZPEH. (1 Sam. xxii. 3.) A town of Moab, where David placed his father and mother during his reverses.

MEDEBA, a city of Moab. (Numb. xxi. 30; Josh. xiii. 16.) It was destroyed about the days of Isaiah, and rebuilt some considerable time before the advent of our Lord.

The plains of MOAB, (Num. xxii. 1; xxxiii. 48—50,) were situated east of Jordan and the Dead Sea, on both sides of the Arnon. The country belonged principally to the Amorites, north of the Arnon, where the Israelites encamped before the passage of the Jordan. Afterwards it fell to the lot of Reuben. The inhabitants were called Moabites, and the country derived its name from Moab.

NIMRIM. (Isa. xv. 6.) A stream in the north part of Moab, near the village of Beth-nimrah, (Num. xxxii. 36,) the ruins of which now bear the name of Nimrein.

KIR, a city of Moab. Isa. xv. 1.) The bulwark or principal fortress of Moab, called Kirharesheth, (Isa. xvi. 7.) Kerek, or Karak, [the modern name of the same place,] is found south of the Dead Sea. Many of the ruins of the ancient fortress are discernible; and a traveller, who was there in 1822, tells us that the population consisted of four hundred Turks, and one hundred and fifty nominal Christians.

KIRJATHAIM. (Josh. xiii. 19.) One of the oldest towns eastward of Jordan. It was once the possession of the Emims, and was then called Shaveh, or the plain of Kiriathaim, (Gen. xiv. 5,) and is afterwards spoken of as a city of Moab. (Jer. xlviii. 23.) There was a town of this name in Naphtali. (1 Chron. vi. 76.)

THE GRECIAN CITIES.

GREECE was first colonized by the Phœnicians and Egyptians—the descendants of the Ethiopians. It was during the 18th dynasty of Egyptian kings, that the first colonization of Greece took place.

The aborigines of Greece, denominated Pelasgi, Heantes, &c. were extremely barbarous. They wandered in woods, without law or government, having but little intercourse with each other. They clothed themselves with skins of beasts; retreated for shelter to rocks and caverns; and lived on acorns, wild fruits, raw flesh, and even devoured the enemies they slew in battle. [Rollin.]

ARGOS. The arrival of Inachus in Greece from Phœnicia, is connected with the foundation of the kingdom of Argos. This event took place B. C. 1857. Money was first made of gold and silver at Argos, B. C. 891.

Inachus is called the son of the Ocean, because he came to Greece by sea. By some he is said to have been the last of the Titans, a Phœnician colony who gave the Greeks the first notions of religion and civilization, and introduced the worship of their own gods, Saturn, Jupiter, Ceres, &c. &c.

The Phœnicians, the Canaanites in scripture, were a commercial people in the days of Abraham. In the time of the Hebrew judges, they had begun to colonize. Their first settlements were Cyprus and Rhodes; thence they passed over and peopled Greece, Sicily, Sardinia, and Spain, and framed likewise establishments on the western coast of Africa.

The city of Athens. (Acts xvii. 15.) The capital of Attica in Greece, situated on the Saronic Gulf, forty-six miles east of Corinth, three hundred south-west of Constantinople, and five miles from the coast.

The foundation of Athens by Anthony, or Cecrops, Egyptians, who conducted thither a colony from the Nile, is dated B. C. 1556. This event had an important connection with the subsequent refinement and literary distinction of Greece. Cecrops, after fixing down in Attica, attempted to civilize the wild and barbarous natives of that region. Constructing twelve small villages, which were afterwards connected with Athens, he prevailed upon the wandering tribes to fix their residences in them. He enacted laws, and introduced the deities and religious worship of the Egyptians. This was the first step towards that civilization which rendered Athens the most distinguished city on the earth. It was distinguished not only for political importance and military power, but for the eloquence, literature, and refinement of its inhabitants. Paul visited it about A. D. 52, and found the people sunk in idolatry and idleness. He preached there, and took occasion to reprove their superstitions, for which he was summoned before the Areopagus.

THEBES. The foundation of the kingdom of Thebes, was laid by the celebrated Cadmus, a Phœnician. The government was monarchical and more despotic than in any other of the Grecian States. The introduction of letters by Cadmus into Greece about B. C. 1519, was a circumstance which contributed most materially to the rapid advances which the Greeks made in knowledge and civilization.

CORINTH. One of the richest cities of Greece, and capital of Achaia. Its commodious haven, and advantageous location, gave it a vast commerce, and immense wealth. During a war with Rome, L. Mummius burnt it to the ground, A. M. 3827. It was afterward re-built under the auspices of Julius Cæsar. It fell into the hands of the Turks, under Mahomet II. Paul preached here. (Acts xviii.) It is now called Corinto.

BYZANTIUM, [now Constantinople,] built by a colony of Athenians, 658 B. C.

THE ROMAN EMPIRE.

THIS empire was colonized by the Phœnicians and Egyptians. The foundation of Rome by Romulus, 752 years B. C., was connected with the rise and establishment of the most powerful empire that has ever existed. He was a wise, courageous and politic prince; and was but eighteen years old. The city was peopled by runaway slaves, and criminals; and at first had neither law, nor rulers, and but few women.

Romulus was the son of Rhea Silvia — a vestal, and was, together with his twin brother, preserved in his infancy, in a remarkable manner. Being, by the death of his brother, at the age of eighteen years, left sole commander of a band of robbers, he began the foundation of what has since been called, "The Eternal City."

It took the name of its founder, and was built upon the Palatine Hill. The city was almost square and about a mile in circumference, containing 1000 houses, or more properly huts. Even the palace of Romulus was built of reeds and thatched with straw. Having become king, he introduced order and discipline, which gradually improved under Numa [a Sabine,] and several succeeding sovereigns. The circumstances in which this people were placed, naturally gave rise to continual animosities, which were commonly settled by battles, in which they were generally victorious. Romulus divided the people into three tribes; and each tribe into ten companies of a hundred men each, headed by a centurion. He divided the land into three parts; one for the support of government; another for the maintenance of religion — and the third portion was divided among the citizens — two acres each. The Romans sent to Athens for Solon's laws, 454 B. C. The first library was erected at Rome, of books brought from Macedonia, 168 B. C. [Rollin.]

GALATIA, a province of Asia Minor,. About 175 B. C. it was reduced to a Roman province. The gospel was planted here by Paul, who wrote an epistle to these churches. (Acts xvi.) Dejotarus, for whom Cicero interceded, in an oration still extant, was king of this country. About A. D. 266, it was overrun by the Goths; and afterward became a province of Turkey. It is now called Natolia.

APPII-FORUM, a place in the south-west of Italy, about fifty miles from Rome, where Paul was met by his Christian friends. (Acts xxviii. 15.) It is now called Fossa Nuova.

PUTEOLI, a city of Campania, in Italy; so called from its hot waters, or the multitude of its wells. Its ancient name was Delus Minor. It stood about eight miles from Naples, and was much frequented on account of its mineral waters. From hence a considerable trade was carried on with Alexandria, in Egypt. Paul halted here seven days, as he went prisoner to Rome. (Acts xxviii. 13.) We find several of its bishops in the primitive councils of the Christian church. The present name of the place is Buzzoli.

SYRACUSE, a famous city, called also Saragossa, on the south-east of Sicily, 22 miles in circumference. It was founded A. M. 3269, and was once the largest and richest city of the Greeks. Archimedes, with astonishing inventions, defended the place from the Romans; but it was taken, and he was slain, about 208 B. C. This city was taken from the Romans by the Saracens in 1090. Here Paul tarried three days, as he went prisoner to Rome. Christianity was early planted here, and still continues, at least in name. The city has wholly lost its ancient splendor. (Acts xxviii. 12.)

THE KINGDOM OF MACEDONIA.

THE founding of MACEDONIA, by Caranus, we date 795 years B. C. Caranus was an Argive by birth, a descendant of Hercules, an African. He established the regal government, which in spite of the dangers that proved fatal to it in most of the Grecian States, subsisted in Macedonia 647 years. The reign of the warlike Philip, first brought Macedonia into notice. In the battle at Cheronea, which was fought 338 years B. C., he subjected the other Grecian communities to his dominion.

The partition of the Macedonian Empire into four great monarchies, took place about twelve years after the death of Philip's warlike son — Alexander the Great, who had conquered most of the world known to the ancients — or 312 years B. C. Ptolemy, Lysimachus, Cassander, and Seleucus, four generals of Alexander — made this division among themselves. To Ptolemy were assigned Egypt, Lybia, Arabia, and Palestine; to Cassander, Macedonia and Greece; to Lysimachus, Bythinia and Thrace; and to Seleucus the remaining territories in Syria as far the river Indus, which was called the kingdom of Syria.

AMPHIPOLIS, a city of Macedonia. (Acts xvii. 1.) It is almost surrounded by the river Strymon, whence its name, which means "a city surrounded." It is now called Emboli.

APOLLONIA. (Acts xvii. 1.) A city of Macedonia, situated at the head of the Ægean Sea, on a promontory between Thessalonica and Philippi.

BEREA, (Acts xvii. 10,) now Veria. A city of Macedonia, about twenty miles west of Thessalonica, near Mount Pindus. The Bereans were honorably distinguished for their diligence in searching the Scriptures, under the preaching of Paul. For this and other causes, it was a place of much interest in the days of the Apostles. (Acts xvii. 10, 15, and xx. 4.) It now contains about 20,000 inhabitants, [chiefly Turks and Greeks,] and produces rice, fruit, and marble, and has manufactures of cotton.

NICOPOLIS, (Tit. iii. 12,) the place where Paul determined to winter, is now called Nicopi, or Nicopoli, a town upon the river Nessus, [now Karasa,] which divided Thrace from Macedonia. Another town of the same name was in Epirus, opposite Actium, to which some have thought the apostle refers in the above passage.

PHILIPPI. (Acts xvi. 12.) A city of Macedonia, formerly called Dathos; but being re-built and greatly magnified by Philip, father of Alexander the Great, it took from him the name Philippi. It is at the head of the Ægean Sea, nine or ten miles north-west of Neapolis. It stood about 70 miles north-east of Thessalonica. It was rendered famous by the defeat of Brutus and Cassius in its neighborhood. Here Paul preached about A. D. 52. Its modern name is Diliba. It is a place of great celebrity in profane history, and is called the chief or first city of that part of Macedonia.

THESSALONICA, the capital of Macedonia. It was anciently called Halis, and Thermæ; but Philip, the father of Alexander the Great, called it Thessalonica, to commemorate his victory over the Thessalians. About A. D. 52, Paul, Silas and Timothy planted a church here. It was at this time a city of great commerce and wealth, and abounded with Jews. The Saracens took it about

A. D. 800; and after various other revolutions, it fell under the power of Turkey. It is at this time one of the chief ports of modern Greece, containing before the late revolution 60,000 inhabitants, of which 12,000 were Jews. Its present name is Saloniki.

THE ISLANDS OF THE MEDITERRANEAN.

CRETE, (Acts xxvii. 7,) now called Candia, Kirid, or Kriti, is an island of the Mediterranean, one hundred and seventy miles long and fifty broad; population 250,000, about equal numbers of Greeks and Turks. Constantinople lies five or six hundred miles north-east of it, and Syria six or seven hundred miles east. It was formerly a rich and powerful kingdom, and is still remarkable for its delightful climate and fertile soil. Oil, corn, fruit trees, and vines are among its principal productions. The city of Candia, which is also the fort and capital of the island, lies on the northern coast. A Christian mission is already established there. Crete was settled, as it is generally supposed, by Philistines from Egypt, part of whom afterwards passed over to Palestine, and are called Caphtorim.

Probably Paul visited this island after his imprisonment at Rome, and established a Christian church there, which he left under the oversight of Titus. (Tit. i. 5.)

The Cretans were once noted for vicious habits. This character was given them by many profane historians.

CYPRUS. (Acts iv. 36.) A large, fertile, and salubrious island of the Mediterranean. It is of a triangular form, two hundred miles long, and sixty in its greatest breadth. Population 120,000, of whom 40,000 are Greeks. Some suppose it to be the same with Chittim. The chief productions of Cyprus are, as formerly, wines, oil, honey and wool. It is a famous place in mythological history, and was distinguished for the licentiousness of its inhabitants. Barnabas was born, and, according to tradition, suffered martyrdom in Cyprus.

SALAMIS, (Acts xiii. 5,) was the principal city and seaport of the island of Cyprus, and received the gospel from Paul and Barnabas, A. D. 44. The ruins of

Salamis were visited in 1835 by two American missionaries. Very little of the ancient town is standing; but
on the outside of the city they found the remains of a
building, two hundred feet in length, and six or eight
high; also a stone church, and portions of an aqueduct,
by which water was brought to the city from a distance
of thirty miles.

PAPHOS. (Acts xiii. 6.) A celebrated maritime city,
lying at the western extremity of the island of Cyprus,
now called Baffa. It was the place where Barjesus, or
Elymas the sorcerer, was struck with blindness; and
where Sergius Paulus was converted to Christianity. In
Paphos, and its vicinity, 25,000 Greeks were massacred
in the late revolution; and it is said that, upon the whole
island, not less than seventy-four villages, containing
18,000 Christians, were destroyed by the Turks. Several interesting incidents of apostolic history occurred
on this island.

MELITA. (Acts xxviii. 1.) This island was settled
by a Phœnician colony, about B. C. 1500. It was a
place of refuge to the ancient Tyrians in their voyages
to Carthage and Spain.

MALTA. An island twelve miles in breadth and twenty in length, lying between Sicily and Africa, about two
hundred miles east of Tunis, and in that part of the
Mediterranean, which, in the apostle's day, was often
called Adria, including the Ionian and Sicilian seas, according to the testimony of Ptolemy and Strabo. Here
Paul and his company were shipwrecked on the passage
to Rome, and very kindly treated by the inhabitants, especially by Publius the governor.

MITYLENE. (Acts xx. 14.) The capital of the ancient island of Lesbos. The whole island is now under
the Turkish power, and is called Mittilene, and the chief
town is called Castra, near which the ruins of the ancient city are discernible. The island lies on the western coast of Asia Minor, nearly opposite Pergamos, and
is about one hundred and seventy miles in circumference. The population is at present 25,000. The chief
productions are wine and figs. Paul passed through
this island on his way from Corinth to Jerusalem. It
was a large and beautiful city, and was famous as the

birth-place of many wise and learned men, as Alcæus, the poet, Sappho, the poetess, Theophanes, the historian, Pittacus, the philosopher, and Diophanes, the orator. On the same island were born, Theophrastus, the sage, and Potamon, the rhetorician. It is now called Castro, and sometimes Metilin. (Acts xx. 14.)

PATMOS. (Rev. i. 9.) An island in the Ægean Sea, now called Patimo or Patmosa, situated near the promontory of Miletus, between Samos and Naxos, about twenty or twenty-five miles in circumference. It was used by the Romans as a place of exile for convicts, and is distinguished as the place to which John the Evangelist was banished by Domitian, A. D. 94. Its soil is very thin and sterile, lying on a rugged rock, probably of volcanic origin. About a mile back from the beach is a chapel, enclosing the cave which, it is said, John occupied when writing the book of Revelation during his banishment.

RHODES. (Acts xxi. 1.) An island of the Mediterranean Sea, north-east of Crete, off the south-west point of Asia Minor, and ranked for dignity and size next to Cyprus and Lesbos, containing a city of the same name. It is forty miles long, and fifteen broad, having a population of eighteen thousand, anciently celebrated for its schools, and for the flourishing state of the arts and sciences, as well as for a colossal statue one hundred and five feet in height, standing astride of the harbor's mouth, so that vessels could pass under it. It stood fifty-six years, and was then overthrown by an earthquake, and the brass of it loaded nine hundred camels, and weighed seven hundred and twenty thousand pounds. In the fifteenth century it was the residence of the knights of St. John of Jerusalem. At this island, Paul touched, on his way from Miletus to Jerusalem. It is supposed by some that the name Rhodes is derived from the multitude of roses produced on the island. The most ancient cities were Lindus, Camirus, and Jalysus.

9

AFRICAN ISLANDS.

AT the mouth of the Red Sea lies the island of Zocotra, belonging to the Arabs. It is a populous and plentiful country, and particularly noted for aloes.

MADAGASCAR is separated from the continent by a channel, called the Channel of Mozambique. This island is 800 miles long, 150 broad, divided into 28 provinces, and watered by some considerable rivers. Its population is estimated at 4,000,000, blacks.

The CAPE VERD islands, so called, are opposite to the most projecting part of Africa. There are ten principal ones, lying almost in a half circle.

The CANARY islands, are still further north, almost opposite to Morocco, but more southerly; famous for Canary wine. The ancients called them the Fortunate Isles. They are ten or twelve in number; the chief are Great Canary, Teneriffe, Gomera and Ferro. Teneriffe is much encumbered with mountains. The Peak is an ascent in the form of a sugar loaf, 15 miles in circumference, and 13,265 feet high. It is a volcano.

The MADEIRAS are three islands, in about 28 degrees north latitude, 100 miles north of the Canaries. The largest, is 180 miles in circumference. The Madeiras are opposite to Morocco: very fruitful, the climate is fine, and there are few reptiles. These islands are famous for an exquisite wine of the same name.

The AZORES, or WESTERN ISLES, lie about midway between the two continents, in about 37 degrees north latitude, nine hundred miles from land. They were discovered by a ship that was driven in that direction by stress of weather. They are nine in number, fertile in corn, wine, and a variety of fruits. The climate is remarkably salubrious. It is said that no poisonous or noxious animal can live on the Azores.

OTAHEITE. The SOCIETY ISLES, are a cluster lying near the 16th degree south latitude, the principal of which is Otaheite. The vegetable productions of these islands are numerous and luxuriant. The inhabitants of Otaheite alone are estimated at 204,000. The people exceed the middle size of Europeans in stature. In their dispositions, they are brave, open, and generous, without either suspicion or treachery. Except a few traces of natural cunning, and some traces of dissimulation, equally artless and inoffensive, they posess the most perfect simplicity of character. Otaheite alone, it is supposed, can send out 1720 war canoes, and 68,000 able men. The chief of each dis'rict superintends the equipping of the fleet in that district; but they must pass in review before the king, so that he may know the state of the whole before they assemble to go on service. They are remarkable for their cleanliness; for both men, women and children constantly wash their whole bodies in running water, three times every day. Their language is soft and melodious and abounds with vowels.

The inhabitants of Otaheite believe in one Supreme Deity, but at the same time acknowledge a variety of subordinate deities; they offer up their prayers without the use of idols, and believe the existence of the soul in a separate state, where there are two situations, of different degrees of happiness. The inhabitants of all these islands are blacks, generally above the middle size, with fine open countenances and good shape. The climate is similar to that of the West Indies.

Africa once contained several kingdoms and states, eminent for the liberal arts, for wealth and power, and the most extensive commerce. The kingdoms of Egypt and Ethiopia, in particular were much celebrated; and the rich and powerful state of Carthage, that once formidable rival to Rome itself, extended her commerce to every part of the then known world.

———

GREECE, EUROPE AND NORTH AND SOUTH AMERICA, WERE SETTLED BY THE DESCENDANTS OF EGYPT. We learn from the ancient history of Europe that the first people known to have lived there were the Grecians, who occupied a small space of country on the Mediterranean. It is supposed to have been near 2500 years from the creation of the world, and about 3396 years to this period, that Greece was first settled by a colony from Egypt, led out by the celebrated Anthony, or Cecrops Egyptians, who conducted thither an Egyptian colony from the Nile, 1556 years B. C.

CHAPTER III.

ANTIQUITY OF AMERICA.

AMERICA, was first settled by the Israelites—Indians who came out from Egypt. [The View of the Hebrews, by Ethan Smith.] America was discovered by Columbus in 1492, and was peopled by Colonies in A. D., 1620, from Europe. The first settlement in New England was made at Plymouth, in the midst of a fertile country.—The Egyptians were an Ethiopian people. [Herodotus.]

The following authors are supposed to have referred to America in their writings:—

M. de Chazelles, when he measured the great pyramid in Egypt, found that the four sides of it were turned [built] exactly to the four quarters of the world, Europe, Asia, Africa and America, above three thousand years ago. During so long a space of time, there has been no alteration in the poles of the earth or the meridians, to have turned the pyramid.

The celebrated Theopompus, a learned historian and orator, flourished in the time of Alexander the Great, the Egyptian hero. In a book entitled "Thaumasia," a sort of dialogue is given between Midas the Phrygian, and Silenus. The book itself is lost, but Strabo refers to it, and Ælianus has given us the substance of the dialogue which follows. After much conversation, Silenus said to Midas that Europe, Asia and Africa were but islands, surrounded on all sides by the sea; but that there was a continent situated beyond these, which was of immense dimensions, even without limits; it was inhabited by men and animals. The land was good, and there were mines of gold, silver, &c. Ælianus referred to a country west of Europe and Africa. [Ælian variar. Historiar., or Ælian's work, in English.] Ælian or Ælianus lived about A. D. 200—230.

HANNO, an African, flourished when the Carthaginins were in their greatest prosperity, but the exact time is unknown. Some place his times 40 and others 140 years before the founding of Rome, which would be about 800 years before our era. [Encyclopædia Perthensis.] He was an officer of great enterprise; having sailed around and explored the coast of Africa, he set out from the Pillars of Hercules, now called the straits of Gibraltar, and sailed westward thirty days. Hence it is inferred by many that he must have visited America, or some of its islands. He wrote a book, which he entitled Periplus, giving an account of his voyages, which was translated and published about 1533, in Greek. [The best account of Hanno and his voyages, with which we are acquainted, is to be found in Marianna's History of Spain.]

Many, and not without tolerably good reasons, believe that an island or continent existed in the Atlantic Ocean about this period, but which disappeared afterwards.

DIODORUS SICULUS says that some "Phœnicians were cast upon a most fertile island opposite to Africa." Of this, he says, they kept the most studied secrecy, which was doubtless occasioned by their jealousy of the advantage the discovery might be to the neighboring nations, and which they wished to secure wholly to themselves. Diodorus Siculus lived about 100 years before Christ. Islands lying west of Europe and Africa are certainly mentioned by Homer and Horace. They were called Atlantides, and were supposed to be about 1000 furlongs from Africa.

PLATO, an Ethiopian and an eminent Greek historian. His account has more weight, perhaps, than any of the ancients. He lived about 400 years before the Christian era. A part of his account is as follows: "In those first times [time of its being first known] the Atlantic was a most broad island, and there were extant most powerful kings in it, who, with joint forces, appointed to occupy Asia and Eniope, and so a most grievous war was carried on, in which the Athenians with the common consent of the Greeks, opposed themselves, and they became the conquerors. But that Atlantic island, by a flood and earthquake, was indeed suddenly destroyed, and so that warlike people were swallowed up." He adds, in another place, " An island in the mouth of the sea, in the passage to those straits, called the Pillars of Hercules, did exist; and that island was greater and larger than Lybia and Asia; from which there was an easy passage over to other islands, and from those islands to that continent, which is situated out of that region." [America known to the Ancients, Vol. x. 8vo., Boston, 1773.]

" NEPTUNE settled in this island, from whose son, Atlas, its name was derived, and divided it among his ten sons. To the youngest fell the extremity of the island, called Gadir, which, in the language of the country signifies fertile or abounding in sheep. The descendants of Neptune reigned here, from father to son, for a great number of generations in the order of primogeniture, during the space of 9,000 years. They also possessed several other islands; and, passing into Europe and Africa, subdued all Lybia as far as Egypt, and all Europe to Asia Minor. At length the island sunk under water; and for a long time afterwards the sea thereabouts was full of rocks and shelves." [Encyclopædia Perthensis, Art. Atlantis.] This account, although mixed with fable, cannot, we think, be entirely rejected; and that the ancients had knowledge of countries westward of Europe, appears as plain and as well authenticated as any passage of history of that period.

ARISTOTLE, or the author of a book which is generally attributed to him, [De mirabil. auscultat. Opera, vol. i. Voltaire says of this book, " On en fesait honneur aux Carthaginois, et on citait un livre d'Aristote qu'il n'a pas composé." Essai sur les Mœurs et l'esprit des nations, chap. cxlv. p. 703, vol. iv. of his works. Edit. Paris, 1817, in 8 vo.] speaks of an island beyond the Straits of Gibraltar; but the passage savors something of hearsay, and is as follows: "Some say that, beyond the Pillars of Hercules, the Carthaginians have found a very fertile island; but without inhabitants, full of forests, navigable rivers and fruit in abundance. It is several day's voyage from the main land. Some Carthaginians, charmed by the fertility of the country, thought to marry and settle there; but some say that the government of Carthage forbid the settlement upon pain of death, from the fear that it would increase in power so as to deprive the mother country of her possessions there." If Aristotle had uttered this as a prediction, that such a thing would take place in regard to some future nation, no one, perhaps, would have called him a false prophet, for the American revolution would have been its fulfilment. This philosopher lived about 384 years B. C.

SENECA lived about the commencement of the vulgar era. He wrote tragedies, and in one of them occurs this passage :—

————"Venient annis
Sæeculia seris, quibus oceanus
Vincula rerum laxet, et ingens
Pateat tellus, Typhisque novos
Detegat orbes ; nec sit terris
Ultima Thule."*

This is nearer prophecy, and may be rendered, in English, thus : "The time will come when the ocean will loosen the chains of nature, and we shall behold a vast country. A new Typhis shall discover new worlds ; Thule shall no longer be considered the last country of the known world."

ST. GREGORY, who flourished in the 7th century, in an epistle to St. Clement, an African bishop, said that, beyond the ocean there was another world.

———

* Medea. Act. 3—v. 375.

CHAPTER IV.

ANCIENT KINGS AND WARS.

ABRAHAM THE PRINCE, A CONQUEROR OF KINGS.

In the days of Amraphet, of Shinar, or Chaldea; Arioch king of Ellasar or Assyria; Chedorlaomer king of Elam or Persia; and Tidal king of Nations, made war with Bera, king of Sodom; and with Bimsha, king of Gomorrah; Shinab, king of Admah; and Shemeber king of Zeboim; and the king of Bela, or Zoar, in that country now called Africa, and Asia. All these were joined together in the valley of Siddim which is the Salt Sea. Twelve years they served Chedorlaomer the king of Persia, and in the thirteenth year they rebelled; and in the fourteenth year, came Chedorlaomer and the kings that were with him, and smote the Rephaims in Ashterothkarnaim, and the Zuzims in Ham, and the Emims in Shaveh-kiriathaim, and the Horites in their Mount Seir unto El-paran, which is by the wilderness. And they returned and came to Enmishphat which is Kadesh, and smote all the country of the Amalekites, and also the Amorites that dwelt in Hazezontamar; and there went out the king of Sodom, and the king of Gomorrah, and the king of Admah, and the king of Zeboim, and the king of Zoar; and they joined battle in the valley of Siddim, with Chedorlaomer the king of Persia, and with Tidal king of Nations, and Amraphet king of Chaldea, and Arioch king of Assyria. The kings of Sodom and Gomorrah fled and fell there, and they that remained fled to the mountain, and took all the goods of Sodom and Gomorrah, and all their victuals, and went their way; and they took Lot, Abraham's brother's son, who dwelt in Sodom, and his goods, and carried them away. And there came one that had escaped, and told Abram the Hebrew, for he dwelt in the plain of Mamre, the Amorite, [an Ethiopian] brother of Eshcol, and brother of Aner, and these were confederate with Abram. And when Abram heard that Lot was taken captive, he armed his trained servants who were in his own house, three hundred and eighteen men, and pursued them unto Dan. And he divided his men against them by night, he and his servants smote them and pursued them unto Habah, which is on the left hand of Damascus, and brought back all the goods again, also his brother Lot, his goods and women and the people. And the king of Sodom went out to meet him, [after his return from the slaughter of Chedorlaomer, and of the kings that were with him,] at the valley of Sheveh, which is the king's dale. And Melchizedek, king of Salem, the priest of the Most High God, brought forth bread and wine: and he blessed him, and said, Blessed be Abram of the Most High God, which hath delivered thine enemies into thy hand. And he gave him tithes of all. And the king of Sodom said to Abram, Give me the persons, and take the goods to thyself. And Abram said to the king of Sodom, I have lifted up mine hand to the Lord, the Most High God, the possessor of heaven and earth, that I will not take from a thread even to a shoe-latchet; and that I will not take any thing that is thine, lest thou shouldst say, I have made Abram rich: save only that which the young men have eaten, and the portion of the men which went with me, Aner, Eshcol and Mamre, let them take their portion. (Gen. xiv. xii. xxiv.; Heb vii.)

THE ETHIOPIAN KINGS OF EGYPT.

1. Menes was the first king of Egypt. We have accounts of but one of his successors — Timans, during the first period, a space of more than two centuries.

2. Shishak was king of Ethiopia, and doubtless of Egypt. After his death

3. Zerah the son of Judah became king of Ethiopia, and made himself master of Egypt and Libya; and in-

tending to add Judea to his dominions, made war upon
Asa. king of Judea. His army consisted of a million of
men, and three hundred chariots of war. (2 Chr. xiv. 9.)

4. Sabachus, an Ethiopian, king of Ethiopia, being
encouraged by an oracle, entered Egypt with a numerous army, and possessed himself of the country. He
reigned with great clemency and justice. It is believed,
that this Sabachus was the same with Solomon, whose
aid was implored by Hosea king of Israel, against Sal-
manaser king of Assyria.

5. Sethon reigned fourteen years. He is the same
with Sabachus, or Savechus the son of Sabacan or Sual
the Ethiopian who reigned so long over Egypt.

6. Tharaca, an Ethiopian, joined Sethon, with an
Ethiopian army to relieve Jerusalem. After the death
of Sethon, who had filled the Egyptian throne fourteen
years, Tharaca ascended the throne and reigned eight
years over Egypt.

7. Sesach or Shishak was the king of Egypt to whom
Jeroboam fled to avoid death at the hands of king Solomon. Jeroboam was entertained till the death of Solomon, when he returned to Judea and was made king of
Israel. (2 Chr. xi. and xii.)

This Sesach, in the fifth year of the reign of Rehoboam marched against Jerusalem, because the Jews had
transgressed against the Lord. He came with twelve
hundred chariots of war, and sixty thousand horse. He
had brought numberless multitudes of people, who were
all Libyans, Troglodytes, and Ethiopians. He seized
upon all the strongest cities of Judah, and advanced as
far as Jerusalem. Then the king, and the princes of
Israel, having humbled themselves and asked the protection of the God of Israel; he told them, by his prophet Shemaiah, that he would not, because they humbled
themselves, destroy them all as they had deserved; but
that they should be the servants of Sesach: in order
that they might know the difference of his service, and
the service of the kingdoms of the country. Sesach retired from Jerusalem, after having plundered the treasures of the house of the Lord, and of the king's house;
he carried off every thing with him, and even also the
300 shields of gold which Solomon had made. [Rollin.]

The following are the kings of Egypt mentioned in scripture by the common appellation of Pharaoh:—

8. Psammetichus Pharaoh, king of Egypt, owed his preservation to the Ionians and Carians. He permitted them to settle in Egypt, whence all foreigners had hitherto been excluded. By assigning them sufficient lands, and fixed revenues, he made them forget their native land; and by his order the Egyptian children were placed under their care to learn the Greek language. Psammetichus engaged in war against the king of Assyria, on account of the limits of the two empires. This war was of long continuance. Ever since Syria had been conquered by the Assyrians, Palestine, being the only country that separated the two kingdoms, was the subject of continual discord; as afterwards between the Ptolemies and the Seleucidæ. They were eternally contending for it, and it was alternately won by the stronger. Psammetichus, seeing himself the peaceable possessor of all Egypt, and having, restored the ancient form of government, [this revolution happened about seven years after the captivity of Manasseh king of Judah,] thought it high time for him to look to his frontiers; and to secure them against the Assyrian, his neighbor, whose power increased daily. For this purpose he entered Palestine at the head of an army.

Perhaps we are to refer to the beginning of this war, an incident related by Diodorus: That the Egyptians, provoked to see the Greeks posted on the right wing by the king himself in preference to them, quitted the service, they being upwards of two hundred thousand men, and retired into Ethiopia, where they met with an advantageous settlement.

Psammetichus died in the 24th year of the reign of Josiah king of Judah; and was succeeded by his son Nechao or Necho — in Scriptures frequently called Pharaoh Necho.

9. Nechao or Pharaoh Necho reigned sixteen years king of Egypt, (2 Chron. xxxv. 20,) whose expeditions are often mentioned in profane history.

The Babylonians and Medes having destroyed Nineveh, and with it the empire of the Assyrians, did there-

by become so formidable that they drew upon themselves
the jealousy of all their neighbors. Nechao, alarmed at
the danger, advanced to the Euphrates, at the head of
a powerful army, in order to check their progress. Josiah, king of Judah, so famous for his uncommon piety,
observing that he took his route through Judea, resolved to
oppose his passage. With this view, he raised all the
forces of his kingdom, and posted himself in the valley
of Megiddo, a city on this side of Jordan, belonging to
the tribe of Manasseh, and called Magdolus by Herodotus. Nechao informed him by a herald, that his enterprize was not designed against him; that he had other
enemies in view, and that he undertook this war, in
the name of God, who was with him; that for this reason he advised Josiah not to concern himself with this
war, for fear it should turn to his disadvantage. However, Josiah was not moved by these reasons: he
was sensible that the bare march of so powerful an
army through Judea, would entirely ruin it. And besides, he feared that the victor, after the defeat of
the Babylonians, would fall upon him, and dispossess
him of part of his dominions. He therefore marched to
engage Nechao; and was not only overthrown by him,
but unfortunately received a wound, of which he died
at Jerusalem, whither he had ordered himself to be carried.

Nechao, animated by this victory, continued his march,
and advanced towards the Euphrates. He defeated the
Babylonians; took Carchemish, a large city in that country; and securing to himself the possession of it, by a
strong garrison, returned to his own kingdom, after having been absent three months from it.

Being informed in his march homeward, that Jehoahaz
had caused himself to be proclaimed king at Jerusalem,
without first asking his consent, he commanded him to
meet him at Riblah in Syria. The unhappy prince had
no sooner arrived there, but he was put in chains by
Nechao's order, and sent prisoner to Egypt, where he
died. From thence, pursuing his march, he came to
Jerusalem, where he gave the sceptre to Eliakim [called
by him Jehoiakim] another of Josiah's sons, in the room
of his brother; and imposed an annual tribute on the

land, of an hundred talents of silver, and one talent of gold. This being done, he returned in triumph to Egypt.

Herodotus, mentioning this king's expedition, and the victory gained by him at Magdolus, [as he calls it] says, that he afterwards took the city Cadytis, which he represents as situated in the mountains of Palestine, and equal in extent to Sardis, the capital at that time not only of Lidya, but of all Asia Minor: this description can suit only Jerusalem, which was situated in the manner above described, and was then the only city in those parts that could be compared to Sardis. It appears besides from scripture, that Nechao, after his victory, won this capital of Judea; for he was there in person, when he gave the crown to Jehoiakim.

10. Psammis Pharaoh reigned over Egypt, and left his kingdom to his son Apries. He gave his daughter in marriage to Solomon, king of Israel; who received her in that part of Jerusalem, called the city of David, till he had built her a palace.

11. Apries, called Pharaoh-Hophra, succeeded his father Psammis, and reigned twenty-five years.

During the first years of his reign, he was as happy as any of his predecessors. He carried his arms into Cyprus; besieged the city of Sidon by sea and land; took it, and made himself master of all Phœnicia and Palestine. So rapid a success elated his heart to a prodigious degree, and, as Herodotus informs us, swelled him with so much pride and infatuation, that he boasted, it was not in the power of the gods themselves to dethrone him; so great was the idea he had formed to himself of the firm establishment of his own power. It was with a view to these arrogant conceits, that Ezekiel put the vain and impious words following into his mouth: "My river is mine own, and I have made it for myself."

12. Amasis, after the death of his father Apries, became the possessor of Egypt in peace. Amasis Pharaoh or Thmosis was according to Plato, a native of the city of Sais. He reigned 40 years; and expelling the shepherd kings, subjected Lower Egypt to his rule. He made an alliance with the Cyrenians, and married a wife among them. He is the only king of Egypt who conquered the Island of Cyprus, and made it tributary.

Long after his reign, Joseph was brought as a slave into Egypt and sold to Potiphar, an officer of Pharaoh.

13. Rameses Miamun — according to Archbishop Usher, was the name of the king who is called Pharaoh in Scripture. He reigned over Egypt sixty-six years; and oppressed the Israelites most greviously. They built for him treasure cities, to receive the abundant products of that fertile land. Rameses Miamun Pharaoh left two sons, Amenophis and Busiris.

14. Amenophis was the Pharaoh in whose reign the Israelites departed out of Egypt; and who was drowned in the Red Sea. Archbishop Usher says that Amenophis left two sons — one named Sesostris, and the other Armais. The Greeks called him Belus, and his two sons Egyptus, and Danaus.

15. Sesostris or Sesosthis Pharaoh was not only one of the most powerful kings of Egypt, but one of the greatest conquerors antiquity could boast of.

16. Pheron the son of Sesostris Pharaoh, succeeded his father in his kingdom, but not in his glory. He reigned fifty years king of Egypt.

17. Proteus was another king of Egypt. According to Herodotus, he must have immediately succeeded the first — since he lived at the time of the siege of Troy, which according to Usher was taken anno mundi 2820.

18. Rhampsinitus was another king of Egypt; and richer than any of his predecessors. He built a treasury.

19. Cheops brother to Cephrenus, reigned fifty years king of Egypt.

20. Cephrenus reigned after his brother fifty-six years. These two kings kept the temples shut during the whole time of their long reigns. They oppressed their subjects.

21. Mycerinus the son of Cheops, reigned but seven years. He opened the temples; restored the sacrifices; and did all in his power to comfort his subjects, and make them forget their past miseries.

22. Asychis, another Egyptian king, was a legislator. But he valued himself for having surpassed all his predecessors in constructing a pyramid of brick more magnificent than any other.

23. Alexander reigned twelve years monarch of Egypt.

The division of his empire into four great monarchies, took place about twelve years after the death of Alexander, — 312 years B. C. Ptolemy, Lysimachus, Cassander, and Seleucus, four generals of Alexander, made this division among themselves, as had been foretold by Daniel. Ptolemy had Egypt, Libya, Arabia, Cœlosyria, and Palestine. Cassander, the son of Antipater, obtained Macedonia and Greece. Lysimachus acquired Thrace, Bithynia, and some other provinces on the other side of the Hellespont and the Bosphorus. And Seleucus had Syria, and all that part of Asia Major, which extended to the other side of the Euphrates, and as far as the river Indus.

24. Lagus was the father of the Ptolemies who reigned in Egypt after Alexander's death.

25. Ptolemy Soter reigned in Egypt thirty-eight years. From him the succeeding king took the title of Ptolemy, as they sometimes did that of Lagides from Lagus his father.

26. Ptolemy, surnamed Soter, made himself master of Jerusalem by stratagem; he entered the city on the Sabbath, under pretence of offering sacrifice, and while the Jews suspected nothing, but spent the day in ease and idleness, he surprised the city without resistance, and made the citizens captives. He sent several colonies of Jews into Egypt, and put great confidence in them.

27. Ptolemeus Philadelphus, son of Ptolemeus Soter, reigned forty years—two of them in the life time of his father. He being a great favorer of learning, built a most magnificent library at Alexander. Demetrius Phalereus, to whom he had committed the care of procuring all sorts of books, and out of all countries, persuaded him to employ seventy-two Jews in translating the Holy Scriptures out of the original Hebrew into the Greek tongue; which was done in the seventh year of his reign. The king also dismissed many captive Jews, and dedicated many presents to the temple of God at Jerusalem.

28. Ptolemy Evergetes reigned twenty-five years.

29. Ptolemy Philopator reigned seventeen years.

30. Ptolemy Epiphanes reigned twenty-five years.

31. Ptolemy Philometer reigned thirty-four years.

After the death of Cleopatra, the Egyptian Queen,

the wife of Ptolemy Philometer, the kingdom of Egypt became a province of Rome under emperor Octavius Augustus. [Rollin.]

The Battle of Philippi was fought 42 years B. C. It was gained by Octavius Cæsar and Antony over the forces of the conspirators against Julius Cæsar, headed by Brutus and Cassius. This decided the fate of the empire.

Octavius, Antony and Lepidus, had formed a triumvirate for their mutual benefit, though the two former were rivals, and alike desirous of supreme authority. To gratify each other's wishes, each consented to sacrifice some of the best of his friends to the vengeance of his associate.

In this way the great Cicero was given up by Octavius to the resentment of Antony. In this manner three hundred senators and three thousand knights were put to death. Octavius, being grand nephew of Julius Cæsar, and his adopted heir, though destitute of military talents, had gained the senate to his interest, and divided with Antony the favor of the people.

As soon as the conspirators were overtaken, Octavius and Antony gave them battle. This happened at Philippi, in Thrace, and Antony obtained the victory. Brutus and Cassius escaped the vengeance of their enemy, by a voluntary death.

The Battle of Actium, and the end of the Roman Commonwealth, took place 31 years B. C. The battle was fought between the naval forces of Octavius, and those of Antony, in which the former was victorius. Octavius became the sole master of the Roman world.

Antony had excited the indignation of the Roman people, on account of his profligacy, and expenditure of the public resources. And having divorced Octavia, his wife, who was sister to Octavius, war between them became inevitable. The object at stake was the empire.

An immense armament, chiefly naval [the land force being merely spectators] came to an engagement near Actium on the coast of Epirus. The conflict was decisive. Cleopatra, the Egyptian queen, to whom Antony was infamously attached, deserted him with her gallies, in the midst of the engagement.

Such was his infatuation that he immediately followed her, leaving his fleet, which, after a contest of some hours, yielded to the squadron of Octavius. Antony and Cleopatra perished miserably, while Octavius was now left without a rival, with the government of Rome in his hands. Egypt which had existed a kingdom from immemorial ages, from this time became a province of Rome.

The empire had now become the largest which the world had ever seen; and Octavius, now named Augustus, holding the principal offices of the state, became the absolute master of the lives and fortunes of the Roman people. During a long administration, he almost obliterated the memory of his former cruelties, and seemed to consult only the good of his subjects.

THE CHARACTER OF JULIUS CÆSAR.

Cæsar was endowed with every great and noble quality, that could exalt human nature, and give a man the ascendant in society: formed to excel* in peace, as well as war; provident in council; fearless in action; and executing what he had resolved with an amazing celerity: generous beyond measure to his friends; placable to his enemies; and for learning, and eloquence, scarce inferior to any man. His orations were admired for two qualities, which are seldom found together, strength and elegance. Cicero ranks him among the greatest orators that Rome ever bred; and Quinctilian says, that he spoke with the same force with which he fought; and if he had devoted himself to the bar, would have been the only man capable of rivalling Cicero. Nor was he a master only of the politer arts, but conversant also with the most abstruse and critical parts of learning; and, among other works which he published, addressed two books to Cicero, on the analogy of language, or the art of speaking and writing correctly. He was a most liberal patron of wit and learning, wheresoever they were found; and out of his love of those talents, would readily pardon those who had employed them against himself: rightly judging that by making such men his friends, he

10

should draw praises from the same fountain from which he had been aspersed. His capital passions were ambition, and love of pleasure; which he indulged in their turns to the greatest excess: yet the first was always predominant; to which he could easily sacrifice all the charms of the second, and draw pleasure even from toils and dangers, when they ministered to his glory. For he thought Tyranny, as Cicero says, the greatest of goddesses; and had frequently in his mouth a verse of Euripedes, which expressed the image of his soul, that if right and justice were ever to be violated, they were to be violated for the sake of reigning. This was the chief end and purpose of his life; the scheme that he had formed from his early youth; so that, as Cato truly declared of him, he came with sobriety and meditation to the subversion of the republic. He used to say, that there were two things necessary, to acquire and support power — soldiers and money; which yet depended mutually upon each other: with money, therefore, he provided soldiers, and with soldiers extorted money; and was, of all men, the most rapacious in plundering both friends and foes; sparing neither prince, nor state, nor temple, nor even private persons, who were known to possess any share of treasure. His great abilities would necessarily have made him one of the first citizens of Rome; but, disdaining the condition of a subject, he could never rest till he made himself a monarch. In acting this last part, his usual prudence seemed to fail him; as if the height to which he was mounted, had turned his head, and made him giddy: for, by a vain ostentation of his power, he destroyed the stability of it: and as men shorten life by living too fast, so by an intemperance of reigning, he brought his reign to a violent end. [Middleton.]

A COMPARISON OF CÆSAR WITH CATO.

As to their extraction, years, and eloquence, they were pretty nigh equal. Both of them had the same greatness of mind, both the same degree of glory, but in different ways: Cæsar was celebrated for his great bounty and generosity; Cato for his unsullied integrity: the former became renowned by his humanity and compassion; an austere severity heightened the dignity of the latter. Cæsar acquired glory by a liberal, compassionate and forgiving temper; as did Cato, by never bestowing anything. In the one, the miserable found a sanctuary; in the other, the guilty met with a certain destruction. Cæsar was admired for an easy yielding temper; Cato for his immovable firmness. Cæsar, in a word, had formed himself for a laborious active life; was intent upon promoting the interest of his friends, to the neglect of his own; and refused to grant nothing that was worth accepting: what he desired for himself, was to have sovereign command, to be at the head of armies, and engaged in new wars, in order to display his military talents. As for Cato, his only study was moderation, regular conduct, and, above all, rigorous severity: he did not vie with the rich in riches, nor in faction with the factious; but, taking a nobler aim, he contended in bravery with the brave, in modesty with the modest, in integrity with the upright; and was more desirous to be virtuous, than appear so: so that the less he courted the same, the more it followed him. [Sallust, by Mr. Rose.]

THE CHARACTER OF CATO.

If we consider the character of Cato without prejudice, he was certainly a great and worthy man; a friend to truth, virtue, liberty; yet, falsely measuring all duty by the absurd rigor of the stoical rule, he was generally disappointed of the end which he sought by it, the happiness both of his private and public life. In his private conduct he was severe, morose, inexorable; banishing all the softer affections, as natural enemies to justice, and as suggesting false motives of acting, from favor, clemency, and compassion: in public affairs he was the same; had but one rule of policy, to adhere to what was right, without regard to time or circumstances, or even to a force that could control him; for, instead of managing the power of the great, so as to mitigate the ill, or extract any good from it, he was urging it always to acts of violence by a perpetual defiance; so that, with the best intentions in the world, he often · did great harm to the republic. This was his general behavior; yet from some particular facts, it appears that his strength of mind was not always impregnable, but had its weak places of pride, ambition, and party zeal; which, when managed and flattered to a certain point, would betray him sometimes into measures contrary to his ordinary rule of right and truth. The last act of his life was agreeable to his nature and philosophy: when he could no longer be what he had been; or when the ills of life overbalanced the good, which, by the principles of his sect, was a just cause for dying; he put an end to his life with a spirit and resolution which would make one imagine, that he was glad to have found an occasion of dying in his proper character. On the whole, his life was rather admirable than amiable; fit to be praised, rather than imitated. [Middleton.]

THE EGYPTIANS RISE AGAINST PERSIA, SUPPORTED BY THE ATHENIANS.

About 3538 A. M., the Egyptians, to free themselves from a foreign yoke which was insupportable to them, revolted from Artaxerxes, and made Inarus, prince of the Libyans, their king. They demanded aid of the Athenians, who having at that time a fleet of two hundred ships at the island of Cyprus, accepted the invitation with pleasure, and immediately set sail for Egypt; judging this a very favorable opportunity to weaken the power of the Persians, by driving them out of so great a kingdom.

Advice being brought Artaxerxes of this revolt, he raised an army of three hundred thousand men, and resolved to march in person against the rebels. But his friends advising him not to venture himself in that expedition, he gave the command of it to Achæmenes, one of his brothers. The latter being arrived in Egypt, encamped his great army on the banks of the Nile. During

this interval, the Athenians having defeated the Persian
fleet, and either destroyed or taken fifty of their ships;
they went again up that river, landed their forces under
the command of Charitimis their general; and having
joined Inarus and his Egyptians, they charged Achæmenes, and defeated him in a great battle, in which that
Persian general, and an hundred thousand of his soldiers
were slain. Those who escaped, fled to Memphis, whither
the conquerors pursued them, and immediately made
themselves masters of two quarters of the city: but the
Persians having fortified themselves in the third, called
the white wall, which was the largest and strongest of
the three, they were besieged in it nearly·three years,
during which they made a most vigorous defence, till
they were at last delivered by the forces sent to their
aid.

Artaxerxes hearing of the defeat of his army, and how
much the Athenians had contributed to it; to make a diversion of their forces, and oblige them to turn their
arms another way, he sent ambassadors to the Lacedæ-
monians with a large sum of money, to engage them to
proclaim war against the Athenians. But the Lacedæ-
monians having rejected the offer, their refusal did not
abate his ardor, and accordingly he gave Megabysus and
Artabazus the command of the forces designed against
Egypt. These generals immediately raised an army of
three hundred thousand men in Cilicia and Phœnicia.
They were obliged to wait till the fleet was equipped,
which was not till the next year. Artabazus then took
upon him the command of it, and sailed towards the Nile,
whilst Megabysus, at the head of the land-army, marched
towards Memphis. He raised the siege of that city, and
afterwards fought Inarus. All the forces on both sides
engaged in this battle, in which Inarus was entirely defeated: but the Egyptians, who had rebelled, suffered
most in this slaughter. After this defeat, Inarus, though
wounded by Megabysus, retreated with the Athenians,
and such Egyptians as were willing to follow him; and
reached Biblos, a city in the island of Prosopitis, which
is surrounded by two arms of the Nile, and both navigable. The Athenians ran their fleet into one of these
arms, where it was secured from the attacks of the ene-

my, and held out a siege of a year and a half in this island. [Rollin.]

THE ANCIENT KINGS.

TIRHAKAH, king of Ethiopia, destroyed by conquest many nations and took their countries and cast their gods into the fire. He having good counsel, was strong for the war, with thousands of chariots, horsemen and soldiers. He took Hamath, Arpad, Sepharvaim, Hena, Ivah, Samaria, Libnah and Lachish, and came out to fight against Judea and Jerusalem; he sent messengers unto Hezekiah, king of Judea, saying, Who are there among all the gods that have delivered their countries out of my hand? And what Lord shall deliver Jerusalem out of my hand? Make an agreement with me by a present and come out to me, and then eat ye every man of his own vine, and every one of his fig-tree, and drink you every one the water of his cistern until I come and take you away to a land like your own land, a land of corn and wine, a land of bread and vineyards, a land of oil, olive and honey, that ye may live and not die. Hast thou not heard long ago what I have done in ancient time? that I have digged and drank strange water and with the soles of my feet have I dried up all the rivers of besieged places? laid waste fenced cities into ruinous heaps? their inhabitants were dismayed and confounded; they were as the grass, as the green herb, as the corn blasted before it be grown up! (2 Kings viii. xix.)

CAMBYSES. The first of this name was a king of Persia, the father of Cyrus the Great. He gave to the young prince such noble instructions as were well adapted to form the great captain and prince; he exhorted him above all things to pay the highest reverence to the gods, and not to undertake any enterprise, whether important or inconsiderable, without first calling upon and consulting them.

Cambyses, the son and successor of Cyrus, carried his army into Egypt. On his arrival there, Amasis, the king, was just dead, and was succeeded by his son Psammenitus, who was made king.

Cambyses, after having succeeded in a battle, pursued the

enemy to Memphis, besieged the city, and soon took it
When Cambyses had resolved to make war upon the Carthaginians, the Phœnicians, who formed the chief strength
of his fleet told him plainly, that they could not serve
him against their countrymen, and this declaration obliged
the prince to lay aside his design.

The Carthaginians, on their side, were never forgetful
of the country from whence they came, and to whom they
owed their origin. A royal city of Ethiopia, Cambyses
named Meroe, for his own sister, after he had taken it.
[Rollin and Strabo.]

CYAXARES, a brother of Cambyses, the uncle of Cyrus
the Great, an Ethiopian, in the sovereignty of the Medes.
This empire he united, besides the Babylonians, which he
vanquished. The Lydians he subjected, and the greatest
part of lesser Asia, and made himself master of Assyria
and Arabia. [Rollin.]

CYRUS, son of Cambyses, king of Persia, by the daughter
of Ahasuerus, king of Media, inherited the crowns both
of Media and Persia, and reigned 30 years. In the first
three chapters of the book of Ezra, we have an account of
God's having disposed Cyrus to promote the re-building of
the city and temple of Jerusalem, who was described by
name nearly 200 years before he appeared. He was a
wise and successful prince, and conquered most of the
east. He mounted the throne of Persia 536 years before
Christ. The God of armies blessed Cyrus, marching before
him and conducting him from city to city, and from province to province, subduing nations before him, and loosen-
ing the loins of kings ; breaking in pieces gates of brass,
cutting asunder the bars of iron, throwing down the walls
and bulwarks of cities, and putting him in possession of
the treasures of darkness, and the hidden riches of secret
places. He ordained Cyrus to be the deliverer of his people, Israel; and to enable him to support with dignity so
glorious a function, the Lord endowed him with all the
qualities which constitute the greatest captain and prince,
and caused that excellent education to be given him which
the heathens so much admired, though they knew neither
the author or the true cause of it. The destruction of
Babylon was foretold by the prophets Isaiah and Jeremiah,
although so strongly fortified, both by nature and art, as to

be thought impregnable. The walls are said to have been 350 feet high, and so broad, that six chariots could go abreast upon them.

Cyrus the Great, the predestined conqueror of Babylon, took it by surprise, whilst the inhabitants, lulled into a false security, were indulging themselves in all the extravagance of riotous and intemperate feasting.

Cyrus spent the last part of his life in consolidating his vast conquests, being greatly beloved not only by his own natural subjects, but by those of the conquered nations. [Rollin.]

AHASUERUS, or ARTAXERXES, (Ezra iv. 7; Esther i. 8,) was king over an hundred and seven and twenty provinces. He reigned from India even unto Ethiopia. This Ethiopia seems to have been the kingdom of Abyssinia, in Africa. One of the wives of Ahasuerus was Esther, the daughter of Abihail, a Jewish captive, whom the king of Media and Persia had taken in the room of Vashti, the queen. In the third year of Ahasuerus's reign, he made a feast unto all his princes and his servants; the power of Persia and Media, the nobles and princes of the provinces being before him. This prince was remarkable for his goodness and generosity. He reigned about forty-nine years. In the beginning of his reign, he fought a bloody battle against his brother Hystaspes, governor of Bactriana, who had revolted; in which a great number of Persian nobles lost their lives. Artaxerxes having at length entirely defeated his enemies, put to death all who had engaged in this conspiracy. By this victory he secured to himself the quiet possession of the empire.

In the revolt of the Egyptians against Persia, supported by the Athenians, Inarus was made their king. The Athenians sent their army to the aid of their besieged countrymen, who sailed up one of the arms of the Nile. The Persian fleet, which kept out at sea, followed them and attacked their rear, whilst the army discharged showers of darts upon them from the banks of the river; thus only a few ships escaped, which opened themselves a way through the enemy's fleet, and all the rest were lost. Here ended the fatal war carried on by the Athenians for six years in Egypt; which kingdom was now united again to the Persian empire, and continued so during the rest of

the reign of Artaxerxes. Megabysus was in the deepest
affliction because Inarus and his Athenians has been delivered up to the king's mother, contrary to the articles of the
treaty, as he had promised that no injury should be done
them. But this inhuman princess, without regard to the
faith of solemn treaties, caused Inarus to be crucified, and
beheaded all the rest. Megabysus left the king's court,
and withdrew to Syria, where he was chosen governor.
His discontent was so great that he raised an army and
revolted openly.

The king sent Osiris, who was one of the greatest lords
of the court, against him with an army of two hundred
thousand men. Megabysus engaged Osiris, wounded him,
took him prisoner, and put his army to flight. Artaxerxes
sending to demand Osiris, Megabysus generously dismissed
him, as soon as his wounds were cured.

The next year Artaxerxes sent another army against him,
the command of which he gave to Menostanes, son to
Artarius the king's brother, and governor of Babylon.
This general was not more fortunate than the former. He
also was defeated and put to flight, and Megabysus gained
as signal a victory as the former.

Artaxerxes finding he could not reduce him by force of
arms, sent his brother Artarius and Amytis his sister, who
was the wife of Megabysus, with several other persons of
the first quality, to persuade the latter to return to his
allegiance. They succeeded in their negotiation; the king
pardoned him, and he returned to court.

Ahasuerus, the king, had a favorite named Haman,
whose mind was filled with pride and cruelty; being enraged because Mordecai, a noble Jew, would not pay homage,
as the rest of the people did, he formed the design of
destroying all the Jews in the Persian dominions on a certain day.

But Esther, being informed by Mordecai of the plot laid
for their destruction, took an opportunity of informing the
king of his treacherous designs, and of unveiling to him
the real character of Haman : upon which the king ordered
him to be put to death, and he was hanged on the very
gibbet which he had erected with the hope of destroying
Mordecai. In commemoration of this event, the feast of
Purim was instituted.

146   LIGHT AND TRUTH.

In the reign of Artaxerxes, Malachi wrote his book, which was the end of vision and prophecy, 397 years B. C., and prophesied the coming of John the Baptist, under the name of Elias.

In the seventh year of the reign of Artaxerxes, Esdras obtained of the king and his seven counsellors an ample commission, empowering him to return to Jerusalem with all such Jews as would follow him thither, in order to settle the Jewish government and religion agreeably to their own laws. Esdras was descended from Saraia, who was high-priest of Jerusalem, when it was destroyed by Nebuchadnezzar, a very learned and pious man, and was chiefly distinguished from the rest of the Jews by his great knowledge.

Some Jews who came from Jerusalem, having informed Nehemiah of the sad fate of that city, that its walls lay in ruins, its gates were burnt down, and the inhabitants thereby exposed to the insults of their enemies, and made the scorn of all their neighbors; the affliction of his brethren, and the dangers with which they were menaced, made such an impression on his mind as might naturally be expected from one of his piety. One day, as he was waiting upon the king, the latter observing an unusual air of melancholy in Nehemiah's contenance, asked him the cause of it. Nehemiah took this opportunity to acquaint him with the calamitous state of his country; owned that was the subject of his grief, and humbly entreated that leave might be given him to go to Jerusalem, in order to repair the fortifications of it. The kings of Persia his predecessors, had permitted the Jews to rebuild the temple, but not the walls of Jerusalem. But Artaxerxes immediately decreed that the walls and gates of Jerusalem should be rebuilt; and Nehemiah, as governor of Judea, was appointed to put this decree into execution. The king, to do him the greater honor, ordered a body of horse, commanded by a considerable officer, to escort him thither. He likewise wrote to all the governors of the provinces on this side the Euphrates, to give him all the assistance possible in forwarding the work for which he was sent. This pious Jew executed every part of his commission with incredible zeal and activity.

It is from this decree, enacted by Artaxerxes in the

twentieth year of his reign, that the walls of Jerusalem were rebuilt. "And the elders of the Jews builded, and they prospered through the prophecying of Haggai the prophet, and Zechariah the son of Iddo. And they builded and finished it, according to the commandment of the God of Israel, and according to the commandment of Cyrus and Darius, and Artaxerxes, king of Persia." Ezra vi.

CYRUS the younger, brother of *Artaxerxes*, formed the project of dethroning him, and with the aid of 13,000 Greeks, engaged him in battle near Babylon. This battle happened about 401 years B. C.

DARIUS, the son of Ahasuerus, (Daniel, ix. 1,) or Artaxerxes, who reigned thirty-six years king of Chaldea, Media and Persia. Before Darius was elected king, he had married the daughter of Gobryas, whose name is not known. Artabarzanes, his eldest son by her, afterwards disputed the empire with Xerxes.

When Darius was seated on the throne, the better to secure himself therein, he married two of Cyrus' daughters, Atossa and Aristona. The former had been wife to Cambyses, her own brother, and afterwards to Smerdis the Magian, during the time he possessed the throne. Aristona was still a virgin, when Darius married her; and of all his wives, was the person he most loved. He likewise married Parmys, daughter of the true Smerdis, who was Cambyses' brother, as also Phedyma, daughter of Otanes. By these wives he had a great number of children of both sexes. And it pleased Darius to set over the kingdom an hundred and twenty princes, which should be over the whole realm.

Daniel was highly esteemed by Darius, who made him first president of the kingdom; this exaltation gave great offence to the nobles, who, not being able to make any just accusation against him, prevailed upon the king to sign a rash decree, that whoever should offer any prayer or petition to either God or man, for the space of thirty days, excepting the king, should be cast into the den of lions.

The enemies of Daniel, observing that, as usual, he addressed his petitions to God, accused him, and insisted upon his incurring the penalty; but the Almighty preserved his faithful servant; and, to the great joy of the king,

Daniel came unhurt out of the lion's den, into which his
accusers were cast, and instantly torn to pieces.

Daniel flourished during the successive reigns of several
Babylonish and Median kings.

The people of God returned from their Babylonish captivity to Jerusalem, under the conduct of Zorobabel.

Darius, first of all, sent Ezra to Jerusalem, and restored the public worship, and the observation of the law.
Nehemiah caused walls to be built round the city, and
fortified it against the attacks of their neighbors. He
caused an edict to be published, in which it was ordained,
that all the victims, oblations, and other expenses of the
temple, be abundantly furnished the Jews, as the priests
should require; it enjoined the priests of Jerusalem, when
they offered their sacrifices to the God of heaven, to pray
for the preservation of the life of the king and the princes,
his children ; denouncing imprecations against all princes
and people, that should hinder the carrying on of the
building of the temple, or that should attempt to destroy it ; by all which, Darius evidently acknowledges, that
the God of Israel is able to overturn the kingdoms of the
world, and to dethrone the most mighty and powerful princes.   By virtue of this edict, the Jews were not only authorized to proceed in the building of their temple, but all the
expenses thereof were also to be furnished to them, out of
the taxes and imposts of the province.

What constitutes the solid glory of Darius' reign is, his
being chosen by God himself, as Cyrus had been before, to
be the instrument of his mercies towards his people, the
declared protector of the Israelites, and the restorer of the
temple at Jerusalem.   The reader may see this part of his
history in the book of Ezra, and in the writings of the
prophets Haggai and Zechariah.

In the beginning of the fifth year of Darius, Babylon revolted, and could not be reduced till after a twenty month's
siege. This city, formerly mistress of the East, grew im-
patient of the Persian yoke, especially after the removing
of the imperial seat to Susa, which very much diminished
Babylon's wealth and grandeur.   The Babylonians, taking
advantage of the revolution that happened in Persia, first
on the death of Cambyses, and afterwards on the massacre
of the Magians, made secretly, for four years together, all

kinds of preparations for war. When they thought the
city sufficiently stored with provisions for many years, they
set up the standard of rebellion : which obliged Darius to
besiege them with all his forces. Now God continued to
accomplis h those terrible threatenings he had denounced
against Babylon: that he would not only humble and bring
down that proud and impious city, but depopulate and lay
it waste with fire and blood; utterly exterminate it, and reduce it to an eternal solitude. In order to fulfill these predictions, God permitted the Babylonians to rebel against
Darius, and by that means to draw upon themselves the
whole force of the Persian empire: and they themselves
were the first in putting these prophecies in execution, by
destroying a great number of their own people, as will be
seen presently. It is probable, that the Jews, of whom a
considerable number remained at Babylon, went out of
the city, before the siege was formed, as the prophets
Isaiah and Jeremiah had exhorted them long before, and
Zechariah very lately, in the following terms : *Thou Sion,
that dwellest with the daughter of Babylon, flee from the
country, and save thyself.*

No sooner was Darius in possession of Babylon, but he
ordered the hundred gates to be pulled down, and all the
walls of that proud city to be entirely demolished, that she
might never be in a condition to rebel more against him,
and in order to hinder the depopulation of the city, he
caused fifty thousand women to be brought from the several provinces of his empire, to supply the place of those,
which the inhabitants had so cruelly destroyed at the beginning of the siege. Such was the fate of Babylon ; and
thus did God execute his vengeance on that impious city,
for the cruelty she has exercised towards the Jews, in falling upon a free people without any reason or provocation ;
in destroying their government, laws and worship ; in for-
cing them from their country, and transporting them to a
strange land ; where they imposed a most grievous yoke of
servitude upon them, and made use of all their power to
crush and afflict an unhappy nation.

DARIUS' EXPEDITION AGAINST THE SCYTHIANS.

AFTER the reduction of Babylon, Darius made great preparations for the war against the Scythians, who inhabited that large tract of land which lies between the Danube and the Tanais. His pretence for undertaking this war was to be revenged of that nation for the invasion of Asia by their ancestors: a very frivolous pretext; and a very ridiculous ground for reviving an old quarrel, which had ceased an hundred and twenty years before. Whilst the Scythians were employed in that irruption, which lasted eight and twenty years, the Scythian wives married their slaves. When the husbands were on their return home, these slaves went out to meet them with a numerous army, and disputed their entrance into their country. After some battles, fought with pretty equal loss on both sides, the slaves were conquered.

I have already observed, that the pretence used by Darius, for undertaking this war against the Scythians, was the irruption formerly made by that people into Asia: but in reality he had no other end therein, than to satisfy his own ambition, and to extend his conquests. He departed from Susa at the head of an army of seven hundred thousand men; and his fleet, consisting of six hundred sail of ships, was chiefly manned with Ionians, and other Grecian nations, that dwelt upon the sea coasts of Asia Minor and the Hellespont. He marched his army towards the Thracian Bosphorus, which he passed upon a bridge of boats: after which, having made himself master of all Thrace, he came to the banks of the Danube, otherwise called the Ister, where he had ordered his fleet to join him. In several places on his march he caused pillars to be erected with magnificent inscriptions, and when the army had passed the Danube upon a bridge of boats, the king was for having the bridge broken down, that his army might not be weakened by leaving so considerable a detachment of his troops, as were necessary to guard it.

Darius, weary of these tedious and fatiguing pursuits, sent an herald to the king of the Scythians, whose name was Indathyrsus, with this message in his name: "Prince of the Scythians, wherefore dost thou continually fly before me? Why dost thou not stop somewhere or other, either to give me battle, if thou believest thyself able to encounter me, or, if thou thinkest thyself too weak, to acknowledge thy master, by presenting him with earth and water?" The Scythians were an high spirited people, extremely jealous of their liberty, and professed enemies to all slavery. Indathyrsus sent Darius the following answer: "If I fly before thee, prince of the Persians, it is not because I fear thee; what I do now, is no more than what I am used to do in time of peace. We Scythians have neither cities nor lands to defend; if thou hast a mind to force us to come to an engagement, come and attack the tombs of our fathers, and thou shalt find what manner of men we are. As to the title of master, which thou assumest, keep it for other nations than the Scythians. For my part, I acknowledge no other master than the great Jupiter, one of my own ancestors, and the goddess Vesta." The farther Darius advanced into the country, the greater hardships his army was exposed to.

Darius deliberated no longer, finding himself under an absolute necessity of quitting his imprudent enterprise. He began then to think in earnest upon returning home; and saw but too plainly that there was no time to be lost. Therefore, as soon as night came, the Persians, to deceive the enemy, lighted a great number of fires, as usual; and leaving the old men and the sick behind them in the camp, together with all their asses, which made a sufficient noise, they marched away as fast as they could, in order to reach the Danube.

Darius, on his return to Sardis after his unhappy expedition against the Scythians, having learnt for certain that he owed both his own safety and that of his whole army to Hystæus, who had persuaded the Ionians not to destroy the bridge on the Danube, sent for that prince to his court, and desired him freely to ask any favor, in recompence of his service. Hystæus hereupon desired the king to give him Mercina of Edonia, a territory upon the river Strymon, in Thrace, together with the liberty of building a city there. His request was readily granted: whereupon he returned to Miletos, where he caused a fleet of ships to be equipped, and then set out for Thrace. Having taken possession of the territory granted him, he immediately set about the execution of his project in building a city.

DARIUS' CONQUEST OF INDIA, &c.

ABOUT the same time, which was in the 13th year of Darius' reign, this prince, having an ambition to extend his dominion eastward, first resolved, in order to facilitate his conquests, to get a proper knowledge of the country. To this end, he caused a fleet to be built and fitted out at Caspatyra, a city upon the Indus, and did the same at several other places on the same river, as far as the frontiers of Scythia. The command of this fleet was given to Scylax, a Grecian of Caryandia, a town of Caria, who was perfectly well versed in maritime affairs. His orders were to sail down the river, and get all the knowledge he possibly could of the country on both sides, quite down to its mouth; to pass from thence into the southern ocean, and to steer his course afterwards to the west, and so return back that way to Persia. Scylax, having exactly observed his instructions, and sailed quite down the river Indus, entered the Red Sea by the straits of Babelmandel; and after a voyage of thirty months from the time of his setting out from Caspatyra, he arrived in Egypt at the same port, from whence Nechao, king of Egypt, had formerly sent the Phœnicians, who were in his service, with orders to sail round the coasts of Africa. Very probably this was the same port where now stands the town of Suez, at the farther end of the Red Sea. From thence Scylax returned to Susa, where he gave Darius an account of all his discoveries. Darius afterwards entered India with an army, and subjected all that vast country. The reader will naturally expect to be informed of the particulars of so important a war. But Herodotus says not one word about it; he only tells us that India made the twentieth province, or government of the Persian empire, and that the annual revenue of it was worth three hundred and sixty talents of gold to Darius, which amounts to near eleven millions of livres, French money, something less than five hundred thousand pounds sterling.

Darius, after his return to Susa from his Scythian expedition, had given his brother Artaphernes the government of Sardis, and made Otanes commander in Thrace, and the adjacent countries along the sea coast, in the room of Megabysus.

From a small spark, kindled by a sedition at Naxus, a great flame arose, which gave occasion to a considerable war. Naxus was the most important island of the Cyclades in the Ægean Sea, now called the Archipelago.

Darius immediately sent away Datis and Artaphernes, whom he had appointed generals in the room of Mardonius Their instructions were, to give up Eretria and Athens to be plundered ; to burn all the houses and temples therein ; to make all the inhabitants of both places prisoners, and to send them to Darius; for which purpose they went provided with a great number of chains and fetters. They set sail with a fleet of five or six hundred ships, and an army of five hundred thousand men. After having made themselves masters of the isles in the Ægean Sea, which they did without difficulty, they turned their course towards Eretria, a city of Eubœa, which they took after a siege of seven days by the treachery of some of the principal inhabitants; they reduced it entirely to ashes, put all the inhabitants in chains, and sent them to Persia. Darius, contrary to their expectation, treated them kindly, and gave them a village in the country of Cissia for their habitation, which was but a day's journey from Susa, where Apollonius Tyaneus found some of their descendants six hundred years afterwards. (Rollin.)

ALEXANDER.

ALEXANDER THE GREAT, the son of Philip, succeeded to the throne of Macedonia, at the age of 20 years. He passed out of Europe into Asia and began to lay waste the Persian empire 330 years B. C., and 206 years from the time of Cyrus the Great.

Alexander marched toward Jerusalem, intending to besiege it. Jaddus the high priest, hearing of it, put on his priestly ornaments, and accompanied with the people all in white, went out to meet him. Alexander, seeing his habit, fell prostrate before him, saying, that whilst he was in Macedonia, a man appeared unto him in the very same habit, who invited him to come into Asia, and promised to deliver the Persian empire into his hands. Af-

11

ter this he went to the temple, and offered sacrifice according to the high priest's direction. They showed him the prophecy of Daniel, that a Grecian should come and destroy the Persians; whereby he was mightily confirmed in his persuasion that he himself was the man. Lastly, he bestowed on the Jews whatever favors they desired and departed.

THE OVERTHROW OF THE PERSIAN EMPIRE.

ITS fate was decided in the battle of Arbela, fought between Alexander and Darius. In this battle Darius is said to have lost 300,000 men. Two other battles had been previously fought between Alexander and the Persian monarch, in both of which the former was successful. Darius soon afterwards being betrayed by one of his own satraps, was cruelly murdered.

Alexander had taken up his father's project of conquering Persia, and was in like manner appointed by the Grecian states commander in chief of their forces. He took with him only 35,000 men, and with this small force he not only conquered Persia, but Syria, Egypt and India, and remained universal monarch of the eastern world. Alexander meditated the design of proceeding to the eastern ocean.

His army refusing to second his wishes, he was obliged to return, after having penetrated to the Ganges. Stung with mortification at the limits assigned to his conquests, which he vainly believed would be commensurate with the globe, he abandoned himself to every excess of luxury. While he tarried at Babylon on his return home, he suddenly died, in a fit of debauch, in the 33d year of his age, and 13th of his reign. [Jos. Ant. 1. 11. c. viii.]

THE HISTORY OF XERXES.

HE was the son of Darius by Atossa, the daughter of Cyrus, who reigned twelve years king of Persia. Xerxes having ascended the throne, employed the first year of his reign in carrying on the preparations, begun by his father, for the reduction of Egypt. He also confirmed to the Jews at Jerusalem all the privileges granted to them by his father, and particularly that which assigned them the tribute of Samaria, for the supplying of them with victims for the temple of God.

In the second year of his reign he marched against the Egyptians, and having reduced and subdued Egypt, he made the yoke of their subjection more heavy; then giving the government of that province to his brother Achæmenes, he returned about the latter end of the year to Susa.

Xerxes, puffed up with this success against the Egyptians, determined to make war against the Grecians. He did not intend, he said, to buy the figs of Attica, which were very excellent, any longer, because he would eat no more of them till he was master of the country.

The war being resolved upon, Xerxes, that he might omit nothing which might contribute to the success of his undertaking, entered into a confederacy with the Carthaginians, who were at that time the most potent people of the west, and made an agreement with them, that whilst the Persian forces should attack Greece, the Carthaginians should fall upon the Grecian colonies that were settled in Sicily and Italy, in order to hinder them from coming to the aid of the other Grecians. The Carthaginians made Amilcar their general, who did not content himself with raising as many troops as he could in Africa, but with the money that Xerxes had sent him, engaged a great number of soldiers out of Spain, Gaul, and Italy, in his service; so that he collected an army of three hundred thousand men, and a proportionate number of ships, in order to execute the projects and stipulations of the league.

Thus Xerxes, agreeably to the prophet Daniel's prediction, having through his power and his great riches stirred up all the nations of the then known world against the realm of Greece, that is to say, of all the west under the command of Amilcar, and of all the east, that was under his own banner, set out from Susa, in order to enter upon this war, in the fifth year of his reign, which was the tenth after the battle of Marathon, and marched towards Sardis, the place of rendezvous for the whole· land army, whilst the fleet advanced along the coasts of Asia Minor towards the Hellespont.

Xerxes had given orders to have a passage cut through mount Athos. This is a mountain in Macedonia, now a province of Turkey in Europe, which extends a great way into the Archipelago, in the form of a peninsula. It is joined to the land only by an Isthmus of about half a league over. It will be, noticed, that the sea in this place was very tempestuous, and occasioned frequent shipwrecks. Xerxes made this his pretext for the orders he gave for cutting through the mountain: but the true reason was the vanity of signalizing himself by an extraordinary enterprize, and by doing a thing that was extremely difficult; as Tacitus says of Nero; *erat incredibilium cupitor.* Accordingly Herodotus observes, that this undertaking was more vainglorious than useful, since he might with less trouble and expense have had his vessels carried over the Isthmus, as was the practice in those days. The passage he caused to be cut through the mountain was broad enough to let two galleys with three banks of oars each pass through it abreast. This prince, who was extravagant enough to believe, that all nature and the very elements were under his command, in consequence of that opinion, wrote a letter to mount Athos in the following terms:

"*Athos, thou proud and aspiring mountain, that liftest up thy head unto the heavens, I advise thee not to be so audacious as to put rocks and stones, which cannot be cut, in the way of my workmen. If thou givest them that opposition, I shall cut thee entirely down, and throw thee headlong into the sea.*"

Xerxes, as we have already related, advanced towards Sardis. Having left Cappadocia and passed the river Halys, he came to Celene, a city of Phrygia, near which is the source of the Mæander. Pythius, a Lydian, had his residence in this city, and next to Xerxes was the most opulent prince of those times. He entertained Xerxes and his whole army with an incredible magnificence, and made him an offer of all his wealth towards defraying the expenses of his expedition. Xerxes, surprised and charmed at so generous an offer, had the

curiosity to inquire to what sum his riches amounted.
Pythius made answer, that having the design of offering
them to his service he had taken an exact account of
them, and that the silver he had by him amounted to two
thousand talents, (which make six millions French
money); and the gold to four millions of Darics, wanting seven thousand (that is to say, to forty millions of
livres, wanting seventy thousand, reckoning ten livres
French money to the Daric.) All this money he offered
him, telling him, that his revenues were sufficient for the
support of his houshold. Xerxes made him very hearty
acknowledgments, entered into a particular friendship
with him, and that he might not be outdone in generosity,
instead of accepting his offers, obliged him to accept of
a present of the seven thousand Darics, which were
wanting to make up his gold a round sum of four millions.

From Phrygia Xerxes marched, and arrived at Sardis,
where he spent the winter. From hence he sent heralds
to all the cities of Greece, except Athens and Lacedæ-
mon, to require them to give him earth and water, which,
as we have taken notice before, was the way of exacting
and acknowledging submission.

As soon as the spring of the year came on, he left Sardis, and directed his march towards the Hellespont.
Having arrived there, he was desirous to see a naval
engagement for his curiosity and diversion. To this end,
a throne was erected for him upon an eminence; and in
that situation seeing all the sea crowded with his vessels,
and the land covered with his troops, he at first felt a
secret joy diffuse itself through his soul, in surveying
with his own eyes the vast extent of his power, considering himself as the most happy of mortals: but reflecting soon afterwards, that of so many thousands, in an
hundred years time there would not be one living soul
remaining, his joy was turned into grief, and he could
not forbear weeping at the uncertainty and instability of
human things.

Xerxes, at vast expense, had caused a bridge of boats
to be built upon the sea, for the passage of his forces
from Asia into Europe. The space that separates the
two continents, formerly called the Hellespont, and now

called the straits of the Dardanelles, or of Gallipoli, is
seven stadias in breadth, which is near an English mile.
A violent storm rising on a sudden, soon after broke
down the bridge. Xerxes hearing this news on his arrival, fell into a transport of passion; and in order to
avenge himself of so cruel an affront, commanded two
pair of chains to be thrown into the sea, as if he meant
to shackle and confine it, and that his men should give
it three hundred strokes of a whip, and speak to it in this
manner:

*Thou troublesome and unhappy element, thus does thy
master chastise thee for having affronted him without reason.
Know that Xerxes will easily find means to pass over thy
waters in spite of all thy billows and resistance.*

The extravagance of this prince did not stop here; but
making the undertakers of the work answerable for
events, which do not in the least depend upon the power
of man, he ordered all the persons to have their heads
struck off, that had been charged with the direction and
management of that undertaking.

Xerxes commanded two other bridges to be built, one
for the army to pass over, and the other for the baggage
and beasts of burden. He appointed workmen more able
and expert than the former, who went about it in this
manner. They placed three hundred and sixty vessels
across, some of them having three banks of oars, and
others fifty oars apiece, with their sides turned towards
the Euxine sea; and on the side that faced the Ægean
sea they put three hundred and fourteen. They then
cast large anchors into the water on both sides, in order
to fix and secure all these vessels against the violence of
the winds, and against the current of the water. On the
east side they left three passages or vacant spaces between the vessels, that there might be room for small
boats to go and come easily, as there was occasion, to
and from the Euxine sea. After this, upon the land on
both sides they drove large piles into the earth, with
huge rings fastened to them, to which were tied six vast
cables, which went over each of the two bridges; two of
which cables were made of hemp, and four of a sort of
reeds, which were made use of in those times for the
making of cordage. Those that were made of hemp

must have been of an extraordinary strength and thickness, since every cubit of those cables weighed a talent. The cables laid over the whole extent of the vessels lengthwise, reached from one side to the other of the sea. When this part of the work was finished quite over the vessels lengthwise, and over the cables we have been speaking of, they laid the trunks of trees, cut purposely for that use, and flat boats again over them, fastened and joined together, to serve as a kind of floor or solid bottom: all which they covered over with earth, and added rails or battlements on each side, that the horses and cattle might not be frightened with seeing the sea in their passage. This was the form of those famous bridges built by Xerxes.

When the whole work was completed, a day was appointed for their passing over. And as soon as the first rays of the sun began to appear, sweet odors of all kinds were abundantly spread over both the bridges, and the way was strewed with myrtle. At the same time Xerxes poured out libations into the sea, and turning his face towards the sun, the principal object of the Persian worship, he implored the assistance of that god in the enterprize he had undertaken, and desired the continuance of his protection till he had made the entire conquest of Europe, and had brought it into subjection to his power: this done, he threw the vessel, which he used in making his libations, together with a golden cup, and a Persian scymitar, into the sea. The army was seven days and seven nights in passing over these straits.

Xerxes directing his march across the Thracian Chersonesus, arrived at Dor, a city standing at the mouth of the Hebrus in Thrace; where, having encamped his army, and given orders for his fleet to follow him along the shore, he reviewed them both.

He found the land army, which he had brought out of Asia consisted of seventeen hundred thousand foot, and of fourscore thousand horse, which with twenty thousand men that were absolutely necessary at least for conducting and taking care of the carriages and the camels, made in all eighteen hundred thousand men. When he had passed the Hellespont, the other nations that submitted to him, made an addition to his army of three hundred thousand men; which made all his land forces together amount to two millions one hundred thousand men.

His fleet, as it was when it set out from Asia, consisted of twelve hundred and seven vessels, or galleys, all of three banks of oars, and intended for fighting. Each vessel carried two hundred men, natives of the country that fitted them out, besides thirty more, that were either Persians or Medes, or of the Sacæ: which made in all two hundred and seventy-seven thousand six hundred and ten men. The European nations augmented his fleet with an hundred and twenty vessels, each of which carried two hundred men, in all four and twenty thousand: these added to the other amount make three hundred and one thousand six hundred and ten men.

Besides this fleet, which consisted all of large vessels, the small galleys of thirty and fifty oars, the transport ships, the vessels that carried the provisions and those that were employed in other uses, amounted to three thousand. If we reckon but eighty men in each of these vessels, one with another, that made in the whole two hundred and forty thousand men.

Thus when Xerxes arrived at Thermopylæ, his land and sea-forces together made up the number of two millions, six hundred and forty-one thousand, six hundred and ten men, without including servants, eunuchs, women, sutlers, and other people of that sort, which usually follow an army, and of which the number at this time was equal to that of the forces: so that the whole number of souls that followed Xerxes in this expedition, amounted to five millions, two hundred eighty-three thousand two hundred and twenty. This is the computation which Herodotus makes of them, and in which Plutarch and Isocrates agree with him. Diodorus Siculus, Pliny, Æ ian and others, fall very short of this number in their calculation: but their accounts of the matter appear to be less authentic than that of Herodotus, who lived in the same age this expedition was made, and who repeats the inscription engraved by the order of the Amphictyons, upon the monument of those Grecians who were killed at Thermopylæ, which expressed that they fought against three millions of men.

For the sustenance of all these persons there must be every day consumed, according to Herodotus' computation, above an hundred and ten thousand three hundred and forty medimnis of flour, (the medimnus was a measure, which according to Budæus was equivalent to six of our bushels,) allowing for every head the quantity of a chœnix, which was the daily portion or allowance that masters gave their slaves among the Grecians. We have no account in history of any other army so numerous as this. And amongst all these millions of men, there was not one that could vie with Xerxes in point of beauty, either for the comeliness of his face, or the tallness of his person.

Artemisa, queen of Halicarnassus, who from the death of her husb nd governed the kingdom for her son, that was still a minor, brought but five vessels along with her; but they were the best equipped, and the lightest ships in the whole fleet, next to those of the Sidonians. This princess distinguished herself in this war by her singular courage, and still more by her prudence and conduct. Herodotus observes, that among all the commanders in the army, there was not one who gave Xerxes so good advice and such wise counsel as this queen: but he was not prudent enough to apply it to his advantage.

A council of war was also held on the side of the Persians, in order to determine whether they should haz rd a naval engagement; Xerxes himself was come to the fleet to take the advice of his captains and officers, who were all unanimous for a battle, because they knew it was agreeable to the king's inclina ion. Queen Artemisa was the only person who opposed that resolution. She represented the dangerous consequences of coming to blows with people much more conversant and more expert in maritime affairs than the Persians; alleging, that the loss of a battle at sea would be attended with the ruin of their land army; whereas by protracting the war, and approaching Peloponnesus, they should create jealousies and divisions among their enemies, or rather augment the division already very great amongst them; that the confederates in that case would not fail to separate from one another, to return and defend their respective countries; and that then the king without difficulty, and almost without striking a stroke, might make himself master of all Greece. This wise advice was not followed, and a battle was resolved upon.

Herodotus gives us also a particular account of the different armor of all the nations this army consisted of. Besides the generals of every nation, who each of them commanded the troops of their respective country, the land army was under the command of six Persian generals; viz., Mardonius, the son of Gobryas; Tirintatechmus, the son of Artabanes, and Smerdonus, son of Otanes, both near relations to the king; Masistus, son of Darius and Atossa; Gergis, son of Ariazes; and Megabysus, son of Zopyrus. The ten thousand Persians, who were called the immortal band, were commanded by Hydarnes. The cavalry had its particular commanders.

There were likewise four Persian generals who commanded the fleet. The Persians had a fleet of above a thousand ships.

Both sides therefore prepared themselves for the battle. The Grecian fleet consisted of three hundred and eighty sail of ships, which in every thing followed the direction and orders of Themistocles. As nothing escaped his vigilance, and as, like an able commander, he knew how to improve every circumstance and incident to advantage, before he began the engagement he waited till a certain wind which arose regularly every day at a certain hour, and which was entirely contrary to the enemy, began to blow. As soon as this wind arose, the signal was given for battle. The Persians, who knew that their king had his eyes upon them, advanced with such courage and impetuosity as were capable of striking an enemy with terror. But the heat of the first attack quickly abated, when they came to be engaged. Every thing was contrary to, and disadvantageous for them: the wind, which blew directly in their faces; the height, and the heaviness of their vessels, which could not move and turn without great difficulty, and even the number of their ships, which was so far from being of use to them, that it only served to embarrass them in a place so strait and narrow, as that they fought in: whereas on the side of the Grecians every thing was done with good order, and without hurry and confusion; because every thing was directed by one commander. The Ionians, whom Themistocles had advised by characters engraven upon stones along the coasts of Eubœa to remember from whom they derived their original, were the first that betook themselves to flight, and were quickly followed by the rest of the fleet. But queen Artemisa distinguished herself by incredible efforts of resolution and courage, so that Xerxes, who saw in what manner she had behaved herself, cried out, that the men had behaved like women in this engagement, and that the women had shewed the courage of men. The Athenians, being enraged that a woman had dared to appear in arms against them, had promised a reward of ten thousand drachmas to any one that should be able to take her alive; but she had the good fortune to escape their pursuit. If they had taken her, she could have deserved nothing from them but the highest commendations, and the most honorable and generous treatment.

The manner in which that queen escaped ought not to be omitted. Seeing herself warmly pursued by an Athenian ship, from which it seemed impossible for her to escape, she hung out Grecian colors, and attacked one of the Persian vessels, on board of which was Damasithymus, king of Calynda, with whom she had some difference, and sunk it: this made her pursuers believe that her ship was one of the Grecian fleet, and give over the chase. [Rollin.]

ARABIAN KINGS.

KING PHILIP the *Great*, the *son* of Amyntas and father of Alexander the Great, an *Arabian*. He mounted the throne of Macedon; the battle of Cheronea was fought by him, 338 years B. C. In this battle, the liberty of all Greece was at stake. He subjected all the Grecian states to his dominion. The reign of this warlike personage first brought Macedon into notice. He met the Grecians at Cheronea, and the fortunes of that day fixed the condition of Greece. It was not, however, his policy to treat them as a conquered people. Their separate and independent government they retained, while he controlled all the national movements in a general council of the states, being chosen generalissimo of the forces of the nation.

ARETAS, an Arabian. He was the first king of the Arabians, who took Damascus and reigned there. His name became common to the Arabian kings both at Damascus and Petræa, as we learn from Josephus in many places.

ZERAH. (2 Chron. xiv., 9.) An Arabian king, who, with an immense army, invaded the kingdom of Judah.

THE ETHIOPIAN KINGS OF BABYLON AND ASSYRIA.

2247 B. C., NIMROD, the Belue of the ancients, [the son of Cush] was the first king of Babylon; a wise and great one in the earth, a mighty man before God, and a king of Assyria. (Gen. x. 8 9, 10.)

NIMUS, or Ninus, the son of Nimrod who succeeded his father and united the kingdom of Babylon and Assyria, by marrying Semiramis the queen.

SEMIRAMIS, a female conqueror and able princess, became Queen of Nations after her husband's death.

NINYAS, the son of Ninus, when of age received the sovereignty from his mother and reigned king of Assyria and Babylon.

AMRAPHEL. (Gen. xiv. 1.) The king of Shinar, (Gen. xi. 2,) or Babylonia, who, confederated, with other kings, made war on Sodom and the other cities of the plain; plundering them, and making prisoners of their inhabitants. Among the captives was Lot, Abraham's nephew.

PUL. (2 Kings xv. 19.) The first king of Assyria, who invaded Canaan, and by a present of one thousand talents of silver, [equivalent to nearly two millions of dollars, in our day,] was prevailed on by Menahem to withdraw his troops, and recognise the title of that wicked usurper. This is the first mention of Assyria in the sacred history after the days of Nimrod, and Pul was the first Assyrian invader of Judea. A town of this name is mentioned in Isa. lxvi. 19; which is supposed, without authority, to be the island of Philæ, in the Nile, not far from Syene, where are found magnificent ruins.

PEKIAH, the son of Pul, succeeded his father and was

king of Assyria. He was slain by Pekah, one of his captains, who usurped his kingdom.

TIGLATH-PILEZER, a king of Assyria, who was called upon by Ahaz, king of Judah, for help against Pekah, king of Israel, and Rezin, king of Damascus. Tiglath-pileser took many cities from the Jews, and carried the inhabitants into captivity. (2 Kings xv. 29; 1 Kings xi.) He died, B. C. 729, and was succeeded by Shalmaneser.

SHALMANESER, (2 Kings xvii. 3,) king of Assyria, was probably the son of Tiglath-pileser. He commenced his reign, B. C. 724, and reigned fourteen years. He found the countries of Israel and Judah entirely open to invasion. He conquered Israel when Hoshea was its king, and three years afterward, finding out a negotiation with Egypt to set themselves free from his yoke, he overrun Israel with his armies, ravaged the country, destroyed the fenced cities, killed many of the inhabitants, captured Samaria, the metropolis, and transported Hoshea and the chief citizens to Media and other eastern parts of his empire. (2 Kings xvii.) Among these was Tobit, whose history is given in the Apocryphal book which bears his name. At this time Hezekiah reigned in Judah; and Sabacus in Egypt. He was succeeded by his son Sennacherib. Some suppose that Shalman (Hos. x. 14) is the same with Shalmaneser.

SENNACHERIB (2 Kings xviii. 13) was king of Assyria when Hezekiah reigned in Judah. The kings of Judah having refused to pay tribute to him, he laid waste their country. Taking part of his army to invade Egypt, he left Rabshakeh in the command of the army in Judah, whose blasphemy and insults we read in 2 Kings xviii. 19. Hezekiah and Isaiah resorted to prayer, and an angel destroyed 185,000 of the Assyrians in one night. the remnant of the invaders returned to Nineveh, where, shortly after, Sennacherib was slain by his sons, as we are told in 2 Kings xviii. During the reign of this monarch, Sevechus was king of Egypt, and Deioces king of Media. About this time, also, Romulus laid the foundation of Rome.

ASARHADDON, or Esarhaddon, (2 Kings xix. 37,) the third son of Sennacherib, who succeeded his father about the 22d year of the reign of Hezekiah, who, after reigning 32 years in Nineveh, obtained the kingdom of Babylon, (2 Kings xix. 37.) and in him the kingdoms of Assyria and Babylon became united; after which he invaded Judah, and carried Manasseh away in chains; which was the occasion of the repentance and reformation of that wicked prince. (2 Kings xxi.) He reigned over Assyria 39 years, and over Babylon 13, and is the same with Sargon, (Isa. xx. 1,) and with Sardanapalus of profane history. He died 668 years before the birth of Christ.

NABOPOLASSER, king of Babylon, having raised an immense army to quell a revolt of the Syrians, Phœnicians, &c., he appointed his son Nebuchadnezzar, to its command, and with it not only subdued those provinces, but overran Canaan, Moab, Ammon, Assyria, Egypt, &c., and made them tributary. He carried to Babylon, among other princes of Judah, Daniel, Hananiah, Mishael, and Azariah; whom he called Belteshazzar, Shadrach, Meshach, and Abednego. These, and other young captives, he caused to be trained up in all the learning of the Chaldeans, that they might serve in the court. (Dan. i.) He died about A. M. 3399.

NEBUCHADNEZZAR, (2 Kings xxiv. 1,) king of Babylon, was son and successor of Nabopolassar. He lived about six hundred years before the birth of Christ, and shared in the administration of the government about two years before his father's decease. He took and destroyed the city of Jerusalem, as had been foretold by the prophets. (2 Kings xxv.)

NEBUZAR-ADAN. (2 Kings xxv. 8.) General of the armies of Nebuchadnezzar. He conducted the siege of Jerusalem to a successful issue, the particulars of which are given in 2 Kings xxv. 8—21.

EVIL-MERODACH. (2 Kings xxv. 27.) Son and successor of Nebuchadnezzar king of Babylon, who reigned during the exile of that monarch from human society. Soon after his permanent accession to the throne, he released Jehoiachin king of Judah from prison, and treated him with great regard through life. (Jer. lii. 31—34.) It is supposed that when Nebuchadnezzar was restored to his reason and his crown, he caused Evil-Merodach to be imprisoned for the abuses of which he was guilty while he administered the government, and that it was then he became acquainted with Jehoiachin as a fellow prisoner. He at last fell a victim to a conspiracy, formed among his own kindred, headed by his brother-in-law Neriglissar, who succeeded him.

BELSHAZZAR, the son of Nebuchadnezzar was king of Babylon, who reigned 17 years. This impious king who was warned of his impending fate by the miraculous hand-writing on the wall, (Daniel v. 5,) was killed by some soldiers of Darius, on the night of his guilty feast. (Dan. v.) His kingdom thenceforth passed over to the Medes and Persians.

JABIN, king of Canaan, to whom the Israelites were captives twenty years. (Judges, iv. 2.)

SISERA, a general of the Canaanites, under Jabin II. Jael invited him into her house, and being instigated of God to destroy this murderous idolater and devoted Canaanite, she drove a nail through his temples.

HEBRON, called originally Arba, or Kirjath-Arba, because Arba, the noted giant, was king of it. It was built on a hill, not long after the flood, (Numb. xiii. 22;) and stood 22 miles south of Jerusalem. Here Anak and his father and sons dwelt, but Caleb receiving it for his inheritance, expelled these giants and called it Hebron, after one of his sons. (Josh. xiv. 13, 14. It was made a city of refuge and given to the priests. David reigned here seven years over Judah, before he was crowned over all Israel. (2 Sam. ii. 11, and v. 3) Here Absalom first set up for king. (2 Sam. xv.) It is now little else than a heap of ruins, compared to its former extent and beauty. The number of houses is estimated at 400. It was visited by Mr. Fisk in 1824, who informs us that its present name is Haleel Rahman.

HIRAM. 1. (2 Sam. v. 11.) A distinguished king of Tyre. He was contemporary with David and Solomon, and on terms of the strictest political and personal friendship with them. Under his reign, the city of Tyre became celebrated for its wealth and magnificence; and the vast supplies he furnished to the kings of Israel show the greatness of his resources. (1 Kings ix. 14; x. 22.)

2. (1 Kings vii. 13.) An eminent artificer of Tyre,

who was employed by Solomon on some of the most
difficult of the fixtures and furniture of the temple, for
which Solomon gave him 20 cities in Galilee. (1 Kings
xi. 11.)

HANUN. (2 Sam. x. 2.) A king of the Ammonites.
We are informed that David had received tokens of
kindness from Nahash, the father and predecessor of
Hanun. After the death of Nahash, David sent messengers to Hanun to comfort him, and to express his respect for the memory of the deceased king. But Hanun
thought, or pretended to think, that David sent them as
spies; so he took them and shaved off one half their
beards, and cut off their garments in the middle, and in
this condition sent them home. David heard of their
situation and sent to meet them, with directions to stay
at Jericho until their beards were grown. This ungen-
erous conduct of Hanun was the occasion of a long war,
in which multitudes of the Ammonites and their allies,
Syrians and others, were slain.

AGAG (Num. xxiv. 7) was a king of the Amalekites.
Some think this was the common name of their kings, as
Pharaoh was the common name of the kings of Egypt.
From the allusion to him in the prophetic passage above
cited, we may suppose him to have been one of the
greatest kings of the earth.

HAMMEDATHA. (Esth. iii. 1.) Haman's father. He
is called the Agagite; and Josephus says he was a descendant from Amalek, and probably of the family or
stock of Agag. If Agag was the common name of their
kings, it is not improbable that an Amalekite would be
called an Agagite, as one of the people of Agag.

ABIMELECH. 1. (Gen. xx. 2, and xxvi. 1.) King of
Gerar, being deceived by Abraham, he sent and took
Sarah, Abraham's wife, to be his wife. God warned
him, however, in a dream, of Sarah's relation to Abraham, and thus withheld him from the commission of sin,
because he did it in ignorance. (Gen. xx. 6.) Abimelech, having rebuked Abraham, restored Sarah to him
with many gifts, and offered him a dwelling-place in any
part of the land. God afterwards remitted the punishment of the family of Abimelech. At a subsequent period, Abimelech [or his successor of the same name]

was deceived, in like manner, by Isaac, respecting his wife Rebekah, while they dwelt in Gerar during a time of famine in Canaan.

NECHO, a famous king of Egypt, mentioned not only in Scripture, but by Herodotus. He conquered Judea in the days of Josiah.

TIRHAKAH, a king of Cush; called in profane history, Thearchon. (2 Kings xix. 9.)

ASTYAGES, king of Media, and grandfather of Cyrus the Great.

OREB, a prince of Midian, defeated and slain by Joshua. (Judges vii. 25.)

BALAK, king of Moab, the son of Zippor, arose and warred against Israel, and promised to bestow riches and honors upon Balaam, if he would go and curse the Israelites. (Num. xxii. 5, 6.)

MESHA, king of Moab, who rebelled against Jehoram, king of Israel, and who sacrificed his son to Baal. (2 Kings iii. 5, 27.)

DEBER, king of Eglon, one of the five kings who besieged Gibeon. (Josh. x. 3.)

HOHAM, king of Hebron, one of the kings defeated by Joshua at Gibeon. (Josh. x. 3.)

MELCHIZEDEK, king of Salem, to whom Abraham paid tithes. (Gen. xiv. 20.)

PIRAM, king of Jarmuth, one of the five kings who besieged Gibeon. (Josh. x. 3.)

JAPHIA, king of Lachish, who besieged Gibeon, but was defeated by Joshua. (Josh. x. 3.)

SIHON, king of the Amorites. (Num. xxi. 23, 24.)

NAHASH, king of the Ammonites. (1 Sam. xi. 1.)

THE KINGS OF ABYSSINIA.

THE Ethiopian kings of Abyssinia anciently sat upon a gold throne, which is a large, convenient, oblong seat, like a small bedstead, covered with Persian carpets, damask, and cloth of gold, with steps leading up to it. It is still richly gilded; but the ancient magnificence is much abridged by the many revolutions and wars.

DOWAGER became queen of Abyssinia after the death

of her husband, the king. She swayed the sceptre with great dignity during the minority of her son.

A. D. 522. DOUNOUDS, or Phineas the son of Dowager, a Jew, the king of Abyssinia, threw Christians into pits of fire who were unwilling to become Jews.

A. D. 523. ELESBOAN or Caleb, a Christian who became king of Abyssinia, subdued the Jews and slew Dounouds their king. [The above is from Joseph Milner and Bruce.]

THE KINGS OF THE HEBREWS.

THE following is a table of the kings of the Hebrews, both before and after their division into the governments of Judah and Israel.

Saul	reigned 40 years.	Solomon reigned 40 years.	
David	" 40 "	Rehoboam " 1 "	

SAUL, (1 Sam. ix. 2,) the first king of Israel, was the son of Kish, of the tribe of Benjamin. His personal appearance was so remarkably fine and noble, as to be particularly mentioned by the sacred historian.

DAVID, the most eminent king of Israel, and one of the most distinguished persons mentioned in the Old Testament, both for his piety, talents, dignity and success. He wrote nearly all the Psalms. Christ, being a lineal descendant, is called "the Son of David." When it is said of him, while yet a youth among the folds, that he was a man "after God's own heart," it means that God chose him to be king over Israel, and would qualify him for that purpose. Under David, the army of 288,000 men was divided into twelve corps, each of which was consequently 24,000 strong, and had its own general. (1 Chron. xxvii.) Under Jehoshaphat this was altered, and there were five unequal corps, under as many commanders. (2 Chron. xvii. 14—19.)

SOLOMON, (2 Sam. v. 14,) king of Israel, was the son and successor of David. His character, and the general condition of the country during his reign, were predicted in remarkable terms, (1 Chron. xxii. 9, 10;) and especially remarkable, as the prediction is supposed to have ultimate and more comprehensive reference to the Messiah and his reign. Soon after the birth of Solomon, the prophet Nathan was sent by divine authority to give him the name of Jedidiah, signifying *beloved of the Lord.*

REHOBOAM, (1 Kings xiv. 21,) son and successor of Solomon, ascended the throne of Judah at the age of forty-one, and reigned seventeen years. At the commencement of his career, he had an opportunity to conciliate the prejudices and discontents which had been excited by the closing acts of his father's reign; but rejecting the wise counsel of the aged, and adopting the precipitate counsel of the young, he inflamed his subjects by the most insolent and tyrannical reply to their petitions and representations, (2 Chron. x. 1—14) and hastened a division of the kingdom. Ten of the tribes revolted, leaving Judah and Benjamin alone in their allegiance to Rehoboam. The latter proposed at once to employ force for the purpose of reducing the rebels, but was divinely admonished to forbear. (1 Kings xii. 24.) Continual wars prevailed, however, between the two parties. (2 Chron. xii. 15.) In about three years after the division of the kingdom, the tribes of Judah followed the tribes of Israel in their idolatrous practices; and for this they suffered the invasion of Shishak, king of Egypt, who desolated the country, and threatened the utter destruction of their city; but upon their repentance, the scourge was stayed, though they suffered immense loss, and were made tributary to the invader. (2 Chron. xii. 2—12. We are told that a history of Rehoboam's reign was written by Shemaiah and Iddo, (2 Chron. xii. 15,) but it has not been preserved. A distinguished modern antiquary has furnished evidence that on the remains of edifices believed to have been erected by this very Shishak, he has discovered several effigies of captive kings, and among them one of Rehoboam, the son and successor of Solomon.

THE KINGS OF JUDAH.

Rehoboam reigned	17 years.		Jotham	reigned	16 years
Abijah	"	3	Ahaz	"	16 "
Asa	"	41	Hezekiah	"	29 "
Jehoshaphat	"	27	Manasseh	"	55 "
Jehoram	"	8	Ammon	"	2 "
Ahaziah	"	1	Josiah	"	31 "
Athaliah	"	6	Jehoiakim	"	11 "
Jehoash	"	40	Jehoiakin	"	3 months
Amaziah	"	29	Zedekiah	"	11 years
Uzziah	"	52			

REHOBOAM, son of Solomon by an Ammonitess, ascended the throne B. C. 970, being then 41 years old;
and reigned 17 years. By following the absurd counsel
of his young companions, he ' caused the revolt of the
ten tribes, an event productive of infinite mischief.

ABIJAH, king of Judah, the son of Jeroboam, and the
only one of his family who died a natural death. (1
Kings xiv. 13.)

ASA, a good king of Judah, who ascended the throne
about A. M. 3049. Respectable chronologists reckon
that it was in his days that the Argonauts made the
voyage up the Hellespont.

JEHOSHAPHAT, (1 Kings xv. 24,) or JOSAPHAT, (Matt.
i. 8,) was the son and successor of Asa king of Judah,
the best of the kings of Judah, ascended the throne A.
M. 3090. He is called king of Israel (2 Chr. xxi. 2)
possibly because his kingdom was a part of the ancient
kingdom of Israel, but probably by mistake; Israel being written for Judah. He was a prince of distinguished
piety, and his reign, which lasted twenty-five years, was
powerful and prosperous. This remarkable commendation is given Jehoshaphat by the sacred historian, that
the more his riches and honor increased, the more his
heart was lifted up in the ways of the Lord. (2 Chron.
xvii. 5, 6.) Among other evidences of his piety and benevolence, we are told that he caused the altars and
places of idolatry to be destroyed, a knowledge of the
law to be diffused throughout the kingdom, and the
places of judicial and ecclesiastical authority to be filled

by the wisest and best men of the land. (2 Chron. xvii.
6, 9; xix. 5—11.) His sin in forming a league with
Ahab, contrary to the counsel of Micaiah, against Ramoth-gilead, (2 Chron. xviii.) was severely censured by
Jehu, and had nearly cost him his life. A few years
after this, the kingdom of Judah was invaded by a confederacy of Edomites, Moabites and others. They collected their forces at Engedi, and threatened to overthrow the kingdom. Jehoshaphat proclaimed a fast; and
the people came from all parts of the kingdom, men,
women, and children, up to Jerusalem; and being assembled in one place, the king himself made supplica-
tion to God for help in their extremity.

JEHORAM, or Joram, (2 Kings viii. 16, 21,) was the
son and successor of Jehoshaphat king of Judah. When
he was thirty-two years of age he was associated with
his father in the government of the kingdom. At the
end of four years, his father died, and he became sole
king. One of the first acts of his government was to
put to death his six brothers and several of the chief
men of the kingdom. (2 Chron. xxi. 4.) To punish
him for this and other abominations of his reign, the
Edomites, who had long been subject to the throne of
Judah, revolted, and secured their independence. One
of his own cities also revolted, and about the same time
he received a writing from Elijah, or, as some suppose,
Elisha, admonishing him.

AHAZIAH. (2 Kings viii. 25.) Called also Azariah,
was a son of Jehoram and Athaliah, and at the age of
twenty-two succeeded his father as king of Judah;
though in 2 Chron. xxii. 2, it is said he was forty-two
years old when he began to reign.

Joram the king of Israel was wounded in a battle
with the king of Syria at Ramoth-gilead, and was carried to Jezreel to be healed. There Ahaziah visited
him, and Jehu, who was left to sustain the siege, [and
who was in the mean time anointed king over Israel,]
came down to Jezreel to execute the judgment of the
Lord upon Joram the son of Ahab, and the representative of the house of Ahab. As soon as his approach
was announced by the watchman, Joram and Ahaziah
went out, each in his chariot, to meet him. And they

met in the portion of Naboth, with which one of Ahab's
daring crimes was so closely associated. Jehu reminded
Joram of the iniquities of his house, and he, suspecting
treachery, warned Ahaziah to flee. Jehu then smote
Joram through the heart with an arrow. He pursued
and slew Ahaziah also, though he had strength to reach
Megiddo, where he died, and was carried thence to Jerusalem, and buried, from respect to the memory of Jehoshaphat his ancestor. In 2 Chron. xxii., the circumstances of the death of Ahaziah are stated differently,
but the variation is not substantial, and therefore requires no particular notice. Athaliah, the mother of
Ahaziah, usurped the kingdom after his death: she was
a cruel and ambitious woman, and endeavored to destroy
all the children of the royal house of Judah. Jehoahash,
daughter of the late king, and wife of Jehoiada the
priest, took Joash, then an infant, and concealed him
from the knowledge of Athaliah, who was slain, after a
cruel usurpation of seven years.

JEHOIACHIN, (2 Kings xxiv. 8,) or Jeconias, (Matt. i.
12,) son and successor of Jehoiakim king of Judah. It
is supposed by some that when he was only eight years
old he was associated with his father in the administration of the government. This supposition is adopted in
order to reconcile the apparent inconsistency of 2 Kings
xxiv. 8; and 2 Chron. xxxvi. 9; but it seems hardly
necessary to resort to such meass to account for a very
natural error or omission of a transcriber, especially in
an immaterial chronological fact of such remote date.
The reign of Jehoiachin terminated at the end of three
months, at which time, the city of Jerusalem was besieged by Nebuchadnezzar.

AMAZIAH. (2 Kings xiv. 1 — 20,) the eighth king of
Judah, the son and successor of Uzziah, or Azariah,
king of Judah. He actually reigned forty-one years,
being associated with his father for twenty-five years before his death. His sole administration of the government was only for sixteen years. His example was holy;
his reign was peaceful and prosperous, and of course
beneficial to the kingdom. His character is peculiarly
described. He did that which was right in the sight of
the Lord, but not with a perfect heart. (2 Chron. xxv.
2; 2 Kings xiv. 3.)

Uzziah, king of Judah, who was struck with a leprosy for offering to burn incense in the temple.

Jotham, a king of Judah, successor to Uzziah. He reigned 16 years, during the latter part of which, Rome was founded.

Ahaz (2 Chron. xxviii. 1) was the son of Jotham, and at the age of twenty succeeded him as king of Judah. Ahaz gave himself up to gross idolatry, and even sacrificed his own children to the gods of the heathen. This course of wickedness brought upon him, and upon his kingdom, severe judgments. They suffered under a succession of disastrous wars, and their allies often proved unfaithful, and involved them in great distress. Ahaz, at last, abandoned himself to the most desperate iniquity, and the kingdom of Judah was brought low, and made waste, because of his great sin. Early in his reign [probably the second year,] the kings of Syria and Israel, who, just at the close of Jotham's reign and life, had confederated for the destruction of Judah, and actually invaded the kingdom with a powerful and victorious army, were about to lay siege to Jerusalem.

Hezekiah, a pious prince of Judah, who by prayer and intercession had his life prolonged, and as a sign of which the sun went back ten degrees. (2 Kings xx. 6, and 11.)

Manasseh, an impious king of Judah, who upon the death of his father Hezekiah, rebuilt the altars of Baal, and re-established idolatry among the Jews. (2 Chron. xxxiii. 3.)

Amon. (2 Kings xxi. 18—26.) The fourteenth king of Judah. He was killed in his palace by his own servants. (2 Kings xxi. 23.)

Josiah, (2 Kings xxi. 24,) the son and successor of Amon king of Judah, began to reign when he was but eight years of age, and was remarkable for his integrity and piety. He gradually abolished the idolatrous customs of his predecessors, and, in the eighteenth year of his reign, began a thorough repair of the temple. In the progress of this work, Hilkiah the high-priest, found a complete copy of the law of Moses; a rare treasure in those days of degeneracy and corruption, when God and his institutions were forsaken and contemned on every side. Josiah himself was but imperfectly acquainted with its contents until they were read to him by one of his officers; and then he was overwhelmed with grief to find how far they and their fathers had departed from the right way. He, however, humbled himself before God, and received the most precious promises of the divine favor. (2 Chron. xxxiv. 26—28.) He then assembled the people, and published the law in their hearing; and they all united with the king in a solemn vow of obedience. After this, he utterly destroyed every vestige of idolatry, both images and temples, and then, by divine command, caused the feast of the passover to be celebrated with unusual solemnity. (2 Chr. xxxv. 3—18.)

JEHOIAKIM. (2 Kings xxiii. 36.) The eldest son of Josiah, and the brother and successor of Jehoaz king of Judah. His original name was Eliakim; but it was changed by order of the king of Egypt, (2 Kings xxiii. 34,) who put him on the throne. The iniquity of his reign is strongly depicted by the historian and prophet, (2 Kings xxiv. 4; 2 Chron. xxxvi. 8; Jer. xxii., xxvi., xxxvi.;) and his end, as Jewish historians inform us, was in strict accordance with the prediction concerning him. For the first four years of his reign, Jehoiakim was subject to the king of Egypt, and paid an enormous tribute. Then he became tributary for three years to Nebuchadnezzar king of Babylon, who at first bound him with chains to carry him to Babylon, but afterwards set him at liberty, and left him at Jerusalem to reign as a tributary prince. The whole time of his reign was eleven years.

JEHOIAKIN was king of Judah at the time Nebuchadnezzar took the city, and was, with his family and most of his people, carried captive to Babylon. (2 Kings xxiv. 14, 15.

ZEDEKIAH, the son of Josiah. When Nebuchadnezzar carried Jehoiachin, king of Judah, prisoner to Babylon, he made Mattaniah king in his stead after he had caused him to swear to be his tributary, and changed his name to Zedekiah. He began to reign when he was twenty-one years of age, and reigned eleven years. His career was marked by crime. He revolted, but was subdued and carried prisoner to Nebuchadnezzar, who caused his children to be murdered before his face, and then his eyes to be plucked out; after which he loaded him with chains, and sent him to Babylon, where he died. (Jer. xxi. xxvii.)

THE KINGS OF ISRAEL.

Jeroboam reigned	22	years.	Jehoahaz reigned	17	years.
Nadab	"	2	"	Jehoash	"	41	"
Baasha	"	24	"	Jeroboam II.	"	41	"
Elah	"	2	"	Zechariah	"	6 months
Zimri	"	7	days.	Shallum	"	1	"
Omri	"	6	years.	Menahim	"	10	years.
Ahab	"	22	"	Pekiah	"	2	"
Ahaziah	"	1	"	Pekah	"	20	"
Joram	"	12	"	Hosea carried captive.
Jehu	"	28	"		

JEROBOAM. The first king of Israel, one of the most wicked rulers that ever lived. He was a distinguished man under Solomon, and was chosen head of the ten tribes which revolted after Solomon's death, A. M. 3029. He reigned in horrible wickedness 22 years. (1 Kings xi., xii., xv.)

NADAB, (1 Kings xv. 25,) son and successor of Jeroboam, king of Israel, reigned two years. His reign was wicked and corrupt, and he was finally assassinated while prosecuting the siege of Gibbethon, a Philistine city.

BAASHA (1 Kings xv. 16) was the son of Abijah, and commander-in-chief of a portion of the army of Israel. When Nadab, king of Israel was besieging Gibbethon, a city of the Philistines, Baasha formed a conspiracy against him and murdered him, and immediately usurped the throne, which he held for twenty-four years. To secure himself against any disturbance from the family of Jeroboam, (the rightful heirs of the throne,) he caused them all to be put to death. By this cruel act he undesignedly fulfilled the prophecy respecting Jeroboam's posterity. (1 Kings xiv. 10.)

Baasha followed in the wicked ways of Jeroboam, and was visited with the most fearful judgments of God. The warning he received of the consequences of his conduct (1 Kings xvi. 1—9) did not induce him to forsake his evil course. His reign was filled with war and treachery, and his family and relatives were cut off, according to the prediction. (1 Kings xvi. 9. 11.)

ELAH. (1 Kings xvi. 6.) Son and successor of Baasha king of Israel. As he was revelling at a friend's house, was assassinated by Zimri, one of the officers of his army. He reigned only two years.

ZIMRI, who slew Elah, king of Israel, and who, when he found that the people had made Omri king, set fire to the palace, and perished in the flames.

OMRI. (1 Kings xvi. 16.) An officer in the army of Israel. He was engaged in the siege of Gibbethon, a Philistine city, when he received intelligence that Zimri, another officer of the army, had assassinated the king, and had usurped the throne. The army, by general acclamation, made Omri king, and raising the siege of Gibbethon, they forthwith marched to Tirzah, where Zimri resided, and captured it. Zimri set fire to the house he occupied, and was consumed. The Israelites were then divided into two parties; but, after a short struggle, Omri prevailed, and took the throne, which he polluted and disgraced through a reign of twelve years. Omri built Samaria, which thereafter became the capital of the ten tribes.

AHAB. (1 Kings xvi. 29.) The son of Omri, and his successor as king of Israel. He reigned twenty-two years, and the seat of his kingdom was at Samaria. He married Jezebel, a Zidonian woman of proverbially wicked character. She was a gross idolater, and Ahab followed her in all her idolatrous practices; became at once a worshipper of Baal, and even made a grove and built an altar for this abominable service. At a very early period of his history, the sacred historian says of him, that he did more to provoke the Lord God of Israel to anger than all the kings of Israel that were before him.

AHAZIAH, (1 Kings xxii. 40,) was the son and successor of Ahab king of Israel. So wicked was he, that when Jehoshaphat king of Judea had joined with him to build a fleet at Ezion-geber for the Tarshish trade, God sent his prophet to tell him, that because of his alliance with Ahaziah, even in this secular enterprise, his fleet should be destroyed; and the ships were accordingly shattered to pieces by the winds.

JORAM, (2 Kings iii. 16,) or Jehoram, (2 Kings iii 1,) successor to Ahaziah, king of Israel, was the second son of Ahab. Though he put away the worship of Baal, he was still a very wicked king. (2 Kings iii. 3.) After the death of Ahab, the king of Moab refused to pay the annual tribute to the king of Israel, which he had been accustomed to pay; and Joram determined for this cause to wage war with him. He secured the aid of Jehoshaphat king of Judah, and they went up through Edom, whose king also joined the expedition. After seven days march, they found themselves likely to be cut off by a severe drought. In this extremity, they besought the help of Elisha the prophet, who had followed the army, (probably under a divine influence.) Elisha at first referred him to the gods of Ahab, his father, and his mother, Jezebel, for succor; but finally, for the sake of Jehoshaphat, he consented to interpose for their relief, and received a command from God to make the valley full of ditches. This was done, and then, without wind or rain, at a particular hour of the next morning, water came, not from the springs, into which they dug, but from Edom, and supplied the army and the country with an abundance of water. (2 Kings iii. 20. Comp. Ex. xvii. 5. 6.)

JEHU, (2 Kings ix. 2.) The son of Nimshi, and grandson of Jehoshaphat, was selected by God to reign over Israel, and to be the instrument of executing his judgments on the house of Ahab. (1 Kings xix. 17. 2 Kings ix. 1—10.) In executing this commission, he commenced with the reigning king, Joram, who was then lying ill at Jezreel. Having been proclaimed king by a few adherents who were with him at Ramoth-gilead, he proceeded towards Jezreel. Upon his approach within sight of that place, Joram despatched two or three messengers to ascertain his design; and finding they did not return, he went out himself to meet him. It happened that they met on the ground of Naboth the Jezreelite, (1 Kings xxi. 1—24;) and Jehu at once charged him with his gross iniquities, and immediately shot him dead in his chariot. (Comp. 1 Kings xxi. 19, and 2 Kings ix. 25.)

JEHOAHAZ succeeded Jehu, his father, and reigned twenty-eight years in Israel, and did not depart from the sins of his predecessors, for which his kingdom was delivered into the hands of Hazael king of Syria, to whom he became tributary; he reigned seventeen years.

JOASH succeeded Jehoahaz, his father, about 835 years B. C., and reigned 16 years over Israel; he did evil in the sight of the Lord. During his reign the prophet Elisha died.

JEROBOAM II., the 13th king of Israel, succeeded his father, Joash, A. M. 3179, and reigned 41 years. He was a very wicked prince, but raised his kingdom to great outward prosperity. (2 Kings xiv. xv.)

ZECHARIAH, or Zachariah, the son of Rehoboam, reigned but six months over Israel. (2 Kings xv.)

MANAHEM, the General of Shallum, in his turn filled the throne; he extorted a thousand talents of silver from the people to buy off Pekah, king of Assyria.

PEKAH, next reigned over Israel. During his reign Tiglath Pileser destroyed many of the cities belonging to the Jews, and carried the people captive into Assyria.

HOSEA, the same with Joshua. (Deut. xxxii. 44.) The son of Elah, and the last of the kings of Israel. (2 Kings xv. 30.) In the ninth year of his reign, the Assyrian king, provoked by an attempt which Hosea made to form an alliance with Egypt, and so throw off the Assyrian yoke, marched against Samaria, and after a siege of three years, took it, and carried the people away into Assyria. (2 Kings xvii. 1—6. Hos. xiii. 16. Mic. 1. 6.)

———

THE GOVERNORS OF JUDEA.

AFTER Judea became a province of the Roman empire, governors or procurators were appointed and sent thither from Rome. This was the office held by Pontius Pilate at the time of our Savior's crucifixion. Sometimes the word governor is used as a general title for ruler.

HEROD, (Matt. ii. 1,) surnamed the Great, was the ancestor of several of the same name, mentioned in the New Testament. He was governor of Judea (then a Roman province) at the time of our Savior's birth. Though he was called king, he was subject to the Roman emperor, and was distinguished for his savage cruelty.

ARCHELAUS. (Matt. ii. 22.) A son of Herod the Great. On the decease of his father, the same year that our Savior was born, Archelaus succeeded to the government of Judea, and reigned there when Joseph and Mary, with the infant Jesus, were returning from Egypt, whither they had gone to escape the fury of Herod. Archelaus, however, was much like his father in the malignity of his temper, and they were therefore still afraid to return.

PONTIUS PILATE, the Roman governor of Judea, was in office 10 years. The character of Pilate was remarkable. When Jesus was arraigned before him, he was not only anxious to avoid trying him, (Luke xxiii. 4. 7,) but he once and again, in the most solemn and impressive manner, even in presence of his malicious and bloodthirsty persecutors, declared his conviction of his perfect innocence. (Luke xxiii. 1. 14. John xix. 6.)

By his covetous and cruel administration he caused himself to be exceedingly hated, both by the Jews and Samaritans. At length, three years after the death of Christ, complaints against him reached the court of the Emperor Caligula, and he was recalled to Rome, tried, and banished to Gaul. Afterwards, through poverty and shame, he committed suicide.

AGRIPPA. (Acts xxv. 13.) Son and successor of Herod the persecutor. (Acts xii. 1.) Porcius Festus, the successor of Felix in the government of Judea, came to Cæsarea; and while there, Agrippa (who was governor or king of several of the eastern provinces of the Roman empire) came, with his sister Bernice or Berenice, to pay him a visit of congratulation upon his accession to office. The conversation between them turning upon Paul, who was then in confinement at Cæsarea, and whose remarkable story must have been very notorious, Festus stated the whole.

FELIX was deputy-governor of Judea. He enticed Drusilla to divorce Azizus, king of Emesa, and then

took her as his own wife. He defeated about 4000 outlaws, headed by an Egyptian impostor, who had posted
themselves in the mount of Olives. (Acts xxi. 38.) During the administration of Felix, Judea was in a constant
turmoil, being infested with robbers and assassins, and
overrun with impostors pretending to be the Messiah. It
was this prince that trembled at the words of Paul, (Acts
xxiv. 25.) He was a bad man, and governed with great
injustice and cruelty. In A. D. 60, he was recalled to
Rome, and Festus was sent in his room. The Jews followed him, and complained to the government of his ex-
tortion and violence. He would have been punished with
death, had not his brother Pallas, by his credit at court,
preserved his life. (Acts xxiii. and xxiv.)

FESTUS succeeded Felix in the government of Judea.
He sent Paul, whom Felix had left bound at Cæsarea,
to Rome, to be tried by Cæsar, to whom he appealed.
(Acts xxv.) Festus was very diligent in his efforts to put
an end to the disturbances and robberies which had become so frequent in Judea, in the reign of Felix, but
took no trouble to investigate the claims of Christianity;
and when Paul spoke of its mysteries, he thought much
learning had made him mad. (Acts xxvi.) He died
about A. D. 62.

THE KINGS OF SYRIA.

THE SYRIAN KINGS numbered twenty-seven. Six, usually called Seleucides, from Seleucus, who reigned the first in
Syria; and thirteen who are called Antiochus; but they
are all distinguished by different surnames. Others of them
assume different names. The last was called Antiochus,
surname Epiphanes, Asiaticus and Commagenes. In his
reign, the celebrated Pompey, an Ethiopian, a Roman
General, reduced Syria into a Roman province, after it
had been governed by kings for the space of two hundred
and fifty years, according to Eusebius.

The Kings and their Reign in Syria.
Seleucus Nicanor, reigned 20 years.
Antiochus Soter, reigned 19 years.
Antiochus Theos, reigned 15 years.

Seleucus Callinicus, reigned 20 years.
Seleucus Ceraunus, reigned 2 years.
Antiochus the Great, reigned 36 years.
Seleucus Philopator, reigned 12 years.
Antiochus Epiphanes, reigned 11 years.

Antiochus Epiphanes succeeded Seleucus in the kingdom of Syria, and reigned eleven years and some months.

Alexander Balas, the son of king Antiochus Epiphanes, enters with an army into Syria; the garrison of Ptolemais set open their gates to him, by reason of their hatred to king Demetrius, who prepares himself for war.

Demetrius desireth an alliance with Jonathan, who makes use of this occasion to repair the fortifications of Jerusalem.

Alexander Balas is no less careful to obtain the friend-ship of Jonathan; and, to oblige him, confers on him the high priesthood.

Jonathan puts on the holy vestment in the seventh month of the 160th year of the kingdom of the Grecians, at the feast of tabernacles. He was the first high priest of the Hasmonean family.

Demetrius and Alexander come to a battle, and Deme-trius is slain.

Alexander Balas finding himself in the peaceable pos-session of the kingdom of Syria, espouseth Cleopatra, the daughter of Ptolemy Philometor king of Egypt. Alexan-der highly honors Jonathan the high priest at his nuptials.

Demetrius Nicanor, eldest son of Demetrius Soter, en-ters into Cilicia with an army. King Alexander Balas gives the command of Syria to Apollonius, who sets upon Jonathan the high priest; Jonathan defeats him, and takes Joppa and Azotus, and burns the temple of Dagon.

Ptolemy Philometor king of Egypt comes to the relief of king Alexander, his son-in-law. Alexander ungrateful-ly sets Ammonius to lie in ambush to kill him. The treachery being discovered, Ptolemy takes away his daugh-ter from Alexander, and marries her to Demetrius. Al-exander having been driven from Antioch, the inhabitants of that place make offer of the kingdom to Ptolemy, but he refuseth it, and persuadeth them to accept of Demetrius for their king.

Alexander returns with a great army. Ptolemy and De-

metrius unite their forces, and overcome him in a pitched
battle; but Ptolemy dies of the wounds which he received,
after he had seen the head of Alexander sent to him by
Zabdiel an Arabian prince. Jonathan besiegeth the citadel at Jerusalem, held by a garrison of Macedonians.
Complaint hereof being made to Demetrius, Jonathan ap-
peaseth him by presents, and obtaineth new favors for the
Jews. Demetrius incurreth the hatred of his soldiers, by
abridging their pay in time of peace.

Tryphon, with some soldiers that revolted from Demetrius, undertakes to establish Antiochus, the son of Alexander Balas, in the kingdom of Syria.

Demetrius is vanquished by young Antiochus and made
to flee into Seleucia. Great honors are, by Antiochus,
conferred on Jonathan, who assists him against Demetrius.

HADADEZER, (2 Sam. viii. 3,) or Hadarezer, (2 Sam. x.
16.) A Syrian king, with whom David had several contests. In one of them he took twenty thousand footmen
and seven hundred horsemen of Hadadezer's army prisoners, besides chariots of war. On another occasion, when
Hadadezer had formed an alliance with a neighboring
province, David again defeated him, and took twenty-two
thousand of his army prisoners. Among the spoils were
gold shields, and a great quantity of brass or copper.

Some years afterwards, Hadadezer and three other Syrian princes formed an alliance to assist the Ammonites
against David; but the whole Syrian army was defeated on
the east bank of the Jordan, by the Israelites, under the
command of Joab. Between forty and fifty thousand of the
enemy were killed, including their principal general; and
they thenceforth became tributary to David. (1 Chron. xix.)

BENHADAD, 1. (1 Kings xv. 18.) King of Syria, in the
time of Asa, king of Judah, with whom he formed an alliance against Baasha, king of Israel. Perhaps he was the
same with Hadad, the Edomite, who rebelled against Solomon. (1 Kings xi. 25.)

BENHADAD. (1 Kings xx. 1.) King, of Syria, and a
son of the preceding. He was a proud, boasting and licentious man, and seemed to be hardened against all re-
bukes. (1 Kings xx. 10—12, 16   He declared war against
Jehoram, king of Israel.

ARETAS. (2 Cor. xi. 32.) The king of Syria, at the

time the governor of Damascus attempted to apprehend
Paul. (Acts ix. 24, 25.

BENHADAD, king of Syria, who besieged Samaria.
(1 Kings xx.)

HAZAEL was anointed king of Syria by Elijah, the
prophet of God. (1 Kings xix. 15. 2 Kings viii.

RESIN, king of Syria. (Isa vii. 5, 1.

THE GOVERNORS OF SYRIA.

ANTIGONUS, governor of Syria, who treated the Jews
with great severity.

CYRENIUS, governor of Syria. He first made it a law
that all the people in his provinces should be taxed.

CÆSAR AUGUSTUS, governor of Syria, sent out a decree
and taxed all the people.

THE KINGS OF ROME.

ROMULUS, the first king of Rome began to reign 745
years B. C., and reigned more than thirty years.

NUMA POMPILIUS was elected the second king 714
years before Christ: he reigned forty-three years.
Numa was of the Sabine nation. This nation was
the most formidable enemy of the early Romans; but
by a wise policy were conciliated; and became united
with the Romans. Numa's disposition was pious and
pacific; and he endeavored to impart the same character
to his people. [The Sabeans or Sabines were the descendants of Cush, an Ethiopian.]

TULLUS HOSTILIUS, the third king, ascended the
throne in 670 B. C. — he reigned thirty years.

ANCUS MARCIUS, grandson of Numa, was elected the
fourth king of Rome, in 637 B. C. He inherited the
piety and virtue of his ancestor, and reigned gloriously
twenty-four years.

TARQUINIUS PRISCUS, son of a former citizen of Corinth, popular from his wealth and liberality, was elected
the fifth king, 614 B. C. He enlarged the senate, and
reigned 38 years.

13

Servius Tullius, an Ethiopian and once a slave, who had married the daughter of Tarquinius, secured, by his own address, and the intrigues of his mother-in-law, his election to the vacant throne in 576 B. C. His popularity originated from his acts of munificence; discharging the debts of the poor; dividing his patrimonial lands among the citizens; improving the city with useful edifices, and extending its boundaries. He reigned 44 years.

Tarquinius Superbus, was the seventh son, and last king of Rome. He married Tullia, the daughter of Servius, and thus secured his elevation to the throne. His disposition was haughty, and produced him the appellation of Superbus [proud,] and his government, systematical tyranny. In him the monarchical government came to an end;—the Romans thenceforward adopting a republican form of government, under Consuls annually elected.

The republican form of government continued till 31 years B. C. when Octavius, or Cæsar Augustus, grandnephew of Julius Cæsar became sole master of the Roman Empire. (Luke ii. 1.)

Jesus, the Savior of mankind was born four years before the commencement of the vulgar era.

A. D. 5. Titus Livius historian died.

Tiberius Cesar (Luke iii. 1) banished the Jews from Rome. He was the son-in-law and successor of Augustus, and though with some apparent virtues, was one of the most infamous tyrants that ever scourged the empire of Rome. He began his reign A. D. 14, reigned during the eventful period of the succeeding twenty-three years, and was finally murdered by suffocation with pillows.

A. D. 37. Caligula, Emperor of Rome.

A. D. 54. Nero, an Ethiopian, Emperor of Rome. A. D. 59, he put his mother, Agrippina, to death. And A. D. 64, raised the first persecution against the Christians—in which St. Paul was put to death. Seneca, the celebrated stoic philosopher was put to death; and Rome burnt by Nero.

A. D. 70. Vespasian, Emperor.

A. D. 78. A great pestilence in Rome,—10,000 dying in one day.

A. D. 79. Titus, Emperor of Rome. Jerusalem taken and destroyed by Titus, Vespasian's son. Nearly 1,500,000 Jews perished on this occasion.

A. D. 81. Domitian, Rome's Emperor. He banished John the evangelist to the island of Patmos.

A. D. 98. Trajan, the Roman Emperor, forbid the Christian assemblies.

Second Century.

A. D. 118. Adrian, Roman Emperor, renewed, but afterward suspended the persecution of the Christians.

A. D. 138. Antoninus Pius, Emperor of Rome.

A. D. 161. Marcus Aurelius Antoninus, Emperor, during whose reign the Christians suffered great persecution.

A. D. 195. Severus was the Roman Emperor.

Third Century.

A. D. 211. Caracalla and Geta, Roman Emperors. Caracalla murders Geta.

A. D. 222. Alexander Severus, Emperor of Rome.

A. D. 235. Maximinus assassinates Severus; and is proclaimed Emperor.

A. D. 238. Gordian, Emperor of Rome.

A. D. 249. Decius, Rome's Emperor.

A. D. 251. Gallus, the Roman Emperor, persecutes the Christians.

A. D. 254. Valerianus, Emperor.

A. D. 268. Claudius, Emperor of Rome.

Fourth Century.

A. D. 306. Constantine, the Great, Emperor of Rome. He becomes a Christian; and stops the persecution of Christianity.

The toleration of Christianity through the Roman Empire took place under Constantine the Great, about 506 years A. C. Constantine fought under the banner of the cross against his enemies, and was successful. Constantine removed the seat of the Roman Empire to Constantinople about 329 years A. C.

Constantine ordered the heathen god Serapis, and a pillar on which are marked the degrees of the Nile, indicating the rise of the water, to be removed into the church of Alexandria in Africa.

A. D. 361.   Julian, Emperor of Rome.
A. D. 375.   Valens was Roman Emperor.
A. D. 381.   Theodosius, the Great, was Emperor of
the East.

Fifth Century.

A. D. 408.   Theodosius 2d, Emperor of the East.

THE LIST OF JUDGES AND TERM OF SERVICE, ABOUT 1400 B. C. — 456 YEARS.

JUDGES. Officers of law and justice. The Jews had
three courts. A court of three or seven petty judges,
who decided small cases.
Othniel judged Israel forty years.
   Oppression of Moab, eighteen years.
Ehud, eighty years.
   Oppression of Philistia, one year.
Shamgar, one year.
   Oppression of Canaan, twenty years.
Deborah and Barak, forty years.
   Oppression of Midian, seven years.
Gideon, forty years.
Abimelech, three years.
Tola, twenty-three years.
Jair, twenty-two years.
   Oppression of Ammon, eighteen years.
Jephthah, six years.
Ibzan, seven years.
Elon, ten years.
Abdon, eight years.
   Oppression of Philistia, Samson last ten, forty years.
Eli, forty years.
   Oppression of Philistia, twenty years.
Samuel, twelve years.
   JUDGES. (Acts xiii. 20.) This was the title of a class
of magistrates among the Israelites. They were appointed
originally by Moses, at the suggestion of Jethro, an Ethio-
pian, prince of Midian, Moses' father-in-law, (Exodus
xviii. 1,) to relieve him of a part of the duties of the
chief magistracy. At an early period after they left Egypt,
a rank of judges was established, the lowest of which were

appointed over ten men, and probably amounted to 60,000 ; then those of fifty, one hundred, and one thousand men ; the final jurisdiction, in all cases of difficulty, being reserved to Moses himself. (Ex. xviii. 21—26.) After they became settled in their respective districts of the promised land, this judiciary system underwent considerable modification. Judges were then appointed for the cities or chief towns.

The book of Judges forms an important part in the history of Israel ; and independently of the ample proofs of its authenticity found in its style, and in its being quoted by both Old and New Testament writers, the transactions it records are confirmed by traditions current among the heathen. Thus we find the memorial of Gideon's transactions preserved by Sanchoniatho.

THE JUDGES OF ISRAEL.

OTHNIEL was raised up to deliver the Israelites from the hands of Chushan-Ethiopians.

EHUD, who delivered the children of Israel from the Moabites.

DEBORAH. 1. (Judg. iv. 4.) A woman of eminent wisdom and holiness, (called a prophetess,) and a judge of the people of Israel. She was the wife of Lapidoth, (though some think the passage should read, a woman of Lapidoth,) and had her judgment-seat under a palm tree, which is hence called by her name. (Judg. iv. 5.) Israel was suffering at that time a most oppressive bondage, under Jabin, a Canaanitish king, to which they were doomed in consequence of their sin. Deborah, by divine direction, called upon Barak, who had probably signalized himself in some way, and commanded him, as from God, to station himself upon mount Tabor, with a prescribed number of men, and she would see to it that Sisera, the commander of the tyrant's army, should fall into his power.

BARAK, (Judg. iv. 6,) was the son of Abinoam, and was distinguished for his share in the conquest of Sisera and the deliverance of Israel from long and severe oppression. A history of the transaction, and a copy of their sublime and triumphal song, are given in Judg. iv. and v.

GIDEON. (Judg. vi. 11.) The son of Joash the Abi-
ezrite, and the same with Jerubbaal the seventh judge of
Israel, a mighty man of valor, and peculiarly favored with
the presence of the Lord. He was a very humble man;
and when the angel proposed to him to go in the strength
of the Lord to save Israel from the hands of the Midianites, he replied, " Behold, my family is poor in Manasseh,
and I am the least of my father's house." The Lord was
pleased to favor Gideon with most remarkable tokens of
his power and grace, which are particularly mentioned in
Judg. vi., vii., viii. He is honorably mentioned, Heb.
xi. 32.

ABIMELECH. 2. (Judg. viii. 31.) A son of Gideon,
who, after the death of his father, persuaded the men of
Shechem to make him king. (Judg. ix. 18.) He afterwards put to death seventy of his brothers who dwelt in his
father's house at Ophrah, leaving only Jotham, the youngest, alive. After several defeats he was at last mortally
wounded by a piece of millstone thrown upon his head by
a woman from the top of a tower in Thebez. That it
might not be said a woman slew him, he called to his
armor-bearer to stab him with his sword, and thus he died.
(Judg. ix. 54—57.)

JEPHTHAH, the tenth judge of Israel, who, in consequence of an extraordinary vow, sacrificed his daughter.
Judg. xi. Some learned men, by altering one of the original words a little, and some considerations connected with
the narrative, infer that he only consigned her to celibacy.
In his day Troy was burnt by the Greeks, about A. M.
2800.

SAMSON. (Judg. xiii. 24.) Son of Manoah, and for
twenty years a Judge of Israel. The circumstances at-
tending the annunciation of his birth are remarkable,
(Judg. xiii. 3 — 23,) and he was distinguished for
his gigantic strength. Contrary to the wishes of his
parents, who were observers of the law, (Ex. xxxiv. 16.
Deut. vii. 3,) he married a woman of Timnath, a Philistine city. On his way to that city, he slew a lion, (Judg.
xiv. 5—9, and he was of the tribe of Daniel. Dr. Clarke
has shown from M. DeLevaar, that he is the original of the
fabled Hercules of heathen mythology. He died 1117
years B. C., aged 40. Judg. xiii. xvi. Heb. xi. 32, 33.

Eli. (1 Sam. ii. 11.) A descendant of Ithamar, the
fourth son of Aaron, and successor of Abdon, as high
priest and judge of Israel. In consequence of his negli-
gence or injudicious management of his two sons Hophni
and Phinehas, he suffered severe chastisement. Samuel
was directed to disclose to Eli the judgments that would
come upon his family, (1 Sam. iii. 13, 14,) chiefly because
of his neglect of paternal duty. The old man received
the intelligence with remarkable submission; but it was
not until twenty-seven years after, that God fulfilled his
threatenings. Then his two sons were both slain in the
same battle with the Philistines, into whose hands the ark
of God fell. The aged priest, then in his ninety-eighth
year, was so overwhelmed when these calamities were made
known to him, that he fell backward from his seat, and
broke his neck. He had governed the Hebrews in all
their concerns, civil and religious, for the long period of
forty years. (1 Sam. iv. 18.)

Samuel, (1 Sam. i. 20,) the son of Elkanah and Hannah, was a celebrated Hebrew prophet, and the last of their
judges. While he was a child, he officiated in some form
in the temple, and was favored with remarkable revelations.

CHAPTER V.

COLORED GENERALS AND SOLDIERS.

MOSES.

MOSES was a General of Egypt.   He was the most distinguished character of ancient times.   Josephus says that after Moses was nourished and brought up in the king's palace, he was appointed General of the Egyptian army, and made war against the Ethiopians and conquered them.   This battle was fought about 1497 years B. C.   Tharbis was the daughter of the Ethiopian king; she happened to see Moses as he led the army near the walls of the city, fighting with great courage.   She admired the subtilty of his undertaking, and believing him to be the author of the Egyptians' success, fell deeply in love with him, and upon consideration of the subject sent to him the most faithful of her servants to discourse with him upon their marriage.   Moses thereupon accepted the offer on condition that she would procure the delivering up of the city to him.   Moses married the king's daughter for the love and affection she had for him, and he obtained the city by her wisdom and artifice. This city had strong walls on every side, and was encircled by the river Nile and Astrapus.   This city was first called Saba, a royal city of Ethiopia.   Cambyses, after he had taken it, named it Meroe, after his own sister. [Rollin and Strabo.]

Moses was learned in all the wisdom of the Egyptians, and mighty in words and in deeds.   (Acts vii. 21, 22.)

HANNO.

HANNO, an African, the father of Hamilcar, was a general of Carthage. He flourished when the Carthaginians were in their greatest prosperity. Some place his time 140 years before the founding of Rome, which would be about 800 years before the era of the whites. This commander-in-chief was sent out with a fleet and army by order of the Carthaginian Senate, to make treaties and settle colonies on the coast of Africa. [Encyclopedia Perthensis. Rollin, Voss, & Hist. Gr. 1. 4.]

HAMILCAR.

HAMILCAR, an African, was the father of Hannibal. The fleet at that time consisted of two thousand ships of war, and upwards of three thousand small vessels of burden. The land forces amounted to no less than three hundred thousand men. These immense forces sailed from Carthage under the command of the celebrated Hamilcar, and were landed at Palermo, (in Latin, Panormus.) This fleet was burnt in the war by the stratagems of Gelon, an able warrior, who was sent to assist Theron the General of Hymera, a city not far from Palermo. The preparations for this war had occupied three years.

Three years after, they appointed Hamilcar their general a second time; and on his pleading his great age for declining the command in this war, they gave him for his lieutenant, Imilcon the son of Hanno, of the same family. The preparations for this war, were equal to the great design, which the Carthaginians had formed. The fleet and army were soon ready, and sailed from Carthage for Sicily. This army consisted of 300,000 men, according to Eporus; but according to Timæus, of six hundred and twenty thousand. The General having died, after the reduction of several cities, Imilcon ended the war by a treaty with Dionysius. [Rollin.]

IMILCON.

IMILCON, an African, a general of Carthage. The following year, Imilcon, being appointed one of the rulers of Carthage, returned to Sicily with a greater army than before. He landed at Palermo, took several cities; and recovered Motya by force of arms. His fleet under the command of Mago, sailed along the coast,—above two hundred ships laden with the spoils of the enemy, and five hundred barques, entered in good order the great harbor of Syracuse. The army according to some authors, consisted of 300,000 foot, and 3,000 horse. In addition to this army, new troops were raised, and placed under the command of Mago, whose father had been lately killed. He was very young, but of great abilities and reputation. He soon arrived in Sicily, and gave Dionysius battle. In this battle, Leptinus, brother of Dionysius and upwards of 14,000 Syracusans were left dead upon the field. By this victory, the Carthaginians obtained an honorable peace, which left them in possession of all they had in Sicily, with the addition even of some strong holds; besides a thousand talents to defray the expenses of the war. Yet Mago, on his return to Carthage was impeached, and died soon after of grief.

HANNIBAL.

HANNIBAL, the Great, an African, a general of Carthage, 218 B. C. Carthage having been at peace 23 years, he led the Carthaginian army and laid siege to Saguntum, a city of Spain, in alliance with the Romans. The Carthaginians, passing through the straits with their fleet, and Hannibal, after taking that place, conceived the bold design of carrying the war into Italy. In the accomplishment of that design, he passed the Pyrenees and finally the Alps, with incredible difficulty, having, when he arrived in Italy, 20,000 foot and 6000 horse. The Romans fell before him. In several pitched battles he utterly routed them, and at Cannæ he made an immense slaughter, 40,000 Romans being left dead on the field. Had he pushed his advantages, and gone immediately to Rome, the fate of the republic would no doubt have been sealed. But he hesitated, and this gave time to the Romans to concentrate their forces, and they in their turn became victorious, by carrying the war into Africa.

SCIPIO AFRICANUS.

Scipio Africanus, an Ethiopian, the Roman general, attacked Hannibal's forces, who had come out against Rome, and gave him battle, about 146 years B. C.; and finally prevailed by carrying the war into Africa. The last punic war terminated with the overthrow of Carthage.

Hannibal to Scipio Africanus at their interview preceding the battle of Zama.

Since fate has so ordained it, that I, who began the war, and who have been so often on the point of ending it by a complete conquest, should now come of my own motion to ask a peace; I am glad that it is of you, Scipio, I have the fortune to ask it. Nor will this be among the least of your glories, that Hannibal, victorious over so many Roman generals, submitted at last to you.

I could wish, that our fathers and we had confined our ambition within the limits which nature seems to have prescribed to it ; the shores of Africa, and the shores of Italy. The gods did not give us that mind. On both sides we have been so eager after foreign possessions, as to put our own to the hazard of war. Rome and Carthage have had, each in her turn, the enemy at her gates. But since errors past may be more easily blamed than corrected, let it now be the work of both you and me to put an end, if possible, to the obstinate contention. For my own part, my years, and the experience I have had of the instability of fortune, incline me to leave nothing to her determination which reason can decide. But much I fear, Scipio, that your youth, your want of the like experience, your uninterrupted success, may render you averse from the thoughts of peace. He whom fortune has never failed, rarely reflects upon her inconstancy. Yet, without recurring to former examples, my own may perhaps suffice to teach you moderation. I am that same Hannibal, who,

after my victory at Cannæ, became master of the greatest
part of your country, and deliberated with myself what
fate I should decree to Italy and Rome. And now, see
the change! Here, in Africa, I am come to treat with a
Roman, for my own preservation, and my country's. Such
are the sports of fortune. Is she then to be trusted because
she smiles? An advantageous peace is preferable to the
hope of victory. The one is in your own power, the other
at the pleasure of the gods. Should you prove victorious,
it would add little to your own glory, or the glory of your
country; if vanquished, you lose in one hour all the honor
and reputation you have been so many years acquiring.
But what is my aim in all this? — that you should content
yourself with our cession of Spain, Sicily, Sardinia and
all the islands between Italy and Africa. A peace on
these conditions will, in my opinion, not only secure the
future tranquillity of Carthage, but be sufficiently glorious
to you, and for the Roman name. And do not tell me
that some of our citizens dealt fraudulently with you in
the late treaty — it is I, Hannibal, that now ask a peace:
I ask it, because I think it expedient for my country; and,
thinking it expedient, I will inviolably maintain it.

Scipio's Answer.

I knew very well, Hannibal, that it was the hope of your
return which embolded the Carthaginians to break the
truce with us, and to lay aside all thoughts of a peace,
when it was just upon the point of being concluded; and
your present proposal is a proof of it. You retrench from
their concessions every thing but what we are, and have
been long possessed of. But as it is your care that your
fellow citizens should have the obligations to you of being
eased from a great part of their burden, so it ought to be
mine that they draw no advantage from their perfidious-
ness. Nobody is more sensible than I am of the weakness
of man and the power of fortune, and that whatever we
enterprise is subject to a thousand chances. If, before the
Romans passed into Africa, you had of your own accord
quitted Italy, and made the offers you now make, I believe
they would not have been rejected. But as you have been
forced out of Italy, and we are masters here of the open
country, the situation of things is much altered. And

what is chiefly to be considered, the Carthaginians, by the late treaty which we entered into at their request, were, over and above what you offer, to have restored to us our prisoners without ransom, delivered up their ships of war, paid us five thousand talents, and to have given hostages for the performance of all. The senate accepted these conditions, but Carthage failed on her part; Carthage deceived us. What then is to be done? Are the Carthaginians to be released from the most important articles of the treaty, as a reward of their breach of faith? No, certainly. If, to the conditions before agreed upon, you had added some new articles to our advantage, there would have been matter of reference to the Roman people; but when, instead of adding, you retrench, there is no room for deliberation. The Carthaginians therefore must submit to us at discretion, or must vanquish us in battle.

POMPEY.

POMPEY, [an Ethiopian,] a Roman general, had early acquired the surname of the Great, by that sort of merit which, from the constitution of the republic, necessarily made him great; a fame and success in war superior to what Rome had ever known in the most celebrated of her generals. He had triumphed, at three several times, over the three different parts of the known world — Europe, Asia and Africa: and by his victories had almost doubled the extent, as well as the revenues of the Roman dominion; for, as he declared to the people on his return from the Mithridatic war, he had found the lesser Asia the boundary; but left it the middle of their empire. He was about six years older than Cæsar; and while Cæsar, immersed in pleasures, oppressed with debts, and suspected by all honest men, was hardly able to show his head, Pompey was flourishing in the height of power and glory; and, by the consent of all parties, placed at the head of the republic.

The taking of Jerusalem by Pompey happened 63 years B. C. This event was connected with the restoration of Hyrcanus to the government of Judea, and the subjection of the country to the Romans. It was made tributary to Rome.

The battle of Pharsalia was fought by Pompey against Cæsar the Great, about 48 years B. C. Cæsar, in his attempt to deprive Pompey of his government, entered Rome before him, and had time to collect an army, with many of the Senate. He immediately left Rome, and marched directly to attack Pompey's lieutenants, who were in Spain, Scipio and Cato. Having subdued them, and being in the mean time appointed dictator, and soon after consul, he had the right of acting in the name of the republic.

By this time, Pompey had raised a numerous army of Roman citizens to oppose Cæsar by force of arms. Cæsar was anxious to bring him to an engagement. He met him in the field of Pharsalia, and entirely defeated his army. Fifteen thousand were slain, and twenty-four thousand surrendered themselves prisoners ; and Pompey, who had been chosen the Roman consul, and was engaged in wars on account of the republic, after conquering various countries, was forced to flee into Egypt, and was slain by Ptolemy the king. This deed was effected by Ptolemy, in order to conciliate the favor of Cæsar, the enemy of Pompey.

How happy would it have been for him to have died in that sickness, when all Italy was putting up vows and prayers for his safety ! or, if he had fallen by the chance of war, on the plains of Pharsalia, in the defence of his country's liberty, he had died still glorious, though unfortunate ; but, as if he had been referred for an example of the instability of human greatness, he, who a few days before commanded kings and consuls, and all the noblest of Rome, was sentenced to die by a council of slaves ; murdered by a base deserter ; cast out naked and headless on the Egyptian strand ; and when the whole earth, as Velleius says, had scarce been sufficient for his victories, could not find a spot upon it at last for a grave. His body was burnt on the shore by one of his freedmen, with the planks of an old fishing boat ; and his ashes, being conveyed to Rome, were deposited privately, by his wife Cornelia, in a vault by his Alban villa. The Egyptians however raised a monument to him on the place, and adorned it with figures of brass, which, being defaced afterwards by time, and buried almost in sand and rubbish, was sought out, and restored by the Emperor Hadrian. [Middleton.]

CIMON.

CIMON was the last of all the Grecian generals, who did any thing, considerable or glorious, against the barbarians. He gained several victories, which reduced Artaxerxes to the necessity of concluding a treaty highly honorable to the Greeks. Greece was first colonized by the Phœnicians and Egyptians.

In A. M. 3554, Cimon stifled the sparks of war which were going to break out among the Greeks; reconciled the two cities, and prevailed with them to conclude a truce for five years. And to prevent the Athenians, who were grown haughty in effect of the many victories they had gained, from having an opportunity, or harboring a design to attack their neighbors and allies, he thought it advisable to lead them to a great distance from home against the common enemy; thus endeavoring, in an honorable way, to inure the citizens to war, and enrich them at the same time. Accordingly he put to sea with a fleet of two hundred sail. He sent sixty of these into Egypt to the aid of Amyrteus, and himself sailed with the rest against the island of Cyprus. Artabazus was at that time in those seas with a fleet of three hundred sail; and Megabysus, the other general of Artaxerxes, with an army of three hundred thousand men, on the coast of Cilicia. As soon as the squadron which Cimon sent into Egypt had joined his fleet, he sailed and attacked Artabazus, and took an hundred of his ships. He sunk many of them, and chased the rest as far as the coasts of Phœnicia. But as if this victory had been only a prelude to a second, he made a descent on Cilicia in his return — attacked Megabysus — defeated him, and cut to pieces a prodigious number of his troops. He afterwards returned to Cyprus with this double triumph, and laid siege to Citium, a strong city of very great importance. His design, after he had reduced that island, was to sail to Egypt, and again embroil the affairs of the Barbarians; for he had very extensive views, and meditated no less a prospect than that of the entire subversion of the mighty empire of Persia. The rumors which prevailed, that Themistocles was to command against him, added fresh fire to his courage; and almost assured of success, he was infinitely pleased with the occasion of trying his abilities with those of that general. But we have already seen that Themistocles laid violent hands on himself about this time.

Artaxerxes, tired with a war in which he had sustained such great losses, resolved, with the advice of his council, to put an end to it. Accordingly, he sent orders to his generals to conclude a peace with the Athenians, upon the most advantageous conditions they could. Megabysus and Artabazus sent ambassadors to Athens to propose an accommodation. Plenipotentiaries were chosen on both sides, and Callias was at the head of those of Athens. The conditions of the treaty were as follows: 1. That all the Grecian cities of Asia should enjoy their liberty, with such laws and forms of government as they should think fit to choose. 2. That no Persian ship of war should be allowed to enter the seas between the Cyanean and Chelidonian islands, that is, from the Euxine sea to the coast of Pamphylia. 3. That no Persian general should march any troops within three day's march of those seas. 4. That the Athenians should not invade any part of the dominions of the king of Persia. These articles being ratified by both parties, peace was proclaimed.

Thus ended this war, which, from the burning of Sardis by the Athenians, had lasted fifty-one years complete, and in which infinite numbers of Persians as well as Greeks had perished.

Whilst this treaty was negotiating, Cimon died, either of sickness, or of a wound he had received at the siege of Citium. When he was near his end, he commanded his officers to sail with the fleet immediately for Athens, and to conceal his death with the utmost care. Accordingly this was executed.

In the 2d century the Jews of Africa, in the city of Cyrene on the Mediterranean, revolted from the Romans, and after slaying 200,000 Greeks and Romans, the Jews were subdued, with a great number massacred, about A. D. 114.

BELISARIUS.

BELISARIUS, an African general. The defeat of the Vandals, in Africa, by Belisarius, occurred A. D. 534.

By this event Africa was recovered to the empire. In the year 536, Belisarius, the great hero of this age, took Rome from the Goths. Though some time elapsed after this event, before the Gothic power was annihilated in Italy, the subjugation of the Ostro Goths, by Belisarius, restored Italy to the empire, A. D. 537.

CONQUESTS OF THE MOORS.—They conquered the whole world known to the ancients. The Saracens or Moors, the descendants of Ishmael, the son of Abraham, by Hagar, an Ethiopian woman, subdued Arabia, Persia, Mesopotamia, Chaldea, Syria, Palestine and the northern part of Africa. Even Sicily, and a part of Europe, became part of their dominion in A. D. 656—666. Their empire was divided into seven kingdoms about A. D. 936.

COL. HENRY DIAZ,

THIS was one of the most remarkable men of his age. In the course of a long and harrassing war with their Dutch masters, the Brazilians had become fatigued, and their resources nearly exhausted. In the midst of their greatest despondency, a stout, active, African (slave,) named Henry Diaz, presented himself in the Brazilian camp. With the air and tone of one whose purpose had been deliberately formed, he proposed to the commander, John Fernandes, to raise a regiment of his own color, and bring them to the rescue of their common country. Although the Portuguese, and other nations of the south of Europe, have never indulged toward the colored race those rancorous prejudices which exist in the United States, yet the sudden appearance, and singular proposal, of this intrepid African, occasioned no small surprise among the Portuguese officers. The arrival of Joan of Arc in the camp of Charles the Seventh could scarcely have produced more wonder. But Diaz, though an enthusiast, made no pretension to miracles. He was well acquainted with the character of his race; and he relied upon his own influence, and tact, to develope the great qualities, which he well knew they possessed. Their situation was indeed wretched and degraded in the ex-

14

treme ; but he had occasionally seen in them, as he felt
within himself, a capacity for high and noble deeds.

When a beggar is offered silver, he is not likely to be
very fastidious about the stamp of the coin; and thus it
was with the Portuguese commander. He readily accepted the proposal of Diaz; but with an incredulous
smile, that plainly implied he considered it no harm for
the blackies to try; just as a father looks and speaks to
little boys, when they ask to hold the plough.

Henry Diaz returned triumphantly to his companions,
to communicate the success of his mission. He exhibited the parchment he had received; and though few
could read the words, all were able to appreciate the
magnitude of the seals, and the magnificence of the flour-
ishes.

The blacks have always shown a readiness to exchange
domestic slavery for the milder servitude, and more ex-
citing scenes of the army. They fear bullets less than
stripes. The history of revolutions in North and South
America, but especially in the latter, furnishes sufficient
proofs of the truth of this remark.

The regiment was soon full, and organized into regular battalions and companies. Such was the talent and
energy of Diaz, and such effective use had he made of
the hours he was enabled to steal from labor and from
sleep, that in less than two months his troops were completely equipped, and in as perfect a state of discipline
as the oldest corps of the army. From miserable, ragged,
servile creatures, they had suddenly started up into
brave and stout men, their faces animated with intelligence and hope, and their eyes glistening like the flash-
ing of the sun upon their bright muskets.

By the fierce and unyielding courage of this regiment,
and the genius and skill of its commander, the Dutch
were repeatedly defeated, after the most severe contests.
The soldiers were never, but once, known to waver from
the rock-like firmness said to distinguish colored troops.
Once, when struggling against a vast superiority of numbers, there was a momentary relaxation of their efforts,
and some symptoms of dismay. Their Colonel rushed
into the midst of the breaking ranks, and exclaiming,
" Are these the brave companions of Henry Diaz !" he

restored their confidence, and secured the victory. By a new and desperate charge, the enemy were completely routed.

After eight years of almost constant warfare, the Dutch were driven from that vast territory, which now forms the empire of Brazil. Of all those rich possessions, which they had expended millions to conquer, by land and by sea, and which their avarice and cruelty had too long desolated, nothing finally remained, but one large, and apparently impregnable fortress, called *Cinco Pontas*, near Pernambuco. It commanded the whole city and neighborhood, and was well provisioned, and garrisoned by an army of five thousand men. Many useless attempts were made to get possession of this important post. It was defended by high and massive walls, and by deep and wide ditches, containing twelve feet of water; and provisions being constantly supplied from Dutch ships, there was no hope of reducing it by famine. Every fresh attack upon it was immediately punished by pouring its powerful batteries on the city and surrounding country. While the enemy possessed this strong hold, the Brazilians were subject to continual irritation and alarm, and could never regard their dear-bought independence as secure.

Here was a subject fit to employ the bold genius and unwearied energy of Henry Diaz!

He sent an officer to the Commander-in-chief, requesting an audience, that he might communicate a plan for taking the *Cinco Pontas.* The General readily granted this request; but with a still smaller hope of any favorable result, than he had entertained, when the slave first proposed his recruiting scheme.

Diaz detailed his plan with characteristic earnestness. The superior officers listened respectfully; for his well-earned reputation effectually protected the speaker from open derision. The result of the conference was, that the General declined adopting the measures proposed, but had no objection that Diaz himself should carry them into effect, with the troops under his command. "Then," replied the brave Colonel, "to-morrow at sunrise, you shall see the Portuguese flag wave on the tower of *Cinco Pontas!*"

As Diaz retired, he overheard his commander say to one of the officers, " *It is a nigger plan.*" He took no notice of the scornful remark; but made preparations for his hazardous enterprise with all possible secrecy and despatch.

His men were ordered to lay aside their muskets— to retain their side-arms — to take a pair of pistols in their belts — and to carry upon their shoulders, a heap of wood, tightly bound together with osier bands. Thus prepared, at two o'clock in the morning, their commander gave directions to march toward the fort. The night was dark, and the column arrived at their destination in perfect safety. Silently and rapidly they deposited their bundles in the deep trench, beginning at the outer margin, and building successive layers toward the wall. As fast as this operation was performed, they filed off, and formed companies, in readiness to scale the wall, as soon as this combined bridge and ladder should be completed. They were obliged to wait but a brief period. The Roman warriors could not have buried the parricide woman under their shields with more celerity, than the soldiers of Diaz filled up the fosse, and formed an ascent to the wall.

Diaz was the first to leap upon the ramparts. The first sentinel he met was laid dead at his feet.

The garrison were sleeping; and before they were completely roused, the Brazilians had gained the greater part of the fortress. As soon as the Dutch recovered a little from their first surprise and confusion, they formed a compact phalanx, and offered desperate resistance. Diaz received a sabre-wound, which shattered the bones of his left arm above the wrist. It was necessary to staunch the blood, which flowed profusely. Finding that it would take the surgeon some time to adjust the bones, and arrange the dressing, he bade him cut off the hand, saying, "It is of less consequence to me than a few moment's time, just now."

This being done, he again rushed into the hottest of the fight; and although the Dutch had greatly the advantage in the use of their artillery and muskets, they could not long withstand the determined bravery of their assailants. Fighting hand to hand, they soon killed, or captured, the whole garrison, and took possession of their immense stores of provision and ammunition.

When the darkness and smoke cleared away, the Portuguese flag was seen waving from the tower of *Cinco Pontas !*

The Commander-in-Chief could scarcely believe the evidence of his own senses. The intrepid Diaz sent an aid-de-camp to say that the fort and prisoners were at the disposition of his Excellency. In a few hours, the General, with a numerous suite entered the fortress, and was saluted by the victorious troops. They found Colonel Diaz reclining on his camp-bed, enfeebled by exertion and loss of blood. He, however, raised himself to a sitting posture, and received the thanks and congratulations of his commanding and brother officers, with the grave and placid air habitual to him. Then looking up archly, he said, "*It was a nigger plan, General; but the Fort is taken.*"

At the request of John the Fourth, Henry Diaz visited Portugal, where he was received with great distinction. The king desired him to choose any reward within his power to bestow. Diaz merely requested that his regiment might be perpetuated, and none admitted to its ranks but those of his own color. This was granted; and a considerable town and territory were appropriated to secure pensions to these brave men and their successors. The town is called Estancia, and is situated a short distance from Pernambuco.

The king conferred knighthood upon Diaz, and caused a medal to be struck in commemoration of the capture of *Cinco Pontas.* It was likewise ordained that the regiment should for ever bear the name of its first commander. It still exists in Pernambuco. Its uniform is white, faced with red, and embroidered with gold. The decorations which Diaz received from John the Fourth, are transmitted to the commander of the regiment, to this day; and at royal audiences they have the privilege of being the first to kiss the sovereign's hand. [Greg. pp. 94. 90. David L. Child, Esq. of Massachusetts.]

COLORED SOLDIERS.

THE brave colored soldiers of America, who fought for the boasted land of equal rights and liberty, in the American war against Great Britain.

In the Revolutionary War on Bunker Hill, in that victorious battle, the colored soldiers fought bravely — standing shoulder to shoulder in regiments with the whites, and gained that great victory over a superior number of British troops. [See the old map of Bunker Hill battle, a slave standing behind his master and shooting down an officer of the British army, and ready for another fire.] Our fathers shed their blood on the shores of Jersey, and faced the British bayonets in the most desperate hour of danger in the Revolution.

Hon. Mr. Burgess of Rhode Island, said on the floor of Congress Jan. 28, 1828 :—

"At the commencement of the Revolutionary War, Rhode Island had a number of this description of people, [slaves.] · A regiment of them were enlisted into the continental service, and no braver men met the enemy in battle; but not one of them was permitted to be a soldier until he had first been made a freeman."

Said the Hon. Mr. Martindale of New York, in Congress, Jan. 22d, 1838 :—

"Blacks who had been slaves, were entrusted as soldiers in the war of the revolution; and I, myself, saw a battalion of them, as fine, martial looking men as I ever saw attached to the northern army in the last war, on its march from Plattsburg to Sackett's Harbor."

Said the Hon. Charles Miner, of Pennsylvania, in Congress, February 7th, 1828 :—

"The African race make excellent soldiers. Large numbers of them were with Perry, and aided to gain the brilliant victory on Lake Erie. A whole battalion of them was distinguished for its soldierly appearance."

The Hon. Mr. Clarke, in the Convention which revised the Constitution of New York, in 1821, said in regard to the right of suffrage of colored men :—

"In the war of the revolution these people helped to fight your battles by land and by sea. Some of your states were glad to turn out corps of colored men, and to stand shoulder to shoulder with them. In your late war they contributed largely towards your most splendid victories. On Lakes Erie and Champlain, where your fleets triumphed over a foe superior in numbers, and engines of death, they were manned in a large proportion with men of color. And in this very house, in the fall of 1814, a bill passed, receiving the approbation of all the branches of your government, authorizing the Governor to accept the service of two thousand free people of color."

On the 20th of March, 1779, it was recommended by Congress to the States of Georgia and South Carolina, to raise 3,000 colored troops who were to be rewarded for their services by their freedom. The delegations from those states informed Congress that such a body of troops would be not only " formidable to the enemy," but would lessen the danger of " revolts and desertions" among the slaves themselves. (See Secret Journal of the Old Congress, Vol. 1, pp. 105 — 107.)

[And are we to be thus looked to for help in the " hour of danger," but trampled under foot in the hour of peace? " No more will we fight against our friends for this oppressed land."]

THE LAST AMERICAN WAR WITH GREAT BRITAIN.

DURING the last war, the slaves and free colored people were called to the defence of the country by General Jackson, and received the following testimony to the value of their services, in which, let it be remarked, they were addressed as *fellow citizens* with the whites:

"Through a mistaken policy you have heretofore been deprived of a participation in the glorious struggle for national rights, in which our country is engaged. This no longer shall exist.

As sons of Freedom, you are now called upon to defend our most inestimable blessing. As Americans, your country looks with confidence to her adopted children, for a valorous support, as a faithful return for the advantages enjoyed under her mild and equitable government. As fathers, husbands, and brothers, you are summoned to rally round the standard of the Eagle, to defend all which is dear in existence.

Your country, although calling for your exertions, does not wish you to engage in her cause, without remunerating you for the services rendered. Your intelligent minds are not to be led away by false representations—your love of honor would cause you to despise the man who should attempt to deceive you. In the sincerity of a soldier, and the language of truth, I address you.

To every noble hearted freeman of color, volunteering to serve during the present contest with Great Britain, and no longer, there will be paid the same bounty in money and lands, now received by the white soldiers of the United States, viz: one hundred and twenty-four dollars in money, and one hundred and sixty acres of land. The non-commissioned officers and privates will also be entitled to the same monthly pay and daily rations, and clothes furnished to any American soldier.

On enrolling yourselves in companies, the Major General Commanding, will select officers for your government, from your white fellow citizens. [General Coffin, with seven hundred of the colored troops beat back the British forces who came up to break through the entrenchment.] Your non-commissioned officers will be appointed from among yourselves.

Due regard will be paid to the feelings of freemen and soldiers. You will not, by being associated with white men in the same corps, be exposed to improper comparisons or unjust sarcasm. As a distinct, independent battalion or regiment, pursuing the path of glory, you will, undivided, receive the applause and gratitude of your countrymen.

To assure you of the sincerity of my intentions and my anxiety to engage your invaluable services to our country, I have communicated my wishes to the governor of Louisiana, who is fully informed as to the manner of enrolments, and will give you every necessary information on the subject of this address.

ANDREW JACKSON,
Major General Commanding."

PROCLAMATION TO THE FREE PEOPLE OF COLOR.

"Soldiers!—When on the banks of the Mobile, I called you to take up arms, inviting you to partake the perils and glory of your white fellow citizens, I expected much from you; for I was not ignorant that you possessed qualities most formidable to an invading enemy. I knew with what fortitude you could endure hunger and thirst, and all the fatigues of a campaign. I know well how you loved your native country, and that you had, as well as ourselves, to defend what man holds most dear—his parents, relations, wife, children and property. You have done more than I expected. In addition to the previous qualities I before knew you to possess, I found, moreover, among you a noble enthusiasm which leads to the performance of great things.

Soldiers!—The President of the United States shall hear how praiseworthy was your conduct in the hour of danger! and the Representatives, of the American people will, I doubt not, give you the praise your exploits entitle you to. Your General anticipates them in applauding your noble ardor.

The enemy approaches; his vessels cover our lakes; our brave citizens are united, and all contention has ceased among them. Their only dispute is, who shall win the prize of valor, or who the most glory, its noblest reward. By order, THOMAS BUTLER, *Aid de Camp.*"

In the last war there was no honor due to Gen. Jackson for arranging his army behind cotton bags in such a manner as to save life. [Belfast Rep. Jour.]

The plan of throwing up an entrenchment between the swamp and the river, at the point where the British were obliged to approach, if they came at all, was not first conceived by Gen. Jackson, nor was the use of the cotton bales a scheme of his, but was a plan of a colored man. He proposed to the General the expediency of defending this strong point, which was so obvious that there could be no hesitation or dispute about it; Jackson therefore ordered it to be built, and thus saved the American army and country.

CHAPTER VI.

DESTRUCTION OF JERUSALEM.

THE GREAT CITY OF JERUSALEM.

Her birth and nativity is of the land of Canaan. The father or founder of Jerusalem was an Amorite, and the mother a Hittite. (Ezekiel xvi. 3.) Amorite, the fourth son of Canaan, and Hittite, the descendants of Ham, the third son of Canaan, (Genesis x. 1Chronicles i.,) a colored people. Glorious things were spoken of this holy city. This noted city was built on two mountains, and contained two parts, called upper and lower city; the former was built on Mount Sion, and the latter on Mount Acra. This city is supposed to have been founded by Melchisedec, and then called Salem or Solyma.

The splendid walls of Jerusalem were very high and broad. The most of this city was surrounded with three walls. In some places, where it was deemed inaccessible, it had only one wall. The wall first built was adorned and strengthened with sixty towers; fourteen towers rested on the middle wall; ninety towers rested on the inside wall, and was most remarkable for its workmanship and grandeur.

The tower Psephina was most celebrated. It was seventy cubits high, had eight angles, and commanded a most beautiful prospect. Here the visitor might, in a clear atmosphere, delight himself with a view of the Mediterranean forty miles to the west, and of most of the Jewish dominions in Arabia and Africa. Some of these towers were nearly ninety cubits high, and famous for their beauty, elegance and curiosities. They were built of white marble, and had the appearance of vast marble blocks. These huge piles gave to the city, in the view of the adjacent country, a most majestic appearance. Near the highest of these towers stood the Royal Palace, of the most commanding elegance. Incredible cost had furnished its pillars, porticos, galleries and apartments. Its gardens, groves, fountains, aqueducts and walks presented the richest and most delightful scenery. This was the beauty and elegance of the north side of Jerusalem. On the east side, stood the temple and the fort of Antonio, over against Mount Olivet. This fort was built on a rock fifty feet in height and of inaccessible steepness, overlaid with slabs of marble. The castle of Antonia stood in the centre of this fortress. The workmanship of this castle made it more resemble a palace than a castle. A tower adorned each square of this fortress — one of which was seventy cubits high, and commanded a full view of the temple.

Jerusalem, the city of the Great King, was originally a city of the Jebusites,* from whom it was taken by King David, and made the capital of Judea. For many centuries it might have been called God's capitol on earth. God said, alluding primarily to this city, The Lord hath chosen Zion to be a habitation for himself. Here will I dwell, for I have desired it, &c. The Lord of Hosts is with us — the God of Jacob is our refuge. In Salem [Jerusalem] stood his Tabernable, and his dwelling place in Zion.

THE UPPER CITY.

The House of the Mighty, the House of David, Zion, or the city of David. The House of Solomon, built for Pharaoh's daughter. Hippodrome and Upper Markets. The Fountain Gate on the west, the Water Gate on the East, the Dung Gate on the N. W., the Fort of Antiochus, &c. &c.

THE LOWER CITY.

The temple was built on Mount Moriah [on the east side] and the fort of Anthony. Bezeta or the New Town, Salem or the Lower Town. The Queen's House, the House of Holens Ophel, Dwellings of the Nethinim. The Fish Gate and Ephraim Gate on the North. The Sheep Gate and Ben-

---

* Jebus, the third son of Canaan, and grandson of Ham. The warlike Jebusites had long defended themselves against the Hebrews. Gen. ix. 15, 16. 2 Samuel v. 6, Josephus.

jamin's Gate on the east. The Corner Gate on the N. W.,
and the Horse Gate on the South. The Fish Market,
Beast Market and Wood Market. The pool of Bethesda,
Theatre, &c.

Jerusalem, formerly the capital of Judea, is now called,
by the Turks, Cudsembaric and Cudscherif; it is about
three miles in circumference, and situated on a rocky
mountain, with very steep ascents on all sides, except to
the north; the valleys being deep, and at some distance,
environed with hills. From the oppressive tyranny of the
Turks, it is now but thinly inhabited.

A DESCRIPTION OF SOLOMON'S TEMPLE.

HIRAM, an Ethiopian king of Tyre, was Solomon's
coadjutor in the construction and furnishing of the temple at Jerusalem.

Solomon sent for Hiram; for he was filled with wisdom
and understanding, skillful to work in gold, silver, brass,
iron, stone, timber, glass, fine-linen, &c.; and to en-
grave any manner of engraving; and to find out every
device which shall be put to him, and he came to Solomon: and Solomon and Hiram made a league together.
Hiram furnished Solomon with cedar and fir trees, olive
and palm trees and algum. He sent also to Solomon six
score talents of gold. He furnished seamen to navigate
Solomon's vessels to Ophir; and such skillful artisans to
prepare the materials for the temple, that there was neither hammer, nor axe, nor any tool of iron heard in the
house while it was building. There were three thousand
and three hundred overseers, and 150,000 workmen engaged on this work. The temple was built upon Mount
Moriah. It was supported by 1453 columns and 2906
pilasters, all hewn from the finest Parian marble. Three
grand columns or pillars were named Wisdom, Strength
and Beauty, wisdom which God gave unto Solomon, and
strength and beauty unto Hiram king of Tyre, whom
God blessed to build and ornament the temple. This
temple was in many respects the most astonishing sight
ever beheld. Its site was partly upon a solid rock originally steep on every side. The foundation was of vast

dimensions, said to be 300 cubits from its lowest base;
it was composed of stones many of them sixty feet in
length. The lower part of the superstructure was composed of blocks of white marble more than sixty feet long
and seven feet by nine in bigness. The circumference
of the whole pile, was four furlongs. In the front were
spacious and lofty galleries, wainscoted with cedar, supported by uniform rows of white marble columns. Josephus asserts that nothing could exceed the exterior parts
of this house of God, for elegant and exquisite workmanship, or in splendor: its solid plates of gold seemed to
strive to outdazzle the rising sun. The part of the building not covered with gold, had at a distance the appearance of pillars of snow, or white marble mountains. And
the grandeur of the internal workmanship of this magnificent edifice was fully equal to its external magnificence.
Nothing superb, costly, or elegant was spared. The
different parts of the world seemed to have vied with
each other, to pour their most costly treasures into this
treasure house of heaven. The lower story of the temple was decorated with the sacred furniture, the table of
the shew bread, the altar of incense, and the candlestick
of pure beaten gold. The altar and table were overlaid
with pure gold. Several doors of this sanctuary were
fifty-five cubits in height, and sixteen in breadth, likewise
overlaid with pure gold. The richest Babylonian tapes-
try of purple, blue, and of exquisite workmanship, waved
within these doors. Gold vines of curious workmanship
with leaves and clusters of grapes of gold were suspended five or six feet from the ceiling. The eastern gate of
the temple was immense, and of pure Corinthian brass,
a most valuable metal. But it would be a task to enu-
merate all the golden works, paintings, and gildings,
vessels of gold, and scarlet, violet, and purple sacerdotal
vestments, and all the piles of incalculable riches in this
temple of Jehovah. The most precious stones, spices
and perfumes, every thing that nature or art or riches
could furnish, were stored within these stupendous and
hallowed walls.

This structure, for beauty, magnificence, and expense,
exceeded any building which was ever erected. It was
built of large stones of white marble, curiously hewn,

and so artfully joined together, that they appeared like one entire stone. Its inner walls, beams, posts, doors, floors and ceilings, were made of cedar and olive wood, and planks of fir; which were entirely covered with plates of gold, with various beautiful engravings, and adorned with precious jewels of many splendid colors. The nails which fastened those plates were also of gold, with heads of curious workmanship. The roof was of olive wood, covered with gold; and when the sun shone thereon, the reflection from it was of such a refulgent splendor that it dazzled the eyes of all who beheld it. The court in which the temple stood, and the courts without, were adorned on all sides with stately buildings and cloisters; and the gates entering therein, were exquisitely beautiful and elegant. The vessels consecrated to the perpetual use of the temple, were suited to the magnificence of the edifice in which they were deposited and used.

Josephus states, that there were one hundred and forty thousand of those vessels, which were made of gold, and one million three hundred and forty thousand of silver; ten thousand vestments for the priests, made of silk, with purple girdles; and two millions of purple vestments for the singers. There were also two hundred thousand trumpets, and forty thousand other musical instruments, made use of in the temple, and in worshipping God.

According to the most accurate computation of the number of talents of gold, silver, and brass, laid out upon the temple, the sum amounts to six thousand nine hundred and four millions, eight hundred and twenty-two thousand and five hundred pounds sterling; and the jewels are reckoned to exceed this sum. The gold vessels are estimated at five hundred and forty-five millions, two hundred and ninety-six thousand, two hundred and three pounds, and four shillings, sterling; and the silver ones, at four hundred and thirty-nine millions, three hundred and forty-four thousand pounds sterling; amounting in all, to nine hundred and eighty-four millions, six hundred and thirty thousand, two hundred and thirty pounds, four shillings. In addition to this, there were expenses for workmen, and for materials brought from Mount Libanus, and the quarries of Zeradatha. There were ten

thousand men per month in Lebanon, employed in falling
and preparing the timbers for the craftsmen to hew them,
seventy thousand to carry burdens; eighty thousand to
hew the stones and timber; and three thousand three
hundred overseers of the work; who were all employed
for seven years; to whom, besides their wages and diet,
king Solomon gave as a free gift, six millions seven hundred and thirty-three thousand, nine hundred and seventy-seven pounds.

The treasure left by David, towards carrying on this
noble and glorious work, is reckoned to be nine hundred
and eleven millions, four hundred and sixteen thousand,
two hundred and seven pounds; to which if we add king
Solomon's annual revenue, his trading to Ophir for gold,
and the presents made him by all the earth, as mentioned
1 Kings x. 24, 25, we shall not wonder at his being able
to carry on so expensive a work; nor can we, without
impiety, question its surpassing all other structures, since
we are assured that it was built by the immediate direction of HEAVEN.

And the king commanded, and they brought great
stones, costly stones, and hewed stones, to lay the foundation of the house. And Solomon's builders and Hiram's builders did hew them, and the stone-squarers: so
they prepared timber and stones to build the house. (1
Kings v. 17, 18.)

When the temple of Jerusalem was finished, the cap-
stone was celebrated, with great joy. "This is the stone
which is become the head of the corner." (Psalm cxviii.
22. Matt. xxi. 42. Mark xii. 10. Luke xx. 17. Acts iv.
11. 1 Kings vi. 27.)

And he set the cherubims within the inner house; and
they stretched forth the wings of the cherubims, so that
the wing of the one touched the one wall; and the wing
of the other cherub touched the other wall; and their
wings touched one another in the midst of the house.

And Solomon made all the vessels that pertained unto
the house of the Lord: the altar of gold, and the table of
gold, whereupon the shew-bread was; and the candle-
sticks of pure gold; five on the right side, and five on the
left, before the oracle; with the flowers, and the lamps,
and the tongs of gold; and the bowls, and the snuffers,

and the basins, and the spoons, and the censers, of pure gold; and the hinges of gold, both for the doors of the inner house, the most holy place, and for the doors of the house, to wit, of the Temple. So Hiram made an end of doing all the work, that he had made king Solomon, for the house of the Lord.

Now, when Solomon had made an end of praying, the fire came down from heaven, and consumed the burnt offering and sacrifices; and the glory of the Lord filled the house. And the priest could not enter into the house of the Lord, because the glory of the Lord had filled the Lord's house.

And when all the children of Israel saw how the fire came down, and the glory of the Lord upon the house, they bowed themselves with their faces to the ground upon the pavement, and worshipped, and praised the Lord, saying, For he is good; for his mercy endureth forever. (2 Chron. vii. 1—4.)

I was glad when they said unto me, Let us go into the house of the Lord. Our feet shall stand within thy gates, O Jerusalem. Jerusalem is builded as a city that is compact together: whither the tribes go up, the tribes of the Lord, unto the testimony of Israel, to give thanks unto the name of the Lord. For there are set thrones of judgment, the thrones of the house of David.

Pray for the peace of Jerusalem: they shall prosper, that love thee. Peace be within thy walls, and prosperity within thy palaces. For my brethren and companions' sakes, I will now say, Peace be within thee. Because of the house of the Lord our God, I will seek thy good. (Psalm cxxii.)

In the year of the world 3029, King Solomon died, and was succeeded by his son Rehoboam. Soon after this, instigated and led on by Jeroboam, the son of Nebat, ten of the tribes revolted from Rehoboam, and set up a separate kingdom, with Jeroboam at their head. In this manner were the tribes of Israel divided, and under two distinct governments, for two hundred and fifty-four years. The ten revolted tribes became weak and degenerated; their country was laid waste, and their government overthrown and extirpated by Salmanezer, King of Assyria. After a series of changes and events,

Nebuchadnezzar, king of Babylon, having besieged Jerusalem, and raised towers all round the city, so that, after defending it for the space of a year and a half, it was, in the eleventh year of the reign of Zedekiah, king of Judah, surrendered and delivered at midnight to the officers of Nebuchadnezzar, who sacked and destroyed the temple, and took away all the holy vessels, together with those two famous brazen pillars; and the remnant of the people that escaped the sword, carried he away captives to Babylon, where they remained servants to him and his successors, until the reign of Cyrus, king of Persia. Cyrus, in the first year of his reign, being directed by that divine power which invisibly led him to the throne of Persia, issued his famous edict for the liberation of the Hebrew captives, with permission that they should return to their native country, and rebuild the city and house of the Lord. Accordingly, the principal people of the tribes of Judah and Benjamin, with the Priests and Levites, immediately departed for Jerusalem, and commenced the great and glorious work.

THE DESTRUCTION OF JERUSALEM.

This City of God, long answered well to its name, Jerusalem, They shall see; Salem, Peace. Long did the church while they walked with God, there see and enjoy peace. But alas, we find recorded of this city, temple, and nation of Jews, a fatal reverse! They found the sentiment in their sacred oracles fulfilled, "The Lord is with you while ye be with him; but if ye forsake him he will cast you off."

The Jews became carnal, and crucified the Lord of Glory; (Simon, a Cyrenian, or African, carried our Savior's cross to the place of crucifixion,) and they fell under the denunciations and the full execution of his wrath. Their lawgiver, Moses, and their prophets had long thundered against them solemn denunciations, that if they should ever become of the character which they did, the most signal judgments of God should cut them off.

The Messiah uttered against them, in consequence of

15

their rejecting him, a new addition of these fatal denunciations, which we find in Matt. xxiv. Mark xiii. Luke xix.
41—44. chap. xxi. and xxiii. 27—30.   These were to
have a primary fulfilment in the desolation of Jerusalem,
and of the Jewish commonwealth.   This primary fulfilment, Christ assured them, should take place in that
generation; and the denunciation was fulfilled.   This
fulfilment, inasmuch as it demonstrated the truth and
divinity of our Savior, exhibited a type of the destruction
of Antichrist, and of the wicked at the end of world; and
shows the danger of rejecting the Son of God, and ought
to be duly noted in the church and frequently contem-
plated.   It is a subject too much neglected and forgotten
in the present Christian world.   I design then to give a
concise description of the event in which Jesus Christ
came in awful judgment upon the infidel Jews, and vindicated his cause against his persecutors and murderers.

This noted city was owned by the warlike Jebusites,
when the Israelites entered Canaan, and contained two
parts called the upper and lower city, built on two mountains, Zion and Acra.   In the higher city they long
defended themselves against the Hebrews.   Here they
remained till king David subdued them, and called their
city the City of David.

Herod the Great, when he repaired or rebuilded the
Temple, added vast strength and embellishments to this
city; which accounts for its superb state and strength
when it was destroyed.

The Hebrew nation possessed this city for many centuries; it was the cradle of the true and only church of
God on earth.   There, glorious things were wrought for
her salvation;   patriarchs had there prayed, sacrificed
and praised; there prophets had prophesied; and the Almighty had often made bare his holy arm.   There his
people had too often apostatized and were expelled from
their Canaan, and again mercifully restored.   There the
Ten tribes of Israel renounced the House or City of
David, and their God, and were hence banished to some
unknown region of the world, while the Jews were still
retained in the covenant of their God.   There, God manifest in the flesh, made his appearance on earth; performed his public ministry; atoned for the sins of the

world; and ascended to glory. There, the first heralds of the Gospel dispensation commenced their ministry; and thence, the wonderful scheme of grace was propagated through the nations.

The Lord blessed the Jews, while they kept his commandments and walked with him. But alas, here were the city and temple to be destroyed for the infidelity, malice, hypocrisy, and persecution of the Lord of Glory and His followers, which characterized its rulers and people. Here, a measure of unprecedented atrociousness was just filled up, which should bring down wrath upon them to the uttermost. This tremendous ruin, our Lord foretold and it was fulfilled.

The last noted entrance into Jerusalem, of Him who was God manifest in the flesh, took place on the Monday before the scene of his suffering. Amidst the acclamation of multitudes, he was hailed king of Zion, with every token of joy and praise. The air rang with their praises, uttered for all the mighty works they had seen. They sang, Hosanna! Blessed be the king that cometh in the name of the Lord! Peace in Heaven and glory in the highest. Our Lord, superior to all their adulation, and knowing how soon the Hosannas of some of them would turn to "Crucify him," and being touched with sympathy and pity for a devoted city, now going to fill up their guilty measure of iniquity, beheld the city and wept over it. He said: "If thou hadst known, even thou, in this thy day, the things which belong to thy peace; but now they are hid from thine eyes. For the days shall come when thine enemies shall cast a trench about thee, and encompass thee around, and keep thee in on every side, and shall lay thee even with the ground, and thy children within thee. And they shall not leave thee one stone upon another, because thou knewest not the time of thy visitations."

The day but one after, Christ went into the temple for the last time, to instruct the people. While he was thus employed, the high priest, elders, Herodians, Sadducees, and Pharisees, gathered in turn around him, with a malicious view to entangle him in his talk. Christ returned such answers, spake such parables, and set home such reproof and conviction to their souls, as not only to astonish and silence them; but to give them some awful prelibation of the final judgment, which awaited them at his bar. He thus, in a free and pungent address to the disciples, administered the most dignified and keen reproofs for the cruelty, hypocrisy, and pride, of the scribes and Pharisees. He foretold the malicious treatment the disciples would meet with at their hands; and then denounced the vengeance on that falling city, which for ages their crimes had been accumulating. He forewarned that this cup of divine indignation should be poured on *that generation.* His tender feelings of soul then melted in a most moving apostrophe: "O Jerusalem, Jerusalem! thou that killest the prophets, and stonest them that are sent unto thee! How often would I have gathered thy children together, even as a hen gathereth her chickens under her wings; and ye would not! Behold, your house is left unto you desolate. For I say unto you, ye shall not see me henceforth, till ye shall say, "Blessed is he that cometh in the name of the Lord." Upon this our Savior left the temple. The disciples took an occasion to speak to Christ of the magnificence of the sacred edifice; how it was adorned with goodly stones and gifts. "Master, [said they,] see what manner of stones and buildings are here." "Jesus said unto them; See ye not all these things? Verily, I say unto you, there shall not be left here one stone upon another, that shall not be thrown down." How very unlikely must such an event have seemed! But it was indeed fulfilled upon that generation.

Jesus and his disciples retired to the Mount of Olives. Here the temple rose before them in all its majestic elegance. The surrounding scenery naturally suggested the conversation which followed. The disciples petitioned;—"Tell us, when shall these things be? and what shall be the sign when all these things shall be fulfilled?" Their minds seem to have been impressed with the preceding discourse; and they fell most readily upon the same subject, and wished to know when such awful events should come; and what warning should announce their approach. Our Lord replied; "Take heed that no man deceive you; for many shall come in my name, saying, I am Christ; and shall deceive many."

As though he had said; This shall be one signal token of the event, both as my denunciations relate to a primary accomplishment in the destruction of Jerusalem, and to a more general and dreadful fulfilment in the destruction of Antichrist in the last days. Impostors shall abound. False religionists shall deceive and ruin many. Let us trace the fulfilment of this and several succeeding predictions.

This was fulfilled in relation to Jerusalem. Not long after Christ's ascension, the Samaritan Dositheus appeared and declared himself the Messiah predicted by Moses. Simon Magus also declared himself " *The Great Power of God.*" Soon after, another impostor appeared from the mongrel Samaritans. The church has ever been annoyed by such kind of Samaritans, who have ever been fruitful in vile impostors, crying " Lo, here; and lo, there." This impostor promised to exhibit to the people sacred utensils said to be deposited by Moses in Mount Gerizim. Here a new decision must be given from heaven, to the question between the Jews and Samaritans, as to the place of worship; a thing of which schismatics have ever been exceedingly fond; to derive some new light on their party question directly from above; as though decisions already given were insufficient.

Armed multitudes sallied forth to follow this Messiah, confident their great deliverer had at last made his appearance. But Pilate, the Roman Governor, checked their fanaticism with the sword, and put their fancied Messiah to death.

Another impostor, Theudas, arose. He had the address to persuade multitudes to follow him into the wilderness, under his promise that he would cause the river Jordan to divide. The Roman procurator, Fadus, with a troop of horse, pursued them; slew the impostor, and many others; and dispersed the faction. Deceivers, under the government of Felix, were multiplied, leading off people into the wilderness under the promise and fanatic l expectation that they should there see signs and wonders. The old serpent often leads fanatical people into wildernesses of error and delusion, under similar expectations. The vigilant eye of the Roman governor rested on these impostors, and was sure to frustrate their designs, as oft as they appeared.

In the year 55, arose a notable Egyptian impostor, named Felix. Thirty thousand followed him, under the persuasion that from mount Olivet they should see the walls of Jerusalem fall to the ground at his command, for their easy capture of the Roman garrison there; and their taking possession of Jerusalem. They were attacked by the Roman governor; four hundred were slain, and the rest dispersed. The Egyptian impostor escaped for his life. In the year 60, another pretended Messiah, appeared, engaging to break the Roman yoke, if they would follow him into the wilderness; but the deceiver and his followers soon fell a sacrifice to the vigilance of Festus, the governor. It would be too unwieldy to mention all the vile impostors of this period. They were a just retribution of righteous Heaven upon the Jews, for having rejected and put to death the true Messiah: and they fulfilled the warning given by our Lord, of a host of deceivers at that period. How prone are men to court deception. Christ had said to the Jews, "I am come in my Father's name, and ye receive me not. If another should come in his own name, him will ye receive." This was fulfilled; and not only then, but in every age to this day. Those who give the best evangelical evidence of their being ambassadors of Christ, many will reject; while the confident and noisy claims of egotists are by them fully allowed. "As in water face answers to face; so the heart of man to man."

Our Lord proceeds; "And ye shall hear of wars, and rumors of wars: see that ye be not troubled: for all these things shall come to pass; but the end is not yet. For nation shall rise against nation; and kingdom against kingdom; and great earthquakes shall be in divers places, and famines, and pestilences; all these are the beginning of sorrows."

The portentous thunders of wars and rumors of wars may be said to have occupied most of the time from the death of our Savior, to the destruction of Jerusalem. The historic pages, which treat of these times, are stained with blood. A war between Herod and Aretas, king of Arabia, opened the bloody scene, after a short season of peace. In Seleucia, the Greeks and Syrians rose against the Jews, who fled thither from the pestilence in Babylon, and slew fifty thousand of them. Five years after, the Jews in Perea and people of Philadelphia contended about the limits of a city, when many of the Jews were slain. Four years after this, an insult being offered to the Jews within the precincts of the temple, by a Roman soldier; and being violently resented, a Roman force rushed upon them, which so terrified the Jews, that they fled in vast disorder, and ten thousand of them lost their lives in the streets. After another four years, the Jews ravaged the country of the Samaritans, in consequence of their having murdered a Galilean, who was going to keep the passover. Many were slain. Soon after, a contention arose between the Jews in Cæsarea and the Syrians, relative to the government of Cæsarea. In the first encounter more than twenty thousand Jews were slain. This contention raged in many cities where the Jews and Syrians dwelt; and mutual slaughter prevailed. And in five other cities the carnage among the Jews was dreadful. At Damascus ten thousand Jews were slain in one hour. And at Scythopolis thirteen thousand were slain in one night. In Alexandria the Jews rose upon the Romans; and had fifty thousand of their people slain, without any regard to infancy or age. Soon after, in a contention at Totapata, forty thousand Jews perished. These contentions rose and increased, till the whole Jewish nation took up arms against the Romans, and brought on themselves their final destruction. Thus the prediction of our Savior quoted, received in those days a striking primary fulfilment.

Our Savior added; "And great earthquakes shall be in divers places." These significant warnings too were accomplished in those days. Two are recorded by Tacitus; one at Rome in the reign of Claudius; another at Apamea, in Syria, where were many Jews. So destructive was the one at the latter place, that the tribute due to the Romans was for five years remitted. One also was terrific at Crete; one at Smyrna; one at Miletus; one at Chios, and one at Samos; in all which places Jews dwelt. These are noted by Philostratus. Soon after, in the reign of Nero, both Tacitus and Eusebius inform, that Hierapolis and Colosse, as well a Laodicea, were overthrown by earthquakes. Another is noted at Rome; one at Campania; and others as tremendous are mentioned as taking place at Jerusalem in the night, just before the commencement of the last siege of that city. Of these, Josephus gives the following account: "A heavy storm burst on them, during the night; violent winds arose, with most excessive rains, with constant lightning, most tremendous thunders, and dreadful roarings of earthquakes. It seemed as if the system of the world had been confounded for the destruction of mankind. And one might well conjecture that these were signs of no common event."

. The *famines* predicted by Christ were likewise fulfilled. The one foretold by Agabus, noted in the Acts of the Apostles, was dreadful and of long continuance. It extended through Greece and Italy; but was most severely felt at Judea, and especially at Jerusalem. The contributions noted as brought by Paul from abroad, to relieve the poor brethren there, were sent during this sore famine. Authors of that time mention two other famines in the empire, previous to the one occasioned by the siege of Jerusalem. .

" Pestilences" too, the Savior, adds. . Two instances of this signal judgment took place before the last Jewish war. The one took place at Babylon, where many Jews resided; the other at Rome, which swept off vast multitudes. Other lighter instances of this calamity occurred, in various parts of the empire; as both Tacitus and Suetonius record.

Our Lord also adds, "And fearful sights and great signs shall there be from heaven." Josephus [who can never be suspected of wishing to favor any prediction of Christ; and who probably knew not of any such prediction, when he wrote,] gives accounts of events, which strikingly answer to this premonition. Speaking of the infatuation of his coun'rymen, in running after impostors, while they neglected the plainest admonitions from heaven, he gives account of the seven following events;

1. He says; "On the 8th of the month Zanthicus, [before the feast of unleavened bread,] at the ninth hour of the night, there shone round about the altar and the

circumjacent buildings of the temple, a light equal to the brightness of the day; which continued for the space of half an hour."

2. "About the sixth hour of the night, [says Josephus,] the eastern gate of the temple was found to open without human assistance." This gate was of solid brass; and so large and heavy, as t require twenty men to close it. And Josephus says, "it was secured by iron bolts, and bars, that were let down into a large threshold consisting of one entire stone." The Jews themselves concluded, from the miraculous nature of this event, that the security of their temple had fled. When the procurator was informed of it, he sent a band of men to close the door; who with great difficulty executed their orders.

3. Again, the same celebrated Jewish author says: "At a subsequent feast of Pentecost, while the priests were going by night into the inner temple, to perform their customary ministrations, they first felt, as they said, a shaking accompanied by an indistinct murmuring; and afterwards voices as of a multitude, saying in a distinct and earnest manner: "Let us depart hence." How striking was this miraculous premonition. It commenced with a *shaking*, to call and fix the attention of these Jewish priests. Then was heard an *indistinct murmur*. This would make them listen with all possible heed. Then they heard the *distinct voices*, as of a multitude in great earnestness and haste;—"*Let us depart hence!*" And their last fatal war with the Romans commenced before the next season for celebrating this feast. .

4. Another sign was the following. The same author says; "A meteor, resembling a sword, hung over Jerusalem, during one whole year." This could not have been a comet, for it was stationary a whole year, and seems, from the words of Josephus, to have been much nearer than a comet, and appeared to be appropriated to that city. This reminds one of the sword of the destroying angel, stretched out over Jerusalem, (1 Chro. xxi. 16.) This stationary position of the sword for a year, was a lively indication that the impending ruin was fatal.

5. Josephus says again, "As the high priests were leading a heifer to the altar to be sacrificed, she

brought forth a lamb in the midst of the temple." Most
striking reproof to those infidel priests who had rejected
the Lamb of God who had shed his blood once for all,
and abrogated the Levitical sacrifices; which yet they
were impiously continuing. This wonder was exhibited
in the temple, the type of the body of Christ, and at the
passover, when at a preceding passover Jesus was ar-
rested and sacrificed; and it took place before the high
priests and their attendants, so that they could never
complain for want of evidence of the fact.

6. This author says: "Soon after the feast of the
passover, in various parts of the country, before the
setting of the sun, chariots and armed men were seen
in the air passing round about Jerusalem." This
strange sight occurring before sunset, and being seen
in various parts of the country, must have been a miraculous portent; a sign from heaven. The Jews had
said, "What sign showest thou, that we may see and
believe." Now they had their signs in abundance; yet
they would not believe.

7. The last and most fearful sign, Josephus relates; that
one Jesus, son of Ananus, a rustic of the lower class,
appeared in the temple at the feast of tabernacles, and
suddenly exclaimed, "*A voice from the east — a voice
from the west — a voice from the four winds — a voice
against Jerusalem and the temple — a voice against the
bridegroom and the brides — a voice against the whole
people!*" These words he continued to exclaim through
the streets of Jerusalem by day and by night, with no
cessation, [unless what was needed for the support of
nature,] for seven years! He commenced in the year
63, while the city was in peace and prosperity, and terminated his exclamations only in his death, amidst the
horrors of the siege, in the year 70. This strange
thing, when it commenced, soon excited great attention,
and this Jesus was brought before Albinus, the Roman
governor, who interrogated him, but could obtain no
answer except the continuation of his woes. He commanded him to be scourged, but to no effect. During
times of festivals, this cry of his was peculiarly loud
and urgent. After the commencement of the siege, he
ascended the walls, and in a voice still more tremendous

than ever, he exclaimed, " *Wo, wo to this city, this temple, and this people!*" And he then added, [for the first time for the seven years,] " *Wo, wo to myself!*" The words were no sooner uttered, than a stone from a Roman machine without the walls, struck him dead on the spot!

Such were the signs in the heavens and in the earth, which just preceded the destruction of Jerusalem. Several of them are recorded by Tacitus as well as by Josephus. The veracity of Josephus as a historian is probably allowed by all. Scaliger affirms that he deserves more credit as a writer than all the Greek and Roman historians put together.

From the conquest of Jerusalem by Pompey, sixty years before Christ, the Jews repeatedly had exhibited a most rebellious spirit against the Romans. The Jews had basely said to Pilate concerning Christ, "If thou let this man go, thou art not a friend to Cæsar." But the fact was, they persecuted Christ because he would not erect a temporal throne in opposition to Cæsar. Any impostor who seemed prepared to do this, they were ready to follow; and were ready to improve every apparent occasion to evince their decided hostility to the Romans. And they hardly needed a prophet's eye to discern that this spirit and conduct, manifested on all occasions, would soon draw against them the Roman sword.

Judas, a Gaulonite, and Suddue, a Pharisee, had rallied the Jews with the idea that their paying tribute to the Romans would not fail to confirm them in the most abject slavery; in consequence of which their enmity often burst forth with malignant violence. Tumults and riots increased; and Florus, the Roman governor of Judea, by his cruel exactions, increased this spirit among the Jews. Eleazer, son of the high priest, persuaded the officers of the temple to reject the offerings of foreigners, and to withhold public prayers for them. The Roman government felt the insult; and a basis was soon found to be laid for a Roman war. Feuds and contentions increased in Judea, till Cestius Gallus marched an army thither from Syria to restore order. His march was marked with blood and desolation. The

city of Zebulon, Joppa, and other villages in his way, he
plundered and burned. Eight thousand four hundred of
the inhabitants of the former place he slew. The district of Narbatene he laid waste, and slew two thousand
of the Jews in Galilee; reduced the city of Lydda to
ashes, and drove the Jews, [who made desperate sallies
upon him,] till he encamped within a hundred miles of
the capital. Soon after, he entered Jerusalem, and
burned some part of the city. But through the treachery
of his own officers, he made an unexpected flight. The
enraged Jews pursued him, and slew about sixty thousand of his men. Many of the rich Jews, alarmed at
the Roman invasion, fled from Jerusalem, as from a
foundering ship. Some suppose many of the Christians now fled to a place called Pella, in the mountains
of Judea.

Nero, the emperor of Rome, being informed of the
defeat of Cestius, gave the command to Vespasian to
press the war against the rebellious Jews. He and his
son Titus soon collected an army of sixty thousand men.
In A. D. 67, he marched from Ptolemais to Judea, mark-
ing his steps with ravages and desolation. Infancy and
age fell before the furious soldiery. All the strong
towns of Galilee and many of those of Judea, fell before
the victorious arms of Vespasian, who slew not less than
one hundred and fifty thousand inhabitants. Signal
vengeance was taken on Joppa, which had in part been
rebuilt, after it had been by Cestius reduced to ashes.
Vespasian was enraged at the frequent piracies of this
people. The Jews of this place fleeing before him,
betook themselves to their shipping. But a furious
tempest overtook those who stood out to sea, and they
were lost. The others were dashed vessel against vessel, or against the rocks. Some in their distress laid
violent hands on themselves. Such as reached the
shore were slain by the enraged Romans. The sea for
some distance was stained with their blood. Forty
thousand are said to have been swallowed up in the
waves, and not one escaped to relate their catastrophe.
Truly this was "distress of their nation, with the sea
and the waves thereof roaring!"

Vespasian returned from Jericho to Cæsarea, to pre-

pare for a grand siege of Jerusalem. Here he received
intelligence of the death of the emperor Nero. This
led him to suspend for the present the execution of his
plan against the Jews. This respite to that devoted
people continued about two years, and but encouraged
them to deeds of greater enormity.

A spirit of faction now appeared in Jerusalem. Two
parties first, and afterwards three, raged there; each
contending with deadly animosity for the precedence.
A part of one of these factions having been excluded
from the city, entered it by force during the night; and
to such madness were they abandoned, that they butch-
ered on that fatal night not less than eight thousand five
hundred men, women and children, whose mangled
bodies appeared the next morning, strewed in the streets
of Jerusalem. These abandoned murderers plundered
in the city, murdered the high priests, Ananus and Jesus,
and insulted their dead bodies. They slew their brethren of Jerusalem as though they had been wild animals.
They scourged and imprisoned the nobles, in hopes to
terrify them to become of their party; and many who
could not be thus won, they slew. In this reign of terror, twelve thousand of the higher orders of the people
thus perished; and no relative dared to shed a mourning
tear, lest this should bring on them a similar fate.
Accusation and death became the most common events.
Many fled, but were intercepted and slain. Piles of
their carcasses lay on the public roads; and all pity, as
well as regard for human or divine authority, seemed
extinguished.

To add to the horrid calamities of the times occasioned
by the bloody factions, Judea was infested by bands of
robbers and murderers, plundering their towns and
cutting in pieces such as made any resistance, whether
men, women or children. Here were exhibited the
most horrid pictures of what fallen man is capable of
perpetrating when restraints are taken off; that they
would turn their own towns and societies into scenes of
horror like kennels of wild animals.

One Simon became commander of one of the factions;
John of another. Simon entered Jerusalem at the head
of forty thousand banditti. A third faction rose: and

discord blazed with terrific fury. The three factions
were intoxicated with rage and desperation, and went
on slaying and trampling on piles of the dead, with an
indescribable fury. People coming to the temple to
worship, were murdered, both natives and foreigners.
Their bodies lay in piles, and a collection of blood defil-
ed the sacred courts.

John of Gischala, head of a faction, burned a store of
provisions. Simon, at the head of another faction, burned another. Thus the Jews were weakening and destroying themselves, and preparing the way for "wrath
to come upon them to the uttermost."

In the midst of these most dismal events, an alarm
was made that a Roman army was approaching the city.
Vespasian becoming emperor, and learning the factious
and horrid state of the Jews, determined to prosecute
the war against them, and sent his son Titus to reduce
Jerusalem and Judea. The Jews, on hearing of the
approach of the Roman army, were petrified with horror. They could have no hope of peace. They had no
means of flight. They had no time for counsel. They
had no confidence in each other. What could be done?
Several things they possessed in abundance. They had
a measure of iniquity filled up; a full ripeness for destruction. All seemed wild disorder and despair. Nothing could be imagined but the confused noise of the warrior, and garments rolled in blood. They knew nothing
was their due from the Romans but exemplary vengeance. The ceaseless cry of combatants, and the horrors of faction had induced some to desire the interven-
tion of a foreign foe to give them deliverance from their
domestic horrors. Such was the state of Jerusalem
when Titus appeared before it with a besieging army.
But he came not to deliver it from its excruciating tortures; but to execute upon it divine vengeance; to fulfil
the fatal predictions of our Lord Jesus Christ, that
"when ye see the abomination of desolation standing
in the holy place—when you see Jerusalem compassed
about with armies—then know that the desolation thereof is nigh." "Wheresoever the carcass is, there shall
the eagles be gathered together." Jerusalem was now
the carcass to be devoured; the Roman eagles had
arrived to tear it as their prey.

The day on which Titus had encompassed Jerusalem was the feast of the passover. Here let it be remembered, that it was the time of this feast, on a preceding occasion, that Christ was taken, condemned and executed. It was at the time of this feast, that the *heifer*, in the hands of the sacrificing priests, brought forth a *lamb*. And just after this feast at another time, that the miraculous besieging armies were seen over Jerusalem, just before sunset. And now, at the time of the passover, the antitype of this prodigy appears in the besieging army of Titus. Multitudes of Jews had convened at Jerusalem from surrounding nations to celebrate this feast. Ah, miserable people! going with intent to feed on the paschal lamb; but really to their own final slaughter, for rejecting "the Lamb of God who taketh away the sins of the world!" The Jews had imprecated the blood of the true Paschal Lamb, [by them wantonly shed,] on themselves and on their children. God was now going in a signal manner to take them at their word. He hence providentially collected their nation, under sentence of death, as into a great prison, for the day of execution. And as their execution of Christ was signal, low, degrading, the death of the cross; so their execution should be signal and dreadful. The falling city was now crowded with little short of two millions of that devoted people. The event came suddenly and unexpectedly to the Jews, as the coming of a thief, and almost like lightning. Josephus notes this, and thus without design, shows the fulfilment of these hints of Christ, that his coming should be like a thief in the night, and like lightning shining under the whole heavens.

The furious contending factions of the Jews, on finding themselves environed with the Roman armies, laid aside, for the moment, their party contentions, sallied out, rushed furiously on their common foe, and came near utterly destroying the tenth legion of the Roman army. This panic among the Romans occasioned a short suspension of hostilities. Some new confidence hence inspired the hopes of the Jews; and they now determined to defend their city. But being a little released from their terrors of the Romans, their factious

resentments again rekindled, and broke out in great fury.
The faction under Eleazer was swallowed up in the
other two, under John and Simon. Slaughter, conflagration and plunder ensued. A portion of the centre of
the city was burned, and the inhabitants became as
prisoners to the two furious parties. The Romans here
saw their own proverb verified: "*Quos Deus vult perdere
prius dementat.*" "Whom God will destroy, he gives
up to madness."

The invading armies knew how to profit by the madness of the Jews. They were soon found by the Jews
to have possession of the two outer walls of their city.
This alarm reached the heart of the factions, and once
more united them against the common enemy. But they
had already proceeded too far to retreat from the effects
of their madness. Famine, with its ghastly horrors,
stared them in the face. It had, as might be expected,
been making a silent approach; and some of the more
obscure had already fallen before it. But even this did
not annihilate the fury of faction, which again returned
with redoubled fury, and presented new scenes of wo.
As the famine increased, the sufferers would snatch
bread from each other's mouths, and devour their grain
unprepared. To discover handfuls of food, tortures
were inflicted. Food was violently taken by husbands
from wives, and wives from husbands; and even by
mothers from their famishing infants. The breast itself
was robbed from the famishing suckling, as our Lord
denounced: "Wo to them that give suck in those
days."

This terror produced a new scene of righteous retribution. Multitudes of the Jews were forced by hunger
to flee to the enemy's camp. Here, instead of pitying
and relieving them, the Romans cut off the hands of
many, and sent them back; but most of them they crucified as fast as they could lay their hands on them; till
wood was wanting for crosses, and space on which to
erect them. Behold here thousands of those despairing
Jews suspended on crosses round the walls of Jerusalem! Verily, the Lord is known by the judgments that
he executeth!" Yea, this did not suffice. Behold two
thousand Jews who had fled to the mercy of their invad-

ers, ripped open alive [two thousand in one night!] by
Arabs and Syrians in the Roman armies, in hopes of
finding gold, which these Jews *had* [or their enemies
fancied they had] *swallowed*, to carry off with them!

Titus being a merciful general, was touched to the
heart at the miseries of the Jews; and in person he ten-
derly entreated the besieged to surrender. But all the
answer he obtained for his tenderness was base revilings.
He now resolved to make thorough work with this obstinate people; and hence surrounded the city with a circum-
vallation of thirty-nine furlongs in length, strengthened
with thirteen towers. This by the astonishing activity
of the soldiers, was effected in three days. Then was
fulfilled this prediction of our blessed Lord, "Thine
enemies shall cast a trench about thee, and keep thee in
on every side."

As the city was now cut off from all possible supplies,
famine became more dreadful. Whole families fell a
sacrifice to it; and the dead bodies of women, children,
and the aged, were seen covering roofs of houses, and
various recesses. Youth, and the middle aged, appeared
like spectres; and fell many of them dead in public
places. The dead became too numerous to be interred.
Many died while attempting to perform this office. So
great and awful became the calamities, that lamentation
ceased, and an awful silence of despair overwhelmed the
city. But all this failed of restraining the more abandoned from most horrid deeds. They took this opportunity to rob the tombs; and with loud, infernal laughter,
to strip the dead of their habiliments of death; and
would try the edge of their swords on dead bodies, and
on some while yet breathing. Simon Georas now vent-
ed his rage against Matthias, the high priest, and his
three sons. He caused them to be condemned, as though
favoring the Romans. The father asked the favor to be
first executed, and not see the death of his sons; but the
malicious Simon reserved him for the last execution.
And as he was expiring, he put the insulting question,
whether the Romans could now relieve him?

Things being thus, one Mannæus, a Jew, escaped to
Titus, and informed him of the consummate wretchedness of the Jews; that in less than three months, one
16

hundred and fifteen thousand and eight hundred dead
bodies of Jews had been conveyed through one gate,
under his care and register: and he assured him of the
ravages of famine and death.   Other deserters confirmed the account, and added, that not less than six hundred
thousand dead bodies of Jews had been carried out
at different gates.   The humane heart of Titus was
deeply affected; and he, under those accounts, and
while surveying the piles of dead bodies of Jews under
the walls, and in the visible parts of the city, raised his
eyes and hands to heaven in solemn protestation, that he
would have prevented these dire calamities; that the
obstinate Jews had procured them upon their own
heads.

Josephus, the Jew, now earnestly entreated the leader,
John, and his brethren, to surrender to the Romans, and
thus save the residue of the Jews.   But he received in
return nothing but insolent reproaches and imprecations;
John declaring his firm persuasion that God would never
suffer his own city, Jerusalem, to be taken by the enemy!   Alas, had he forgotten the history of his own nation, and the denunciations of the prophets ?   Micah, the
Moor, had foretold that in this very calamity they would
presumptuously "lean upon the Lord, and say, Is not
the Lord among us?   No evil shall come upon us."   So
blind and presumptuous are hypocrisy and self confidence!
"The temple of the Lord, the temple of the Lord, the
temple of the Lord, are these."

The famine in the city became, as might be expected,
still more deadly.   For want of food the Jews ate their
belts, sandals, skins of their shields, dried grass, and
even ordure of cattle.   *Now it was that a noble Jewess,
urged by the insufferable pangs of hunger, slew and prepared for food her own infant child !* She had eaten half
the horrible preparation, when the smell of food brought
in a horde of soldiery, who threatened her with instant
death, if she did not produce to them the food she had in
possession.   She being thus compelled to obey, produced
the remaining half of her child!   The soldiers stood
aghast; and the recital petrified the hearers with horror; and congratulations were poured on those whose
eyes death had closed upon such horrid scenes.   Human-

ity seems ready to sink at the recital of the woful events
of that day.   No words can reach the horrors of the situation of the female part of the community at that period.   Such scenes force upon our recollection the tender
pathetic address of our Saviour to the pious females who
followed him, going to the cross : "Daughters of Jerusalem, weep not for me ; but weep for yourselves and
for your children ; for behold the days are coming, in
which they shall say, Blessed are the barren, and the
wombs that never bare, and the breasts that never gave
suck."   Moses had long predicted this very scene.—
"The tender and delicate woman among you, (said he,)
who would not venture to set the sole of her foot on the
ground for delicateness ; her eye shall be evil towards
her young one, and toward her children, which she shall
bare ; for she shall eat them, for want of all things, secretly in the siege and straitness wherewith thine enemy shall distress thee in thy gates."   Probably the history of the world will not afford a parallel to this.   God
prepared peculiar judgments for peculiarly horrid crimes!
"These be the days of vengeance; that all things that
are written may be fulfilled."   Josephus declares, that
if there had not been many credible witnesses of that awful fact, he never would have recorded it; for, said he,
"such a shocking violation of nature never has been per-
petrated by any Greek or barbarian."

While famine thus spread desolation, the Romans finally
succeeded in removing part of the inner wall, and in possessing themselves of the high and commanding tower of
Antonia, which seemed to overlook the temple.   Titus with
his counsel of war had formed a determination to save the
temple, to grace his conquest, and remain an ornament to
his empire.   But God had not so determined.   And
" though there be many devices in man's heart; nevertheless, the counsel of the Lord, that shall stand."   A Roman
soldier, violating the general order of Titus, succeeded in
hurling a brand of fire into the golden window of the
temple; and soon [as righteous heaven would have it!] the
sacred edifice was in flames.   The Jews perceiving this,
rushed with horrid outcries to extinguish the fire.   Titus,
too, flew to the spot in his chariot, with his chief officers
and legions.   With loud command, and every token of

anxiety, he enforced the extinguishing of the fire; but in vain. So great was the confusion, that no attention was paid to him. His soldiers, deaf to all cries, assiduously spread the flames far and wide; rushing at the same time on the Jews, sword in hand, slaying and trampling down, or crushing them to death against the walls. Many were plunged into the flames, and perished in the burning of the out buildings of the temple. The fury of the Roman soldiers slaughtered the poor, the unarmed, and the rich, as well as men in arms. Multitudes of dead bodies were piled round about the altar, to which they had fled for protection. The way leading to the inner court was deluged with blood.

Titus, finding the fire had not yet reached the inner temple, entered it with his superior officers, and surveyed its magnificence with silent admiration. He found it to exceed all he had heard. This view led him to renew his efforts to save this stupendous pile of building, though so many of the out buildings were gone. He even entreated his soldiers to extinguish the flames, and appointed an officer to punish any who should disobey. But all his renewed efforts were still in vain. The feelings of his soldiery were utterly unmanageable. Plunder, revenge and slaughter had combined to render them deaf and most furious. A soldier succeeded in firing the door posts of the inner temple, and the conflagration soon became general.

One needs a heart of steel to contemplate the scene which followed. The triumphant Roman soldiers were in a most ungovernable rage and fury. They were indeed instruments prepared for their work, to execute the most signal vengeance of Heaven; the flame of which was now reaching its height! The Romans slew of the Jews all before them : sparing neither age, sex or rank. They seemed determined to annihilate the Jewish race on the spot. Priests and common people — those who surrendered, and those who still fought — all were alike subjects of an indiscriminate slaughter. The fire of the temple at length completely enveloped the stupendous pile of building. The fury of the flames exceeded description. It impressed on distant spectators an idea that the whole city was in flames. The ensuing disorder and tumult, Josephus pronounces to have been such as to baffle all description. The outcry of the Roman legions was as great as they could make. And the Jews, finding themselves a prey to the fury of both fire and sword, exerted themselves in the wildest accents of screaming. The people in the city, and those on the hill, mutually responded to each other in groans and screeches. People who had seemed just expiring through famine, derived new strength from unprecedented scenes of horror and death, to deplore their wretchedness. From mountain to mountain, and from places distant, lamentations echoed to each other.

As the temple was sinking under the fury of the raging element, the mount on which it stood seemed in that part of it, [says the historian,] to "impress the idea of a lake of liquid fire!" The blood of the slain ran in rivulets.— The earth around became covered with the slain; and the victorious Romans trampled over those piles of the dead, in pursuit of the thousands who were fleeing from the points of their swords. In a word, the roar and crackling of fire; the shrieks of thousands in despair; the dying groans of thousands, and the sights which met the eye wherever it was turned, were such as never before had any parallel on earth. They probably as much exceeded all antecedent scenes of horror, as the guilt which occasioned them, in their treatment of the Lord of Glory, exceeded all guilt ever before known among men.

A tragical event had transpired worthy of particular detail. Before the temple was wrapped in flames, an impostor appeared among the Jews, asserting a divine commission; and that if the people would follow him to the temple, they would see signs, wonders and deliverance. About six thousand, mostly women and children, followed him, and were in the galleries of the temple, waiting for this promised deliverance, when fire was set to that building. Not one escaped. All were consumed in the conflagration of the sacred edifice! What multitudes are by false prophets plunged in eternal fire!

The place of the temple now presented a vast pile of ruins. Here terminated the glory and existence of this stupendous building, this type of the body of Christ and of his church; this type of the Millennium, and of heaven. Here it reached its close, after the period of one thousand and thirty years, from the time of its dedi-

 sation by Solomon; and of six hundred and thirty-nine
years, from its being rebuilt in the days of Haggai, after
he seventy years captivity. It is singular, that it should
be reduced to ashes not only soon after the feast of the
passover, which convened so many thousands of Jews to
Jerusalem to meet the ruins of their city and nation;
but that it should be consumed on the same month, on
the same day of the month, on which the Babylonians
had before destroyed it by fire.

Josephus records another striking event, which seemed
a sign of the destruction of Jerusalem. He says: [ad-
dressing the Jews who survived this ruin] "The fountains flow copiously for Titus, which to you were dried
up. For before he came, you know that both Siloam and
all the springs without the city failed; so that water was
brought by the amphora, [a vessel.] But now they are
so abundant to your enemies, as to suffice for themselves
and their cattle. This wonder you also formerly experienced, when the king of Babylon laid siege to your
city."

The priests of the temple, after the destruction of their
sacred edifice, betook themselves — those who had thus
far escaped the general slaughter — to the top of one of
its broken walls, where they sat mourning and famishing.
On the fifth day, necessity compelled them to descend,
and humbly to ask pardon of the Roman general. But
Titus at this late period rejected their petition, saying;
"As the temple, for the sake of which, I would have spared
you, is destroyed: it is but fit the priests should perish
also." All were put to death.

The obstinate leaders of the great Jewish factions, be-
holding now the desperateness of their cause, desired a
conference with Titus. One would imagine they would
at least now lay down their arms. Their desiring an interview with the triumphant Roman general, appeared as
though they would be glad to do this. But righteous
heaven designed their still greater destruction. Titus,
after all their mad rebellions, kindly offered to spare the
residue of the Jews, if they would now submit. But
strange to relate, they refused to comply. The noble
general then, as must have been expected, was highly
exasperated; and issued his general order that he would

grant no further pardon to the insurgents. His legions
now were ordered to "*ravage and destroy.*" With the
light of the next morning, arose the tremendous flame of
the castle of Antonia, the council chamber, register's office, and the noble palace of the Queen Helena. These
magnificent piles were reduced to ashes. The furious
legions, [executioners of divine vengeance, Ezek. ix. 5,
6,] then flew through the lower city, of which they soon
became masters, slaughtering and burning in every
street. The Jews themselves aided the slaughter. In
the royal palace, containing vast treasures, eight thousand four hundred Jews were murdered by their seditious
brethren. Great numbers of deserters from the furious
leaders of faction, flocked to the Romans; but it was
too late. The general order was given, all should be
slain. Such therefore fell.

The Roman soldiers, however, being at length weary
with butchery, and more than satisfied with blood, for a
short time sheathed their swords, and betook themselves
to plunder. They collected multitudes of Jews — husbands, wives, children and servants, formed a market:
and set them up at vendue for slaves. They sold them
for any trifle; while purchasers were but few. Their
law-giver, Moses, had forewarned them of this; Deut.
xxviii. 68: "And ye shall be sold for bondmen and bond-
women; and no man shall buy you." Tremendous indeed must the lot of those be, who reject the Messiah,
and are found fighting against the Son of God. Often
had these Jews heard read [but little it seems did they
understand the sense of the tremendous passage] relative
to the Jewish rejectors of Christ, " He that sitteth in
the Heavens shall laugh; the Lord shall have them in
derision. Then shall he speak unto them in his wrath,
and vex them in his sore displeasure. Yet have I set my
king upon my holy hill of Zion. Thou shalt break them
with a rod of iron; thou shalt dash them in pieces like a
potter's vessel." "Thus saith the Lord, say, a sword, a
sword is sharpened, and also furbished: it is sharpened to
make a sore slaughter; it is furbished that it may glitter;
[said God by the prophet, Ezek. xxi., alluding to this very
event;] the sword is sharpened, and it is furbished to
give it into the hand of the slayer. Cry and howl, son

of man; smite upon thy thigh; smite thy hands together, and let the sword be doubled a third time; the sword of the slain. I have set the point of the sword against all their gates, that their hearts may faint, and their ruins be multiplied: Ah, it is made bright! it is wrapped up for the slaughter." Such, and much more, were the divine denunciations of this very scene, which the infidel Jews would not escape, but would incur! And even a merciful God shrunk not from the execution! Let anti-Christian powers, yea, let all infidels and gospel despisers, consider this and tremble!

The whole lower city now in the possession of the Roman legions, after the respite noted, was set on fire. But the insolence of the devoted Jews in a part of the higher city remained unabated. They even insulted and exasperated their enemies, as though afraid the work of vengeance might not be sufficiently executed.

The Romans brought their engines to operate upon the walls of this higher branch of the city, still standing; which soon gave way before them. Before their demolition, Titus reconnoitred the city, and its fortifications; and expressed his astonishment that it should ever fall before his arms. He exclaimed, "Had not God himself aided our operations, and driven the Jews from their fortresses, it would have been absolutely impossible to have taken them. For what could men and the force of engines have done against such towers as these?" Yes, unless their Rock had sold them for their iniquities, no enemy could have prevailed against Jerusalem. Josephus, who was an eye witness of all the scene, says: "All the calamities, which ever befell any nation, since the beginning of the world, were inferior to the miseries of the Jews at this awful period."

The upper city, too, fell before the victorious arms of the Roman conquerors. Titus would have spared all who had not been forward in resisting the Romans; and gave his orders accordingly. But his soldiers, callous to all the feelings of humanity, slaughtered the aged and sick, as well as the mass of the people. The tall and most beautiful young men, however, were spared by Titus to grace his triumph at Rome. Of the rest, many above the age of seventeen were sent in chains to Egypt to be disposed of as slaves. Some were reserved to be sacrificed on their amphitheatres, as gladiators; to be slain in sham fights, for the sport of their conquerors. Others were distributed through the empire. All who survived, under the age of seventeen, were exposed for sale.

The triumphant general commanded what remained of the city, to be razed to its foundation, except three of the most stately towers, Mariamne, Hippocos, and Phasael. These should stand as monuments of the magnificence of the place, and of his victory. A small part of the wall of the city at the west, also, he commanded should be spared, as a rampart for his garrison. The other parts of the city he wished to have so effectually erased, as never to be recognized to have been inhabited. The Talmud and Maimonides relate that the foundations of the temple were so removed, that the site of it was ploughed by Terentus Rufus. Thus our Savior predicted, that "there should not be left one stone upon another."

One awful occurrence is noted as transpiring during these scenes; that eleven thousand Jews, under the guard of one Fronto, a Roman general, were, owing to their own obstinacy, and to the scarcity of provisions, *literally starved to death!*

Josephus informs that eleven hundred thousand Jews perished in this siege of Jerusalem, that two hundred and thirty-seven thousand perished in that last war in other sieges and battles; besides multitudes who perished by famine and pestilence: making a total of at least fourteen hundred thousand. Some hundreds of thousands, in sullen despair, laid violent hands on themselves. About ninety-seven thousand were captured, and dispersed. Relative to the two great leaders of the Jewish factions, Simon and John, they were led to Rome, to grace the triumph of Titus; after which Simon was scourged, and executed as a malefactor; and John was committed for life to a dungeon. Thus ended their violent factious contentions.

The Roman army, before they left Jerusalem, not only demolished the buildings there, but even dug up their foundations. How fatal was the divine judgment on this devoted city. Five months before, it was the wonder of the world; and contained, at the commencement of the siege, more than a million and a half of Jews, natives and visitors; now it lay in total ruins, with not "one stone upon another;" as Christ had denounced. These ruins Eusebius informs us, he beheld. And Eleazer is introduced by Josephus as exclaiming: "Where is our great city, which it was believed God inhabited." The prophet Micah, a Moor, had predicted: "Therefore shall Zion for your sakes be ploughed as a field, and Jerusalem shall become heaps, and the mountain of the Lord's house as the high places of the forest." A captain of the army of Titus, did, in fact, plough where some part of the foundation of the temple had stood, as the Talmud records, and thus fulfilled this prediction.

Jesus Christ had foretold of this destruction, that "there should be great tribulation, such as was not since the beginning of the world." And of the event Josephus says·
"If the misfortunes of all nations from the beginning of the world, were compared with those which befel the Jews, they would appear far less." Again; "No other city ever suffered such things; as no other generation from the beginning of the world, was ever more fruitful in wickedness."

Other parts of Judea were still to be subdued. Macherus was attacked. Seventeen hundred Jews surrendered and were slain; also three thousand fugitives taken in the woods of Jardes. Titus at Cæsarea celebrated in great splendor the birth day of his brother Domitian. Here a horrid scene, according to the bloody customs of those times, was presented. To grace this occasion, more than two thousand five hundred Jews fell; some by burning — some by fighting with wild beasts — and some by mutual combat with the sword.

Massada was besieged. The Jewish commander, in despair, induced the garrison first to destroy their stores, and then themselves. They (nine hundred and sixty in number) consented to the horrid proposal. Men, women, and children took their seats upon the ground, and offered their necks to the sword. Ten men were selected to executed the fatal deed. The dreadful work was done. One of the ten was then chosen to execute the nine, and then himself. The nine being put to death, and fire being set to the place, the last man plunged his dagger into his own heart.

Seven persons, [women and children,] found means to conceal themselves, and escape the ruin. When the Romans approached, these seven related to them these horrid events.

Most of the remaining places now, through sullen despair, gave up all opposition, and submitted to the conquerors. Thus Judea became as a desolate wilderness; and the following passage in Isaiah had at least a primary accomplishment; " Until the cities be wasted without inhabitant; and the houses without man; and the land be utterly desolate; and the Lord have removed man far away, and there be a great forsaking in the midst of the land."

A line of prophecies is found in the sacred oracles, which relate to a signal temporal destruction of the most notorious enemies of the kingdom of Jesus Christ. Those were to have a two fold accomplishment; first upon the Jews; and secondly upon the great Antichrist of the last days, typified by the infidel Jews. Accordingly those prophecies in the Old Testament are ever found in close connection with the Millennium. The predictions of our Savior, in Matt. xxiv. Mark xiii. and Luke xxi. are but a new edition of these sacred prophecies. This has been noted as " *the destruction of the city and temple foretold.*" —It is also a denunciation of the destruction of the great Antichrist in the last days. The certainty of this will appear in the following things, as New Testament writers decide. The Thessalonians, having heard what our Lord denounced, that all those things he had predicted should take place on *that generation*, were trembling with the apprehension, that the *coming* of Christ predicted, would then very soon burst upon the world. Paul writes to them, (2 Thes. ii.) and beseeches them by this coming of Christ, not to be shaken in mind, or troubled with such an apprehension. For that day, [that predicted coming of Christ, as it related to others beside the Jews,] was not to take place on that generation. It was not to come till the Antichristian apostacy came first; that man of sin was first to be revealed. This long apostacy was to be accomplished before the noted coming of Christ in its more important sense be fulfilled. After the Roman government, which hindered the rise of the

man of sin, should be taken out of the way, Paul says,
" Then shall that wicked one be revealed whom the Lord
shall consume with the spirit of his mouth, and destroy
with the brightness of his coming." Here then, is the
predicted coming of Christ, in its more interesting sense,
in the battle of that great day, which introduces the Mil-
lenium. Here is a full decision that these noted denunciations of Christ alluded more especially, though not
primarily, to a coming which is still future.

The same is decided by Christ himself, in Rev. xvi.
After the sixth vial, in the drying up of the Turkish
Euphrates, three unclean spirits of devils, like frogs, go
forth to the kings of the earth, and of all the world, to
gather them to the great battle. The awful account is
interrupted by this notice from the mouth of Christ; verse
15, "Behold, I come as a thief. Blessed is he that
watcheth and keepeth his garments; lest he walk naked,
and they see his shame." This is as though our Lord
should say; now the time is at hand, to which my predictions of coming as a thief, principally alluded. Now
is the time when my people on earth shall need to watch,
as I directed, when predicting my coming to destroy first
the type of Antichrist, and secondly the antitype.

The predictions in the prophets, which, received an
incipient fulfilment in the destruction of Jerusalem, were
to receive a more interesting fulfilment in Christ's coming to destroy his antichristian foes. Hence it is that
the seventh vial is called (Rev. xvi. 14,) "the battle of
the great day of God Almighty;" clearly alluding to
that great day noted through the prophets. And of the
same event it is said, Rev. x. 7; "the mystery of God
shall be finished, as he hath declared to his servants, the
prophets." Here again the allusion clearly is to the
many predictions in the prophets of the destruction of the
enemies of Christ's kingdom, which were to receive an
incipient fulfilment in the destruction of Jerusalem; and
a far more interesting one, in the sweeping from the
earth the last antichristian powers, to introduce the mil-
lennial kingdom of Christ. We accordingly find those
predictions through the prophets clearly alluding to the
last days, and the introduction of the Millennium.

Viewing the destruction of Jerusalem then, as but a

type of an event now pending upon antichristian nations, we peruse it with new interest; and it must be viewed in the light of a most impressive warning to this age of the world. The factions, madness, and self-ruin of the former, give but a lively practical comment upon the various predictions of the latter. Three great and noted factions introduced the destruction of Jerusalem. And of the destruction of Antichrist we read [perhaps alluding to that very circumstance] Rev. xvi. 19; "And the great city was divided into three parts." Then it follows; "and the cities of the nations fell; and great Babylon came in remembrance before God to give unto her the cup of the wine of the fierceness of his wrath." In the desolation of Gog and his bands, faction draws the sword of extermination. "I will call for a sword against him throughout all my mountains, saith the Lord God; every man's sword shall be against his brother." (Ezek. xxxviii. 21.)

The great coalition against the Jews, in the time of Jehoshaphat, was destroyed by the sword of mutiny and faction: (See 2 Chron. xx.) And in allusion to this very battle which God fought for his church, the vast coalitions of Antichrist, in the last days, when the Jews are restored, is said to be gathered "to the valley of Jehoshaphat:" (See Joel iii.) The various circumstances of the destruction of Jerusalem afforded a lively incipient comment on the many denunciations of the battle of that great day of God Almighty, which awaits the antichristian world; while it is fully evident, that the passages more especially allude to the tremendous scenes of judgment, which shall introduce the Millennium.

DESTRUCTION OF THE JEWS.

THE number of people that perished at Jerusalem, by the sword, fire, sea, wild beasts, famine and pestilence, amounts to one million four hundred thousand. Ninety-seven thousand were captured and dispersed among the nations. [Josephus.]

CHAPTER VII.

THE PRESENT STATE OF JUDAH AND ISRAEL.

THE HEBREWS OR ISRAELITES, THE JEWS.

" He shall assemble the outcasts of Israel, and gather together the dispersed of Judah." The black Jews of Cochin in the East Indies, Doctor Buchanan gives an account of. The Most High speaks of gathering his ancient people from the east and from the west. Dr. Buchanan informs us that the black Jews have a tradition that they arrived in the East Indies not long after the Babylonish captivity. And he adds, " what seems to countenance this tradition is, they have copies of those books of the Old Testament which were written before the captivity, but none of those whose dates are subsequent to that event." It seems most probable, then, that these black Jews are descendants of the Jews who turned their course to that region of the East when they were liberated from Babylon, instead of returning to Jerusalem. Some of the Jews manifestly did thus part from their brethren, and migrate to the East. These were the Jews who abounded in the eastern as well as the western provinces of Persia, in the days of Ahasuerus, Haman, Esther and Mordecai, when the impious decree was obtained against them by Haman.

Ahasuerus then " reigned over one hundred and twenty-seven provinces, even from India to Abyssinia 'or Ethiopia," Esther i. 1 — in Africa.

The Jews appear at that time to have been scattered in all these provinces. Thence these black Jews became planted in India, and they had their Bible, as far as it was written, before the captivity.

The black Jews at Hindostan, in Asia, having descended from the ten tribes, they called themselves Jews. The Jews have been strict to retain the knowledge of their descent. The tribes of Israel were threatened with the famine of the word which has been already noted, Amos viii. 11, 12. Here the ten tribes, in their long banishment, should wander from "north to south, and from sea to sea," running to and fro to find communication from heaven, but should remain destitute of the word of life, till about the time of their restoration. The black Jews in Asia have all the sacred writings which were given before the Babylonish captivity.

Mr. Largon gives the following account of some people discovered by him, in Hindostan.

1. These people, in dress and manners, resemble the natives so much as not to be distinguished from them, but by attentive observation and inquiry.

2. They have some Hebrew names, with local terminations.

3. Some of them read Hebrew, and they have a faint tradition of the cause of their original exodus from Egypt.

4. Their common language is Hindoo.

5. They keep idols, and worship them; and use idolatrous ceremonies, intermixed with Hebrew.

6. They circumcise their children.

7. They observe the kippoor or great expiation day of the Hebrews.

8. They call themselves Jehudi.

9. They say the Arabian Jews are their brethren; grant this to be a fact; and they, no doubt, are of the descendants of Judah.

10. They use a Jew's prayer : Hear, O Israel; the Lord thy God is one Lord; Deut. vi. 4.

11. They have no priest, Levite or Nasi among them; though they have elders and a chief in each community.

12. They expect the Messiah: and that when he comes he will go to Jerusalem, whither they shall return to be dispersed no more."

For these reasons, Mr. Jaratt views this people as of the ten tribes. Should they prove to be thus, they may be descendants of the small part of Israel, who stayed behind, according to the Indian tradition.

The Hindoos, it appears, have a national literature, abounding in numerous works on theology, law, jurisprudence, politics, geography, astronomy and other sciences; and many of them are said to have settled opinions on all these subjects, founded on the basis of custom, education, and continued patient investigation.

HINDOOSTAN — BOUNDARIES AND EXTENT. — Hindoostan, called also India on this side of the Ganges, lies between 8 and 31 degrees north latitude, and is bounded on the north by Tartary and Thibet; east by Assam and Arracan; south by the sea; and west by the river Indus; 1,800 miles long, and 1,600 broad.

CLIMATE.—The climate towards the north is temperate; but hot in the south. It rains almost constantly for three months in the year.

RIVERS.—The Indus, the Ganges, and the Burrampooter, far exceed the other rivers of Hindoostan in magnitude. The Ganges is one of the finest rivers in the world. It is revered by the Hindoos as a deity, who is to wash away all their sins. Its whole course is 2,100 miles; it empties into the sea by several mouths.

PRODUCTIONS.—The vegetable products of Hindoostan are almost innumerable, and extremely luxuriant. The grain most cultivated is rice. All kinds of fruit, suited to the climate, are produced here in abundance. The domestic animals are buffaloes, sheep, camels and elephants. Of wild quadrupeds are the rhinoceros, the Bengal tiger, monkies, wild boars, &c. The mines of Golconda have long been celebrated for diamonds.

POPULATION, &c.—The inhabitants of Hindoostan are computed at about 10,000,000 Mahometans, and 100,000,000 Hindoos. The Mahometans, or Mussulmans, are represented to be of a warlike character. The Hindoos, or Gentoos, are of a black complexion; their hair is long, their person straight and elegant, and their countenances open and pleasant. They differ materially from all other nations, by being divided into tribes or casts. The four principal are the Bramins, Soldiers, Laborers and Mechanics; and these are subdivided into a multiplicity of inferior distinctions.

THE AFRICAN JEWS.—It may be asked, how came they Jews. Josephus informs us the nation and name of Africa were derived from Abraham, by Keturah, by whom he had six sons — men of courage and sagacious minds. Now Abraham, the Jew, contrived to settle his sons and grandsons in colonies, and they took possession of Troglodytes, and named it Africa. And the country of Arabia to the Red Sea. The black Jews of Hindoostan call the Arabian Jews brethren.

Are ye not as children of the Ethiopians unto me, O children of Israel, saith the Lord. Have not I brought Israel out of the land of Egypt, and the Philistines (Ethiopians) from Caphtor, and the Syrians from Kin, Amos ix. 7. Israel shall return, and come unto Zion, the city of our God. We, the Indians and Ethiopians, say to them that are of fearful hearts, Be strong, fear not; behold, your God will come, Isa. xxxv. 4.

THE CLAIM OF POSTERITY.—It is natural and scriptural, that the posterity of great men be called after their father, down to the latest generation. The Hebrews are called after Heber, their great father, from whom all the Hebrews descended. The Israelites are called after their great father Israel. The Jews are descendants from Judah, their great father, and are called after him in Africa and Asia.

The Edomites or Indians, are descendants from Edom or Esau, and are called after their great father, &c. All Christians are the children of Christ Jesus by faith, and therefore, should be called after him.

THE INDIAN TRIBES IN AMERICA.

Columbus, the discoverer of America, was inflamed with a love of what he saw among the natives; and declared in a communication to the king and queen of Spain, that there was not a better people in the world than these — none more affectionate and mild; they love their neighbors as themselves; always speaking and smiling; and use every person with kindness.

17

De Las Casas, who spent much time in New Spain, says of the natives : Did they not receive the Spaniards who first came among them, with gentleness and humanity? Did they not show more joy, in proportion, in lavishing treasures upon them, than the Spaniards did greediness in receiving them ? But our avarice was not yet satisfied, "though they gave us their riches and lands; we would take from them their wives, and children, and liberties." To blacken the characters of these people, their enemies asserted that they were scarce human. "But it is we (adds the author) who ought to blush for having been less men, and more barbarous than they." The natives are said to have been free from the European vices of blasphemy, lying and stealing, and to have lived in peace until the Europeans came among them ; "Like Judas, with a kiss the natives they betrayed."

Arguments in favor of the native Americans being the descendants of Israel.—O Israel, Israel, whom they have scattered among the nations."

"The Lord shall assemble the outcasts of Israel, and gather together the dispersed of Judah from the four corners of the earth."

"Woe unto them who have robbed me, and have enriched themselves in land and blood and the souls of men."

These natives all appear to have had one origin. Their language appears to have been Hebrew. The Indians have had their Ark of the covenant; have been in the practice of circumcision; and have acknowledged one, and only one God. They have one tribe, answering in various respects to the tribe of Levi ; and they have something answering to the Jewish "cities of refuge." Indian pyramids resemble the "high places of ancient Israel. Phylacteries, or ancient Hebrew writing, have been found on "Indian Hill," in Pittsfield.

In addition to various other arguments, and many traditions, a table of words and phrases is furnished by Doctor Boudinot, Adair, and others — to which several have been added from good authority — to show how clearly the Indian language is derived from the Hebrew. Some of these Indian words have been taken from one tribe — and some from another. In a long continued heathen state, destitute of all aid from letters, a language must roll and change.

And it is strange that after the lapse of 2500 years, a single word should be preserved among such a people — under such circumstances.

English.	Indian.	Hebrew or Chaldaic.
Jehovah,	Yahewah,	Jehovah.
God,	Ale,	Ale Aleim.
Jah,	Yah or Wah,	Jah.
Shiloh,	Shilah,	Shiloh.
Heaven,	Chemim,	Shemim.
Farther,	Abba,	Abba.
Man,	Ish Ishte,	Ish.
Woman,	Ishto,	Ishto.
Wife,	Awah,	Eweh Eve.
Thou,	Keah,	Ka.
His Wife,	Liani,	Lihene.
This Man,	Uwah,	Huah,
Nose,	Nichiri,	Neheri.
Roof of a House,	Taubana-Ora,	Debonaoun.
Winter,	Kora,	Korah.
Canaan,	Canaai,	Canaan.
To pray,	Phale,	Phalac.
Now,	Na,	No.
Hind part,	Kesh,	Kish.
Do,	Jennais,	Jannon.
To blow,	Phaubac,	Phauhe.
Rushing wind,	Rowah,	Ruach.
Ararat,	Ararat,	Ararat.
Man of God,	Isto allo,	Ishda alloah.
Waiter of high-priest,	Sagan,	Sagan.

Parts of Sentences.

Very hot,	Heru hara or hala,	Hara hara.
Praise to the First Cause,	Halleluwah,	Hallelujah.
Give me food,	Natoni bomen,	Natoui bamen.

Authors and authorities adduced to prove the Tribes of Israel in America.

Archaeologia Americana, p. 138. Adair, pp. 80, 88–9, 92, 95, 98, 112, 116, 121, 123, 147, 154. Don Alonzo De Ericilla, p. 158.

Boudinot, pp. 87, 91, 93, 96, 98, 100, 116, 120, 123, 125, 133, 134, 138. Bartram, pp. 123, 113, 125. Bultric, p. 130. Beatty, pp. 96, 98, 116, 119.

Charlevoix, pp. 85, 174. Colden, pp. 94, 106. Cushman pp. 105, 174. Clavigero, p. 118. Chapman, pp. 123, 157. Carver, pp. 123, 164. Columbus, p. 132. Commissioners, p. 137. Casas, p. 176.

Dodge and Blight, p. 104.

Edwards, pp. 86, 89, 162. Esdras, p. 74.

Frey, p. 118.

Giddings, pp. 88, 102. Gookin, p. 107.

Hunter, p. 162. Humbolt, p. 177. Herman, p. 140. Heckewelder, p. 107. Hebard, p. 101. Hutchinson, pp. 93, 174.

Immanuel de Moraez, p. 97.

Jarvis, p. 79.

Long, pp. 141, 160. Lewis and Clark, pp. 106, 124.

McKenzie, pp. 97, 114–15. Morse, pp. 91, 129, 142. Mather, p. 127. Melverda and Acasta, p. 162.

Occum, p. 106.

Pratz, pp. 87, 175. Pedro de Cicca, p. 88. Penn, pp. 107, 174. Pixley, pp. 111, 113, 130.

Robertson, p. 153.

Sauard, p. 72. Smith, (colored,) pp. 117, 126, 134, 136, 174, 175. Schoolcraft, p. 145.

Ulloa, p. 88.

Williams, pp. 88, 101, 110, 114. Williams, (Roger,) p. 107.

"View of the Hebrews, by Ethan Smith," compiled from these histories.

According to these authors and scriptures of truth, the natives of America are the Israelites, the Jews; and as they are oppressed and driven from the land, a wo—a curse will follow, and who of us can stand.

Can a rational doubt be entertained whether the above Indian words, and parts of sentences, were derived from their corresponding words and parts of sentences in Hebrew? If so, their adoption by savages at this distant time and place, would appear miraculous. Some one or two words might happen to be the same, among distant, different nations. But that so many words, and parts of sentences too, in a language with a construction peculiar to itself, should so nearly, and some of them exactly correspond, is never to be admitted as resulting from accident.

And if these words and parts of sentences are from their corresponding Hebrew, the Indians must have descended from the ten tribes of Israel.

Some of the Creek Indians called a murderer Abe; probably from Abel, the first man murdered, whose name in Hebrew imports, mourning. And they called one who kills a rambling enemy, Noabe; probably from Noah, importing rest, and Abe. He thus puts his rambling enemy to rest. The Caribbee Indians and the Creeks had more than their due proportion of the words and parts of sentences in the above table.

Rev. Dr. Morse, in his late tour among the western Indians, says of the language: " It is highly metaphorical; and in this and other respects, they resemble the Hebrew. This resemblance in their language, (he adds,) and the similarity of many of their religious customs to those of the Hebrews, certainly gave plausibility to the ingenious theory of Dr. Boudinot, exhibited in his interesting work, the *Star in the West.*"

Dr. Boudinot informs that a gentleman, then living in the city of New York, who had long been much conversant with the Indians, assured him that, being once with the Indians at the place called *Cohocks*, they showed him a very high mountain at the west, the Indian name of which, they informed him, was Ararat. And the Penobscot Indians, the Dr. informs, call a high mountain by the same name.

Dr. Boudinot assures us that he himself attended an Indian religious dance. He says: "They danced one round; and then a second, singing hal-hal-hal, till they finished the round. They then gave us a third round, striking up the words, le-le-le. On the next round, it was the words, lu-lu-lu, dancing with all their might. During the fifth round, was sung, yah-yah-yah. Then all joined in a lively and joyful chorus, and sung *halleluyah;* dwelling on each syllable with a very long breath, in a most pleasing manner." The Doctor adds : " There could be no deception in all this. The writer was near them — paid great attention — and every thing was obvious to the senses. Their pronunciation was very guttural and sonorous; but

distinct and clear." How could it be possible that the wild
native Americans, in different parts of the continent,
should be found singing this phrase of praise to the Great
First Cause, or to Jah — exclusively Hebrew, without having brought it down by tradition from ancient Israel? The
positive testimonies of such men as Boudinot and Adair,
are not to be dispensed with, nor doubted. They testify
what they have seen and heard. And I can conceive of no
rational way to account for this Indian song, but that they
brought it down from ancient Israel, their ancestors.

Mr. Faber remarks: "They (the Indians) call the lightning and thunder, *Eloha*; and its rumbling, *Rowah*, which
may not improperly be deduced from the Hebrew word,
Ruach, a name of the third person of the Holy Trinity,
originally signifying the air in motion, or a rushing of the
wind." Who can doubt but their name of thunder, Eloha,
is derived from a Hebrew name of God, Elohim? Souard,
(quoted in Boudinot,) in his Literary Miscellanies, says of
the Indians in Surinam, on the authority of Isaac Nasci, a
learned Jew residing there, that the dialect of those Indians, common to all the tribes of Guiana, is soft, agreeable,
and regular. And this learned Jew asserts, that their sub-
stantives are Hebrew. The word expressive of the soul,
(he says,) is the same in each language, and is the same
with breath. "God breathed into man the breath of life,
and man became a living soul." This testimony from
Nasci, a learned Jew, dwelling with the Indians, must be
of signal weight.

Dr. Boudinot, from many good authorities, says of the
Indians: "Their language in their roots, idiom, and particular construction, appears to have the whole genius of
the Hebrew; and what is very remarkable, it has most of
the peculiarities of that language; especially those in which
it differs from most other languages."

Governor Hutchinson observed, that "many people (at
the time of the first settlement of New England) pleased
themselves with the conjecture, that the Indians in America are the descendants of the ten tribes of Israel."
Something was discovered so early, which excited this
pleasing sentiment. This has been noted as having been
the sentiment of Rev. Samuel Sewall, of Vice President
Willard, and others. Governor Hutchinson expresses his

doubt upon the subject, on account of the dissimilarity of the language of the natives of Massachusetts, to the Hebrew. Any language, in a savage state, must, in the course of 2,500 years, have rolled and varied exceedingly. This is shown to be the case in the different dialects, and many new words introduced among those tribes, which are acknowledged to have their language radically the same.

The following facts are enough to answer every objection on this ground. The Indians had no written language. Hence the English scholar could not see the spelling or the root of any Indian word. And the guttural pronunciation of the natives was such as to make even the Hebrew word, that might still be retained, appear a different word; especially to those who were looking for no Hebrew language among them. And the following noted idiom of the Indian language was calculated to hide the fact in perfect obscurity, even had it been originally Hebrew, viz.: the Indian language consists of a multitude of monosyllables added together. Every property or circumstance of a thing to be mentioned by an Indian, must be noted by a new monosyllable added to its name. Hence it was that the simple words *our loves*, must be expressed by the following long Indian word, *Noowomantammoonkanunonnash.* Mr. Colden, in his history of the five nations, observes, "They have few radical words. But they compound their words without end. The words expressive of things lately come to their knowledge, (he says,) are all compounds. And sometimes one word among them includes an entire definition of the thing."* These things, considered of a language among natives, 2,500 years after their expulsion from Canaan, must answer every objection arising from the fact, that the Indian language appears in some things very different from the Hebrew. And they must render it little less than miraculous, (as Mr. Adair says it is,) that after a lapse of so long a period among savages, without a book or letters, a word or phrase properly Hebrew should still be found among them. Yet such words and phrases are found. And many more may yet be found in the compounds of Indian words. I have just now observed, in dropping my eye on a Connecticut Magazine for 1803, a

---

* See the Connecticut Magazine, Vol. III. p. 367.

writer on the Indians in Massachusetts, in its earliest days,
informs, that the name of a being they worshipped was
Abamocko. Here, without any perception of the fact, he
furnishes a Hebrew word in compound. Abba-mocko;
father-mocho. As a tribe of Indians in the south call God,
Abba-mingo-ishto; Father chief-man. In the latter, we
have two Hebrew words: Abba, father; and Ish, man.
Could we make proper allowance for Pagan pronunciation,
and find how the syllables in their words ought to be
spelled, we might probably find many more of the Hebrew
roots in their language.

It is ascertained that the Indians make great use of the
syllables of the names of God, as roots of compound words.
Dr. Boudinot says: " Y-O-he-wah-yah and Ale, are roots
of a prodigious number of words through their various dialects." Wah being a noted name of God with the Indians, it seems often to occur in their proper names. Major
Long informs us, in his expedition to the Rocky Mountains, that the name of God with the Omawhaw tribe is
Wahconda. The Indians have their Wabash river, their
Wa-sasheh tribe, (of which the word Osage is but a French
corruption,) their Wa-bingie, Wa-ping, Wa-masqueak, Wa-
shpelong, and Wa-shpeaute tribes; also their Wa-bunk, a
name of the sun. A friend of mine informs me, that while
surveying, in his younger life, in the state of Ohio, he obtained considerable acquaintance with the Indians there.
That they appeared to have a great veneration for the sun,
which they called Wahbunk. If bunk is an Indian name
for a bed, as some suppose, it would seem that with those
Indians, the sun was Jehovah's bed, or place of residence.
The Indians have had much of an idea of embodying the
Great Spirit in fire. It is an idea which resulted from the
scene on the fiery top of Sinai, and from ancient Hebrew
figures, (as Paul informed in his epistle to the Hebrews,)
that "Our God is a consuming fire." No wonder then
those Indians in Ohio, as did the ancient Peruvians, embodied their Great Spirit in the sun. And no wonder their
veneration for that visible supposed residence of the Great
Spirit should be mistaken by strangers for worship paid to
the sun.

The Indians have had their imitation of the ark of the
covenant in ancient Israel. Different travellers, and from

different regions unite in this. Mr. Adair is full in his account of it. It is a small square box, made convenient to carry on the back. They never set it on the ground, but on logs in low ground where stones are not to be had; and on stones where they are to be found. This author gives the following account of it. "It is worthy of notice, (he says,) that they never place the ark on the ground, nor sit it on the bare earth when they are carrying it against an enemy. On hilly ground, where stones are plenty, they place it on them. But in level land, upon short logs, always resting themselves, (i. e., the carriers of the ark,) on the same materials. They have also as strong a faith of the power and holiness of their ark, as ever the Israelites retained of theirs. The Indian ark is deemed so sacred and dangerous to touch, either by their own sanctified warriors, or the spoiling enemy, that neither of them dare meddle with it on any account. It is not to be handled by any except the chieftain and his waiter, under penalty of incurring great evil; nor would the most inveterate enemy dare to touch it. The leader virtually acts the part of a priest of war, pro tempore, in imitation of the Israelites fighting under the divine military banner."

Dr. Boudinot says of this ark, "It may be called the ark of the covenant imitated." In time of peace it is the charge of their high priests. In their wars, they make great account of it. The leader, (acting as high priest on that occasion,) and his darling waiter, carry it in turns. They deposit in the ark some of their most consecrated articles. The two carriers of this sacred symbol, before setting off with it for the war, purify themselves longer than do the rest of the warriors. The waiter bears the ark during a battle. It is strictly forbidden for any one, but the proper officer, to look into it. An enemy, if they capture it, treat it with the same reverence.

Dr. Boudinot says, that a gentleman who was at Ohio in 1756, informed him, that while he was there, he saw among the Indians a stranger who appeared very desirous to look into the ark of that tribe. The ark was then standing on a block of wood, covered with a dressed deer skin. A centinel was guarding it, armed with a bow and arrow. The centinel finding the intruder press-

ing on, to look into the ark, drew his arrow at his head,
and would have dropped him on the spot; but the stranger perceiving his danger, fled.   Who can doubt the origin of this Indian custom?   And who can resist the evidence it furnishes, that here are the tribes of Israel?
See Num. x. 35, 36, and xiv. 44.

The American Indians have practised circumcision.
Doct. Beaty, in his journal of a visit to the Indians in
Ohio, between fifty and sixty years ago, says that "an
old Indian (in answer to his questions relative to their
ancient customs, the Indian being one of the old beloved
wise men,) informed him that an old uncle of his, who
died about the year 1728, related to him several customs
of former times among the Indians, and among the rest,
that circumcision was long ago practised among them,
but that their young men made a mock of it, and it fell
into disrepute and was discontinued."   Mr. M'Kenzie
informs, that in his travels among the Indians, he was
led to believe the same fact, of a tribe far to the north-
west; as stated in the "Star in the West."   His words
(when speaking of the nations of the Slave and Dog-rib
Indians,) are these; "Whether circumcision be practised among them, I cannot pretend to say; but the appearance of it was general among those I saw."   The
Indians cautiously conceal their special religious rites
from strangers travelling among them.   Mr. M'Kenzie
then would not be likely to learn this fact from them, by
any statement of the fact, or by seeing it performed.
But he says, "The appearance of it was general."
Doctor Boudinot assures that the eastern Indians inform
of its having been practised among them in times past;
but that latterly, not being able to give any account of
so strange a rite, their young men had opposed it, and it
was discontinued.   Immanuel de Moraez, in his history
of Brazil, says it was practised among the native Brazilians.   These native inhabitants of South America were
of the same origin with the Indians of North America.

The Rev. Mr. Bingham of Boston informed the writer
of these sheets, that Thomas Hopoo, the pious native of
a Sandwich Island, informed him while in this country,
before he returned with our missionaries to his native
region, that he himself had been circumcised; that he

perfectly remembered his brother's holding him, while his father performed upon him this rite.

Mr. Bingham also informed that the pious Obookiah, of the same race, pleased himself that he was a natural descendant of Abraham, and thought their own language radically Hebrew. It is believed by men of the best information that the Sandwich Islanders and the native Americans are of the same race. What savage nation could ever have conceived of such a rite, had they not descended from Israel?

The native Americans have acknowledged one, and only one God; and they have generally views concerning the one Great Spirit, of which no account can be given, but that they derived them from ancient revelation in Israel. Other nations destitute of revelation have had their many gods. But little short of three hundred thousand gods have existed in the bewildered imaginations of the pagan world. Every thing, almost, has been deified by the heathen. Not liking to retain God in their knowledge, and professing themselves to be wise, they became fools; and they changed the glory of the one living God into images of beasts, birds, reptiles and creeping things. There has been the most astonishing inclination in the world of mankind to do thus. But here is a new world of savages, chiefly if not wholly free from such wild idolatry. Doctor Boudinot (being assured by many good witnesses,) says of the Indians who had been known in his day, "They were never known [whatever mercenary Spanish writers may have written to the contrary] to pay the least adoration to images or dead persons, to celestial luminaries, to evil spirits, or to any created beings whatever." Mr. Adair says the same, and assures that "none of the numerous tribes and nations, from Hudson's Bay to the Mississippi, have ever been known to attempt the formation of any image of God." Du Pratz was very intimate with the chief of those Indians called "the Guardians of the Temple," near the Mississippi. He inquired of them the nature of their worship. The chief informed him that they worshipped the great and most perfect Spirit; and said, "He is so great and powerful, that in comparison with him all others are as nothing. He made all things that we see, and all things that we cannot see." The chief went on to speak of God as having made little spirits, called *free servants,* who always stand before the Great Spirit ready to do his will. That "the air is filled with spirits; some good, some bad; and that the bad have a chief who is more wicked than the rest." Here it seems is their traditional notion of good and bad angels; and of Beelzebub, the chief of the latter. This chief being asked how God made man, replied, that "God kneaded some clay, made it into a little man, and finding it was well formed, he blew on his work, and the man had life and grew up!" Being asked of the creation of the woman, he said, "their ancient speech made no mention of any difference, only that the man was made first." Moses' account of the formation of the woman, it seems had been lost.

Mr. Adair is very full in this, that the Indians have but one God, the Great Yohewah, whom they call the great, beneficent, supreme, and holy Spirit, who dwells above the clouds, and who dwells with good people, and is the only object of worship." So different are they from all the idolatrous heathen upon earth. He assures that they hold this great divine Spirit as the immediate head of their community; which opinion he conceives they must have derived from the ancient theocracy in Israel. He assures that the Indians are intoxicated with religious pride, and call all other people the accursed people; and have time out of mind been accustomed to hold them in great contempt. Their ancestors they boast to have been under the immediate government of Yohewah, who was with them and directed them by his prophets, while the rest of the world were outlaws, and strangers to the covenant of Yohewah. The Indians thus please themselves (Mr. Adair assures us) with the idea that God has chosen them from the rest of mankind as his peculiar people. This, he says, has been the occasion of their hating other people; and of viewing themselves hated by all men. These things show that they acknowledge but one God.

The Peruvians have been spoken of as paying adoration to the sun, and as receiving their race of Incas, as children of the sun, in their succession of twelve monarchies. The Indians have had much of an apprehen-

sion that their one Great Spirit had a great affinity to fire.
And the Peruvians, it seems, went so far as to embody
him in the sun. Here seems a shred of mixture of the
Persian idolatry, with the theocracy of Israel. As the
more ancient Israelites caught a degree of the idolatrous
distemper of Egypt, as appears in their golden calf; so
the ten tribes, the time they resided in Media, and before
they set off for America, may have blended some idea of
fire with their one God. But the veneration the Peruvians had for their Incas, as children of the Most High,
seems but a shred of ancient tradition from Israel, that
their kings were divinely anointed; and is so far from
being an argument against their being of Israel, that it
operates rather in favor of the fact.

Doctor Boudinot informs of the southern Indians of
North America, that they had a name for God, which
signifies, "the great, the beloved, holy cause." And
one of their names of God, is *Mingo-Ishto-Abba; Great
Chief Father*. He speaks of a preacher's being among
the Indians at the south, before the American revolution,
and beginning to inform them that there is a God who
created all things. Upon which they indignantly replied,
"Go about your business, you fool! do not we know
there is a God, as well as you?"

In their sacred dances, these authors assure us the
Indians sing "Halleluyah Yohewah;"— praise to Jah
Jehovah. When they return victorious from their wars,
they sing, Yo-he-wah; having been by tradition taught
to ascribe the praise to God.

The same authors assure us, the Indians make great
use of the initials of the mysterious name of God, like the
tetragrammation of the ancient Hebrews; or the four
radical letters which form the name of Jehovah; as the
Indians pronounce thus, Y-O-He-wah. That like the
ancient Hebrews, they are cautious of mentioning these
together, or at once. They sing and repeat the syllables
of this name in their sacred dances thus; Yo-yo, or ho-
ho-he-he-wah-wah. Mr. Adair upon the same, says;
"After this they begin again; Hal-hal-le-le-lu-lu-yah-
yah. And frequently the whole train strike up, hallehu-
hallelu-halleluyah-halleluyah." They frequently sing
the name of Shilu (Shilo, Christ) with the syllables of

the name of God added; thus, " Shilu-yo-Shilu—yo-Shilu -he–Shilu-he–Shilu-wah–Shilu-wah." Thus adding to the name of Shilu the name of Jehovah by its sacred syllables. Things like these have been found among Indians of different regions of America. Syllables and letters of the name of God have been so transposed in different ways; and so strange and guttural has been the Indian pronunciation, that it seems it took a long time to perceive that these savages were by tradition pronouncing the names of the God of Israel. Often have people been informed, and smiled at the fact, that an Indian, hurt or frightened, usually cries out *wah!* This is a part of his traditional religion; O Jah! or O Lord !

Doctor Williams upon the Indians' belief of the being of God, observes; " They denominate the deity the Great Spirit; the Great Man above; and seem to have some general ideas of his government and providence, universal power and dominion. The immortality of the soul was every where admitted among the Indian tribes."

The Rev. Ithamar Hebard, formerly minister of this place, related the following: That about fifty years ago, a number of men were sent from New-England by the government of Britain into the region of the Mississippi, to form some treaty with the Indians. That while these commissioners were there, having tarried for some time, an Indian chief came from the distance of what he calls several moons to the westward. Having heard that white men were there, he came to inquire of them where the Great Being dwelt who made all things. And being informed, through an interpreter, of the divine omnipresence, he raised his eyes and hands to heaven with great awe and ecstacy, and looking round, and leaping, he seemed to express the greatest reverence and delight. The head man of these commissioners had been a profane man; but this incident cured him, so that he was not heard to utter another profane word on his tour. This was related to Mr. Hebard by one Elijah Wood, who was an eye witness of the scene, and who was afterward a preacher of the gospel. The son of Mr. Hebard, a settled minister, gives this relation.

Let this fact of the Indians generally adhering to one, and only one God, be contrasted with the polytheism of the world of pagans, and heathen besides; with the idle

THE INDIAN TRIBES IN AMERICA.

and ridiculous notions of heathen gods and goddesses; and who can doubt of the true origin of the natives of our continent? They are fatally destitute of proper views of God and religion. But they have brought down by tradition from their remote ancestors, the notion of there being but one great and true God; which affords a most substantial argument in favor of their being the ancient Israel.

It is agreed that within about eighty years, a great change has been produced among the Indians. They have in this period much degenerated as to their traditional religion. Their connexions with the most degenerate part of the white people, trading among them, and their knowledge and use of ardent spirit, have produced the most deleterious effects. They have felt less zeal to maintain their own religion, such as it was; and to transmit their own traditions. Remarkable indeed it is, that they did so diligently propagate and transmit them, till so competent a number of good testimonies should be furnished to the civilized and religious world, relative to their origin. This must have been the great object of divine Providence in causing them so remarkably to transmit their traditions through such numbers of ages. And when the end is answered, the cause leading to it may be expected to cease.

This may account for the degeneracy of some Indians far to the west, reported in the journals of Mr. Giddings, in his exploring tour. He informs, "They differ greatly in their ideas of the Great Spirit; one supposes that he dwells in a buffalo, another in a wolf, another in a bear, another in a bird, another in a rattlesnake. On great occasions, such as when they go to war, and when they return, he adds, they sacrifice a dog, and have a dance. On these occasions they formerly sacrificed a prisoner taken in the war; but through the benevolent exertions of a trader among them, they have abandoned the practice of human sacrifice. There is always one who officiates as high priest. He practises the most rigid abstinence. He pretends to a kind of inspiration, or witchcraft; and his directions are obeyed.

"They all believe, he adds, in future rewards and punishments; but their heaven is sensual. They dif-

fer much in their ideas of goodness. One of their chiefs
told him, he did not know what constituted a good man ;
that their wise men in this did not agree.

"Their chiefs, and most of their warriors, have a war
sack, which contains generally, the skin of a bird, which
has a green plumage ; or some other object, which they
imagine to have some secret virtue."

Here we learn that those far distant savages have (as
have all the other tribes) their Great Spirit, "who made
every thing," though in their bewildered opinion he
dwells in certain animals. On going to war, or returning, they must sacrifice; and for victory obtained, must
have their religious dance. They must have their high
priest, who must practice great abstinence, and pretend
to inspiration; and hence must be obeyed. They have
brought down their traditional notions of these things;
and of future rewards and punishments. The ark of their
warlike chieftains, it seems, has degenerated into a
sack ! but this (like the ark of the other tribes) must contain their most sacred things; "green plumage, or some
other objects which they imagine to have some secret
virtue." Here these Indians furnish their quota of evidence, in these more broken traditions, of their descent
from Israel.

These tribes in the west are more savage, and know
less of the old Indian traditions. Mr. Giddings says,
"As you ascend the Missouri and proceed to the west, the
nearer to the state of nature the savages approach, and
the more savage they appear." This may account for
their *ark's* degenerating into a *sack;* and for their verg-
ing nearer to idolatry in their views of the Great Spirit,
viewing him as embodied in certain animals.

A chief of the Delaware Indians far in the west, visited by Messrs. Dodge and Blight, Jan. 1824, from the
Union Mission, gave the following information to these
missionaries. The chief was said by these missionaries
"to be a grave and venerable character, possessing a
mind which (if cultivated) would render him probably not
inferior to some of the first statesmen of our country."
On being inquired of by them whether he believed in the
existence of a Supreme Being ? he replied; "Long ago,
before ever a white man stepped his foot in America, the

Delawares knew there was one God; and believed there
was a hell, where bad folks would go when they die;
and a heaven where good folks would go. He went
on to state (these missionaries inform) that "he believed there was a devil, and he was afraid of him.
These things (he said) he knew were handed down by
his ancestors long before William Penn arrived in Pennsylvania. He said, he also knew it to be wrong if a
poor man came to his door hungry and naked, to turn
him away empty For he believed God loved the poor-
est of men better than he did proud rich men. Long
time ago, (he added,) it was a good custom among his
people to take but one wife, and that for life. But now
they had become so foolish, and so wicked, that they
would take a number of wives at a time, and turn them
away at pleasure!" He was asked to state what he
knew of Jesus Christ, the Son of God. He replied that
"he knew but little about him For his part, he knew
there was one God. He did not know about two Gods."
This evidence needs no comment to show that it appears
to be Israelitish tradition, in relation to the one God, to
heaven, hell, the devil, and to marriage, as taught in the
Old Testament, as well as God's estimation of the proud
rich, and the poor. These things he assures us came
down from their ancestors, before ever any white man
appeared in America. But the great peculiarity which
white men would naturally teach them (if they taught any
thing,) that Jesus Christ, the Son of God, is the Savior
of the world, he honestly confesses he knew not this part
of the subject.

The following is an extract of a letter from Mr. Cal-
vin Cushman, missionary among the Choctaws, to a
friend in Plainfield, Mass., in 1824.

"By information received of father Hoyt respecting
the former traditions, rites and ceremonies of the Indians of this region, I think there is much reason to believe they are the descendants of Abraham. They have
had cities of refuge, feasts of first truits, sacrifices of
the firstlings of the flocks, which had to be perfect, without blemish or deformity, a bone of which must not be
broken. They were never known to worship images,

18

nor to offer sacrifice to any god made with hands. They
all have some idea and belief of the Great Spirit. Their
fasts, holy days, &c. were regulated by *sevens*, as to time,
i. e. seven sleeps, seven moons, seven years, &c. They
had a kind of box containing some kind of substance
which was considered sacred, and kept an entire secret
from the common people. Said box was borne by a number of men who were considered pure or holy, (if I mistake not such a box was kept by the Cherokees.) And
whenever they went to war with another tribe they carried this box; and such was its purity in their view, that
nothing would justify its being rested on the ground. A
clean rock or scaffold of timber only, was considered
sufficiently pure for a resting place for this sacred coffer.
And such was the veneration of all the tribes for it, that
whenever the party retaining it was defeated, and obliged to leave it on the field of battle, the conquerors would
by no means touch it." This account well accords with
accounts of various others from different regions of the
Indians. But it is unaccountable upon every principle
except that the Indians are the descendants of Israel.

It is probable that while most of the natives of our
land had their one Great Spirit, some of this wretched
people talked of their differemt gods. Among the natives
on Martha's Vineyard, in the beginning of Mayhew's
mission among them, we find Mioxo, in his conversation
with the converted native, Hiaccomes, speaking of his
thirty-seven gods; and finally concluding to throw them
all away, to serve the one true God. We know not
what this insulated native could mean by his thirty-seven
gods. But it seems evident from all quarters, that such
were not the sentiments of the body of the natives of
America.

The ancient natives on Long Island talked of their
different subordinate gods. Sampson Occum, the noted
Indian preacher, says, "the Indians on Long Island
imagined a great number of gods." But he says, "they
had (at the same time) a notion of one great and good
God, who was over all the rest." Here, doubtless,
was their tradition of the holy angels which they had
become accustomed to call gods under the one great God.

The North American Reviewers speak of the fact, that the natives of our land acknowledged one supreme God. They inquire, " If the Indians in general have not some settled opinion of a Supreme Being, how has it happened that in all the conferences or talks of the white people with them, they have constantly spoken of the Great Spirit; as they denominate the Ruler of the universe?"

Lewis and Clarke informs us of the Mandans, (a tribe far toward the Pacific) thus: " The whole religion of the Mandans consists in a belief of one Great Spirit presiding over their destinies. To propitiate whom, every attention is lavished, and every personal consideration is sacrificed." One Mandan informed that lately he had eight horses; but that he had offered them all up to the *Great Spirit*. His mode of doing it was this; he took them into the plains, and turned them all loose; committing them to the Great Spirit, he abandoned them for ever. The horses, less devout than their master, no doubt took care of themselves.

Heckewelder (a venerable missionary among the Indians 40 years, noted in Doct. Jarvis' discourse before the New York Historical Society, and who had a great acquaintance with the wide spread dialect of the Delaware language,) says: " Habitual devotion to the great first cause, and a strong feeling of gratitude for the benefits he confers, is one of the prominent traits which characterize the mind of the untutored Indian. He believes it to be his duty to adore and worship his Creator and Benefactor."

Gookin, a writer in New England in 1674, says of the natives, "generally they acknowledge one great supreme Doer of good." Roger Williams, one of the first settlers of New England, says: "He that questions whether God made the world, the Indians will teach him. I must acknowledge (he adds) I have in my concourse with them, received many confirmations of these two great points — 1. That God is. 2. That he is a rewarder of all that diligently seek him. If they receive any good in fishing, hunting or harvesting, they acknowledge God in it."

Surely, then, the natives of the deserts of America must have been a people who once knew the God of

Israel! They maintained for more than two millenaries, the tradition of him, in many respects correct. What possible account can be given of this, but that they were descendants of Israel, and that the God of Israel has had his merciful eye upon them, with a view in his own time to bring them to light, and effect their restoration?

The celebrated William Penn gives accounts of the natives of Pennsylvania, which go to corroborate the same point. Mr. Penn saw the Indians of Pennsylvania before they had been affected with the rude treatment of the white people. And in a letter to a friend in England, he thus writes of those natives: " I found them with like countenances with the Hebrew race; and their children of so lively a resemblance to them, that a man would think himself in Duke's place, or Barry street, in London, when he sees them." Here, without the least previous idea of those natives being Israelites, that shrewd man was struck with their perfect resemblance of them; and with other things which will be noted. He speaks of their dress and trinkets as notable, and like those of ancient Israel; their ear-rings, nose jewels, bracelets on their arms and legs, rings (such as they were) on their fingers; necklaces, made of polished shells found in their rivers and on their coasts; bands, shells and feathers ornamenting the heads of females, and various strings of beads adorning several parts of the body.

Mr. Penn adds to his friend, "that he considered this people as under a dark night; yet they believed in God and immortality, without the help of metaphysics. For he says they informed him that there was a great king, who made them — that the souls of the good shall go to him." He adds: "Their worship consists in two parts, sacrifice and cantico, (songs.) The first is with their first fruits; and the first buck they kill goes to the fire." Mr. Penn proceeds to describe their splendid feast of first fruits, one of which he had attended. He informs, " all that go to this feast must take a piece of money, which is made of the bone of a fish." " None shall appear before me empty." He speaks of the agreement of their rites with those of the Hebrews. He adds, " They reckon by moons; they offer their first ripe fruits; they have a kind of feast of tabernacles; they are said to lay their altars with twelve stones; they mourn a year; they have their separations of women; with many other things that do not now occur." Here is a most artless testimony, given by that notable man, drawn from his own observations, and accounts given by him; while the thought of this people's being actually Hebrew, probably was most distant from his mind.

*Their having a tribe, answering in various respects to the tribe of Levi, sheds further light on this subject.** The thought naturally occurs, that if these are the ten tribes, and they have preserved so many of their religious traditions, should we not be likely to find among them some tradition of a tribe answering to the tribe of Levi? If we should find something of this, the evidence of their being the tribes of Israel would indeed be more striking. Possibly this is furnished. The *Mohawk* tribe were held by the other tribes in great reverence; and the other tribes round about them had been accustomed to pay them an annual tribute. Mr. Boudinot gives the following account of them. "Mr. Colden says, he had been told by old men (Indians) in New England, that when their Indians were at war formerly with the Mohawks, as soon as one (a Mohawk) appeared, the Indians would raise a cry, from hill to hill, *a Mohawk! a Mohawk!* upon which all would flee as sheep before a wolf, without attempting to make the least resistance. And that all the nations around them have for many years entirely submitted to their advice, and paid them a yearly tribute. And the tributary nations dared not to make war or peace, without the consent of the Mohawks." Mr. Colden goes on to state an instance of their speech to the governor of Virginia, in which it appears the Mohawks were the correctors of the misdoings of the other tribes.

Now, could any thing be found in their *name* which might have an allusion to the superiority of the tribe of Levi, we should think the evidence very considerable, that here are indeed the descendants of the part of that tribe which clave to the house of Israel. And here, too,

---

* Some of this tribe probably remained with the ten tribes.

evidence seems not wholly wanting. The Hebrew word *Mhhokek*, signifies an interpreter of the law, superior. We have, then, a new view of the possible origin of the Mohawks!

Several prophetic traits of character given of the Hebrews, do accurately apply to the aborigines of America. Intemperance may be first noted. Isaiah, writing about the time of the expulsion of Israel from Canaan, and about to predict their restoration says, Isa. xxviii. 1 — " Wo to the crown of pride, the drunkards of Ephraim, (Ephraim was a noted name of the ten tribes of Israel.) The crown of pride, the drunkards of Ephraim, shall be trodden under feet. For all tables shall be full of vomit and filthiness; so that there is no place clean."

In the course of the descriptions of their drunkenness, that of their rejection and restoration is blended; that the Lord by a mighty one would cast him down to the earth; and their glorious beauty should be like that of a rich flower in a fertile valley, which droops, withers and dies. But in time God would revive it. "In that day shall the Lord of hosts be for a crown of glory, and for a diadem of beauty unto the residue of this people." None who know the character of the Indians in relation to intemperance, need to be informed that this picture does most singularly apply to them.

Doctor Williams, in his History of Vermont, on this trait of Indian character, says: "no sooner had the Indians tasted of the spirituous liquors brought by the Europeans, than they contracted a new appetite, which they were wholly unable to govern. The old and the young, the sachem, the warrior and the women, whenever they can obtain liquors, indulge themselves without moderation and without decency, till universal drunkenness takes place. All the tribes appear to be under the dominion of this appetite, and unable to govern it."

A writer in the Connecticut Magazine assures us of the Indians in Massachusetts, when our fathers first arrived there: "As soon as they had a taste of ardent spirits, they discovered a strong appetite for them, and their thirst soon became insatiable."

Another trait of Hebrew character which singularly applies to the Indians, is found in Isa. iii. "The bravery of their tinkling ornaments about their feet; their cauls, and round tires like the moon; their chains, bracelets, mufflers, bonnets, ornaments of the legs; head-bands, tablets, ear-rings, rings, and nose jewels; the mantles, the wimples, and the crisping pins." One would imagine the prophet was here indeed, describing the natives of America in their full dress! No other people on earth probably bear a resemblance to such a degree.

This description was given just before the expulsion of Israel. And nothing would be more likely than that their taste for these flashy ornaments should descend to posterity. For these make the earliest and deepest impressions on the rising generation. And many of the Indians exhibit the horrid contrast which there follows.

Mr. Pixley, of the Union mission, being out among the Indians over Sabbath, thus wrote in his journal:— "I have endeavored to pay a little attention to the day, (the Sabbath) by building a fire in the woods, and there reading my Bible. In reading the third chapter of the prophet Isaiah, I found in the latter part of the chapter a striking analogy between the situation of this people, and the condition of the people about whom the prophet was speaking, which I never before discovered. They are represented by the prophet as sitting on the ground; having their secret parts discovered; having given to them, instead of a sweet smell, a stench; instead of a girdle, a rent; instead of well set hair, baldness; instead of a stomacher, a girding of sackcloth; and *burning* instead of beauty. In all these particulars, except that of baldness, the prediction of the prophet is amply fulfilled in this people. And even this exception would be removed, if we might suppose that their shaving their heads with a razor, leaving one small lock on the crown, would constitute the baldness hinted. And certainly if any women in the world labor to secure their own bread and water, and yet a number of them be attached to one man to take away their reproach, you will find it among this people, whether the prediction may or may not be applied to them."

The Indians being in tribes, with their heads and names of tribes, affords further light upon this subject.

The Hebrews not only had their tribes and heads of tribes, as have the Indians, but they had their animal emblems of their tribes. Dan's emblem was a *serpent*; Issachar's an *ass*; Benjamin's a *wolf*; and Judah's a *lion*. And this trait of character is not wanting among the natives of this land. They have their wolf tribe; their tiger tribe; panther tribe; buffalo tribe; bear tribe; deer tribe; raccoon tribe; eagle tribe; and many others. What other nation on earth bears any resemblance to this? Here, no doubt, is Hebrew tradition.

Various of the emblems given in Jacob's last blessing have been strikingly fulfilled in the American Indians. "Dan shall be a serpent by the way; an adder in the path, that biteth the horse heels, so that the rider shall fall backwards. Benjamin shall ravin as a wolf; in the morning he shall devour the prey; and at night he shall divide the spoil." Had the prophetic eye rested on the American aborigines, it seems as though no picture could have been more accurate.

Their having an imitation of the ancient city of refuge, evinces the truth of our subject. Their city of refuge has been hinted from Mr. Adair. But as this is so convincing an argument, no nation on earth having any thing of the kind, but the ancient Hebrews and the Indians, the reader shall be more particularly instructed on this article. Of one of these places of refuge, Mr. Boudinot says: "The town of refuge called *Choate* is on a large stream of the Mississippi, five miles above where Fort Loudon formerly stood. Here, some years ago, a brave Englishman was protected, after killing an Indian warrior in defence of his property. He told Mr. Adair that after some month's stay in this place of refuge, he intended to return to his house in the neighborhood; but the chiefs told him it would prove fatal to him. So that he was obliged to continue there, till he pacified the friends of the deceased by presents to their satisfaction. "In the upper country of Muskagee, (says Doctor Boudinot,) was an old *beloved town*, called *Koosah*—which is a place of safety for those who kill undesignedly."

"In almost every Indian nation (he adds) there are several peaceable towns, which are called *old beloved*, *holy, or white towns.* It is not within the memory of the oldest people, that blood was ever shed in them; although they often force persons from them, and put them else-where to death." Who can read this, and not be satisfied of the origin of this Indian tradition.

THE TRUE CHRISTIANS IN THIS LAND ARE INDIANS.

A council of chiefs' reply to the missionary in 1805, at the Six Nations, by Sagnym Whathah, alias Red Jacket [Philanthropist.]

Friend and Brother : — It was the will of the Great Spirit, that we should meet together this day. He orders all things; and has given us a fine day for our council. He has taken his garment from before the sun, and caused it to shine with brightness. Our eyes are opened, that we may see clearly; our ears are unstopped, that we have been able to hear distinctly, the word you have spoken. For all these favors we thank the Great Spirit — and him only.

Brother, listen to what we say. There was a time when our forefathers owned this great island; their seats extended from the rising to the setting sun — the Great Spirit had made it for the use of the Indians. He had created the buffalo, the deer, and other animals for food. He had made the bear and the beaver; their skin served us for clothing. He had scattered them over the coun-try, and taught us how to take them. He had caused the earth to produce corn for bread. All these he has done for his red children, because he had loved them.

If we had disputes about our hunting ground, they were generally settled without the shedding of blood. But an evil day is come upon us; your forefathers crossed the great waters, and landed on this island. Their num-ber was small. They found us friends and not enemies. They told us that they had fled from their own coun-try through fear of wicked men, and had come here to enjoy their religion. They asked for a small seat. We took pity on them, and granted their request, and they sat down among us. We gave them corn and meat, and in return they gave us poison. The white people having now found our country good, tidings were sent back and more came among us. Yet we did not fear them. **We** took them to be friends. They called us brothers; we believed them, and gave them a larger seat. At length their number so increased, that they wanted more land —they wanted our country. Our eyes were opened: and we became uneasy. War took place. Indians were hired to fight against Indians; and many of our people were destroyed. They also distributed liquor amongst us — which has slain thousands.

Brother: — once our seats were large, and yours were small. You have now become a great people; and we have scarcely a place left to spread our blankets. You have got our country, but are not satisfied. You want to force your religion upon us.

Brother, continue to listen. You say you are sent to instruct us how to worship the Great Spirit, agreeably to his mind; and, that if we do not take hold of the religion which you teach, we shall be unhappy hereafter. How do we know this to be true? We understand that your religion is written in a book. If it was intended for us as well as you, why has not the Great Spirit given it to us? and not only to us, but why did he not give to our forefathers the knowledge of that book, with the means of rightly understanding it? We only know what you tell us about it: and having been s often deceived by white people, how shall we believe what they say?

Brother, you say there is but one way to worship and serve the Great Spirit. If there is but one religion, why do you white people differ so much about it? why not all agree, as you can all read the Book.

Brother, we do not understand these things. We are told that your religion was given to your forefathers; and has been handed down from father to son. We also have a religion, which was given to our forefathers; and has been handed down to us. It teaches us to be thankful for all favors received; to love each other, and be united. We never quarrel about religion.

Brother, the Great Spirit made us all. But he has made a great difference between his white and his red children. He has given us different complexions, and different customs. To you he has given the arts — to these he has not opened our eyes. Since he has made so great a difference between us in other things, why may he not have given us a different religion? The

Great Spirit does right. He knows what is best for his children.

Brother, we do not want to destroy your religion; or to take it from you. We only want to enjoy our own.

Brother, we have been told that you have been preaching to the white people in this place. These people are our neighbors. We will wait a little, and see what effect your preaching has had upon them. If we find it makes them honest, and less disposed to cheat Indians, we will then consider again of what you have said.

Brother, you have now heard our answer; and this is all we have to say at present. As we are about to part, we will come and take you by the hand; and we hope the Great Spirit will protect you on your journey, and return you safe to your friends.

Whole families of Christian Indians were murdered in cool blood by the whites. This circumstance is but one in a thousand:—

Upon the banks of the Ohio, a party of two hundred white warriors, in 1757, or about that time, came across a settlement of Christian Indians, and falsely accused them of being warriors; to which they denied, but all to no purpose; they were determined to massacre them all. They, the Indians, then asked liberty to prepare for the fatal hour. The white savages then gave them one hour, as the historian said.

They then prayed together; and in tears and cries, upon their knees, begged pardon of each other, of all they had done. After which they informed the white savages that they were now ready. One white man then begun with a mallet, and knocked them down, and continued his work until he had killed fifteen with his own hand; then saying it ached, he gave his commission to another. And thus they continued till they had massacred nearly ninety men, women and children, all these innocent of any crime. What sad tales are these, for us to look upon the massacre of our dear fathers, mothers, brothers and sisters; and if we speak, we are then called savages for complaining. Our affections for each other are the same as yours; we think as much of ourselves as the whites do of themselves.

THE ABORIGINAL INDIANS OF AMAZONIA.—These natives, like all other Americans, are of a good stature—have handsome features — long black hair, and copper complexions. They are said to have a taste for the imitative arts, especially painting and sculpture, and make good mechanics. They spin and weave cotton cloth, and build their houses with wood and clay, and thatch them with reeds. Their arms, in general, are darts and javelins — bows and arrows, with targets of cane or fish skins. The several nations are governed by their chiefs or cassiques.

America was originally peopled by Christian nations, which lived mostly by hunting and fishing. The Europeans, who first visited these shores, treated the natives as wild beasts of the forests, and hunted the Indians down with dogs and guns!"

The native inhabitants of America are of a copper-color, (red, black and white,) have black, thick, straight hair, flat noses, high cheek bones, and small eyes. They paint the body and face of various colors, and eradicate the hair of their beards and other parts, as a deformity. Their limbs are not so large and robust, as those of the Europeans. They endure hunger, thirst and pain with astonishing firmness and patience; and, though cruel to their enemies, they are kind and just to each other.

GEORGIA.—The Indian tribes within the vicinity of this district, are the Cherokees and Chickasaws. The Cherokees have been a warlike and numerous nation; but by continual wars, in which it has been their destiny to be engaged with the northern Indian tribes, they were reduced at the commencement of the last war, to about 2,000 fighting men.

The Creek Indians represent this as the most blissful spot on earth. They say it is inhabited by a peculiar race of Indians, whose women are incomparably beautiful. They were called daughters of the sun, who kindly gave to strangers. Their husbands were fierce men, and cruel to their enemies.

The people of God, who were murdered by thousands, — men, women and children,— under the act made by Congress, in cold blood murder, to obtain their land. Woe unto the nation — the United States of America.

The islands of Cuba and Hispaniola were discovered by Columbus. After having built several houses on these islands, he returned to Spain.

Hispaniola contained three millions of natives; the inhabitants of Cuba were above six hundred thousand.

Bartholomew de las Casas, bishop of Chiapa, who was an eye witness to these desolations, relates, that they hunted down the natives with dogs. This race of men, almost naked, and without arms, were pursued like wild beasts in the forests, devoured alive by dogs, shot to death, or surprised and burnt in their habitations.

He farther declares, from ocular testimony, that they frequently caused a number of these native inhabitants to be summoned by a priest to come in, and submit to the Christian religion, and to the king of Spain; and that after this ceremony, which was only an additional act of injustice, they put them to death without the least remorse.

"Vengeance is mine, and I will repay saith the Lord." Thus we see the Island of Hispaniola, or St. Domingo was taken from the white Spaniards, or French, and given to the blacks; and so shall the island of Cuba be taken away, and given to the blacks and Indians of the island.

The following is a true copy of a Speech, composed by a North American Indian, without any assistance, or correction of any one, but those of his own color. [Theological Magazine.]

" *To the great Sachem and Chiefs of the State of* ———, *now sitting around the Great Council fire at* ———.

"Brothers, Before you cover your council fire, we beg your attention to the voice of your brethren. The different tribes of ——— speak to you, in remembrance of the friendship you have manifested towards them in all our treaties.

"We, ourselves, have held councils at different times, to contemplate the welfare of our nations, because we cannot but groan to see our situation. It is almost melancholy to reflect upon the ways of our forefathers.

"Brothers, You are, also, sometimes sorry to see the deplorable situation of our Indian brethren, for which you have given us so many good counsels, though we feel ourselves willing to follow your counsel, but it has made no effect as yet. Our situation is still miserable. Our ancestors were conquered immediately after you came over to this land, by the strong *Hero*, who does still reign among the Indian tribes with tyranny; who has robbed us of every thing that was precious in our eyes. But we need not mention every thing particular, how this tyrant has used us; for your eyes have been open to behold our dismal situation. By the power of our enemy, our eyes have been blinded; our young men seem to become willing slaves to this despotic hero. So, by that, we displease the Great Good Spirit, and could not become civilized people. In looking back, we see nothing but desolation of our mighty men; in looking forward, we foresee the desolation of our tribes.

"Our chiefs have used their endeavors to reform their respective people, but having seen no success, they seem discouraged, and hang down their heads.

"Brothers, In remembrance of your kind promises, we unite our cries to you for help. Perhaps you are ready to think, what man that must be, that has abused so much of our brethren? Never was such hero or tyrant heard, that ever meddled with Indians. But in litterally, he is your own begotten son, and his name you call RUM. And the names of his officers are BRANDY, WINE and GIN, and we know you have power to control him; and as we desire to live in peace, and to become civilized nations, we earnestly entreat you to use your power and wisdom, to prevent all people who may cause RUM and all other spirituous liquors to come into the hand of our tribes, throughout your state. In your compliance with this our request, we will ever acknowledge your friendship, is from your brethren, chiefs and warriors of —— nation.

Done at ——, on the 5th day of March, 1796.

J. S.
C. T.
W. T.
N. C.
U. A., &c."

Extract of a Speech, delivered by an Indian Chief called Little Turtle.

"Brothers and friends, when our forefathers first met on this island, your red brothers were very numerous, but since the introduction amongst us of what you call spirituous liquors, and what we think may be justly called poison, our numbers are greatly diminished; it has destroyed a great part of your red brothers.

"Brothers and friends, we plainly perceive the very evil which has destroyed your red brethren, is not an evil of our own making; we have not placed it among ourselves, it is an evil placed among us by the white people, we look to them to remove it out of our country. We tell them, brethren, bring us useful things, bring goods that will clothe us, our women, our children; and not this evil liquor, that destroys our health, destroys our lives; but all we can say is of no service, nor gives relief to your red brethren. It causes our young men to say, We had better be at war with the white people; the liquor which they introduce into our country is more to be feared, than the gun or the tomahawk.

"Brothers, when our young men have been out a hunting, and are returning home loaded with skins and furs, on their way it happens that they come along where some of this whiskey is deposited: the white man who sells it, tells them to take a little drink; some of them will say no, I do not want it. They go on till they come to another house, where they find more of the same kind of drink, it is there offered again, they refuse again the third time, but finally, the fourth or fifth one accepts of it, and takes a drink, and getting one, he wants another, and then a third, and a fourth, till his senses have left him; after his reason comes back to him, when he gets up, and finds where he is, he asks for his peltry, the answer is, you have drank them. Where is my gun? It is gone! Where is my shirt? You have sold it for whiskey! Now, brethren figure to yourselves what condition this man must be in. He has a family at home; a wife and children, who stand in need of the profits of his hunting. What must be their wants, when he himself is without a shirt?"

CHAPTER V.

THE ARTS AND SCIENCES.

EARLY DISCOVERIES, INVENTIONS, &c.

The discoveries, inventions and improvements made by the Egyptians and Ethiopians, in early times, must have been very great. The Arts and Sciences were studied in the first age of the Egyptian monarchy. Previous to the invention of the alphabet, the Egyptians had discovered and systematized a method of transmitting ideas by hieroglyphics. It was a representation of thought, by figures of animals and other things, to whom the Chinese are indebted.

Memnon, an Egyptian, invented the first letters. The celebrated Cadmus introduced them into Greece. It is said these characters or letters were Egyptian, and Cadmus himself was a native of Egypt, and not of Phœnicia; and the Egyptians, who ascribe to themselves the invention of every art, and boast a greater antiquity than any other nation, give to their Mercury the honor of inventing letters. Most of the learned agree, that Cadmus carried the Phœnician, Egyptian, or Syrian letters into Greece about 1519 years B. C., and that these letters were Hebraic. The Hebrews are a small nation of that country, under the general name of Syrians. The alphabet which he introduced into Greece, consisted of sixteen letters. And the mode of writing was alternately from left to right and from right to left, [as the Arabians and Moors now write.] He is said to have taught the people navigation and the principles of commerce, the manner of cultivating the vine, and the art of forging and working metals. The introduction of Cadmus' letters into Greece, was a great advance which the Greeks made in knowledge and civilization.

Palamedes invented four letters at the siege of Troy, 1134 years B. C., and Simonides invented four more many years afterwards.

The Grecian and Roman alphabets were derived from these letters, which were the same as the Samaritan, and were used by the Jews, Ethiopians, before the Babylonish captivity.

The ancient books, rolls, volumes or scrolls were formed in Egypt, and a kind of paper was made from the stalk of an Egyptian vegetable called papyrus or paper reed, which is still found in various parts of India. The stalk was slit with a needle, into plates or layers, as broad and thin as possible. Some of them were ten or fifteen inches broad. These strips were laid side by side, upon a flat horizontal surface, and then immersed in the water of the Nile; which not only served as a kind of sizing, but also caused the edges of the strips to adhere together as if glued. The sheets thus formed were dried in the sun, and then covered with a fine wash, which made them smooth and flexible. They were finally beaten with hammers, and polished. Twenty or more of these sheets were sometimes connected in one roll.

A sealed book, was a roll fastened together by a band or string, and a seal affixed to the knot.

Book of the generation signifies the genealogical history, or records of a family or nation.

The pen or style was made of some hard substance; perhaps not unlike the instruments used by glaziers to cut glass. [Jer. xvii. 1.] Upon tablets of wax an instrument was used, one end of which was pointed, to mark the letters, and the other broad and flat, to make erasures. Pens or styles of copper are now used by the Ceylonese. On soft substances, like linen or papyrus, the marks were painted with a fine hair pencil, as is practised among the Chinese to this day. Hence the word *style*, signifying one's manner of writing — easy *style*, elegant *style*, &c.

Most of the eastern nations now use the reed-pen. Ink was prepared from a variety of substances; and

those who were skilful in writing wore an ink-horn fastened to the girdle, [Ezek. ix. 2,] which is the present
mode among the Persians and the Moors of Barbary.

The Egyptians invented the art of embalming the
dead, viz., the Kings, Queens, Prophets, Priests, Rulers,
&c., &c. After death they were embalmed and put into
a pyramid or tomb, built of marble, stone or brick, richly ornamented with men, beasts, birds and reptiles, engraved or carved work.

Coffins were used in Egypt and Babylon, but are unknown in the east, even at the present day, except when
a body is to be conveyed to a distant place.

The embalming was not general among the Jews,
though spices, &c. were used in their burials. [2 Chron.
xvi. 14. John xix. 40.] Jacob and Joseph, whose bodies
were embalmed, both died in Egypt, where the art of embalming was very skilfully practised. In Jacob's case,
we are told that Joseph commanded his servants, the
physicians, to embalm his father, and then he was placed
in a coffin, in Egypt. And thence his body was carried
to Machpelah, in Canaan, and buried. [Gen. l. 2, 7, 8.]

Raiment was at first made of the skins of beasts, [Gen. iii.
21 ;] but the art of spinning and weaving was soon invented,
[Ex. xxviii. 42,] and even embroidering, [Ex. xxxv. 35.]

Linen. [Lev. xiii. 47.] This cloth was much celebrated
in ancient times. The best linen was anciently made in
Egypt, as their country afforded the finest flax, [Prov. vii.
16,] and Solomon, it seems, bought linen yarn in Egypt.
[1 Kings x. 28.] It is supposed that linen was anciently
used for writing on, and the letters formed with a pencil.
It was much valued and used in ancient as in modern
times. Fine white linen is, in Scripture, the emblem of
innocence, or moral purity. [Rev. xv. 6.]

The era of Sesostris was called the second age. During
this age, architecture, and the arts of war were chiefly cultivated. Owing to the oppression of the times, many Egyptians left their native country, and settled colonies in other
lands, carrying with them their arts and sciences. From
Sesostris to Amasis, was the third age — one of luxury
and conquest.

It was the Egyptians that discovered the elementary principles; studied the sciences and arts, and the phenomena,

and laws of nature ; gave names to the planets, and furnished the archetype of those civil and religious systems, which prevailed in that quarter of the world, and have since spread into every civilized nation.

The celebrated Prometheus was the first that struck fire with a flint.

The first ship was built in Egypt by the Egyptians.

The first pump was invented by the celebrated Archimedes, in Egypt; and in Egypt the first libraries were formed.

The library of Alexandria, in Egypt, previous to its being burned in the time of Pompey's reign, was the richest in the world. . It contained four hundred thousand valuable volumes in MSS. Egypt was considered, by all the ancients, as the most renowed school for wisdom and politics; and the source from whence most arts and sciences were derived. This kingdom bestowed its noblest labors and finest arts upon the improvement of mankind ; and Greece was so sensible of this, that its most illustrious men, as Homer, Pythagoras, Plato, and even its great legislators,— Lycurgus, the reformer of the Spartan Republic, and Solon, the legislator of Athens, and the wisest men of Greece, and many others travelled into Egypt to complete their studies, and draw from that fountain whatever was rare and valuable in every kind of learning.

At Alexandria was the chief school in Egypt, where the arts and sciences were taught.

Philosophy, The art of knowledge, natural or moral.

Mathematics, The science which contemplates whatever is capable of being numbered or measured.

Jurisprudence, The science of law.

Medicine, The science of healing.

Magic, The art of putting in action the power of spirits.

The principles of geometry were discovered by the celebrated Euclid, an Ethiopian, and were written in Greek.

The admeasurement of the lands, annually disturbed by the overflowing of the Nile, induced to the cultivation of geometry by the Egyptians.

Geometry treats of the powers and properties of magnitudes in general, where length, breadth, and thickness are considered, from a point to a line, from a line to a superficies, and from a superficies to a solid.

A point is a dimensionless figure; or an indivisible part of a space.

A line is a point continued, and a figure of one capacity, namely, length.

A superficies is a figure of two dimensions, namely, length and breadth.

A solid is a figure of three dimensions, namely, length, breadth, and thickness.

THE ADVANTAGES OF GEOMETRY.—By this science the architect is enabled to construct his plans, and execute his designs; the general to arrange his soldiers; the geographer to give us the dimensions of the world, and all things therein contained; to delineate the extent of the seas, and specify the divisions of empires, kingdoms and provinces. By it, also, the astronomer is enabled to make his observations, and to fix the duration of times and seasons, years and cycles.

In fine, geometry is the foundation of architecture, and the root of the mathematics.

THE MORAL ADVANTAGES OF GEOMETRY. —Geometry is the first and noblest of sciences. By it we may curiously trace nature, through her various windings, to her most concealed recesses. By it we may discover the power, the wisdom, and the goodness of the grand art of the universe, and view with delight the proportions which connect this vast machine.

By it we may discover how the planets move in their different orbits, and demonstrate their various revolutions. By it we account for the return of seasons, &c.

THE RECKONERS OF TIME.—Derivation of the names of the days, and times of the beginning of the day, among the ancient blacks.

Sunday derived its name from the sun; Monday from the moon; Tuesday from the word Tuisco; Wednesday from Woden — the name of a heathen deity; Thursday from Thor; Friday from Friga; and Saturday from Saturn.

The Athenians and Jews began their day at sunsetting; a custom followed by the Austrians, Bohemians, Silesians, Italians and Chinese.

The Babylonians, Persians, Syrians, and most of the eastern nations, began their day at sun-rise.

The Egyptians and Romans began their day at midnight, and are followed by the English, Americans, French, Germans, Dutch and Portuguese.

The Arabians began their day at noon.

The following arts and sciences were first discovered by the Egyptians and Ethiopians :—The art of reading, writing, letters and figures, building, making, moulding, carving, casting, forging, engraving, carding, spinning, weaving, dying, sawing, ploughing, planting, reaping, threshing, winnowing, grinding, preserving, embalming, navigation, fighting, &c., &c.

ART OF WAR, AND SOLDIERS OF EGYPT.— Herodotus says that two thousand guards attended annually upon the kings of Egypt. Four hundred thousand soldiers were kept continually in pay — all natives of Egypt: and trained in the exactest discipline. Shishak, king of Egypt, came up against Jerusalem with 120 chariots, and 60,000 horsemen, and soldiers without number. [2 Chron. xii. 3.] They were inured to the fatigues of war, by a severe and rigorous education. There is an art of disciplining the body as well as the mind: and this art was well known to the Egyptians; we have lost it by our sloth. Foot, horse and chariot races were performed in Egypt with wonderful agility; and the world could not show better horsemen than the Egyptians. The profession of arms was in great repute among them. After the sacerdotal families, the most illustrious, as with us, were those devoted to a military life. They were not only distinguished by honors, but by ample pecuniary rewards. Every soldier was furnished with a quantity of land, and was exempted from all tax or tribute. Besides this privilege, each soldier received a daily allowance of five pounds of bread, two of flesh, and a pint of wine. This allowance was sufficient to support part of their family. Such an indulgence made them more affectionate to the person of their prince, and the interests of their country, and more resolute in the defence of both; and, as Diodorus observes, it was thought inconsistent with good policy, and even common sense, to commit the defence of a country to men who had no interest in its preservation.

Military laws were easily preserved in Egypt, because sons received them from their fathers; the profession of war, as all others, being transmitted from father to son.

Those who fled in battle, or discovered any signs of cowardice, were only distinguished by some particular mark of ignominy; it being thought more advisable to restrain them by motives of honor, than by the terrors of punishment.

But notwithstanding this, I will not pretend to say, that the Egyptians were a warlike people. It is of little advantage to have regular and well-paid troops; to have armies exercised in peace, and employed only in mock fights; it is war alone, and real combats, which form the soldier. Egypt loved peace, because it loved justice, and maintained soldiers only for its security. Its inhabitants, content with a country which abounded in all things, had no ambitious dreams of conquest. The Egyptians extended their reputation in a very different manner, by sending colonies into all parts of the world, and with them laws and politeness. They triumphed by the wisdom of their counsels, and the superiority of their knowledge; and this empire of the mind appeared more noble and glorious to them, than that which is achieved by arms and conquests. But nevertheless, Egypt has given birth to illustrious conquerors.

THE HISTORY OF MUSIC.—The origin of the ancient music, with the perfect knowledge we have, not only of the instruments, but of the system by which those instruments were tuned, and the manner in which they were performed. Jubal was "the father of all such as handle the harp and the organ," the son of Lamech, who first lived in tents, and a brother of Noah; the celebrated Tubalcain, "an instructor of every artificer in brass and iron." Thus early did the necessities of man establish the right of property, and originate the mechanic arts. And the Patriarchal government which existed in the Antedeluvian ages, the knowledge and experience acquired in a life of many centuries, must have been favorable to a high degree of perfection in these arts, and the science of music.

The celebrated Egyptians — the descendants of the Ethiopians, were the first who acquired a knowledge of music, after the flood of waters was upon the earth, and bestowed the honor of its parentage upon the Trismegistus, or *thrice illustrious*, Egyptian Mercury. "The Nile," says Apollodorus, "after having overflowed the whole country of Egypt, when it returned within its natural bounds, left on the shore a great number of dead animals of various kinds, and, among the rest, a tortoise; the flesh of which being dried and wasted by the sun, nothing was left within the shell but nerves and cartilages, which, braced and contracted by desiccation, were rendered sonorous. Mercury, walking along the banks of the river, chanced to strike his foot against the shell of this tortoise, was pleased with the sound it produced, and upon reflection, conceived the idea of a *lyre*, which instrument he afterwards constructed in the form of a tortoise, stringing it with the dried sinews of dead animals."

The flute, or monaulos, according to Plutarch, was the invention of Apollo; while Athenæus [in Juba's Theatrical History] attributes its origin to the gréat Egyptian ruler and legislator, Osiris. Its first shape is said to have been that of a bull's horn; and Apuleius, speaking of its uses in the mysteries of Iris, call it the *crooked flute*.

The celerated Egyptians or Africans of Egypt, were, at a very early age, a people who took an elevated stand in the civilized world, and were familiar with all the varieties of knowledge which flourished in those days. The influence of civilization extended to the people inhabiting the adjoining countries.

About 285 years B. C., the distinguished Dionysius, of Alexandria, began his astronomical era on Monday, June 26, being the first who found the solar year to consist exactly of 365 days, 5 hours, and 49 minutes.

ASTRONOMY.

The Ptolemaic System was so called from Ptolemeus, an Ethiopian, a celebrated astronomer of Pelusium, in Egypt, who adopted and defended the prevailing system of that age. This Egyptian astronomer lived 130 years B. C. He supposed the earth immovably fixed in the centre of the universe, around which moved the sun and the planets from east to west, once in twenty-four hours, in the following order: the Moon, Mercury, Venus, the Sun, Mars, Jupiter, Saturn, Herschel; and beyond these were placed the fixed stars.

Astronomy was first attended to by the shepherds, on the beautiful plains of Egypt and Babylon. The Ethiopians, shepherds of Egypt and Chaldea, first acquired the knowledge of the stars, and designated them by proper names. The Thebans, says Diodorus, consider themselves the most ancient people of the East, and assert that philosophy and the science of the stars originated with them.

Astronomy is the science which describes the heavenly bodies—the sun, planets, fixed stars and comets. Assisted by astronomy we can observe the magnitude and calculate the periods and eclipses of the heavenly bodies. By it we learn the use of globes, the system of the world, and the preliminary law of nature. While we are employed in the study of this science, we must perceive unparalleled instances of wisdom and goodness through the whole creation, and trace the glorious Author by his works.

SUN, the great source of light and heat; brought into existence on the fourth day of creation. The diameter of the sun is about 800,000 miles. His distance from our earth is ninety-five millions of miles; so that light, which flies at the inconceivable swiftness of two hundred thousand miles in a second, requires eight minutes to reach our earth! A cannon ball shot thence, and moving with unabated swiftness, viz., (according to Durham,) a mile in eight and a half seconds, would take about thirty years to reach our earth.

MOON, or *lesser light*, is a planet revolving round the earth, and reflecting the light of the sun.

The use of the Globes was first found out by the Egyptians. The Globes are two artificial spherical bodies, on the convex surface of which are represented the countries, seas, and various parts of the earth, the face of the heavens, the planetary revolutions and other particulars.

Their principal use, beside serving as maps to distinguish the outward parts of the earth, and the situation of the fixed stars, is to illustrate and explain the phenomena arising from the annual revolution, and the diurnal rotation, of the earth round its own axis. They are the noblest instruments for improving the mind, and giving it the most distinct idea of any problem or proposition, as well as enabling it to solve the same. Contemplating these bodies, we are inspired with a due reverence for the Deity and his works, and are induced to encourage the studies of astronomy, geography, and navigation, and the arts dependent on them, by which man has been so much benefitted.

Maps, globes, and the signs of the Zodiac, invented by Anaximander, the scholar of Thales.

RHETORIC.

This science was first taught by the celebrated Apollinarii, of Africa. Victorinus, of Africa, had professed Rhetoric many years at Rome, and was held in such high reputation that a public statue was erected to his honor in that city.

Rhetoric teaches us to speak copiously and fluently on any subject, not merely with propriety alone, but with all the advantages of force and elegance, wisely contriving to captivate the hearer by strength of argument and beauty of expression, whether it be to entreat or exhort, to admonish or applaud.

The Egyptians first acquired the knowledge of Logic, Arithmetic and orders of Architecture.

Logic teaches us to guide our reason discretionally in the general knowledge of things, and directs our inquiries after truth. It consists of a regular train of argument, whence we infer, deduce, and conclude, according to certain premises laid down, admitted, or granted; and in it are employed the faculties of conceiving, judging; reasoning and disposing; all of which are naturally led on from one gradation to another, till the point in question is finally determined.

Arithmetic teaches the powers and properties of numbers, which is variously effected, by letters, tables, figures and instruments. By this art, reasons and demonstrations are given for finding out any certain number, whose relation or affinity to another is already known or discovered.

ARCHITECTURE.

From the first formation of society, order in architecture may be traced. When the rigor of seasons obliged men to contrive shelter from the inclemency of the weather, we learn that they first planted trees on end, and then laid others across, to support a covering. The bands which connected those trees at top and bottom, are said to have given rise to the idea of the base and capital of pillars, and from this simple hint originally proceeded the more improved art of architecture. By order in architecture is meant a system of proportions, and ornaments of columns and pilasters;—or, it is a regular arrangement of the projecting parts of a building, which, united with those of a column, form a beautiful, perfect, and complete whole.

SHIPS.—Noah's ark was probably the first vessel of this kind ever formed.

The first ship that was built was called the Egyptian Argus. She was brought into Greece from Egypt by Danaus, who arrived at Rhodis, with his five daughters.

By order of Nechao or Pharaoh Necho, king of Egypt, some Phœnicians sailed from the Red Sea round Africa, and returned by the Mediterranean.

The tribes of Zebulon and Dan appear to have early engaged in commerce.

Solomon, king of Israel, married Psammis, or Nechao Pharaoh's daughter, and was furnished by Hiram with seamen to navigate vessels to Ophir. The account of these voyages we have in 1 Kings ix. 26–28; and also chapter x. 5–22. Once in three years the king's navy came, bringing from Ophir gold and silver, ivory, apes, and peacocks.

Ezion Geber, the port from whence they set out, lies on the Red Sea, at the upper part. Down this sea they came, and along the coast of Africa, till they reached the country now called Sofala; but then known under the name of Ophir. They were three years in going and returning, and after king Solomon, Jehoshaphat sent out vessels to trade by sea.

The Trojans were powerful at sea, but the Tyrians and Sidonians for many ages were much more so; and after them, the Carthaginians. The Greeks were also in their turns famous by sea. Their navigation, however, was very imperfect, as, even in the time of Paul, vessels passing from Judea to Italy, frequently wintered on the way. The vessels were small, and generally had oars, as well as sails. The compass being unknown, they dared not go out of sight of land.

The ancients of Gebal, and the wise men thereof, were in thee thy caulkers; all the ships of the sea, with their mariners, were in thee, to occupy thy merchandise. (Ezek. xxvii. 9.)

The Phœnicians, an Ethiopian nation, greatly improved the art of navigation. But the world is indebted to the Ethiopians for blessings greater even than their alphabet, geometry, and navigation. These great principles would have been useless if unapplied, and if wrongly applied, worse than useless. The knowledge of its use gives an instrument its value; and this knowledge accompanied these principles. It was the true, *practical wisdom* of the Egyptians, by which the Grecian legislators raised their state to such dignity. The wisdom of the Egyptians pointed out the correct application of these principles, which it had first shown important, invaluable; and doubtless suggested many of the improvements which the Grecians afterwards made upon them. But for the Egyptians, Greece might have remained a country of barbarians to this day; the world, in consequence, in want of the rich stores of Grecian lore, and Rome, uncivilized by the arts and sciences of Greece, might have risen and fallen, distinguished only for its glory in blood and military horrors. The Egyptian sciences, and the religious feelings which the Grecians imbibed while studying in Egypt, and which they carefully cherished and diffused in their own country, are the parents of the boasted civilization and of much of the mental and physical enjoyments of those who, while they participate in them, are manifesting their grateful emotions in their barbarous, soul-sickening treatment of the offspring of their benefactors.

PYRAMIDS.—A Pyramid is a solid or hollow body having a large and generally a square base and terminating in a point.

There were three pyramids in Egypt more famous than the rest, one whereof deserved to be ranked among the seven wonders of the world; they did not stand very far from the city of Memphis. I shall take notice here only of the largest of the three. This pyramid, like the rest,

was built on a rock, having a square base, cut on the
outside of so many steps, and decreasing gradually quite
to the summit. It was built with stones of a prodigious
size, the least of which were thirty feet, wrought with
wonderful art, and covered with hieroglyphics. According to several ancient authors, each side was eight
hundred feet broad and as many high. The summit of
the pyramids, which to those who viewed it from below,
seemed a point, was a fine platform, composed of ten or
twelve massy stones, and each side of that platform sixteen or eighteen feet long.

M. de Chazelles, of the Academy of Sciences, who
went purposely on the spot in 1693, gives us the following dimensions.

The side of the square base,   110 fathoms.
The fronts are equilateral triangles, and ⎱ 12,100 square
  therefore the superficies of the base is ⎰   fathoms.
The perpendicular height,   77 3-6 fathoms.
The solid contents,   313,590 cubical fathoms.

An hundred thousand men were constantly employed
about this work, and were relieved every three months
by the same number. Ten complete years were spent
in hewing out the stones, either in Arabia or Ethiopia,
and in conveying them to Egypt; and twenty years more
in building this immense edifice, the inside of which
contained numberless rooms and apartments. There
was expressed on the pyramid, in Egyptian characters,
the sums it cost only in garlic, leeks, onions, and the
like, for the workmen; and the whole amounted to sixteen hundred talents of silver, (about £25,000 sterling,)
that is, four millions five hundred thousand French livres;
from whence it was easy to conjecture what a vast sum the
whole must have amounted to.

Pliny gives us, in a few words, a just idea of these
pyramids, when he calls them a foolish and useless ostentation of the wealth of the Egyptian kings; *Regum
pecuniæ otiosa ab stulta ostentio;* and adds, that by a just
punishment, their memory is buried in oblivion; the
historians not agreeing among themselves about the
names of those who first raised those vain monuments.
*Inter eos non constant a quibus factæ sint, justissimo casu
obliteratis tantæ vanitatis auctoribus.* In a word, accord-

ing to the judicious remark of Diodorus, the industry of
the architects of those pyramids is no less valuable and
praiseworthy, than the design of the Egyptian kings con-
temptible and ridiculous.

But what we should most admire in these ancient monuments, is, the true and standing evidence they give of
the skill of the Egyptians in astronomy; that is, in a
science which seems incapable of being brought to perfection, but by a long series of years, and a great number of observations. M. de Chazelles, when he measured the great pyramid in question, found that the four
sides of it were turned exactly to the four quarters of the
world, and consequently showed the true meridian of that
place. Now, as so exact a situation was in all probability purposely pitched upon by those who piled up this
huge mass of stones, above three thousand years ago, it
follows, that during so long a space of time, there has
been no alteration in the heavens in that respect, or
(which amounts to the same thing) in the poles of the
earth or the meridians. This is M. de Fontenelle's
remark in his eulogium of M. de Chazelles.

What has been said concerning the judgment we ought
to form of the pyramids, may also be applied to the Labyrinth, which Herodotus, who saw it, assures us was still
more surprising than the pyramids. It was built at the
most southern part of the lake of Mœris, whereof mention will be made presently, near the town of Crocodiles, the same with Arsinoe. It was not so much one
single palace, as a magnificent pile composed of twelve
palaces, regularly disposed, which had a communication
with each other. Fifteen hundred rooms, interspersed
with terraces, were ranged round twelve halls, and discovered no outlet to such as went to see them. There
were the like number of buildings under ground. These
subterraneous structures were designed as the burying
place of the kings, and (who can speak this without confusion and without deploring the blindness of man!) for
keeping the sacred crocodiles, which a nation, so wise in
other respects, worshipped as gods.

In order to visit the rooms and halls of the labyrinth,
it was necessary, as the reader will naturally suppose,
for people to take the same precaution as Ariadne made

Theseus use, when he was obliged to go and fight the
Minotaur in the labyrinth of Crete. Virgil describes it
in this manner:—

> And as the Cretan labyrinth of old,
>
> With wand'ring ways, and many a winding fold,
>
> Involved the weary way without redress,
>
> In a round error, which denied recess;
>
> Not far from thence he grav'd the wond'rous maze,
>
> A thousand doors, a thousand winding ways.

These Pyramids are among the most stupendous
works of man. They are the most ancient, too, having
been built before any accounts were written; beyond
the knowledge of history. Some regard them as the
work of the children of Israel when in bondage in
Egypt. Their purpose, too, is equally obscure: whether
as sepulchres for their kings, or as places for worship
at the top, a high place, as was the custom with many
nations; or as a cavern inside, which was the mode pre-
ferred by others. Their shape and solidity render them
very durable. Those who built them thought to render
themselves famous to posterity, but we do not now even
know their names.

The village of Gizeh, near Cairo, has those most eminent. Four of these are placed near together; the
largest of which covers eleven acres of ground. Its
height is 500 feet. The only room discovered in it is
about the middle, thirty-four feet long and seventeen
broad, which has nothing in it but a large stone chest,
without a lid, large enough for the body of a man; but
whether one was ever in it we cannot tell.

The Pyramids were inseparably associated with the
name of Egypt; they were formerly reckoned among the
seven wonders of the world, and they are now justly
ranked among the most remarkable monuments which
have ever been erected by the hand of man. It was
generally supposed that there were only three Pyramids,
this being the number at Gizeh, usually visited by travellers; but within fifty miles of that place were one hundred others, and it was supposed that upwards of two
hundred of these singular burial places were scattered
over Egypt and Nubia. We shall, however, confine

ourself to a description of the pyramids at Gizeh, and a description of one will serve for all the rest.

When a person first visited the Pyramids, he was struck with the vastness of their size, and the wonderful perfection of their structure; although of great antiquity, they exhibit no signs of decay. The extraordinary durability he conceived to arise from three causes, viz., the solidity of their foundation, a solid rock—the peculiarity of their form, being best calculated for duration—and the dryness of the climate, there not being alternate seasons of moisture and heat, which tended to produce mineral decomposition. The Pyramids were situated outside the boundaries of Egypt proper, being about three miles from the spot where terminates the inundation of the Nile. They were doubtless built there in conformity with an Egyptian law, mentioned by Plutarch, prohibiting the burial of any person on a spot of land capable of giving sustenance to the living. Thus the Pyramids and Catacombs, those immense sepulchres above and below the surface of the earth, were built outside of the territories which were overflowed by the waters of the Nile.

Of the origin of the Pyramids nothing positively was known. Of all the monuments of ancient greatness, the origin of none is involved in so great obscurity. Tradition has only preserved the names of the kings by whom they were supposed to have been built. They contain neither within them nor about them any pictorial or hieroglyphic emblems—from which an inference is drawn that the Pyramids were erected before this kind of writing was discovered. All the other Egyptian monuments were covered with hieroglyphics.

The size of the Pyramids was so great that it was almost impossible to conceive of their magnitude. Much discrepancy existed in the various estimates of their size made by travellers—they varying in their measurements from 564 to 800 feet. This discrepancy could be accounted for, from the fact that the Pyramids were exposed to the winds of the desert and were sometimes half buried in the sand. But when the wind blew in an opposite direction, the sand was carried away, and the Pyramids appeared in their proper dimensions. The statements of Herodotus were probably to be relied on; he found the base of the Pyramid of Cheops to measure 800 feet square—the perpendicular height 686 feet—and the slope from the outer part of the base to the top, 720 feet. By these measurements their size might be estimated. A French *savant* who accompanied Bonaparte to Egypt, in 1800, had made an estimate, that if the solid contents of the Pyramid of Cheops were turned into a quarry, and cut up for building, it would furnish materials for constructing a wall around the whole kingdom of France, six feet high, and one foot thick! Mr. Lyell, the celebrated English geologist, has calculated this Pyramid contained a mass of stone weighing *six millions of tons!* Now the shipping of the United States amounted to 1,800,000 tons; but supposing it to amount to 2,000,000, it would require all the vessels of every description in America, to make three voyages to Egypt, before they could bring away all the materials of which the Pyramid of Cheops was built. One of the other Pyramids at Gizeh was equal to it in size; the third was somewhat smaller. The various Pyramids scattered through Egypt and Nubia might average about half their size.

The base of the largest Pyramid covers 11 acres. The stones are above thirty feet in length, and the layers are 208; 360,000 men were employed in its erection.

CATACOMBS.—The Catacombs of Egypt were vast excavations in the solid rock, intended for the reception of the embalmed bodies of the people of Egypt. Those Catacombs were of various sizes, averaging half a furlong in width and a furlong in length. It was the custom when an individual died, to cause his body to be embalmed. It was then taken to the burial place and placed upon its feet. Rows of the dead were thus formed—some attention being paid to uniformity of size —and the whole surface of the Catacomb would be thus closely covered; insomuch that at this day some of these burial places appear to be *paved with human skulls.* Another layer of bodies was placed on top, and then another, until the excavation could contain no more. Some of these burial places contained 100,000 bodies, and probably none less than 10,000. It was estimated that there were now upwards of *two hundred millions of the embalmed bodies of the old Egyptians in the Catacombs of Egypt.*

SPHYNX.—The great Sphynx of Egypt laid partly buried in sand at the base of the Pyramids. This emblematic figure was common in Egypt; the sphynx being composed of the body of a lion and the bust of a virgin. The ancient Egyptians adored the Nile, and the learned men were consulted to design an emblem of this noble river—and as the inundation of the Nile took place when the sun was passing out of Leo into Virgo, the Sphynx was devised as emblematic of the inundation of the Nile. The size of the great Sphynx was enormous—it being 160 feet in length on the back, and 30 feet from the top of the forehead to the chin; its eye was a little cavern, and its under lip appeared like a spacious shelf, on which a person might lay at length. The feet, with the claws, projected 52 feet — and the whole length of the Sphynx was about 200 feet. In addition to its vast size, the scale of its proportions had been very much admired; but its face had been much mutilated by the Arabs, and consequently had lost all the beauty which, according to history, it originally possessed.

LABYRINTH.—The Egyptian Labyrinth was a wonderful work of art, which was thought to have been the model of the famous Labyrinth of Crete. It was composed, according to Herodotus, of twelve courts, all of which were covered; their entrances were opposite to each other, six to the north and six to the south. One wall enclosed the whole. The apartments were of two kinds—1500 above the surface of the ground, and as many beneath—in all 3000. The ceilings and walls were all of marble, the latter richly adorned with the finest sculpture; around each court were pillars of the whitest and most polished marble. At the point where the labyrinth terminates, stands a pyramid 160 cubits high, having large figures of animals engraved on its outside, and the entrance to it is by a subterraneous path.

There was little doubt that for whatever purpose the Labyrinth was built, it was subsequently used for initiating the Egyptian priest into the rites and mysteries and

20

impostures of their religion. Before any candidates were admitted to the priesthood, their resolution and fortitude were put to severe tests — as would be fully seen in "The Epicurean," a work by Thomas Moore, in which a detailed and accurate description was given of these initiations. [Mr. Buckingham's Lectures on Egypt.]

THE LAKE OF MŒRIS.

The noblest and most wonderful of all the structures or works of the kings of Egypt, was the lake of Mœris: accordingly, Herodotus considers it as vastly superior to the pyramids and labyrinth. As Egypt was more or less fruitful in proportion to the inundations of the Nile; and as in these floods the too general flow or ebb of the waters were equally fatal to the lands; king Mœris, to prevent these inconveniencies, and correct, as far as lay in his power, the irregularities of the Nile, thought proper to call art to the assistance of nature; and so caused the lake to be dug, which afterwards went by his name. This lake was about three thousand six hundred stadia, that is, one hundred and eighty French leagues in circuit, and three hundred feet deep. Two pyramids, on each of which stood a colossal statue, seated on a throne, raised their heads to the height of three hundred feet, in the midst of the lake, whilst their foundations took up the same space under the water; a proof that they were erected before the cavity was filled, and a demonstration that a lake of such vast extent was the work of man's hands, in one prince's reign. This is what several historians have related concerning the lake Mœris, on the testimony of the inhabitants of the country. And the Bishop of Meaux, in his discourse on Universal History, relates the whole as fact. With regard to myself, I will confess, that I do not see the least probability in it. Is it possible to conceive, that a lake of an hundred and eighty leagues in circumference, could have been dug in the reign of one prince? In what manner, and where, could the earth taken from it be conveyed? What should prompt the Egyptians to lose the surface of so much land? By what arts could they fill this vast tract with the superfluous waters of the

Nile? Many other objections might be made. In my opinion, therefore, we ought to follow Pomponius Mela, an ancient geographer; especially as his account is confirmed by several modern travellers. According to that author, this lake is but twenty thousand paces, that is, seven or eight French leagues in circumference. *Mœris aliquando campus, nunc lacus, viginti millia passuum in circuitu patens.*

This lake had a communication with the Nile, by a great canal, four leagues long, and fifty feet broad.— Great sluices either opened or shut the canal and lake, as there was occasion.

The charge of opening or shutting them amounted to fifty talents, that is, fifty thousand French crowns.— The fishing of this lake brought the monarch immense sums; but its chief use related to the overflowing of the Nile. When it rose too high, and was like to be attended with fatal consequences, the sluices were opened; and the waters, having a free passage into the lake, covered the lands no longer than was necessary to enrich them.— On the contrary, when the inundation was too low, and threatened a famine, a sufficient quantity of water, by the help of drains, was let out of the lake, to water the lands. In this manner the irregularities of the Nile were corrected; and Strabo remarks, that, in his time, under Petronius, a governor of Egypt, when the inundation of the Nile was twelve cubits, a great plenty ensued; and even when it rose but to eight cubits, the dearth was scarce felt in the country; doubtless, because the waters of the lake made up for those of the inundation, by the help of canals and drains.

The lake Mœris—an immense reservoir, of artificial construction—which was designed and executed when the twelve kings reigned over the twelve several districts called Nomes. During a period of profound peace, a Congress was held, in which they deliberated on the means of erecting a public monument, which should not only redound to their own glory, but subserve the interests of the great body of the Egyptian people. For this purpose, they concluded to construct the Lake Mœris, to assist in irrigating the country, and to remedy the evils caused by the inequality in the inundations of the

Nile. This lake was constructed on the Lybian side; and canals were cut to convey the waters to and from that great river, and by this means the soil could always be overflowed whenever the Nile did not rise as high as it was wont. This important work was planned with much care and calculation. To be of great service it was necessary that it should be of vast extent; and accordingly it was the most stupendous work ever undertaken by the hand of man—being, according to Diodorus Siculus, 420 miles in circumference—according to Strabo, 450—and according to Herodotus, 500! It was situated about 350 miles from the sea, and 10 miles from the banks of the Nile — being nearly in the centre of Egypt.

In order to convey to posterity the fact that this immense lake was constructed by the hand of man, two pyramids were erected within it, each of 400 cubits in height, one half of each being submerged in the water, and the other half rising above the surface. As these pyramids must have been built before the waters were let into the lake, they afford conclusive proof that it was of artificial construction. It was calculated that the fertility of Egypt was increased one-fourth by means of this wonderful artificial lake, and thus amply repaid the expenses of its construction.

It was supposed that the vast quantity of soil which must have been removed in order to form the lake, was used to construct the banks of the lake and the embankments of the canals, and the remainder was conveyed to the Nile, and swept away by the currents towards the ocean, and probably assisted in forming the Delta. The Lake is now diminished in size, being only about 150 miles in circumference, and is gradually diminishing.

Near to the shore of Lake Mœris stood a pyramid, built of brick, on which was an inscription implying that it was constructed of the earth taken from the lake. It was in a very dilapidated state, and the pyramids in the centre of the lake were nearly destroyed by the combined action of the water and air.

Mr. Buckingham described a light house which stood in "olden time" on the river of the Nile.

TEMPLES OF EGYPT.

All the Egyptian temples have two massive towers in front —standing as it were an advanced guard— built in the form of a semi-pyramid, and supporting an immense gateway. The famous temple of Tentyra, of exceeding beauty, was dedicated to Isis. Its architecture was peculiar, the massive capitals having on each side a face of Isis. This temple was not large, compared with many of the temples in Egypt, but was about double the size of the largest cathedrals in England, being 400 feet long, 200 broad, and 60 or 70 high. Its portico was very remarkable, it being carved with hieroglyphics and figures of the Egyptian deities, and bearing on the surface of one of the pillars a representation of the zodiac and the celestial hemisphere. This was regarded with much interest by the French savans, who thought that a clue could thus be obtained to the Egyptian records of the age of the world. It was copied, and sent to various scientific societies. But the learned expositors of this zodiac, interpreted the hieroglyphics differently, in order to support the particular theory of each individual, and hence this curious zodiac threw no light on the age of the world. This zodiac has since been removed, and is now in the Louvre at Paris.

The Egyptian Temple of Hermopolis, the body of which was in ruins, but the portico remains entire, strikes the stranger not only with admiration, but with awe. The massiveness of the pillars, the high and overhanging cornice, the mysterious hieroglyphics, all combine to produce a feeling of intense veneration and sublimity.

The Temple of Apollinopolis is on the bank of the Nile, and is remarkable for its great size. It has two massive towers in front—standing as it were an advanced guard—built in the form of a semi-pyramid, and supporting an immense gateway. On the summit of the gateway which connects the two towers of the temple of Apollinopolis they were constructed— a very elevated spot. The temple of Apollinopolis is 2,000 feet long—500 feet broad, and the walls are covered on every part with the most perfect specimens of sculpture. The pillars of the portico are each as large as Pompey's Pillar — ten and a half feet in diameter — and no two are exactly alike — a favorite mode of building with the Egyptians. In this temple are seen representations of the views which the Egyptians entertained of a future state; as the passage of the souls across the dark river — some of whom are seen ascending the steps leading to the higher regions — and several superior beings are holding in their hands tablets, and noting down the good and bad actions of those who seek to pass, that they may be brought forward at the final judgment. In the neighborhood are a number of sepulchres, on the walls of which are representations of human sacrifices — rites which some suppose have never been performed by any nation.

THE EXPLANATION OF FIVE GRAND VIRTUES.

TRUTH.—Truth is a divine attribute, and the foundation of every virtue. To be good and true, is the first lesson we are taught in Scripture. On this theme we contemplate, and by its dictates endeavor to regulate our conduct: hence, while influenced by this principle, hypocrisy and deceit are unknown among us; sincerity and plain dealing distinguish us; and the heart and tongue join in promoting each other's welfare, and rejoicing in each other's prosperity.

JUSTICE.—Justice is that standard, or boundary of right, which enables us to render to every man his just due, without distinction. This virtue is not only considered with divine and human laws, but is the very cement and support of civil society; and as justice in a great measure constitutes the real good of man, so should it be the invariable practice of every friend, never to deviate from the minutest principles thereof. * * * * *

TEMPERANCE.—Temperance is that due restraint upon our affections and passions, which renders the body tame and governable, and frees the mind from the allurements of vice. This virtue should be the constant practice of every man; as he is thereby taught to avoid excess, or contracting any licentious or vicious habit, the indulgence of which might lead him to ruin.

PRUDENCE.—Prudence teaches us to regulate our lives and actions agreeably to the dictates of reason, and is that habit by which we wisely judge, and prudentially determine on all things relative to our present as well as to our future happiness. This virtue should be the peculiar characteristic of every man.

FORTITUDE.—Fortitude is that noble and steady purpose of the mind, whereby we are enabled to undergo any pain, peril or danger, when prudentially deemed expedient. This virtue is equally distant from rashness and cowardice; and, like the former, should be deeply impressed upon the mind of every man, as a safe guard or security against any illegal attack that may be made, by force or otherwise, to extort from him any of those valuable secrets with which he has been so solemnly intrusted.

THE GRECIAN PHILOSOPHERS.

Plato, an Ethiopian, was an eminent Grecian philosopher, called the Divine.

Socrates, a Grecian philosopher — the best of the wise men.

Thales, of Miletus, travelled into Egypt — acquired the knowledge of geometry and philosophy, and returned to Greece.

THE ROMAN PHILOSOPHERS.

BOETHIUS, a Roman platonic philosopher.

Epictetus a stoic philosopher, who was once a slave to Epaphroditus, an officer of the Emperor Nero's Guards.

Seneca, Nero's tutor, the celebrated Roman stoic philosopher. He was put to death by Nero.

CHAPTER IX.

MODERN EMINENT COLORED MEN.

MODERN EMINENT COLORED MEN.

The distinguished colored president of the South American states, General Guerrero, late president of Mexico, was a colored man; so is General Alvarez, one of the most distinguished of the Mexican generals, and some of the most prominent men of the Mexican Congress are mulattos. General Paez, the distinguished president of Venezuela, is also a colored man. General Piar, who bore a conspicuous part in the commencement of the Columbian revolution, was a mulatto. General Sucre, the commander-in-chief at the battle of Ayacucho, in 1824, the most remarkable ever fought in South America, was a black man. In 1826 he was elected president of Bolivia.

Colored lawyers and physicians are found in all parts of Europe, and some of the highest offices in the state are filled by black men.

Alex. Dumas, a black man, was one of the most literary characters of the West India Islands, and a general of artillery. General Dumas for a long time commanded a legion in the French army, and was one of Bonaparte's favorite generals of division, and named by him the "Horatius Cocles of the Tyrols." His son, a mulatto, is deemed second only in literature to Victor Hugo, and it is said he has received the distinguished honor of being elected a member of the French Institute.

Geoffroy L'Islet, a mulatto, originally an officer of artillery in the French army, was elected a corresponding member of the Academy of Sciences at Paris, and was living a few years since.

Scipio Africanus, an African, in his boyhood, was one of the playmates of Louis Phillippe, the present king of the French, and was one of the family of the Duke of Orleans, [Egalite.] Scipio afterwards became an officer in the French army, under Joubert, and was killed with that officer at the battle of Novi, in 1779.

Pellet, a highly respected and popular officer in the National Guards of France, is a dark mulatto.

The celebrated Kina, a black, was a favorite officer in the British army, and who, on a visit to London, received the most flattering attentions in honor of his services in the West Indies.

Annibal, an African, was a general and director of artillery in the army of Peter the Great, who conferred upon him, as a mark of honor, the order of Saint Alexander Neuski. His son, a mulatto, was, in 1784, a lieutenant general of artillery in the Russian service.

It is a fact well known, that some of the highest officers in the Turkish and Persian empires have been filled by blacks and mulattos.

Some of the most distinguished officers in the Brazilian army are blacks and mulattos.

"Prejudice against color" has never existed in Great Britain, France, Spain, Portugal, the Italian States, Prussia, Austria, Russia, or in any part of the world where colored persons have not been held as slaves. Indeed, in many countries, where multitudes of Africans and their descendants have been long held slaves, no prejudice against color has ever existed. This is the case in Turkey, Brazil, and Persia. In Brazil there are more than two millions of slaves. Yet some of the highest offices of state are filled by the black men. Some of the most distinguished officers in the Brazilian army are blacks and mulattos.

There are distinguished lawyers, professors, physicians, &c., [blacks and mulattos,] in Lisbon and other parts of Portugal, in France and England, in the West Indies, and in all parts of the civilized world, except the United States and Texas.

The celebrated M. Pay, a mulatto, was one of the most popular lawyers at the royal court of Martinique.

The celebrated Mentor, a black, a native of Martinique,

was one of the members of the French national assembly between forty and fifty years since.

The distinguished Price Watkis, a mulatto, recently deceased, for the last ten years of his life was at the head of the Jamaica bar, and for a long time a distinguished member of the assembly.

Mr. Osborn, a mulatto, was elected to the assembly by the parish of St. Andrews. Mr. Osborn was, a few years since appointed, by the Governor, a magistrate of the parish in which he resided, and a judge of the court room of common pleas.

Richard Hill, a dark mulatto, has been for a number of years at the head of the special magistracy in Jamaica, a body of about sixty magistrates, and their official organ of communication with the government. When Lord Sligo was governor of Jamaica, Mr. Hill was his official Secretary, and an inmate of his family. His lordship, when in New York in the summer of 1839, on his return to England, speaking of Mr. Hill, said, " with no gentleman in the West Indies was I, in social life, on terms of more intimate friendship."

The distinguished A. De Castro, a mulatto, was aid-de-camp to the governor general of the Danish West Indies, and, also, his son is aid-de-camp to the governor of St. Thomas.

The secretary of the governor of Antigua, in 1837, was a mulatto; so is a Mr Athill, who was at the same time postmaster-general of Antigua, and a member of assembly.

The celebrated Gustavus Vasa, a black, was born at Benin. He resided many years in London, where he mingled with refined society, and was highly respected. His son, Sancho, was assistant librarian to Sir Joseph Banks, and secretary to the Vaccine Institution.

The celebrated George Washington Jefferson, a mulatto from St. Domingo, who resides near Brighton, England, associates with the most respectable society, and is a director in a bank there.

Edward Jordan, a mulatto, has been for many years editor of the ablest and most influential paper published in Jamaica. Mr. J. has also been, for some years, a leading member of the Jamaica assembly, and alderman of the city of Kingston.

The celebrated Prince Sanders was a dark mulatto. He was a native of Boston, but resided many years in London, where he was a great favorite in fashionable circles — was invited to breakfast with the Prince Regent, and received flattering attentions from distinguished literary characters.

Hundreds of the Roman Catholic clergy are black and colored men. These ministers to congregations are made up indiscriminately of blacks and whites. For a century past, a considerable portion of the Roman Catholic clergy in the Cape de Verd Islands have been blacks.

The distinguished Capitein, a black, a native of Guinea, was graduated with great applause at the University of Leyden, in Holland, and afterwards became a clergyman.

The distinguished Girard, a young man of color from Gaudaloupe, who received, amongst other prizes, the prize of honor. Villemain, the minister of public instruction, placed the crown or wreath on Girard's head, embraced him, and delivered to him his prizes amidst the unanimous applauses of the collegians and spectators. Girard was then invited to dine with the king, and he spent three days with the royal family at St. Cloud.

The celebrated Thomas Jenkins, a black, a native of Guinea, was, for a number of years, a teacher of a parish school near Edinburgh, in Scotland; he afterwards entered the university, where he distinguished himself for scholarship. He was so great a favorite with the faculty, that the professors generally relinquished their fees to assist him in his education. He eventually became a preacher, and was deputed, by the British Society, for promoting Christian knowledge as a missionary to Mauritius, where he still resides.

The celebrated Ignatius Sancho was a black — the associate of Garrick, and the friend and correspondent of Sterne.

The celebrated Correa de Serra was a black, and the Secretary of the Portuguese academy.

A SELF-TAUGHT MAN.—At a meeting of the Synod of Alabama, on the third week in January, 1840, contributions were called for to purchase a colored man, [a slave,] of extraordinary character. It was stated that he was a good classical scholar, and wholly self-taught. He is a blacksmith; and it was stated on the floor of the Synod, by members and others, who knew him, that he first learned the letters of the alphabet, by inducing his master's children and others, to make the letters, one at a time, on the door of his shop. In this way he familiarized himself with the letters and their names. He then learned to put them together and make words, and soon he was able to read. He then commenced the study of arithmetic, and then English grammar and geography. It was also stated that he is now able to read the Greek Testament with ease — has some knowledge of the Latin Language, and even commenced the study of the Hebrew language, but relinquished it in consequence of not having suitable books. It was stated that he studied nights till 11 or 12 o'clock, and that in conversing with him, they felt themselves in the presence of their equal. He is between 30 and 35 years of age, and is willing to go out as a missionary to Africa, under the Assembly's Board. [Newburyport Herald.]

CHAPTER X.

THE GREAT HISTORICAL AGES.

THE ANCIENT AND MODERN DISTINGUISHED HISTORIANS AND WRITERS, THE DESCENDANTS OF AFRICA AND ASIA.

EVERY age has produced heroes and politicians; all nations have experienced revolutions; and all histories are nearly alike, to those who seek only to furnish their memories with facts; but whoever thinks, or, what is still rare, whoever has taste, will find but three ages in the history of the world. These three happy ages are those in which the arts were carried to perfection; and which, by serving as the era of the greatness of the human mind, are examples for posterity.

The first of these ages to which true glory is annexed, is that of Philip and Alexander, or that of a Pericles, a Demosthenes, an Aristotle, a Plato, an Apelles, a Phidias, and a Praxiteles, &c.

The second age is that of Cæsar and Augustus, distinguished likewise by the names of Lucretius, Cicero, Titus, Livius, Virgil, Horace, Ovid, Varro, Vitruvius, &c.

The third is that which followed the taking of Constantinople by Mahomet II., a Moor.

ANCIENT HISTORIANS.

THE Old Testament was written in Africa, and Cœlo Syria in the land of Moab, and translated into the Greek tongue, from the Hebrew, by the Egyptian and Jerusalem Jews, by order of Ptolemy Philadelphus, an Ethiopian, king of Egypt.

The Greek translation of the Old Testament was first
began, at least, in Egypt; thence it found its way into
Ethiopia. Greek was understood by superior persons
there, and from this translation it is highly probable that,
without any other teacher, the Ethiopians obtained the
knowledge of the true God, and thus became first prose-
lyted to Judaism, and then converted to Christianity.

Next to the historical books of the Old Testament,
the most ancient history worthy of perusal is that of
Herodotus, the father of profane history, which is in nine
books. In the second book of his History of Egypt,
and the manners of the Egyptians, he states that the
Egyptians were black, and their hair frizzly, &c. Herodotus has been translated by Beloe, in four volumes.

Livy, the prince of Roman historians, wrote a work
of 132 books. Many of these are lost; those which are
extant have been translated by Baker. In this work are
found the lives of Hannibal, Scipio Africanus, Flamin-
ius, Paulus Æmilius, the elder Cato, the Gracchi, Marius,
Scylla, the younger Cato, Sertorius, Lucullus, Julius
Cæsar, Cicero, Pompey and Brutus, Ethiopians or
Africans.

Plutarch; translated by Langhorne.

Polybius wrote a general history of the Greeks and
Romans, in forty books; translated by Hampton.

The works of Appian originally consisted of twenty
books of the history of Rome from the earliest period.

Sallust, the first philosophical Roman historian. This
work has been translated into English by Murphy, by
Stuart, and by Rose.

Xenophon's History of Greece, translated by Smith.

The History of Arrian, translated by Rook.

Thucydides, an eminent Greek historian; translated
by Smith.

Dionysius Halicarnassus wrote a history of Rome;
translated by Spelman.

Ephorus and Temæus.

Tacitus; translated by Murphy.

Cornelius Nepos and Appianus Alexander.

The celebrated Justin, an African, wrote his first
apology for the Christians about 136 years after Christ.
His history is translated by Turnbull.

Eusebius, the father of Ecclesiastical History, was born in Cæsarea, of Palestine, the inhabitants of which were descendants of Ham.

Pausanias, Aristoteles, Isocrates, Diogenes Laertius, Athenæus.

Procopius, a Roman historian, and last of the classical writers.

Strabo, an Ethiopian, a celebrated historian. His Ancient Geography was written in Greek. We hope this work will be translated into English.

Eratosthenes, an African poet of Cyrene.

Josephus, a Jewish historian, wrote his book in Greek. It has been translated into English

Euclid, an Ethiopian, a Greek writer in Geometry. Three hundred years before Christ, he was at the head of the most celebrated mathematical school in the world.

Archimedes, a celebrated disciple of Euclid.

Julius Cæsar, an African.

Plato, an Ethiopian, a wise and learned Grecian writer.

Proclus, a learned Platonist.

Origen and Cyprian, learned Christian writers.

Photius, a learned Christian writer and philosopher.

Lactantius, an elegant writer, and an able defender of Christianity.

ANCIENT POETS.

THE first kind of poetry that was among the Romans was the verses made by Numa, a prince of Rome, which the Salian priests sung in his time. Pythagoras, either in the same reign, or, if you please, some time after, gave the Romans a tincture of poetry as well as philosophy; for Cicero assures us that the Pythagorians made great use of poetry and music.

Callimachus, an African poet of Cyrene.

Orpheus, Musæus, and Linus, were before Homer's time.

Homer, an Ethiopian, the greatest of the Grecian poets; a historian likewise.

Anacreon, a Greek poet, and father of the Anacreontic verse.

Pindar, the chief of the Grecian lyric poets.

Lucilius, an early Roman poet.

Lucretius, a Roman didactic poet.

Virgil, the prince of Roman poets.

Horace, the greatest of the Roman lyric poets.

Boethius, also distinguished in other departments of literature.

Claudian, an elegant Latin poet.

Aleman, a lyric poet.

Æschylus, Sophocles, and Euripides, distinguished Athenian poets.

David, Solomon, Asaph, and the Hebrew prophets, were poets unequalled by any others, of whatever name or nation. The blacks were the ancient poets and learned historians.

We recommend our colored and Indian brethren to procure the true copies, translated from the Hebrew, Greek and Latin, by our friends, the unprejudiced French, Spanish and English historians.

The celebrated Homer was an Ethiopian, the greatest of the Grecian poets, and a historian. He travelled into Egypt, from whence he brought into Greece the names of their gods, and the chief ceremonials of their worship. &c. Homer divided the Ethiopians into two parts, and Strabo maintains that the division line to which he alluded was the Red Sea. Homer's poems were introduced into Greece about 886 years before Christ. He was among the first and probably the most eminent of all the writers of heathen antiquity. The literary world down to this day have bowed to his authority, and owned the force of his genius. His poems have been taken as the model of all similar poems, written since his day. It had a powerful influence over the Grecian mind, inspiring them to many of their noblest actions.

Smyrna, a celebrated city of Ionia, built by the Amazonians, the descendants of Ham, was famous as early as the time of Homer, whose birthplace it claims to be. Then Smyrna was in all its glory, abounding in all the works of art and learning.

Hanno, the father of Hamilcar, was an African writer and a general. There is still extant a Greek version of a treatise drawn up by Hanno in the Punic tongue, relating to a voyage he made by order of the Carthaginian Senate, with a considerable fleet, round Africa, for the settling of different colonies in that part of the world.

Hamilcar, an African writer and a General of Carthage, was a man of profound wisdom and knowledge, who honored his native country as much by his pen as with his sword. His fleet consisted of two thousand ships of war, and upwards of three thousand small vessels of burden, and his land forces amounted to three hundred thousand men.

The celebrated Hannibal, the son of Hamilcar, was an African writer and a great general of Carthage. He in all respects was an ornament to that city, for he was well acquainted with polite literature, and director of artillery. He led the Carthaginians across the Alps, and in the heart of Italy displayed a military bravery and skill, unsurpassed by the most distinguished Roman commanders.

The celebrated Mago, supposed to have been Hannibal's brother, was a distinguished African writer and a general of Carthage. He did as much honor to the city with his pen as by his victories. He wrote twenty-eight volumes upon husbandry, in the Punic language. These volumes were so highly esteemed by the Romans, that the Roman Senate ordered them to be translated into the Greek, by Cassius Dionysius, of Utica, a city in Africa, from whose version we may suppose the Latin was made. These volumes were found in the libraries of Africa, when Carthage was taken by the Romans.

Clitomachus, an African, called in the Punic language Asdrubal, the brother of Hannibal. He was a great philosopher, and a commander of the Carthaginian army. He succeeded the distinguished Carneades, whose disciple he had been, and maintained in Athens the honor of the Academic sect.

The famous Tertullian flourished at Carthage in the second and third century. He was the first Latin writer of the Church of Christ whose works have come down to us. Among his writings was an admirable apology for the Christian religion. He wrote many books in Latin.

21

Terence, an African, a native of Carthage, was the most elegant and refined of all the dramatic writers who appeared on the Roman stage.

The celebrated Cicero, an African, wrote several valuable books, viz., Clitomachus, Homo, Acutus diligens, Ut Pœnus, and Valde Studiosus. In one of which he composed a piece to console the unhappy citizens of Carthage, who by the ruin of their city were reduced to slavery under the Romans.

The celebrated elder Cato, an African. Cicero, Quintilian and Pliny celebrated the writings of the elder Cato, whose principal works were historical. We have his Fragment [De Re Rustica] on Agriculture, in which he was imitated by Varro, one of the earliest of the good writers among the Romans, and a man of universal erudition of the variety of his talents. We may judge not only from the splendid eulogium of Cicero, but from the circumstance of Pliny's having recourse to his authority, in every book of his natural history.

The celebrated Phædrus, an African, wrote fables in Iambic verse. He flourished, and formed his style of writing under Augustus; and his book, though it did not appear till the reign of Tiberius, deserves, on all accounts, to be reckoned among the works of the Augustan age. Fabulæ Æsopeæ was probably the title which he gave his fables.

Afranius. We have a very great loss in the works of Afranius, for he was regarded, even in the Augustan age, as the most exact imitator of Menander. He owns, himself, that he had no restraint in copying him; or any other of the Greek comic writers.

St. Cyprian, an African writer. The powers of genius and arts of eloquence were introduced by him alone of the learned among the Pagan writers. He was capable of pleasing their taste.

The celebrated Origen, an African. The history written by this learned father, is still extant: viz., The Philocalia of Origen, consisting of scriptural questions and Origen's Comments.

The celebrated Eusebius of Cæsarea, in Phœnicia. He was one of the most learned of all Christian historians. He was in Africa, Egypt, Thebais, Palestine, Phœnicia,

&c., when martyrs were put to death. Many of the modern historians refer to him.

Plautus. He was the first that consulted his own genius, and confined himself to that species of dramatic writing, for which he was the best fitted by nature.

The celebrated St. Augustine, an African, was born in the city of Tagasta, in Algiers, [the ancient Numidia.] His father's name was Patricius, a pagan, and continued till near his death. Manica, his mother, was renowned for her Christian piety. St. Augustine wrote several valuable histories, some of them related to the Donatists, and the narrative of Passidonius, &c.

A short View of Augustine's City of God.

This great and extensive work is in itself so remarkable a monument of genius, learning, and piety united, and deserves so well both of the classical scholar and the theologian, that the reader will either expect some account of it, or at least excuse me if I attempt it. Ecclesiastical antiquity has been too much depreciated in our times, and students in divinity have been discouraged from the study of the fathers. In truth, a selection of them ought to be made ; to praise or dispraise the primitive writers, in general, is obviously absurd. But Augustine's City of God deserves an unqualified commendation. The young student who shall meditate upon it with deep attention, will find it richly to repay his labor, and the following review of its plan and contents may teach him what he is to expect from it.

The capture of Rome by Alaric the Goth, and the subsequent plunder and miseries of the imperial city, had opened the mouths of the Pagans, and the true God was blasphemed on the account. Christianity was looked on as the cause of the declension of the empire ; and however trifling such an argument may appear at this day, at that time it had so great a weight, that it gave occasion to Augustine, in his zeal for the house of God, to write this treatise.

The work itself consists of twenty-two books. The first states the objections made by the pagans, and answers them in form. It was a remarkable fact, that all who fled

to the church called the Basilicæ of the Apostles, whether
Christians or not, were preserved from military fury. The
author takes notice of this singular circumstance, as a
proof of the great authority of the name and doctrine of
Christ, even among pagans, and shows that no instance
can be found in their history, where many vanquished people were spared out of respect to their religious worship. He justly observes, therefore, that the evils accom-
panying the late disaster ought to be ascribed to the usual
events of war, the benefits to the power of the name of
Christ. His thoughts on the promiscuous distribution of
good and evil in this life are uncommonly excellent. "If
all sin, he observes, were now punished, nothing might
seem to be reserved to the last judgment. If the Divinity
punished no sin openly, now his providence might be denied. In like manner in prosperous things, if some petitions for temporal things were not abundantly answered,
it might be said that they were not at God's disposal. If
all petitions were granted, it might be thought that we
should serve God only for the sake of worldly things."
And in a number of elegant allusions he goes on to show
the benefit of afflictions to the righteous, and the curse
which accompanies them to the wicked.* He mentions
also the propriety of punishing the godly often in this life,
because they are not sufficiently weaned from the world,
and because they do not rebuke the sins of the world as
they ought, but conform too much to the taste of ungodly
men. He answers the objections drawn from their suffer-
ings in the late disaster. "Many Christians, say they, are
led captive. It would be very miserable, he owns, if they
could be led to any place where they could not find their
God." In the same book he excellently handles the subject of suicide, demonstrates its cowardice, and exposes
the pusillanimity of Cato. He mentions the prayer of
Paulinus, bishop of Nola, who had reduced himself to
poverty for the sake of Christ, when the barbarians laid
waste his city: "Lord, suffer me not to be tormented on
account of gold and silver; for, where all my wealth is,

---

*Pari motu exagitatum and exhalat horribiliter cœnum, et suaviter fra-
grat unguentum, &c. It is a just recommendation of this treatise, that its
Latinity is of a superior taste to that of his other works, which were written to the populace ; this was meant for the perusal of philosophers.

thou knowest." For there he had his all, where the Lord
hath directed us to lay up our treasure, and he strougly in-
sists, as the fullest answer to objections, that the saint loses
nothing by all his afflictions.

Having sufficiently spoken to the particular occasion, he
proceeds in the second book, to wage offensive war with
the pagans, and shows, that while their religion prevailed,
it never promoted the real benefit of men. In this book
he proves his point with respect to moral evils. Immoral
practices were not discouraged or prohibited in the least
by the popular idolatry, but, on the contrary, vice and fla-
gitiousness were encouraged. He triumphs in the peculiar excellence of Christian institutes, because, by them instruction was constantly diffused among the body of the
people, of which the whole system of pagan worship was
void. His observations on stage-plays,* and on the vicious
manners of the Romans, even in the best times of their
republic, as confessed by Sallust, or, at least deduced by
fair inference from his writings, are extremely worthy of
attention, nor have I seen a more just estimate any where
of Roman virtue, than is to be found in this and some following books. The classical reader will do well to at-
tend to his remarks, after he has made himself master of
the historical facts. And, it is only one instance among
many of the unhappy propensity of the age to infidelity,
that the specious sophisms of Montesquieu, concerning the
virtue of the Roman republic, are so much sought after,
and held in such veneration, while the solid arguments of
Augustine are scarce known among us. He eloquently
describes what sort of felicity a carnal heart would desire,
and in the description, shows the unreasonableness of its
wishes. In the same book will be found some valuable remains of Cicero de Republica, a most profound and ingenious treatise, of which a few fragments are preserved by
Augustine, and which are introduced by him, to show,
that, by Cicero's confession, the Roman state was completely ruined before the times of Christianity. The book
concludes with a pathetic exhortation to unbelievers.

In the third book he demonstrates that the Pagans had
no more help from their religon against natural evils than

---

* By Roman laws, players could not be admitted into Roman citizenship.

they had against moral. He recounts the numberless miseries endured by the Romans long before the coming of Christ. Such as would by malice have been imputed to the Christian religion had it then existed, some of which were more calamitous than any thing which they had lately sustained from the Goths.

In the fourth book he demonstrates that the Roman felicity, such as it was, was not caused by their religion. Here he weighs the nature of that glory and extent of empire with which the carnal heart is so much captivated, and demonstrates, in the most solid manner, that a large extended empire is no more an evidence of felicity than immense property is in private life; and whoever has been fascinated by political writers, ancient or modern, into an admiration of this false glory, may see it excellently combatted by the reasonings of Augustine. The Pantheistic philosophy, of which the old sages are full, is ridiculed, and the futility of all the popular religions exposed. In the conclusion he gives a short view of the dispensations of Providence toward the Jews, and shews, while they continued obedient, the superiority of their felicity to that of the Romans.

In the fifth book he describes the virtue of the old Romans, and what reward was given to it here on earth —shadowy reward for shadowy virtue. He gives an excellent account of the vice of vain glory, and contrasts it with the humility of Christians. He demonstrates that it was the true God who dispensed his mercies and judgments toward the Romans. Nor have I seen a more striking view of the emptiness of warlike grandeur, than in the account which he gives of the condition of the victors and the vanquished, and in the demonstration that the latter were no way inferior to the former in point of real happiness, except in the crisis of battle.

In the same book he argues against Cicero, and shews the consistency of the prescience of God with the free agency of man, and, in this and some other parts of his works, the discerning reader may see some traces of that ingenious work, namely, Jonathan Edwards' Inquiry on Free-Will He takes notice of the total defeat sustained by Rhadagasus, the barbarous pagan in Italy, and reminds the Gentiles how insultingly they had declared beforehand, that he would certainly be victorious. His observations on the ill success of the pious Emperor Gratian, and the prosperity of Constantine and Theodosius, deserve also our attention.

Having shewn, in the five first books, that paganism could do nothing for men in temporal things, in the five following books he proves that it was as totally insignificant with respect to the next life. Here we meet with some valuable fragments of the very learned Varro, who divides religion into three kinds, the fabulous, the philosophical, and the political. Here, too, we have a clear and historical detail of the opinions of the ancient philosophers.

Of the remaining books, the four first describe the beginning, the four middle the progress, and the four last the issues of the two states, namely, the City of God and the world ; the history of both, and the different genius and spirit of each, are throughout conceived with great energy by the author, and are illustrated with copiousness and perspicuity.

The eleventh book begins with a just and solid view of the knowledge of God by the Mediator, and the authority of the Scriptures. A number of questions, which respect the beginnings of things, rather curious than important, follow. Among these there is, in the twelfth chapter, an occasional comparison of the felicity of the just in this life with that of Adam before his fall, which deserves a better character. His metaphysics concerning the origin of evil are interspersed. But the greater part of the book may be omitted with little loss to the reader. Yet his censure of Origen in the twenty-third chapter deserves attention.

In the twelfth book the question concerning the origin of evil is still more explicitly stated; and the opinions of those who pretend to account for the origin of the world in a manner different from the Scriptures, and to give it an antiquity much superior to that which is assigned to it in them, are refuted.

The thirteenth book describes the fall of man; but questions of little or no moment are interspersed; and the subtilty of the learning of his times meeting with his argumentative mind leads him here, as in various other parts of his writings, into trifling disquisitions. I do not reckon of this sort, however, his account of the difference between an animal and spiritual body, because it throws some good light on the fifteenth chapter of the First Epistle to the Corinthians.

The fourteenth book contains matter more interesting than the foregoing three, though it is not without unimportant speculations. A just idea of the magnitude of the first sin is given, and the justice of God is excellently vindicated. In the close of this book he contrasts the two states in a very graphical manner. "Two sets of affections have produced two states: self-love produced an earthly one to the contempt of God; the love of God produced an heavenly one to the contempt of man. That glories in man, this in the Lord. That seeks glory from men; to this, God, the witness of the conscience, is the greatest glory. That exalts the head in its own glory; this says to its God: THOU ART MY GLORY, AND THE LIFTER UP OF MY HEAD. In that the lust of power reigns; in this men serve one another in love, governors in providing, subjects in obeying. That loves its own strength, this says to its God, I will LOVE THEE, O LORD, MY STRENGTH. In that wise men live according to man, and pursue the goods of body or mind, or both, or, if they know God, honor him not as God, nor are thankful. In this human wisdom is of no account, godliness is all, in which the true God is worshipped, and the reward in the society of saints and angels is expected, that God may be all in all."

In the fifteenth book he enters upon the second part of the history of the two states, namely, their progress. He describes very justly the two types, Sarah and Agar, and illustrates the spirit and genius of the two sects by the cases of Cain and Abel. He confutes those who would make the lives of the antediluvians of shorter duration than that assigned them in Scripture. His reflections on the ark and the deluge are just, though to us they can contain little that is new, and, in the last chapter, he shews that the literal and allegorical sense of Scripture ought both to be supported, without depreciating either.

The sixteenth book carries on the history of the City.

of God from Noah to David, and contains important instruction throughout, especially to those who have not read the same things in modern authors.

The seventeenth book may be called the prophetic history. He shews a double sense must necessarily be affixed to the words of the prophets, in which sometimes the literal, sometimes the spiritual, and sometimes both senses are applicable. He justly observes, therefore, that the Scriptures are to be understood in a tripartite sense. And he gives an admirable instance of his views in Hannah's song in the first book of Samuel, in which a king is prophesied of, at a time when no king was in Israel. His comment on the Psalms are excellent also to the same purpose. These views are so remote from the usual mode of reasoning in our times, that they will not easily find credit in the world. But I will venture to affirm, that the more men study the Scriptures, the more they will see the justness of Augustine's remarks, and the necessity of admitting them.

In the eighteenth book he displays much learning in describing the times of the world coeval with those of the church of God, to the birth of Christ. He proves the superior antiquity of prophetic authority to that of any philosophers. The remarkable harmony of the sacred writers in the promotion of one system, and the endless discordancies of philosophers, are ably contrasted. Yet, he proves from the earliest times that the citizens of the new Jerusalem were not confined absolutely to Jewry.

In speaking of the times of Christ and the propagation of the gospel, he observes: "In this malignant world, in these evil days, whilst the church is procuring future dignity by present humility, and is disciplined by the incentives of fear, the torments of pain, the fatigue of labors, and the dangers of temptations, rejoicing only in hope, when her joy is sound, many reprobates are mixed with the good; both are collected into the gospel-net, and both, included in this world as in a sea, swim promiscuously till they reach the shore, where the bad shall be severed from the good, and in the good, as in his temple, God shall be all in all." Christ chose disciples meanly born, obscure, and illiterate, that whatever great things they should do, he might be in them, and do all.

One he had among them, whose evil he turned to good, by making it an instrument of his passion, and affording an example to his church of enduring evil. His holy church being planted, so far as his bodily presence required, he suffered, died, rose again, shewing, by his passion, what we ought to sustain for the truth, by his resurrection what to hope for in eternity; and this is an additional lesson to the great mystery of redemption, by which his blood was shed for the remission of our sins. He proves that the faith of the gospel is strengthened by the dissensions of heretics; and, after some observations on Antichrist, as just as might be expected in his time, he concludes with a remark on a pagan prophecy, which affirmed that the Christian religion would only continue three hundred and sixty-five years. "What may be doing, says he, at the end of this period in other parts of the world, it may be needless to inquire. I will mention what I know: in the renowned city of Carthage, the imperial officers, in the year following the predicted extinction of Christianity, overturned the temples of the idols, and broke the images. And for the space of thirty years since that time, the falsity of the pagan divination being notorious, occasion hath been given to render the progress of the gospel still more triumphant."

The four last books describe the issues of the two states. The nineteenth deserves the studious attention of every scholar, who would accurately distinguish between theology and philosophy. He contrasts the ideas of happiness exhibited by both with great clearness, and while he does justice to all the good that is found in secular systems, he points out their fundamental errors. The principles of evangelical virtue are stated ; the miseries of life are described, and both the true relief against them which the gospel proposes is exhibited, and the false consolations of philosophy are justly exposed. In fine, the reader will find here the mass of secular philosophy reduced to order, its errors detected, and the very picture of the Christian state and genius delineated.

The twentieth book undertakes to describe the last judgment. But as the vigorous and discursive genius of the author led him to handle a multitude of intricate questions, and to undertake the exposition of some of the

most difficult prophecies in the Scripture, for which the
early times in which he lived were unequal, through
want of the evidence of their accomplishment, almost
the whole is very uninteresting.

In the two last books he gives his ideas of the punishment of the wicked, and of the happiness of the righteous
in a future state.   The former, though it has a mixture
of curious questions, more subtile than important, will
from the eleventh chapter to the end deserve a careful
perusal.   I have not seen, in so small a compass, a
sounder answer to the objections of men against the
divine justice in punishing sin eternally, than is to be
found in the eleventh and twelfth chapters.   It appears
that the Lord's prayer was daily used by the church in
his time, and though he seems to give an unsound inter-
pretation of our Lord's words, of making FRIENDS OF THE
MAMMON OF UNRIGHTEOUSNESS, yet he confesses his in-
terpretation would be dangerous in practice ; and he
protests against the ideas of those who imagine they can
atone for their sins by alms.   He refutes various pre-
sumptions of men, who expect to escape the damnation
of hell, without a sound conversion.

In the last book, which describes the eternal rest of
the City of God, he thinks proper to dwell a little on the
external evidences of Christianity, and in speaking of
miracles, he describes, in chapter eight, some which
were wrought in his own time. One of them, the healing
of a disorder, seems peculiarly striking, because it was
in answer to prayer. I have again to regret the scholas-
tic and subtile taste of his times, interwoven with most
important matter. The twenty-second chapter gives as
striking a proof, drawn from facts, of human apostacy as
I have seen. The reflections in the two next chapters
are also admirable. And he closes with a delightful
view of the eternal felicity of the church of God.

Should the very imperfect sketch I have given of this
work, one of the greatest efforts of genius and learning
in any age, induce any classical scholars to peruse it
with candor and attention, and, by the blessing of God,
to imbibe some portion of the heavenly spirit of the
author, I shall have cause to rejoice.

The Life of St. Augustine was written by POSSIDIUS,

sometimes called *Passidoius*, (an African) a pious priest
of his diocese, afterwards Bishop of Calama.

St. Augustine lived seventy-six years, forty of which.
he had been a presbyter, or bishop. This holy man died
in the triumph of faith, at the city of Hippo, in Africa,
A. D. 430, and left his valuable library for the church of
Christ.

The Epistle to Egyptius is full of charity, and
describes the greatness of the Christian graces in a manner much resembling that of St. Augustine's Epistle to
Theodorus.

Vigilius, an African, was of Thapsus ; he was a man
famous for his writings. He composed a number of
treatises, under the names of the most renowned Fathers. The creed, called that of Athanasius, is ascribed
to him.

Mark, the Hermit of Africa, a writer on the spiritual
life and labor of man, describes the conflict truly solemn
for eternity.

Rammohun Roy, the Hindoo philosopher and theologian, was a native of Bengal, and has rendered himself
conspicuous both in India and Europe, by his talents and
learning, and discovers a familiar and profound acquaintance with the various living languages, and is said to be
well read in the Greek and Hebrew. By his writings in
most of these he has proved himself to be one of the most
learned and remarkable men of the present age.

Victorinus, of Africa, was a Christian historian. He
wrote against the Arians and the Manichees. In his
treatise against the latter, he addresses his friend Jus-
tinius, who had been deceived by them, in this manner :
" In vain do you macerate yourself with excessive mortification ; for after you have worn away yourself by
your austerities, your flesh will return to the devil, in
darkness. I advise you to acknowledge that God Almighty created you, that you may be truly the temple of
God according to the words of the Apostle. You are
the temple of God; and his Spirit dwelleth in you! If
you have not the honor to be the temple of God, and to
receive the Holy Spirit in you, Jesus Christ is come not
to save, but to destroy you."

Optatus, of Africa, wrote an able treatise against the

Donatists. He was the author of many other sensible writings.

Apollinarii — father and son — of Africa. The father a presbyter, and the son a reader in the Church. Both skilled in Greek Literature; the father taught Grammar, the son Rhetoric. Epiphanius, a professor of philosophy, was united with them in the closest intimacy. These men were doubtless persons of superior capacity. The son, particularly, was one of the greatest men of his time, in learning, genius, and powers of argument. His answer to Porphyry is looked on as the best defence of Christianity against Paganism. He it was who, in Julian's time, endeavored to compensate to the Christian world, the loss of the classical authors, from the study of whom they were debarred by the persecution of that Emperor. He wrote poems and dialogues in imitation of Sophocles and Plato, on scriptural subjects. His translation of the Psalms into Greek verse, which remains to this day, is highly commended.

Didymus, of Africa, may be fairly matched with Apollinarius in greatness of understanding and accomplishments, though he lost his sight at the age of five years. He became so vigorous and successful a student that he was renowned for his skill in Philosophy, Rhetoric, and Geometry. He filled the chair of the famous school at Alexandria with vast applause. Origenism was his favorite system, though, as far as appears, he continued always sound. His treatise on the Holy Spirit, the Latin translation of which, by Jerome, has only come down to us, is perhaps the best the Christian world ever saw on the subject. And whatever has been *said since that time* in defence of the *Divinity* and Personality of the Holy Ghost, seem, in substance, to be found in that book.

Theophilus, Paulinus, Alpius, Sulpicius Severus, Florentius, Isidore, Cassian, Hilary, Vincentus Primasius, Timotheus, Ælumus, Honoratus, Politian, Antony, and Faustus, learned Christian writers of Africa.

The celebrated Victor, of Africa. His history of the African persecutions is very affecting, and who himself suffered for righteousness sake, will deserve to be added to this list. Joseph Milner, A. M., has made much use

of his history in writing the history of the Church of
Christ.

Jason, an African, of Cyrene, wrote five books of
2 Mac. ii, Acts ii, 10, the history of the second book of
Maccabees being an abstract and breviary of the five
books of Jason, a Jew, of Cyrene.

MODERN HISTORIANS.

DE VASTEY, an African, and once, we believe, a slave,
an eloquent man of St. Domingo, who published several
works. The following are extracts from his pen : —

"Every species of calumny and absurdity has been
invented to palliate the atrocious injustice of white men,
toward those whom they have tormented and persecuted
for ages.

"Posterity will find it difficult to believe, that in an enlightened age like ours, there are men, who call themselves
philosophers, willing to reduce human beings to an equality with brutes, merely for the sake of sanctioning the
abominable privilege of oppressing a large portion of
mankind. While I am now writing, I can scarcely re-
frain from laughter, at the absurdities which have been
published on this subject. Learned authors, and skilful
anatomists, have passed their lives in discussing facts as
clear as daylight, and in dissecting the bodies of men
and animals, in order to prove that I, who am now writing, belong to the race of Ourang-Outangs! Edward
Long gravely advances, as a proof of the moral inferior-
ity of the black man, that our vermin are black, and that
we eat wild-cats. Hanneman maintains that our color
originates in the curse pronounced by Noah against Canaan; others affirm that it was a mark fixed upon Cain,
for the murder of his brother Abel. For myself, I see
strong reasons to believe that the white men are the real
descendants of Cain; for I still find in them that primitive hatred, that spirit of envy and of pride, and that
passion for riches, which the Scriptures inform us led
him to sacrifice his brother.

"I smile while I ask whether we are still in those
ages of ignorance and superstition, which saw Coperni-
cus and Galileo condemned as heretics and sorcerers?

Or whether we are really living in an age of light, which has given birth to so many great men, who have immortalized their country by illustrious works?"

Benoit, of Palermo, an African, called by historians the "Holy Black," was among the most eulogized and honored saints in the Roman Catholic Church of the age in which he lived. He died at Palermo, A. D. 1589.

Francis Williams, an African, was born in Jamaica, about the close of the 17th century. He was sent to England, and there entered the University of Cambridge. After his return to Jamaica, he opened a school for instruction in Latin and Mathematics. He wrote many pieces in Latin verse, in which he discovered great talents.

Don Juan Latino, an African, was a distinguished teacher of the Latin language at Seville, in Spain, during the last century.

John Capitein, an African, was born in Africa, and was carried to Holland, and there employed himself in painting. He acquired the elements of the Latin, Greek, Hebrew, and Chaldaic languages, and afterwards entered the University of Leyden, where he devoted himself to the study of Theology. Having studied the regular academic term, he received his degrees while in Holland. He published an elegy in Latin verse, two Latin dissertations, one on the calling of the Gentiles, and the other on slavery, and a small volume of sermons in the Dutch language.

Anthony William Amo, an African. He was born in Guinea, and brought to Europe when very young, under the patronage of the Princess of Brunswick. He pursued his studies at Halle, in Saxony, and at Williamberg, where he greatly distinguished himself by his talents and good conduct. In 1734, he took the degree of Doctor in Philosophy at the University of Williamberg. He was skilled in the Greek and Latin languages, and was well acquainted with the ancient and modern systems of philosophy. His lectures upon philosophy were well received. In 1744 he supported a Thesis at Williamberg, and published a dissertation on the absence of sensation in the soul, and its presence in the human body. He was appointed Professor, and the same year supported a

Thesis on the distinction which ought to be made between the operations of mind and those of sense.

Lakman, an African, was a distinguished man. He wrote some fables, which are yet extant, and have some celebrity. He is surnamed, in Arabia and among the Eastern nations, "the Wise," and by the Mahometans he is believed to have been a Prophet. To Lakman's opinions Mahomet frequently appeals, in the Koran, in support of his own. He died and was buried near Jerusalem.

Kislar Aga, an African, was a man of great wisdom and profound knowledge. In 1730 he was chief of the eunuchs of the Grand Seignior at Constantinople.

Job Ben Solomon, an African, a son of the Mahometan King of Bunda, on the Gambia. He was captured in 1730, and sold in Maryland, U. S.; he afterwards found his way to England, (*a land of freedom;*) here, his talents, dignified air, and amenity of character, procured him many friends; he was received at the Court of St. James with high distinction, and among others, by Sir Hans Sloane, for whom he translated several Arabic manuscripts. He is said to have been able to repeat the Koran from memory.

Captain Paul Cuffee, an African, the youngest son of John Cuffee, was sold in this country a slave; in time he obtained his freedom. He afterwards purchased a farm, and having married one of the native Indians, brought up a family of ten children respectably, on one of the Elizabeth Islands, near New Bedford, Massachusetts. In the year 1773, when Paul was about fourteen years of age, his father dying left a widow with six children to the care of him and his brothers. He advanced in knowledge, in arithmetic and navigation. He commanded his own vessel in its voyages to many ports in the Southern States, the West Indies, England, Russia, and to Africa. The beginning of his business in this line was in an open boat; he was at length enabled to obtain a good sized schooner, then a brig, and afterwards a ship. In the year 1806 he owned a ship, two brigs, and several small vessels, besides considerable property in houses and land. He employed his time in teaching navigation to his own family, and to the young men of the neighborhood. Even on his voyages, when opportunity offered, he instructed those under his care in that useful art. He was so conscientious that he would not enter into any business, however profitable, that might have a tendency to injure his fellow-men. He had a store of West India goods, and seeing the dreadful effects of drunkenness, he would not deal in ardent spirits on that account. In Westport, the town where he lived, there was no school; and, as he was anxious that his children should obtain an education, he built a school-house on his own land at his own expense, and gave his neighbors the free use of it, being satisfied in seeing it occupied for so useful and excellent a purpose.

In many parts of his history we may discover that excellent trait of character which rendered him so eminently useful, a steady perseverance in laudable undertakings. His mind had long been affected with the degraded, oppressed, and miserable condition of his brethren in this country; and, his heart yearning toward them, he sought to relieve them, believing it to be his duty to use a part of what God had given him for their benefit.

As a private man he was just and upright in all his dealings. He was an affectionate husband, a kind father, a good neighbor, and a faithful friend. He was pious without ostentation, and warmly attached to the principles of the Society of Friends of which he was a member. Such was his reputation for wisdom and integrity that his neighbors consulted him in all their important concerns. What an honor conferred on us! The most respectable men in Great Britain and America were not ashamed to seek him for counsel and advice. He lived and died a Christian.

DAVID WALKER, an African, was a distinguished Friend, a good writer, and a warm advocate for the oppressed and miserable condition of his brethren in slavery. His celebrated appeal in behalf of his brethren is highly esteemed by wise men; he was a man of a strong mind and great talents. The city of Boston, Mass., was his place of residence, where he died.

WILLIAM APES, an Indian, was a minister of the gospel

22

of Christ our Lord. "Oh Israel, or Indians, my people," like the prophet of old, he was constrained to cry out, "oh that my head were waters, and mine eyes fountains of tears, that I might weep day and night for the slain of the daughters of my people, Israel or Indians, whom they have scattered among the nations and parted my land." In his history of the native tribes of Indians, he shows his talents, his knowledge of the Scriptures, and the wrongs inflicted on his people by this nation; the worth of souls, and the judgments of God that will fall upon this people as a nation.

Hosea Easton.—This individual was born at North Bridgewater, Mass. He, with three brothers, met a premature grave, on account of the cursed prejudices existing against them in their town, by reason of their complexion. His father was born in Middleboro', Mass., and served eight months in the service of his country, in times when "men's souls were tried." His "Treatise on the civil and political condition of the colored population of the United States," is a profound production, and gives a true sketch of the condition of this class of people.

FEMALE WRITERS.

Cornelia, the daughter of Scipio Africanus, was distinguished for virtue, learning, and good sense. She wrote and spoke with uncommon elegance and purity. Cicero and Quinctilian bestow high praise upon her letters; and the eloquence of her children was attributed to her careful superintendence.

Hypatia, the daughter of Theon, of Alexandria, in Africa, succeeded her father in the government of the Platonic school, and filled with reputation a seat where many celebrated philosophers had taught. The people regarded her as an oracle, and magistrates consulted her in all important cases.

Phillis Wheatley.—This distinguished colored young woman was brought a slave from Africa to America, in the year 1761, when between seven and eight years of age, and sold to Mr. John Wheatley, a respectable citizen of Boston, in whose family she continued to reside. According to his testimony, "without any assistance from school education, with only what she was taught in the family, in sixteen months from the time of her arrival, she attained the English language, to which she was before an utter stranger, to such a degree, as to read any, the most difficult parts of the sacred writings, to the great astonishment of all who heard her." The records of school education may be safely challenged to show an equal improvement in an equal time. Her master further stated that, "as to her writing, her own curiosity led her to it; and this she learned in so short a time, that in the year 1765 she wrote a letter to the Rev. Mr. Occum, the *Indian* minister, while he was in England." Thus, in about four years from the time when this interesting little girl was seized by some lawless gang of free-booters in Africa, torn from her parents and friends, and carried into a foreign land, a stranger to its manners and its language, and when she was only eleven years old, while she was laboring as a slave, without the advantages of a school education, by her own efforts and mental energy, she had so far advanced in improvement as to write a respectable letter to an Indian minister, then in a foreign country, who had previously been educated at Dartmouth College, in New Hampshire.

After she had obtained a very respectable command of the English language, as her writings testify, she was not content with this acquisition. Her master further states, "she has a great inclination to learn the Latin tongue, and has made some progress in it."

In 1772, when she was about seventeen years of age, and had been ten years in America, her poetical productions, which were written as an amusement in her leisure hours, became known to her friends, who earnestly advised to their publication. Though nothing was further from her thoughts, while composing them, than such a use of them, yet, in deference to their judgment, and in compliance with their wishes, it was done.

The publisher, justly fearful lest the fact should be questioned that these poems were really written by Phillis, very prudently procured the following attestation: "We, whose names are underwritten, do assure the world, that the poems specified in the following page, (referring to the table of contents in the manuscript)

were (as we verily believe) written by Phillis, a young
African girl, who was, but a few years since, brought an
uncultivated barbarian from Africa, and has ever since
been, and now is, under the disadvantage of serving as
a slave in a family in this town. She has been examined
by the best judges, and is thought qualified to write
them." This certificate was signed by the existing
Governor and Lieutenant Governor of Massachusetts,
and by all the most distinguished civilians and clergy of
Boston. Among the names is that of John Hancock, the
president of the first American Congress.

As the little volume of poems here referred to is, at
the present time, rarely to be met with, a few extracts
from it may be interesting to our readers, and will be
honorable to African genius.

Phillis evinces that her reading had been considerably
extensive, for she often alludes to the classic writers of
antiquity in a way which shows that she was not ignorant
of their works. The following allusion to the writings
of Homer is found in one of her poems:

> While Homer paints, lo! circumfused in air
> Celestial gods in mortal forms appear;
> Swift as they move hear each recess rebound,
> Heav'n quakes, earth trembles, and the shores resound.
> Great sire of verse, before my mortal eyes,
> The lightnings blaze across the vaulted skies,
> And as the thunder shakes the heavenly plains,
> A deep-felt horror thrills through all my veins.
> When gentle strains demand thy graceful song,
> The length'ning line moves languishing along.
> When great *Patroclus* courts Achilles' aid,
> The grateful tribute of my tears is paid;
> Prone on the shores he feels the pangs of love,
> And stern *Pelides'* tend'rest passions move.

Though Phillis had doubtless read with satisfaction
Pope's translation of Homer, a work which is exceedingly rich in poetic imagery, yet the mythology and exploits of the heathen were not the subjects on which she
delighted most to dwell. The following is the commencement of a poem on the death of the Rev. George Whitefield, written in 1770, when she was about fifteen years

of age. This poem was sent, by the friends of Phillis, to the Countess of Huntingdon, the distinguished patroness of Whitefield in England; and it procured from that lady an invitation to Phillis to visit England, which she did, by the consent of her master. Though she was introduced to many distinguished persons, and treated with much attention in England, she returned to America the same modest, unassuming young woman as when she left it. What would have completely overset some minds in such circumstances, produced no unfavorable influence upon her.

Hail, happy saint, on thine immortal throne,
Possest of glory, life, and bliss unknown;
We hear no more the music of thy tongue,
Thy wonted auditories cease to throng.
Thy sermons in unequall'd accents flow'd,
And every bosom with devotion glow'd;
Thou didst in strains of eloquence refin'd
Inflame the heart, and captivate the mind.
Unhappy we the setting sun deplore,
So glorious once, but ah! it shines no more.

Behold the prophet in his towering flight!
He leaves the earth for heaven's unmeasured height,
And worlds unknown receive him from our sight.
There Whitefield wings with rapid course his way,
And sails to Zion through vast seas of day.

The following is the commencement of a poem on the works of Providence:

Arise, my soul, on wings enraptur'd rise,
To praise the monarch of the earth and skies,
Whose goodness and beneficence appear,
As round the centre moves the rolling year,
Or when the morning glows with rosy charms,
Or the sun slumbers in the ocean's arms:
Of light divine be a rich portion lent,
To guide my soul, and favor my intent:
Celestial muse, my arduous flight sustain,
And raise my mind to a seraphic strain.

Phillis's harp was early unstrung on earth, but, it is hoped, to be tuned to sublimer melody in heaven. She died in 1784, aged about 31 years. Her name has obtained an honorable place in the most respectable biographical dictionaries; and those works would probably be searched in vain for an instance of equal improvement under equal disadvantages.

It is not improbable that some native poet may yet strike the lyre in Africa, with a note as much more elevated than that of Phillis, as the opportunities for improvement there are likely to be superior to those which she enjoyed. In that interesting country intellectual and moral improvement should go hand in hand; and a community may yet arise which the people of the United States will delight to acknowledge as founded by their benevolence, and reared by their exertions. Many African minds are capable of high cultivation, and may yet be made to send out from Africa the cheering radiance of intelligence and virtue in a region now overspread with an intellectual and moral midnight.

MARIA STEWART, whose talents and love of virtue, dignified air, and amenity of character procured her many friends; and whose mind being awakened with the sense of duty she owed to God, wrote a powerful appeal in behalf of the degraded and oppressed people which are in this land of Christianity; saying, Come ye poor and needy, despised, and afflicted outcast people unto God. "Many daughters have done virtuously, but thou excelleth them all. Favor is deceitful, and beauty is vain; but a woman that feareth the Lord, she shall be praised. Give her of the fruit of her hands, and let her own work praise her in the gates."

BURNING OF THE LIBRARIES.

It has already been said, that in very early times Egypt was the land of science; it was a great character, therefore, to give Moses, when it is said of him, Acts vii. 22, that "he was learned in all the wisdom of Egypt."

When the Ptolemies, descendants of Alexander's famous general, ruled in Egypt, they brought all the taste and elegance of Grecian philosophy into the country. One of them, Ptolemy Soter, founded a library in Alexandria, and gathered a hundred thousand volumes; to which were added, in the course of years, so many as made up seven hundred thousand in the time of Julius Cæsar; by whose soldiers more than half of them were destroyed. The library was, however, filled again, and kept with great care, as a treasure of all that human intellect had ever produced most worthy. But, in the year 642, when the Saracens or Moors conquered Egypt, who were Mahomedans, and who reverenced the Koran, their general, Omar, ordered the rich collection to be burnt, like an ignorant barbarian, as he was; saying, " If there is any thing in these books besides what is in the Koran, it is false; and if it is only the same, we don't want them while we have that." For some months, therefore, the books of this most ancient and magnificent library were used to cook their victuals, and to warm their baths.

CHAPTER XI.

THE ANCIENT ARABIANS.

The Arabians a people of color, are the only people who have preserved their descent, their language, independence, manners, and customs from the earliest age; and to whom we are to look for examples of patriarchal life and habits. The tribes in general choose to pitch their tents — whether on a hill or plain — so as to form a circular encampment. A collection of black tents thus arranged, is said to present a pleasing and beautiful appearance to the distant traveller. Tents were first made it is thought of skins of animals, fastened to a long pole set perpendicularly into the ground, — and the covering was drawn away from the bottom of the pole so as to form a small round dwelling. Subsequently tents were enlarged and made oblong. Tents were first invented in the family of Jubal — brother of Noah, and son of Lamech. The covering of the large tents, was made of goat's hair, and was black. This fact beautifully illustrates the passage in the Song of Solomon : " I am black as the tents of Kedar." Kedar was the second son of Ishmael : and Isaiah frequently personifies the Arabians under the name of Kedar. (Isa. 20th and 60th chap.) " The curtains of Solomon " was a shelter in Arabia — a cavern whither the Arabian shepherds gathered their herds and flocks at night, for refuge. Tents are very portable dwellings; and are therefore conveniently adapted to the habits of those wandering tribes whose occupation leads them to frequent removals to different parts of the country.

When they remove from one place to another, they take their tents with them ; and when they stop, they erect them again ; this they call " pitching their tents."

It appears, that about the time of the Hebrews' bondage

in Egypt, a number of the Arabian tribes passed the Red Sea at the straits of Babelmandel. And the Ludims in ages still earlier, settled in that country. The language of the ancient Arabians, and of the modern Abyssinians, and many of their laws were much the same with those of the ancient Egyptians. The Arabians seem to have been originally divided into a great number of tribes — with kings at the head of each. It is supposed that they worship Ammon, the offspring of Lot, in the person of their chief deity.

MAHOMET, an Arabian, was founder of the religion which is called by his name. He was born in Mecca, Arabia, on the Red Sea, anno domini, 569.

The religion of which he was the author, was a system of Asiatic and Arabian voluptuousness, grafted on the morality of the Gospel and partly upon some of the rites of Judaism. The Koran which he wrote in detached portions, embodies the substance of his religion, and is the sacred book of the Mussulmen. Mahomet never laid down his arms from the time he captured Mecca, till he subdued all Arabia, and a part of Syria; impressing his religion wherever he extended his conquests. He died in the midst of his successes, at the age of 61, A. D.

AVIENNA, an Arabian philosopher and physician.

THE ARABIC LANGUAGE.

THE Hebrew language — the most ancient in the world, after gradually pervading in Samaria and Chaldea, was carried into the country of Arabia, by Kahtang, an ancient Arabian king, and a descendant of Ishmael; and either formed the root of the Arabic, or, by a commixture with it, both in respect to idiom and verbal expression, gave birth to a language as new as compounded. The Arabic is now divided into many dialects, which vary from each other no less in construction than in pronunciation. It is, however, notwithstanding these diversities, so generally understood in Africa and most parts of Asia, that, according to the statement of an able and respectable writer on the subject, a traveller who possesses a thorough knowledge of this language, may pass from the shores of the Mediterranean to the Cape of Good Hope; may cross the widest part of the African continent from east to west; may follow the course

of the Nile, and from Morocco to the eastern shores of
China, opposite the islands of Japan, and find himself every
where understood.

The Arabic language, independently of its different dialects, is divided into two principal parts — the *Lisan en-
nahwi*, or grammatical language; and the *Lisan-elamma*,
or vulgar tongue. The former of these is the pure ancient
Arabic, and forms in itself a dialect of the Hebrew; sufficient indications of which appear in the resemblance of the
characters of one to those of the other. The latter is used
in the three Arabias; and is likewise spoken, with some
variation of dialect, over great part of the East, from Egypt
to the court of the Great Mogul.

By the Eastern nations, the Arabic language is esteemed
the richest and most energetic of any in the world; and it
is taught in their schools, as Greek and Latin are in the
academies of Europe and America. But its distinguishing
honor is, that it is the language in which the *Koran* was
written, and the only one in which the Turks will allow the
sacred text to be publicly read. They regard it as the language of Paradise; and since it comprises several millions
of words, think, and certainly not without reason, that no
one can be perfectly master of its treasures. The great
number of its synonymes forms one of the distinguishing
features of this language. To express the article *honey*, it
has more than eighty different words — possesses two hundred names for the *serpent*, five hundred for the *lion*, a
thousand for the *camel*, and a thousand and some hundreds
for a *sword*.

The modern Arabic is written from right to left, and its
alphabet is composed of twenty-eight letters; being six
more than are contained either in that of the Samaritan, or
of the Chaldean.

The Arabs have also a character called *Lamalif*, composed of *Lam* and *Alif*; the power of which is equivalent
to the sound *la*, in English. The numeric value of the
letters corresponds with that of the Hebrew characters;
i. e. from *Alif* to *Ra*, is from one to ten; *Za* is twenty,
and *Sin* is thirty, and so forth; while the six extra characters are employed, as are the Hebrew elongations and finals,
in carrying on the series from four hundred, where the
twenty-second letter stops, to one thousand. Indeed, these

latter six characters are varied from their primitives, only by their points, in appearance; and only by a gutteral, or aspirate, in sound.

The Arabians use five orthographical points for the government of their characters. *Hamra*, placed on the letters *Alif*, *Waw*, and *Ya*, doubles the vowel: *Wesla*, or *Ousla*, is put over *Alif*, to indicate that its own sound is merged in that of the succeeding letter. *Medda* is placed on *Alif*, to render it long; and it is also employed as a mark, or sign.

The Saracens, or Moors from Arabia, brought into Europe the figures in Arithmetic, and the Letters of the Alphabet, about 991 years A. C.

THE WORD NEGRO.

NEGRO is derived from the Latin term *niger* — meaning *black*.

The following terms and definitions are in the American edition of Dr. Walker's Dictionary.

Moor — a marsh, a fen; a negro.

Marsh — a fen, a bog, a swamp; a plant.

Moorish — fenny, marshy.

Negro — blackmoor.

In Dr. Johnson's Dictionary — American edition, by Rev. Joseph Hamilton, M. A., 1810 — we find these words thus defined:

Black — dark, cloudy, mournful, wicked.

Black — a negro, the dark color, mourning.

Moor — a negro, marsh, fen, bog.

Moorish or Moory — marshy, fenny.

Negro — a blackmoor, (a Moor.)

In the Dictionary for schools, by Dr. Webster, American edition, we find these words thus defined:

Negro, an *African* by birth, or a descendant of one of full blood.

Moor, a black man, a marsh.

Marsh, low ground.

Negro, a blackmoor, a slave, a mean wretch.

Moor, a black, marsh, watery ground.

Marsh, a fen, a bog, a swamp, watery ground.

. In Dr. Webster's definition of the complexion of the

skin, he calls it the blood of Africa, or their descendants — as follows :

Mangroon, is all black, a full blood, (a whole negro.)

Sambo, is three quarters blood, (three quarters negro.)

Mulatto, is one half blood, (one half negro.)

Quadroon, is one quarter blood, (one quarter negro.)

Mestizo, is a half quarter blood, (a half quarter negro.)

Niger, a Latin word, was formerly used by the Moors — the old Romans, to designate any black, inferior object, &c., a plant, a marsh, flat, moist ground, bog, or animal.

Micah, the Morasthite (a prophet of the Moors,) prophesied in the days of Hezekiah, king of Judah; and spake to all the people of Judah, (the Moors,) saying, thus saith the Lord of hosts: Zion shall be ploughed like a field, and Jerusalem shall become heaps, (a forest.)

Micah showeth the wrath of God against Jacob for idolatry. (Jer. xxvi. 18. Micah i. 1.)

Moserath was built by the Moors, in the Desert of Paran, in the land of Amalek, and was the ancient encampment of Israel in the days of Moses.

In the Moorish war of Adel, in Africa, some of the books of Moses were burnt.

Moriah, a hill adjacent to Jerusalem, on the northeast. Here Abraham offered his son. Gen. xxii. When Solomon built the temple on it, it became included in the city. 2 Chron. iii. 1.

The appellation of Moor is given to those successors of Mahomet — Pagans, Christians, and Jews — who extended their empire through North Africa, South Europe, and the islands of the Mediterranean. The Moors gained the highest reputation, both in Arts and Arms, of all the nations of the East. The mechanic and the fine arts, especially sculpture and painting, were in a very low state in Europe, when the Moors turned their attention to them, and cultivated them with great success.

The Moors had founded in Africa the empire of Morocco, which was governed by a viceroy, named Muca. Muca sent his general Tariff into Spain, who, in a single memorable engagement, stripped the Gothic king Roderigo of his life and crown, and subdued the country, A. D. 713. The kingdom of the Moors flourished in the.

south of Spain, for the space of two centuries, in full
vigor. Abdalrahman fixed the seat of his government at
Cordova, and made it a place of the utmost splendor and
magnificence. Spain's conqueror, satisfied with the sovereignty of the country, left the Goths, who had long
been masters of Spain, in possession of their property,
laws, and religion. And by the marriage of Abdallah,
the Moor, with the widow of the Gothic king, the two
nations became united. In A. D. 732, the Moors penetrated from Spain into France, and defeated the duke of
Aquitain. The siege of Constantinople by the Moors
occurred A. D. 672. Their fleet passed through the un-
guarded channel of the Hellespont, and disembarked
their troops seven miles from the city. But after a thirty
years' war, and the loss of 30,000 Moslems, they were
compelled to relinquish the enterprise. And by a treaty
between the two empires, 'the Faithful' were reduced
to submit to the payment of a heavy annual tribute. This
badge of servitude was however soon shaken off, and the
succeeding emperors were unable to enforce it.

Jerusalem was taken by the Saracens, or followers of
Mahomet, A. D. 637.

Alexandria, in Egypt, is taken by the Saracens, and
the grand library there burnt, by order of Omar, their
caliph or prince, A. D. 640.

The Caliph Omar, the third in succession from Mo-
hammed, reduced Jerusalem under his subjection. This
Omar was afterwards assassinated at Jerusalem, in 643.

The Saracens continued masters of Jerusalem till the
year 1099, when it was taken by the Crusaders, under
Godfrey of Bouillon. They founded a new kingdom, of
which Jerusalem was the capital, and which lasted
eighty-eight years, under nine kings. At last this kingdom was utterly ruined by Saladin; and though the
Christians once more obtained possession of the city,
they were again obliged to relinquish it. In 1217, the
Saracens were expelled by the Turks, who have ever
since continued in possession of it.

Seventeen times has Jerusalem been taken and pil-
laged; millions of men have been slaughtered within its
walls. No other city has experienced such a fate. This

protracted and almost supernatural punishment betokens unexampled guilt.

THE MOORS.—Their dress is handsome; a sort of short shirt with wide sleeves, over which comes a cloth vest, fastened with small buttons and loops, embroidered richly with gold and silver; they wear linen drawers, with broad silk scarfs round their waist, in which they stick a large knife, with a curiously ornamented handle.

The word *negro* is considered insulting, and is used as an epithet of contempt to the colored people. It has been long used by our common enemies in America. It is not only/insulting, but very improper for any one to make use of it. Our friends, the friends of Christ, would do well to consider this, and never write or publish it again to the world. Let it be remembered that it is as *wicked* for a Christian to swear as to call a disciple of Christ a *negro*. Men of Africa were chosen by Christ our Lord to go and preach the everlasting gospel to every creature. See the sons of Africa who came to Antioch, preaching the Lord Jesus. Acts xi. 20. Men of Cyprus, an island of Africa, and of Cyrene, a city on the Mediterranean, in Africa.

In the third century the Church of Christ was ably defended by the celebrated sons of Africa, Origen and Cyprian, learned Christian writers, commonly called Fathers, and St. Chrysostom, and St. Augustine, learned and eloquent Fathers in the Church of Christ, and many others.

I am authorized by the word of God to say, whosoever makes use of the word *negro*, applying it to us as a people, after the *light* and *truth* have been proclaimed, are neither friends to God nor man. "I say unto you, inasmuch as ye have done it unto one of the least of these, my brethren, ye have done it unto *me*." Matt. xxv. 40.

To call a person a negro, in the East, is expressive of the highest contempt.

The dark Spaniard is proud of his descent from the African Moor, who first taught Europe the use of the Arabic figures, &c. The Arab of Africa, the most majestic of men, with his piercing eye and flowing beard, is the descendant and representative of Abraham.

THE HAIR OF MEN'S HEADS.

Our common enemies in America call *frizzle* or *curly hair*, on the head of an African, *wool*.

The Dictionary of Dr. Walker calls the fleece of a sheep, *wool*. Cloth, called woollen, is made of *wool*.

Daniel's vision of God's kingdom : "The ancient of days did sit, whose garment was white as snow, and the hair of his head like the pure wool." Dan. vii. 9.

A description of Christ: "His head is as the most fine gold, his locks are bushy, and black as a raven." Solomon's Song, v. 11.

Frizzle, friz'zl. v. a. to curl in short curls.

THE ROCK OF GIBRALTAR.

Mount Calpe, or Gibraltar, or in other words, the Rock of Gibraltar, taken by the Spaniards from the Moors, was celebrated among the ancients as one of the Pillars of Hercules; and, as he was the fabled god of strength, Gibraltar may with propriety be termed his pillar. The English took it from the Spanish. It is now called the Key of the Mediterranean Sea; and is probably one of the strongest fortresses in the world. Gibraltar is a celebrated promontory, more than 1400 feet high, at the southern extremity of Spain, belonging to Great Britain.

THE MOORISH CASTLE.

This castle was taken from the Moors by the Spanish. It is now called Gibraltar Castle, or by the name of the Spanish Castle. This castle is not very large, but it bears the marks of great age, and has not, in fact, been opened for several hundred years, even from the time it was first taken from the Moors. There are various and marvellous reasons told for keeping it closed. One reason was that the sentinels stationed at this castle for eight or ten days in succession, when the relief guard came in the morning, were found dead on the ramparts; and after twenty or thirty men had been thus singularly cut off from the Spanish ranks, it was resolved to search the castle. They marched with a file of soldiers to the castle gate, and were just putting the key to the lock when some terrible disease caused the death of more than one-half of those who were actors in this enterprise. The Moors say the reason this castle was not opened by the Spanish was that the plague was in it.

The Jews, since their expulsion, had offered to cover the rock with silver dollars, laying them flat-wise on the ground, provided that the rock would be given up to them; but the terms were not accepted; yet, if they would cover it with the dollars edge down it should be given up to them; this the Jews would not do. The Jews pretend to say that the Moorish Castle contains inspired writings, never yet published; that they never would be till they were published by the Jews; that there were no people in existence who could find them, provided the castle was opened for that express purpose, unless it was a Jew; and that no Jew would or could ever do it unless he was master of the soil where those papers were concealed; that as soon as they could effect this, Jewish honor would be restored; the eyes of millions opened to the gross calumnies now circulated against a people, so long the *proverb* and *song* of a heartless world, and for more than seventeen hundred years counted the abomination of the earth; and that in offering to purchase the rock, they were not merely endeavoring to regain a place and name among the nations of the earth, but that other motives, more important, actuated them.

ABDUHL RAHHAHMAN, called the Moorish Prince, was a native of the celebrated city of Timbuctoo, in Central Africa, of which city, and province connected with it, his grand-father was king.

Abduhl's father, when a young man, was sent to conquer the Soo Soos, a nation living at the distance of twelve hundred miles from Timbuctoo. He succeeded, and established a new kingdom, called Footo Jallo, and founded its capital Teembo, now known as one of the largest cities of that continent. He removed his family from Timbuctoo to his newly acquired kingdom, when the Prince Abduhl was about five years of age. At twelve years of age the Prince was sent to Timbuctoo to obtain an education — being the rightful heir to the throne, in

preference to his elder brother, whose mother was a Soo
Soo, while his own was a Moor. While the Prince was
at Timbuctoo, his grand-father being far advanced in
life, resigned his throne to his son, an uncle of the
Prince. The family were all Mahometans.

When the Prince was nineteen years of age, Dr. Cox,
an American citizen, and surgeon on board a ship which
arrived at Sierra Leone, having gone on a hunting expedition into the interior, and lost himself in the woods,
found, on his return to the coast, that his vessel had
sailed. He then undertook an excursion into the country, and arrived at length, sick and lame, in the territory
of Foota Jallo. Being the first white man seen in that
country, he was carried as a great curiosity to the king,
Abduhl's father, at Teembo. The King entertained him
for six months with the greatest hospitality; and during
this time he was an inmate of the Prince's house, adjoining that of his father. When the Doctor was perfectly
restored to health, he was dismissed by the King, and
furnished with clothes, gold, ivory, and an escort of
armed men to protect him to Sierra Leone. In the inte-
rim his ship had providentially returned, and the Doctor
arrived safely in America. Would the Christians in the
Southern part of the United States do the same to an
Ethiopian or Indian?

The Prince (Abduhl Rahhahman) a colonel in his father's cavalry, was sent with a party of seventeen hundred
men to retaliate upon the Hebohs — who had very much
annoyed the trade of the people of Foota Jallo with the sea
coast. On the return of the Prince after a successful campaign, he was taken prisoner by the Hebohs, who surprised
him and his party by ambush. He was sold to the Man-
dingoes; and they in turn sold him to a slave ship at the
mouth of the Gambia; thence he was carried to Dominique;
and thence to Natchez, where he was sold to Colonel Foster. About sixteen or eighteen years after this transaction,
as the Prince was selling sweet potatoes in Washington, a
neighboring town, he met the Doctor Cox who had been
his old acquaintance in Africa, and an inmate of his dwelling at Teembo; and who immediately recognized him.
The Doctor, in the fulness of his gratitude to the Prince,
went to Col. Foster, and offered him one thousand dollars

23

as a ransom for the Prince; but Foster valued him so highly for the salutary influence he exerted over the slaves, that he rejected this proposal. But such intreaties were made by a son of Dr. Cox, and others, that Col. Rabhahman and his wife received their freedom in the spring of 1828. The Prince, having been born in 1760, was now about sixty-six years of age; forty of which he had passed in bondage. His character was remarkably exemplary. When he visited New York and the other northern Atlantic cities, he brought with him letters of recommendation from Mr. Clay and other distinguished gentlemen who had cultivated his acquaintance. He became a member of the Baptist church during the year previous to his manumission. The Prince embarked with his wife on board the Harriet, which left Hampton Roads in January, 1829, for Liberia; and he arrived at Monrovia in Africa, with his wife, May 5th, 1829; and died on the 9th of the same month, with a Liberia seasoning fever.

The city of Timbuctoo is situated in the middle of Africa; and has been the object of the European's curiosity for many years. The slave-traders from the North, East, and West, have spoken of it, and their accounts have been rather marvellous. Several travellers have attempted to reach it, but none have been able to get so far; and some have sacrificed their lives to the difficulties of the journey. The Prince Abduhl describes the city as surrounded by large and high walls. The government maintains a standing army; and the people are well advised in arts and sciences.

Honor to the memory of Abduhl, and peace to his ashes. His honesty and humanity, the "noblest work of God." He was man's victim, but nature's nobleman.

> "The palm's rich nectar, and lie down at eve
> In the green pastures of remembered days,
> And walk — to wander and to weep no more —
> On Congo's mountain-coast, or Gambia's golden shore."

CHAPTER XI.

HISTORY OF THE PROPHETS.

THE ancient prophets whom God in his wisdom chose from the different nations and tribes to prophesy unto the people his word, and teach them his commands. " For the Lord thy God will raise up unto thee a prophet from the midst of thee, of thy brethren." (Deut. xviii. 15.)

The term prophecy was regarded as under the direction of the Holy Spirit. So it is said that Judas and Silas were prophets; and in Acts xiii. 1, that there were in the church at Antioch certain prophets and teachers.

Isaiah, Jeremiah, Ezekiel, and Daniel, are called the greater prophets, from the size of their books, and the extent and importance of their prophecies. The others are called the minor or lesser prophets.

The supposed chronological arrangement of the prophecies, and the order in which they may be most intelligibly read, is as follows:

Jonah	B. C. 856—784
Amos	810—785
Hosea	810—725
Isaiah	810—698
Joel	810—660
Micah	758—699
Nahum	720—698
Zephaniah	640—609
Jeremiah	628—586
Habakkuk	612—598
Daniel	606—534
Obadiah	588—583
Ezekiel	595—536
Haggai	620—518
Zechariah	520—518
Malachi	436—420

The Prophet Noah.—Noah, the son of Lamech, was a prophet of the antediluvian world. A knowledge of the deluge was made known to him about 120 years before the flood. He was a just man and a faithful preacher of righteousness. He warned the people of their destruction by a flood. God commanded Noah to build the ark, or great ship, and Ham, a mighty man, helped to build the ark at God's command. The posterity of Noah who inhabited the earth after the flood, were a colored people, and their language was Hebrew. [See the Historical books of the ancients.] This language was originally given to man by his Creator, and afterwards broken into a multitude of tongues at Babel. The Hebrew, it is almost certain, was the language of Adam and Eve, and it is certain their complexion was black, or dark red. Their country was called the land of Ethiopia (Gen. ii. 13.)

Abraham.—The prophet Abraham, the son of Terah. The Lord God called Abraham about 1921, B. C. He was 75 years old, and the tenth lineal descendant from Shem, born in Chaldea, the land of Nimrod. He was a faithful preacher of righteousness, and a father of many nations.

Lot.—Righteous Lot, the son of Haran, Abraham's brother's son, who prayed for his brethren of Sodom and Gomorrah, in the border of Canaan, a wicked people of a black complexion, whom the Lord threatened he would destroy, and their cities, for their wickedness, for their transgressions had come up before him. The angel made known the will of the Lord to Lot, for him and his family to escape from the city; and Lot spake unto his sons-in-law to flee for their lives, for the Lord would destroy their city; but they mocked and obeyed him not, and perished in the flames of fire that were rained down from the clouds upon all the inhabitants except Lot, his wife, and two daughters, who fled unto the mountain. Lot's wife looked back, and became a pillar of salt, for disobeying the command of God, but Lot with his daughters entered into Zoar, and from there into the mountains of Arabia, and dwelt in a cave.

There was no man in these mountains but Lot, that his daughters might be married, and bear seed. Now the daughters of Lot made their father drink wine, and they lay with him, and he perceived it not when they lay down nor when they rose up. Thus were both of the daughters of Lot with child by their father. The first born bore a son, and she called his name Moab, the father of the Moabites, who inhabited the land of Moab. And the younger bore a son, and she called his name Ben-ammi, the father of the Ammonites, who inhabited the land of Ammon. (Gen. xix., Ruth iv., 1 Kings xi. 1.)

MOSES.—The prophet Moses, the son of Amram, a Hebrew of the tribe of Levi, a prophet of Egypt, and a leader of the Israelites. He wrote five Books, viz., Genesis, Exodus, Leviticus, Numbers, and Deuteronomy, [called the Books of Moses,] in the land of Midian and Moab. The Law of God delivered by Moses unto the tribes of Israel. And it came to pass, when Moses had made an end of writing the words of this law in a book, until they were finished, that Moses commanded the Levites, which bore the ark of the covenant of the Lord, saying, take this book of the law, and put it in the side of the ark of the covenant of the Lord your God, that it may be there for a witness against thee. (Deut. xxxi. 24—26.)

And Moses led the Israelites forty years in the wilderness, and died about 1447 years B. C., on mount Hor, in the sight of Canaan. (Gen., Exod., Num. xxvi. 59.)

The prophet Oleodemus, who was also called Malchus, wrote a history of the Jews, in agreement with the history of Moses, their legislator.

JOSHUA.—The prophet Joshua, the son of Nun. The Lord appointed Joshua to succeed Moses, and he should lead the people into the promised land, the land of Canaan, of wine and honey. Joshua led Israel and conquered many nations. Achan, the son of Carmi, the son of Zabdi, the son of Zerah, the son of Judah, of the tribe of Israel. This Ethiopian transgressed against the law of God, written by Moses, and he was stoned to death in the valley of Achor, by the Israelites. (Joshua vii., 2 Chron. xiv. 9.)

Aaron is called the prophet of Moses, (Ex. vii. 1,) because he declared the communications of Moses to the people.

The Book of Judges forms an important part in the history of Israel; and independently of the ample proofs of its authenticity, found in its style, and in its being quoted by o th Old and New Testament writers, the transactions it records are confirmed by traditions current among the heathen. Thus we find the memorial of Gideon's transactions preserved by Sanchoniatho.

The Book of Ruth is thought to have been written by Samuel, and forms a sort of appendix to the book of Judges. The principal scope of the book is to record the genealogy of Christ in David's line. Compare Ruth iv. 18—22, with Matt. i. 5, 6. The adoption of Ruth, a heathen, converted to Judaism.

SAMUEL.—The prophet Samuel, the son of Elkanah, an Ephrathite, the descendant of Egypt. He was dedicated to the Lord from his birth, and brought up in the temple, under the care of Eli, the high priest. Samuel was commanded by the Lord to take a vial of oil and pour it upon the head of Saul, and anoint him king over Israel; and he did so. But Saul was rejected from reigning over Israel for his wickedness; and the Lord said unto Samuel, fill thine horns with oil, and anoint David, the son of that Ephrathite of Bethlehem-judah, whose name was Jesse, king of Israel; and he did so. (1st and 2d Samuel.) Samuel anointed Saul, 1117 B. C.

ESTHER THE QUEEN.—Hadassah, or Esther, the daughter of Abihail, and cousin of Mordecai, the Jew. Ahasuerus, the king, who reigned from India (or Abyssinia) into Ethiopia, over a hundred and seven and twenty provinces in Africa. He loved Esther above all the women in his kingdom, and she obtained grace and favor in his sight more than all the virgins; so he married her, set the royal crown upon her head, and made her Queen about 467 years B. C.

HAMAN.—Haman, an Agagite, of the race of the Amalekites, the descendants of Ham, a great favorite of king Ahasuerus, offended at Mordecai because he falls not down and adores him, as others do, resolves to be revenged of the whole nation of the Jews. Haman obtains an edict from the king that all Jews, without respect to sex or age, upon the 13th day of the month Adar, be put to death in all the provinces of the king's domains. Hereupon, Mordecai, Esther, and all the Jews, humble themselves before the Lord, by fasting and prayer; three days and nights did they neither eat nor drink. Esther entertaining the king and Haman at a banquet, maketh suit for her own life and her people's and accuseth Haman. The king understanding it, she obtained favor of him ; then the king's decree was reversed, and the enemies of the Jews were destroyed by an edict from the king, throughout the provinces of Abyssinia, ancient Ethiopia. (Map of Africa. Book of Esther.)

Job.—Job, a perfect, blameless and holy man, who lived about 1500 years B. C. The words of Job to his friends : " My skin is black upon me." (Job xxx. 30.) Thus he speaks of himself, for he was an Arabian shepherd, who dwelt in the land of Uz,* with seven thousand sheep, three thousand camels, five hundred yoke of oxen, five hundred she asses, and a very great household. There were born unto him seven sons and three daughters. He was a perfect and upright man, and there was a day when his sons and daughters were eating and drinking wine in their eldest brother's house, and behold there came a great wind from the wilderness and smote the four corners of the house, and it fell upon them, and they died. The Sabeans, the descendants of Cush, fell upon Job's servants with the edge of the sword and slew them, and drove away his oxen and asses with them. The Chaldeans [Ethiopians] made out three bands, and fell upon the camels, and carried them away and slew his servants. There were four messengers who came unto Job and told him, saying they only escaped alone to tell him; great was the affliction of Job, but he complained not against God, so the Lord blessed the latter end of Job, more than his beginning, for he had fourteen thousand sheep, and six thousand camels, and a thousand yoke of oxen, and a thousand she asses. He had also seven sons and three daughters.

David.—The Psalm of David constitute the nineteenth in the order of the books of the Old Testament, and their right to a place in the canon has never been disputed. They consist of inspired hymns and songs, meditations and prayers, chiefly of David. It is supposed they were collected into one book by Ezra, though without any regard to chronological order. They are a complete and perfect manual of devotional exercises ; and there is scarcely a grief or disease of the soul, for which there is not in this divine

---

* The Book of Job. Calmet and others make Uz, his country, to have been Arabia Deserta.

book a present comfortable remedy always to be found by those who rightly seek it.

They are sometimes called The Psalter, from the psaltery, a musical instrument used to accompany them when sung.

The titles of the Psalms sometimes have reference to a choice of tunes, or instruments, or contain some directions to persons appointed to set them to music, or to the leaders of the choir, or something peculiar in the subject, season, or style of the composition. The conjectures as to their meaning are various.

This book was once published in five parts, each concluding with a doxology, viz. i.— xli.; xlii.— lxxii.; lxxiii. — lxxxix.; xc.— cvi.: cvii.— cl.; but it is cited as one book, in Luke xx. 42.

The original collection would seem to have comprised psalms i.— lxxii. [See the subscription, Ps. lxxii. 20. And for a chronological arrangement of the Psalms, with the occasion which led to the composition of them, see Life of David, by Am. S. S. Union, pp. 273—275.]

SOLOMON.—The Song of Solomon, the wise man. The words of Solomon, the son of David, to his friends: "I am black, but comely, [graceful] oh ye daughters of Jerusalem. Look not upon me because I am black as the tents of Kedar, as the curtains of Solomon." Here Solomon describes his color to be as beautiful as the tents of Kedar, whose tents were made of black goat's hair; also travellers tell us camel's hair was used for the covering of tents; that appear beautifully to the distant traveller; so was Solomon to Israel, " as the curtains of Solomon." There was a shelter, a cover from injury, or cave, in Arabia, where the shepherds with their flocks at night, fled for protection. So did Israel and all the kings of that country flee unto Solomon for wisdom and knowledge.

Solomon's history is full of interest, and amply given in Scripture. He was the author of several books, besides those in the Bible, viz. 3000 Proverbs, 1005 Songs.

Ecclesiastes, or [as the name signifies,] the Preacher, is the twenty-first in the order of the books of the Old Testament, and was written by Solomon, besides works on botany, and commerce.

We are told of the book of the acts of Solomon, (1 Kings

xi. 41, and elsewhere,) that his acts were written in the book of Nathan, the prophecy of Abijah, and the visions of Iddo against Jeroboam, (2 Chron. ix. 29;) but no other knowledge of these books has come down to us; and perhaps they were chiefly genealogical, and were destroyed with other Jewish writings in the frequent revolutions of the country.

Solomon was anointed king of all Israel, according to Newton, 1019 B. C., and he died in the year of the world 3029.

Isaiah, the prophet, the son of Amos, was an Ethiopian, who prophesied unto Egypt and Ethiopia. As God commanded him, saying, Go and loose the sackcloth from off thy loins, and put off thy shoes from thy feet, walk naked and barefoot, he did so, three years, for a sign and a wonder unto Egypt and Ethiopia, preaching unto his brethren the word of God; but they obeyed not the word of the Lord by the mouth of the prophet; and were led away, young and old, naked and barefoot, into captivity. (Isa. 20.) As they were black, so was he; as he was naked, so were they. Led naked and barefoot, young and old, into captivity! Even unto this day, from Africa, their descendants are led away, by a wicked people, into slavery. But it shall come to pass that the Lord shall set his hand again, the second time, to recover the remnant of his people which shall be left, from Assyria, from Egypt, from Pathros, from Cush, from Shinar or Chaldea, from Elam, from Hamath, and from the Islands of the Sea, the Lord shall set up an ensign for the nations, and shall assemble the outcasts of Israel, and gather together the dispersed of Judah, from the four corners of the earth. (Isa. 11.) Whom the Lord of hosts shall bless, saying, blessed be Egypt, my people, and Assyria, the works of my hands, and Israel mine inheritance. (Isa. 19.) For they shall cry unto the Lord, because of the oppressors, and he shall send them a Savior and a great one, and he shall deliver them. (Isa. xix. 20.) The children of Judah, and the children of Egypt and Ethiopia, ye have sold. Behold, I will raise them out of the place whither ye have sold them, and will return your recompense upon your own heads. (Joel iii. 7.) And they shall take them captive whose

captives they were, and they shall rule over their oppressors. And it shall come to pass in that day that the
Lord shall give thee rest from thy sorrow and from thy
fear, and from the hard bondage wherein thou wast made
to serve. (Isa. xiv. 2.)

Isaiah began to prophesy 760 years B. C.

JEREMIAH, the prophet, was the son Hilkiah. The
words of Jeremiah to his friends; thus saith the prophet,
chap. viii. 21 : " I am black." Here he describes himself
to be black. Lamentation v. 10. " Our skin was black
like an oven;" here he describes his people, "They are
black unto (or on) the ground, mourning because of the
terrible famine." (Jer. xiv.) "Our necks are under
persecution, we labor and have no rest; we have given
the hand to the Egyptians and to the Assyrians, to be
satisfied with bread."

The princes of Judah and Jerusalem assembled at the
king's house, in the scribe's chamber, to counsel against
the prophet Jeremiah. And Jehudi, the son of Netha-
niah, the son of Shelemiah, the son of Cushi, and Deba-
iah the son of Shemiah, and Jedediah the son of Pashur,
and Jucal the son of Shelemiah, and Pashur the son of
Malchiah, and others, heard the words that Jeremiah
had spoken unto all the people, saying, " Thus saith the
Lord, he that remaineth in this city shall die by the
sword, the famine, and the pestilence; but he that goeth
forth to the Chaldeans (Ethiopians) shall live, for he
shall have his life saved; but this city shall surely be
given into the hands of the King of Babylon's army,
which shall take it."

The princes said unto Zedekiah, the King, " We be-
seech thee, let this man, the prophet, be put to death."
The king said, " Behold, he is in your hands." Then
took they Jeremiah, and cast him into the dungeon, or
pit, and they let him down with cord, into the dungeon,
and there was no water, but mire; so Jeremiah sunk in
the mire. And when Ebed-melech, the Ethiopian, one
of the eunuchs which was in the king's house, heard that
they had put Jeremiah in the dungeon, he spake to Zedekiah, the king, saying, My Lord, O king, these men
have done evil in all that they have done to Jeremiah,
the prophet, whom they have cast into the dungeon, and

he is like to die for hunger. Then Zedekiah, the king, commanded Ebed-melech, saying, Take from hence [or this place] thirty men; away with thee, and take up Jeremiah, the prophet, out of the dungeon before he die. And they drew up Jeremiah with cords, up out of the dungeon. (Jer., chap. 37, 38 and 39.) Jeremiah began to prophesy 631 years B. C.

DANIEL.—The prophet Daniel, the son of David, a wise man, who was surnamed Belteshazzar, by the king. He was carried captive to Babylon, in the fourth year of Jehoiakim, by Nebuchadnezzar, king of Babylon. Daniel was enabled by God to interpret a remarkable dream of the king's, in which was made known to him the fate of his kingdom in after-times; and was exalted by him to great power and dignity. Daniel also explained for Belshazzar, the king of Babylon, the grandson of Nebuchadnezzar, the hand-writing legibly traced upon the wall by a miraculous hand: MENE, MENE, TEKEL UPHARSIN; which none of the wise men being able to interpret, thus spake Daniel to the king, saying, "Thy days are numbered; thou art weighed in the balance and found wanting; thy kingdom is given to the Medes, and Persians." Accordingly, that very night, the city was taken by Darius the Mede, [the son of Ahasuerus, an Ethiopian,] and Belshazzar slain. Daniel was highly esteemed by Darius, who made him first president of the kingdom, for his excellent spirit. This exaltation gave great offence to the princes, governors, counsellors, and captains of the realm, who, being unable to make any just accusation against him, prevailed upon the king Darius to sign a rash decree, that whoever should offer any prayer or petition to either God or man, for the space of thirty days, [excepting the king] they should be cast into the den of lions.

The enemies of Daniel observing that as usual he addressed his petitions to God, accused him, and insisted upon his incurring the penalty; but the Almighty preserved his faithful servant, and, to the great joy of the king, Daniel came unhurt out of the lion's den, into which his accusers were cast, and instantly torn to pieces. Daniel prophesied about 555 years B. C.

HOSEA.—The prophet Hosea was the son of Beeri.

The word of the Lord came unto him in the days of Uzziah, Jotham, Ahaz, and Hezekiah, king of Judah, and in the days of Jeroboam, king of Israel; and he prophesied against the people and their cities, for their idolatry, about 785 years B. C.

JOEL.—The prophet Joel was the son of Pethuel. The word of the Lord came to him to prophesy of the judgments of God against the enemies of his people, about 800 years B. C. He prophesied the desolation of Judah by the Chaldeans.

AMOS.—The prophet Amos was the son of the herdman of Tekoa, and father of Isaiah. The word of the Lord came unto him as he followed the flock, and said unto him, "Go and prophesy unto my people Israel ; publish it in the palaces at Ashdod and in the land of Egypt, saying unto them, Prepare to meet thy God, O Israel. Are ye not as children of the Ethiopians unto me, O children of Israel, saith the Lord." Amos prophesied about 787 years B. C.

OBADIAH.—The prophecy of Obadiah is the thirty-first in the order of the books of the Old Testament. It relates to the judgments impending over Edom. Thus saith the Lord God concerning Edom, We have heard a rumor from the Lord, and an ambassador is sent among the heathen. And saviours shall come upon mount Zion to judge the mount of Esau; and the kingdom shall be the Lord's. (Jer. xliv. 7—10, and 14. Obad. i. 9.) These portions of prophecy are supposed to have relation to events still future, the restoration and prosperity of the Jews.

JONAH.—The prophet Jonah, the son of Amittai, lived in the time of Jeroboam, the king of Israel. The word of the Lord came unto him, saying, "Arise, go to Nineveh, that great city, and cry against it, for their wickedness is come up before me." But his heart failed him, and he went down to Joppa, and there found a ship, and took his passage on board, bound to Tarshish. The sailors supposing him to be the occasion of a severe tempest which overtook them, threw him overboard, when he was immediately swallowed by a great fish; and after three days cast upon the shore. He then proceeded upon his mission. The Ninevites repented, and were spared, about 802 years B. C.

MICAH. — Micah, the prophet, who lived in the latter days of Isaiah and Hosea. The Book of Micah is one of the most important prophecies in the Old Testament. The words of the Lord that came to Micah, the Morasthite, a Moor, who prophesied in the reigns of Jotham, Ahaz, and Hezekiah, kings of Judah, against Judah and Jerusalem. "Hear all ye people; hearken, O Earth, and all that therein is, and let the Lord God be witness against you, for the transgression of Jacob, is it not Samaria, and the high places of Judah, are they not Jerusalem; therefore I will make Samaria as an heap of the field," &c. "The inhabitant of Maroth waiteth carefully for good, but evil came down from the Lord unto the gate of Jerusalem." Micah prophesied of the captivity of the Moorish tribes, and their deliverance by Cyrus the Great; also, previous to the coming of the Messiah Christ, the Lord, of the "seed of the woman" to the line of Shem, the descendants of Abraham, the tribe of Judah, and the house of David. Micah sheds further light, by designating the very place of his birth, (ch. v. 2) with other important circumstances of his kingdom and glory.

NAHUM. — The prophet Nahum, the Elkoshite, was a native of Galilee, and prophesied, in the reign of Hezekiah, against Nineveh, about 758 years B. C. "Wo to the bloody city, it is all full of lies and wickedness, the noise of the whip, and the noise of the rattling of the wheels, and of the prancing horses, and of the jumping chariots. The horsemen lifteth up both the bright sword and the glittering spear, and there is a multitude of slain and a great number of carcases, and there is no end of their corpses." "Nineveh is laid waste; who will bemoan her; whence shall I seek comforters for thee." "Ethiopia and Egypt were her strength; Put and Lubim were thy helpers. Yet was she carried away, she went into captivity; her young children also were dashed in pieces at the top of all the streets."

HABAKKUK prophesied about 609 years B. C. He complained of the iniquity of the land, the judgments upon the Chaldeans; he saw the tents of Cushan in affliction.

ZEPHANIAH. — The prophet Zephaniah, an Ethiopian. The word of the Lord came unto Zephaniah the son of

Cushi, the son of Jedediah, the son of Amariah, the son of Hizkiah, in the days of Josiah, the son of Amon, king of Judah. He exhorted the Jews to repentance, and predicted the destruction of cities and nations. "I will utterly consume all things from off the land, saith the Lord. Men and beasts, the fowls of the heaven, and the fish of the sea; I will also stretch out mine hand upon Judah, and upon all the inhabitants of Jerusalem. Howl ye inhabitants of Maktesh, for all the merchant-people are cut down. Gaza shall be forsaken, and Askelon a desolation. They shall drive out Ashdod at the noon-day, and Ekron shall be rooted up. Wo unto the inhabitants of the sea-coast, the nation of the Cherethites, the word of the Lord is against you. O Canaan, the land of the Philistines, I will even destroy thee. Therefore, as I live, saith the Lord of hosts, the God of Israel, surely Moab shall be as Sodom, and the children of Ammon as Gomorrah. Ye Ethiopians, ye shall be slain by the sword. And he will stretch out his hand against the North and destroy Assyria, and will make Nineveh a desolation." Zephaniah prophesied 630 years B. C.

HAGGAI.—Haggai, the first of the three prophets who flourished after the Jewish captivity, in the second year of Darius Hystaspes, about 520 years B. C. He was born in Chaldea, and began his public work of prophesy-ing about seventeen years after the return from Babylon. He, together with Zechariah, excited and encouraged the Jews to finish the temple, assuring them that Messiah should appear in the flesh, teach in the courts of the new temple, and render it more glorious than the first. (Ezra v. i. 2; Haggai i. and ii.; Zech. iv.)

ZECHARIAH.—The prophet Zechariah, who is expressly called the son of Barachiah, (Zech. i. 1,) was one of the minor prophets who returned from Babylon, with Zerub-babel, and began to prophesy about two months after Haggai. He and Haggai zealously encouraged the Jews to rebuild the temple and city, the work on which had been suspended for several years. He wrote the book which bears his name, and has been called the chief of the minor prophets.

IDDO.—Iddo, a prophet of Judah, who seems to have been the historian of his day, and whose record and genealogies are mentioned in Scripture. 2 Chron. ix. 29, and xii. 15. His writings never made a part of the canon of the Old Testament. Indeed, had every thing done or said by holy men, according to the will of God, been inserted in the Bible, it would have made the book too large to be useful. Josephus is of opinion that this was the prophet sent to Jeroboam at Bethel, and slain by a lion on his return. 1 Kings xiii. Whether he was the grandfather of Zechariah, is uncertain. Zech. i. 1. There were several other persons of this name. 1 Chr. xxvii. 21; Ezra viii. 17.

Malachi.—The prophet Malachi wrote his book, which was the end of vision and prophecy, 397 years B. C. He lived in the reign of Artaxerxes, the king of Persia, and prophesied the coming of John the Baptist, under the name of Elias, and was the last of the prophets of the Old Testament. He flourished after the rebuilding of Jerusalem and the temple by Nehemiah, and was cotemporary with Plato, the philosopher; Cimon, the Athenian general; Amyrtæus, king of Egypt, and Darius Nothus, king of Persia. With him, the prophetical office seems to have ceased for nearly 400 years; that is, till Messiah came. About 40 years after the delivery of his prophecy was born Aristotle, the philosopher.

Prophetess.—(Ex. xv. 20.) Prophetess signifies not only the wife of a prophet, (Isa. viii. 3,) but also a woman that has the gift of prophecy. Among these were Miriam, Deborah, Hannah, and Anna.

Miriam led the concert (Ex. xv. 20, 21) that she is reckoned as a prophetess.

Philip, the evangelist, had four daughters, virgins, which did prophesy. (Acts xxi. 9.)

The apostles and prophets: Jesus Christ himself being the chief corner stone. (Eph. ii. 20; Rev. xviii. 20.)

The names of the books that were written on skin-parchment, which are not recorded in the Bible, were written by these prophets, viz:

The Book of Nathan the prophet.

The Book of Gad the seer or prophet. (1 Chr. 29: 29.)

The Book of Jasher. (2 Sam. 1: 18.)

The Book of Shemaiah the prophet.

The Book of Iddo the seer or prophet. (2 Chron. 12: 15, &c.)

There was a prophet for every tribe and nation under heaven, to prophesy to them the word of God.

THE SHEPHERDS OF ANTIQUITY.

ABEL, the son of Adam, was the first shepherd, a keeper of sheep, a righteous man.

The Ethiopian shepherds of Egypt and Chaldea first acquired a knowledge of the stars, while guarding their flocks by night. Their employment led them to contemplate the stars. While their flocks, in the silence of the night, were enjoying sweet repose, the spangled sky would naturally invite the attention of the shepherds. The observation of the heavenly bodies afforded them amusement, and, at the same time, assisted them in travelling in the night. A star guided the shepherds to the manger where our blessed Saviour was born. By the aid of a lively imagination, they distributed the stars into a number of constellations, or companies, of which they gave the names of the animals which they represented; and from them we have received the science of astronomy.

The Canaanites or Phœnicians were shepherds; the Cushans or Samarians were shepherds; the Syrians were shepherds; the inhabitants of Lower Egypt were originally shepherds; and those of Upper Egypt, in the best of the land of Goshen or Rameses, were shepherds. The Arabian shepherds brought to Jehoshaphat presents of their flocks; seven thousand and seven hundred rams, and as many he-goats. The shepherds watched their flocks day and night, and guarded them with their dogs.

"All the flocks of Kedar (Arabians) shall be gathered together; they shall come up with acceptance on mine altar; and I will glorify the house (or people) of my glory." (Isa. 60: 7.)

> While shepherds watched their flocks by night,
> All seated on the ground,
> The Angel of the Lord came down,
> And glory shone around.

The prophecy of Christ, the Good Shepherd. — "And there were in the country of Canaan, called Judea, shepherds abiding in the field, keeping watch over their flocks by night; and lo! the Angel of the Lord came upon them, and the glory of the Lord shone round about them, and they were sore afraid; and the angel said unto them, Fear not, for behold, I bring you good tidings of great joy which shall be to all people, for unto you is born this day, in the city of David, a Savior, which is Christ the Lord. For thus it is written by the prophet in Bethlehem, in the land of Judea, (or Canaan,) art not thou the least among the princes of Judea : for out of thee shall come a Governor that shall rule my people Israel; and this shall be a sign unto you: ye shall find the babe wrapped in swaddling clothes, lying in a manger; and suddenly there was with the angel Gabriel a multitude of the heavenly host (a great number) praising God, and saying, Glory to God in the highest, and on earth, peace, good will toward men. And it came to pass as the angels were gone away from them into heaven, the shepherds said one to another, Let us now go even unto Bethlehem, and see this thing which is come to pass, which the Lord hath made known unto us. And they came with haste, and found Mary and Joseph with the babe lying in a manger; and when they had seen it they made known abroad the saying which was told them concerning the child, and all that heard it wondered at those things which were told them by the shepherds, and the shepherds returned (home) glorifying and praising God in the highest, for all these things that they had heard and seen, as it was told them by the angels, of the birth of the Messiah the Shepherd of Israel, who would lead his people as a flock." (Matthew, Luke, and John.)

"The Lord is my shepherd; I shall not want. He maketh me to lie down in green pastures: he leadeth me beside the still waters. He restoreth my soul: he leadeth me in the paths of righteousness for his name's sake. Yea, though I walk through the valley of the shadow of death, I will fear no evil: for thou art with me; thy rod and thy staff they comfort me. Thou preparest a table before me in the presence of mine enemies: thou anointest my head with oil; my cup runneth over. Surely goodness and mercy shall follow me all the days of my life: and I will dwell in the house of the Lord for ever." (Psalm xxiii.)

24

The Command and Law of God. — " Ye fathers! bring up your children in the nurture and admonition of the Lord." (Eph. vi. 4)

" And if a stranger sojourn with thee in your land, ye shall not vex him. But the stranger that dwelleth with you shall be unto you as one born among you, and thou shalt love him as thyself." (Lev. xix. 23.)

" Children, obey your parents in all things: for this is well pleasing unto the Lord." (Cor. iii. 20.)

" Honor thy father and thy mother." (Ex. xx. 12. Eph. vi. 1.)

" The law is not made for a righteous man, but for the lawless and disobedient, for the ungodly and sinners, for the unholy and profane, for murderers of fathers and murderers of mothers, for man-slayers, for whore-mongers, for them that defile themselves with mankind, for MANSTEALERS." (1 Tim. i. 9, 10.)

" Thou shalt not steal." (Exodus xxi. 16.) " He that stealeth a man and selleth him, or if he be found in his hand, he shall surely be put to death." (Exodus xx. 15.)

" Masters give unto your servants that which is just and equal." (Col. iv. 1.)

" Wo unto you lawyers! for ye have taken away the key of knowledge: ye entered not in yourselves, and them that were entering in ye hindered." (Luke xi. 52.)

" Behold ! the hire of the laborers who have reaped down your fields, which is of you kept back by fraud, crieth: and the cries of them which have reaped are entered into the ears of the Lord of Sabaoth." (Jas. v. 4.)

" Parents, bring up your children to obey and honor you."

It is a truth — you'll find it so —
As the twig is bent, the tree will grow !

THE GENERATION OF JESUS CHRIST.

MARY, the mother of our Lord, was the daughter of Eli, or Joachim, of the family of David.

SHEM, the second son of Noah, was born A. M. 1558, about 98 years before the deluge, from whom descended the Jews, and through them the Messiah. He had five sons, who peopled the finest provinces of the East. The languages of these nations are still called the *Shemitish* languages, including the Hebrew, Chaldee, Syriac, Arabic, Ethiopic, &c.

ABRAM, ABRAHAM, (Gen. xi. 27,) was the son of Terah, and was born at Ur, a city of Chaldea, in the beginning of the kingdom of Nimrod. (Gen. x. 10.) Abram left Ur, and removed to the land of Canaan. He remained at Haran.

SARAH, or SARAI, (Gen. xi. 31,) was the sister-in-law and wife of Abraham.

ISAAC, (Gen. xxi. 3,) the son of Abraham and Sarah, was born A. M. 2108, in Canaan. Isaac, at the age of 40, married Rebekah, the daughter of Bethuel, the sister of Laban, and begat Jacob.

JACOB, the second son of Isaac, and founder of the Jewish nation, was born A. M. 2167, and married Leah, (Gen. xxix. 16,) the daughter of Laban, the Syrian, and begat Judah. He removed to Egypt, with his family, at the request of Joseph, and died, after having dwelt in Goshen 17 years.

AMORITES, (Gen. x. 16,) a Syrian tribe descended from Canaan, and among the most formidable of the tribes. They were of gigantic stature and great courage, (Amos ii. 9,) and inhabited one of the most fertile districts of the country, being bounded on three sides by the rivers Arnon, Jabbok, and Jordan. The Israelites asked permission of their king to travel through their territory.

JUDAH, (Gen. xxix. 35,) the fourth son of Jacob and Leah, was born in Mesopotamia about A. M. 2249, and married the daughter of Shuah, or Shua, the Canaanitess, one of the posterity of Ham. The sons of Judah which were born unto him, were three, by the daughter of Shuah, Er, Onan, and Shelah.

"And Judah took a wife for Er, his first born, whose name was Tamar; and Er marrieth Tamar.

And Er, Judah's first-born, was wicked in the sight of the Lord; and the Lord slew him.

And Judah said unto Onan, Go in unto thy brother's wife and marry her, and raise up seed to thy brother.

And Onan knew that the seed should not be his.

And the thing which he did displeased the Lord;
wherefore he slew him also.

Then said Judah to Tamar, his daughter-in-law, Remain a widow at thy father's house till Shelah my son be
grown; for he said, Lest peradventure he die also, as his
brethren did. And Tamar went and dwelt in her father's
house.

Judah acknowledged to Tamar, and said, She hath
been more righteous than I; because that I gave her not
to Shelah my son.

And Judah begat Phares, or Pharez, of Tamar, his
daughter-in-law. (Gen. xxxviii. 1 Chron. ii.)

And Pares begat Esrom, and Esrom begat Aram, and
Aram begat Aminadab, and Aminadab begat Naasson,
and Naasson begat Salmon, and Salmon begat Booz of
Rachab. (Matt. i.)

RECHAB, RECHABITES. (Jer. xxxv. 16, 18.) The Re-
chabites were a tribe of Kenites, or Midianites. "The
Kenites that came of Hemath, the father of the house of
Rechab." (1 Chron. ii. 55.)

HAMATHITES, the descendants of Ham, are mentioned
as having once occupied the southern border of the province of Canaan. (1 Chron. iv. 40.) They were people
of color.

The word *house* is used to denote a family, (Gen. xii.
17, 1 Tim. v. 8,) a race, or lineage, (Luke ii. 4, 1 Kings
xiii. 8.)

KENITES, (1 Sam. xv. 6.) descended from Jonadab, or
Jehonadab, the son or descendant of Rechab, (2 Kings x.
15,) from which last they derive their name. (Comp. Num.
x. 29—32, with Judges i. 16, and iv. 11.) Jonadab appears
to have been zealous for the pure worship of God, and was
associated with Jehu in the destruction of the idolatrous
house of Ahab. He established a rule for his posterity,
that they should possess neither land nor houses, but should
live in tents, and should drink no wine or strong drink. In
obedience to this rule, the Rechabites continued a separate
but peaceable people, living in tents, and removing from
place to place, as circumstances required. When Judea
was first invaded by Nebuchadnezzar they fled to Jerusalem for safety, where it pleased God, by the prophet Jeremiah, to exhibit them to the wicked inhabitants of Jerusa-

lem, as an example of constancy in their obedience to the mandates of an earthly father. (Jer. xxxv. 2—19.)

Some highly interesting facts are known respecting the present condition of the Rechabites. They still dwell in the mountainous tropical country to the northeast of Medina. They are called Beni Khaibr, sons of Heber; and their land is called Khaibr. They have no intercourse with their brethren, the Jews, who are dispersed over Asia; and are esteemed as false brethren, because they observe not the law . These persons cannot accompany a caravan, because their religion permits them not to travel on the Sabbath; yet their country is so surrounded by deserts, that unless in a caravan, it can neither be entered or left safely.

A late traveller inquired of a Jew about them, and whether they ever came to Jerusalem; and the Jew proved that they came to that city in the time of Jeremiah, by reading ch. xxxv. of his prophecy. This Jew stated that these persons, who were unquestionably the descendants of the Rechabites, are now known to drink no wine; to have neither vineyards, field, nor seed; and to be wandering nomades, dwelling like Arabs in tents; and they have never wanted a man to stand before the Lord, but have maintained strictly and constantly the worship of the true God. (Josh. vi. 17—25.) The faith of Rahab is commended, (Heb. xi. 31; James ii. 25;) and it is supposed she married into a noble family of the tribe of Judah. (Matt. i. 5.) The term Rahab is used poetically as descriptive of Egypt, in Ps. lxxxvii. 4; lxxxix. 10; Isa. li. 9.

Naomi and her husband Elimelech retired to the land of Moab, because of a famine in Canaan, where their two sons married—Chilion, Orpah, and Mahlon, Ruth. After about ten years, Elimelech and his sons died without leaving any children, and Naomi, Ruth's mother-in-law, returned home to the land of Canaan, where Ruth, one of the ancestors of our Saviour, married Boaz, who lived in the days of Gideon, about 300 years before Homer flourished.

Boaz, or Booz, married Ruth, (Ruth i. 4,) a Moabitish woman, and begat Obed, and through Boaz is traced the regular succession of Jewish Kings. (Matt. i. 5.) Boaz was a man of wealth, and of great respectability; and, from his conduct towards his poor kinswoman, Ruth, we suppose him to have been a man of strict integrity, and of an estimable character, as she soon found favor in the eyes of a kinsman, whom she afterwards married, by which event she became the ancestor of the royal family of David. And Obed begat Jesse.

JESSE, (1 Chron. ii 13.) The son of Obed, and father of David. Hence he is called the root of David; and the ancestor of the Messiah. (Isa. xi. 1, 10.) Christ describes himself as the root and the offspring of David, (Rev. v. 5; xxii. 16,) in reference to his two-fold nature; in one of which, he was the Creator and the source of all being, (John i. 3,) and in the other, he was born of a woman of a descendant of the family of David. (Matt. i. 5—16.)

DAVID (1 Sam. xvi. 13,) was the son of Jesse, of the tribe of Judah. He was born in Bethlehem, B. C. 1085, and was, both in his prophetical and regal character, an eminent type of the Messiah. David was a "ruddy" complexion, a dark red. (1 Sam. xvii. 42.) While he was employed as a shepherd in his father's fields, God sent Samuel to Bethlehem, with instructions to anoint David as king of Israel, in the place of Saul, who had incurred the divine displeasure, and was therefore to be deposed. He was then about twenty-two years old. He did not succeed at once to the throne, but first became Saul's armour-bearer. (1 Sam. xvi. 14—23.) Then he retired to Bethlehem, but soon appeared as the champion of the Israelites, against Goliath, a famous giant of the Philistines, whom he slew. (1 Sam. xvii.) This victory greatly advanced his reputation, and secured him a high place in the court and camp of the king. In this situation, he formed a friendship with Jonathan, the king's son, which is memorable for its strength and sacredness. (1 Sam. xviii. 1—5.)

David the king, begat Solomon of Bathsheba, the daughter of Eliam, of her that had been the wife of Uriah the Hittite. (2 Sam. xi. and xii.)

HITTITES, (1 Kings xi. 1.) The posterity of Heth, the second son of Canaan, blacks. (Herodotus.) Their settlements were in the southern part of Judea, near Hebron. (Gen. xxiii. 3.) They are also spoken of as inhabiting the mountains of Judah. (Num. xiii. 29;) and again as in the neighborhood of Bethel. (Judg. i. 26.) Probably they maintained a sort of independence, (1 Kings x. 29; 2 Kings vii. 6;) and they seem to have retained their distinctive name to a late period. (Ezra ix. 1, 2.)

And Solomon begat Rehoboam of Naamah, the daughter of Pharaoh, women of the Moabites, Ammonites, Edomites, Zidonians, and Hittites. The testimony of history proves these nations colored. And Pharaoh's daughter came up out of the city of David unto her house, which Solomon had built for her. (1 Kings vii., ix., and xi.)

REHOBOAM, the son of Solomon by Pharoah's daughter, an Ammonitess woman, ascended the throne B. C. 970, being then 41 years old, and reigned 17 years.

Roboam begat Abia, and Abia begat Asa, and Asa begat Josaphat, and Josaphat begat Joram, and Joram begat Ozias, and Ozias begat Joatham, and Joatham begat Achaz, and Achaz begat Ezekias, and Ezekias begat Manasses, and Manasses beget Amon, and Amon begat Josias, and Josias begat Jechonias and his brethren, about the time they were carried away to Babylon. And after they were brought to Babylon, Jechonias begat Salathiel, and Salathiel begat Zorobabel, and Zorobabel begat Abiud, and Abiud begat Eliakim, and Eliakim begat Azor, and Azor begat Sadoc, and Sadoc begat Achim, and Achim begat Eliud, and Eliud begat Eleazer, and Eleazer begat Matthan, and Matthan begat Jacob, and Jacob begat Joseph, (Matt. i. 16—18,) the husband of Mary, the mother of Jesus, who is called Christ.

THE BIRTH OF CHRIST.

JOHN THE BAPTIST was the son of Elizabeth (cousin to the Virgin Mary) and Zacharias. His birth had been miraculously foretold by the angel Gabriel to Zacharias whilst he was officiating in the temple.

As John was designed to be the forerunner of the Messiah, the angel informed Zacharias, that he should live with the austerity of a Nazarite, and act under the influence of the Holy Spirit of God; that he should call the children of Israel to repentance, and in the power of Elijah should prepare the world for the reception of the Messiah.

The birth of our Savior, called the Lord Jesus Christ, the Messiah, the Mediator, the Redeemer of the world, took upon himself the human form, and was born of the Virgin Mary, December the 25th. According to the best authorities, it may be dated 2188 years from the founding of the kingdom of Egypt, and 846 years from the founding of the city of Carthage.

Christ, the Lord, was born in Bethlehem, in the land of Judea, in the city of David, (Luke ii.) they being of the house and lineage of David, to be registered in the chief city of their tribe, in the land of Canaan, the country now called Judea.

Joseph, of Galilee, was the reputed father of Jesus Christ. (John vi. 42.)

Cyrenius, an Ethiopian governor of Syria, first made the taxing of the people. [Luke ii.]

The treasury of Cæsar Augustus, governor of Syria, being greatly exhausted, he commanded that all his subjects, including the inhabitants of the conquered provinces, should have their names enrolled, in order to be taxed.

And all went to be taxed, every one into his own city. And Joseph also went up from Galilee, out of the city of Nazareth, into Judea, unto the city of David, which is called Bethlehem, (because he was of the house and lineage of David,) to be taxed, with Mary his espoused wife, being great with child.

CHAPTER XIII.

PERIODS, &C.

PERIOD I. will extend from the creation of the world 4004 years B. C. to the deluge 2348 B. C.; to this period we give the name of antedeluvian.

Period II. extends from the deluge 2348 B. C. to the calling of Abraham, 1921 B. C.; this is the period of Confusion of languages.

Period III. From the calling of Abraham, 1921 B. C., to the Founding of Athens, 1556 B. C.; this is the period of the Egyptian bondage.

Period IV. From the Founding of Athens, 1556 B. C., to the Dedication of Solomon's Temple, B. C. 1004; this is the period of the Trojan war.

Period V. From the Dedication of Solomon's Temple, 1004 B. C., to the Founding of Rome, 752 B. C.; this is the period of Homer.

Period VI. From the Founding of Rome, 752 B. C., to the War between the Greeks and Persians, 496 B. C.; this is the period of the Roman kings.

Period VII. From the War between the Greeks and Persians, 496 B. C., to the Birth of Alexander, an Egyptian, 256 B. C.; this is the period of Grecian glory.

Period VIII. From the Birth of Alexander, 356 B. C. to the Destruction of Carthage, 146 B. C.; this is the period of Roman military renown.

Period IX. From the Destruction of Carthage, 146 B. C. to the first campaign of Julius Cæsar, 80 B. C.; this is the period of the Civil War between Marius and Scylla.

Period X. From the First campaign of Julius Cæsar, 80 B. C., to the Nativity of Jesus Christ; and the commencement of the Christian era; this is the period of Roman Literature.

Period XI. From the Nativity of Jesus Christ, to the Reign of Constantine the Great, A. D. 309; this is the period of the Toleration of Christianity, which took place under Constantine.

Period XII. From the Toleration of Christianity, A. D. 306, to the Extinction of the Western empire, A. D. 476; this is the period of the Northern invasions.

Period XIII. From the extinction of the Western empire, A. D. 476, to the flight of Mahomet the Arabian, A. D. 622; this is the period of the Justinian Code; and of the wars of Belisarius.

Period XIV. From the Flight of Mahomet, A. D. 622, to the Crowning of Charlemagne at Rome, A. D. 800; this is the period of the Establishment of the Moors' dominion.

CHRONOLOGICAL TABLE,

FROM A. D. 826 TO 1791.

826 HAROLD, king of Denmark, dethroned by his subjects for being a Christian.

828 Egbert, king of Wessex, unites the Heptarchy, by the name of England.

838 The Scots and Picts have a decisive battle, in which the former prevail, and both kingdoms are united by Kenneth.

867 The Danes began their ravages in England.

896 Alfred the Great, after subduing the Danish invaders, (against whom he fought fifty-six battles by sea and land,) composes his body of laws; divides England into counties, hundreds and tythings; erects county courts, and founds the university of Oxford.

915 The university of Cambridge founded.

991 The figures in Arithmetic are brought into Europe by the Saracens from Arabia.
Letters of the alphabet were hitherto used.

996 Otho III. makes the empire of Germany elective.

999 Boleslaus, the first king of Poland.
    Paper, made of cotton rags, were in use in 1000;
    that of linen rags in 1170; the manufactory intro-
    duced into England, at Dartford, 1588.

1015 Children forbidden, by law, to be sold by their pa-
    rents in England.

1017 Canute, king of Denmark, gets possession of Eng-
    land.

1041 The Saxon line restored under Edward, the Con-
    fessor.

1043 The Turks (a nation of adventurers from Tartary)
    become formidable, and take possession of Persia.

1054 Leo IX., the first pope that kept an army.

1057 Malcolm III., king of Scotland, kills the tyrant,
    Macbeth, at Dunsinane, and marries the princess
    Margaret, sister to Edgar Atheling.

1065 The Turks take Jerusalem from the Saracens.

1066 The battle of Hastings, fought between Harold
    and William, duke of Normandy, in which Harold
    is conquered and slain, after which William be-
    comes king of England.

1070 Musical notes invented.

1076 Justices of Peace first appointed in England.

1080 Doomsday-book began to be compiled, by order of
    William, from a survey of all the estates in Eng-
    land, (and finished in 1086.)
    The Tower of London, built by ditto, to curb his
    English subjects, numbers of whom fly to Scotland,
    (same year.)

1096 The first crusade to the Holy Land was begun un-
    der several Christian princes, to drive the infidels
    from Jerusalem.

1110 Edgar Atheling, the last of the Saxon princes, dies
    in England.

1118 The order of the Knights Templars, instituted to
    defend the sepulchre at Jerusalem, and to protect
    Christian strangers.

1163 London Bridge, consisting of nineteen small arches,
    first built of stone.

1172 Henry II., king of England, (and first of the
    Plantagenets,) takes possession of Ireland; which,
    from that period, has been governed by an English
    viceroy, lord-lieutenant.

1176 England was divided, by Henry, into six circuits, and justice was dispensed by itinerant judges.

1180 Glass windows began to be used in private houses in England.

1182 Pope Alexander III. compelled the kings of England and France to hold the stirrups of his saddle when he mounted his horse.

1165 The great conjunction of the sun, and moon, and all the planets, in Libra, happened in September.

1182 The battle of Ascalon, in Judæa, in which Richard, king of England, defeats Saladin's army, consisting of 300,000 combatants.

1194 *Dieu et mon Droit*, was first used as a motto by Richard, on a victory over the French.

1200 Chimnies were not known in England.
Surnames now began to be used; first among the nobility, (same year.)

1208 London incorporated, and obtained their first charter, for electing their lord-mayor and other magistrates, from king John.

1215 Magna Charta was signed by king John and the barons of England.

1227 The Tartars, a new race of heroes, under Gingis-Kan, emerged from the northern parts of Asia, and overrun all the Saracen empire.

1233 The houses of London, and other cities in England, France and Germany, are still thatched with straw.

1264 According to some writers, the commons of England were not summoned to parliament till now.

1273 The empire of the present Austrian family began in Germany.

1282 Llewellyn, prince of Wales, was defeated and killed by Edward I., who united that principality to England.

1284 Edward II., born at Caernarvon, was the first prince of Wales.

1298 The present Turkish empire begun in Bithynia, under Ottoman.
Tallow candles were so great a luxury, that splinters of wood were used for lights (the same year.)

1302 The mariner's compass was invented, or improved, by Gioia, of Naples.

1307 The beginning of the Swiss Cantons.

1308 The popes were removed to Avignon, in France, for 70 years.

1310 Lincoln's Inn Society established.

1314 The battle of Bannockburn, between Edward II. and Robert Bruce, which established the latter on the throne of Scotland.

Gold first coined in Christendom 1320; ditto in England 1344.

1337 The first comet, whose course is described with an astronomical exactness.

Gunpowder and guns were first invented by Swartz, a monk of Cologne, in 1340; Edward III. had four pieces of cannon, which contributed to gain him the battle of Cressy, in 1346. Bombs and mortars were invented in the same year.

1340 Oil painting was first made use of by John Vaneck.

1344 The first creation of titles by patents, used by Edward III.

The order of the Garter was instituted in England, by Edward III., 1349; altered in 1557, and consists of 26 knights.

1356 The battle of Poictiers, in which king John, of France, and his son were taken prisoners by Edward, the Black Prince.

1357 Coals were first brought to London.

1358 Arms of England and France were first quartered by Edward III.

John Wickliffe, an Englishman, began about 1362 to oppose the errors of the church of Rome with great acuteness and spirit.

1386 A company of linen weavers, from the Netherlands, established in London.

Windsor castle was built by Edward III., (same year.)

1391 Cards invented in France for the king's amusement.

1399 Westminster Abbey built and enlarged. Westminster Hall ditto.

Order of the bath instituted at the coronation of Henry IV., in 1399; renewed in 1725, consisting of 38 knights.

1410 Guildhall, London, was built.
1415 The battle of Agincourt gained over the French,
by Henry V. of England.
     About 1430, Laurentius, of Haerlem, invented the
art of printing, which he practised with separate
wooden types. Guttemburgh afterwards invented
cut metal types; but the art was carried to perfection by Peter Schoeffer, who invented the mode of
casting the types in matrices. Frederic Corsellis
began to print at Oxford, in 1468, with wooden types;
but it was William Caxton who introduced into
England the art of printing with fusile types, in 1474.
1446 The Vatican Library founded at Rome.
     The sea breaks in at Dort, in Holland, and drowns
100,000 people, (the same year.)
1453 Constantinople taken by the Turks, which ended
the eastern empire, 1123 years from its erection by
Constantine the Great, and 2206 years from the
foundation of Rome.
1460 Engraving and etching in copper was invented.
1483 Richard III., king of England, and last of the
Plantagenets, was defeated and killed at the battle of Bosworth, by Henry (Tudor) VII., which
puts an end to the civil wars between the houses of
York and Lancaster, after a contest of 30 years,
and the loss of 100,000 men.
1486 Henry VII. establishes fifty yeomen of the guards,
the first standing army.
1491 William Grocyn publicly teaches the Greek language at Oxford.
1492 America was first discovered by Columbus, a Ge-
noese, in the service of Spain.
1494 Algebra first known in Europe.
1497 The Portuguese first sailed to the East Indies by
the Cape of Good Hope.
     South America was discovered by Vespucius, from
whom it has its name, (the same year.)
1499 North America was discovered for Henry VII., by
Cabot.
1505 Shillings first coined in England.
1509 Gardening introduced into England from the Netherlands, whence vegetables were imported.

1517 Martin Luther began the Reformation.
1520 Henry VIII., for his writings in favor of Popery, receives the title of Defender of the Faith from his Holiness.
1534 The Reformation took place in England, under Henry VIII.
The first English edition of the Bible authorized 1539; the present translation finished 1611.
1539 Cannon began to be used in ships.
Silk stockings first worn by the French king in 1543; first worn in England by queen Elizabeth in 1561.
1561 Pins first used England, (before which time the ladies used skewers.)
1544 Good lands were let in England at one shilling per acre.
1545 The famous council of Trent began and continued 18 years.
1546 First law in England, establishing the interest of money at ten per cent.
1549 Lords lieutenants of counties instituted in England.
1550 Horse guards instituted in England.
1558 Queen Elizabeth began her reign.
1560 The Reformation in Scotland completed by John Knox.
1563 Knives first made in England.
1569 Royal Exchange first built.
1572 The great massacre of Protestants at Paris.
1579 The Dutch shake off the Spanish yoke, and the republic of Holland begun.
English East India Company incorporated in 1579; established 1600.
1580 Sir Francis Drake returns from his voyage round the world, being the first English circumnavigator.
1582 Pope Gregory introduces the new style in Italy; the 6th of October being counted 15.
1583 Tobacco first brought from Virginia into England.
1587 Mary, queen of Scots, was beheaded by order of Elizabeth, after 18 years' imprisonment.
1588 The Spanish Armada destroyed by Drake, and other English admirals.

Coaches were first introduced into England in 1589; hackney act in 1693; increased to 1000 in 1770.

1597 Watches first brought into England from Germany.

1603 Queen Elizabeth (the last of the Tudors) died, and nominated James VI. of Scotland (and first of the Stuarts) as her successor; which united both kingdoms, under the name of Great Britain.

1605 The gunpowder-plot was discovered at Westminster.

1608 Galileo, of Florence, first discovers the satellites about the planet Saturn, by a teslescope then just invented in Holland.

1610 Henry IV. is murdered at Paris, by Ravaillac, a priest.

1611 Baronets first created in England, by James I.

1614 Napier, of Marcheston, in Scotland, invents the logarithms.
Sir Hugh Middleton brings the New River to London, from Ware, (the same year.)

1625 King James dies, and is succeeded by his son, Charles I.
The island of Barbadoes, the first English settlement in the West Indies, was planted, (the same year.

1635 Regular posts established from London to Scotland, Ireland, &c.

1640 The massacre in Ireland, when 40,000 English Protestants were killed.

1642 King Charles impeaches five members, who had opposed his arbitrary measures, which begins the civil war in England.

1643 Excise on beer, ale, &c., first imposed by parliament.

1649 Charles I., (aged 49,) was beheaded at Whitehall, January 30.

1654 Cromwell assumes the protectorship.

1658 Cromwell dies, and is succeeded in the protectorship by his son Richard.

1660 King Charles II. is restored by Monk, commander of the army, after an exile of twelve years in France and Holland.

1662 The Royal Society established at London, by Charles II.

1665 The Plague rages in London, and carries off 68,000 persons.

1666 The great fire of London began September 2, and continued three days, in which were destroyed 13,000 houses, and 400 streets.
Tea first used in England in the same year.

1668 St. James' Park was planted, and made a thoroughfare for public use, by Charles II.

1678 The habeas corpus act passed.

1680 A great comet appeared, and, from its nearness to our earth, alarmed the inhabitants. It continued visible from November 3, to March 9.
William Penn, a quaker, receives a charter for planting Pennsylvania the same year.

1683 India stock sold from 360 to 500 per cent.

1685 Charles II. dies, aged 55, and is succeeded by his brother, James II.

1688 The Revolution in Great Britain, begins November 5. King James abdicates, and retires to France, December 3.

1689 King William and Queen Mary, daughter and son-in-law to James, are proclaimed February 16.
The land-tax passed in England the same year.
The toleration act passed in England the same year.
Several bishops are deprived, for not taking the oath to king William the same year.

1690 The battle of Boyne, gained by William, against James in Ireland.

1692 The English and Dutch fleets, commanded by admiral Russel, defeat the French fleet off La Hoge.

1693 Bayonets at the end of loaded muskets first used by the French, against the confederates in the battle of Turin.
Bank of England established, by king William the same year.
The first public lottery was drawn the same year.

1694 Queen Mary dies at the age of 33, and William reigns alone.

25

Stamp duties were instituted in England the same year.

1696 The peace of Ryswick.

1709 Charles XII., of Sweden, begins his reign.

1701 Prussia erected into a kingdom.

Society for the propagation of the Gospel in foreign parts established the same year.

1702 King William dies, aged 50, and is succeeded by queen Anne, daughter to James II.

1704 Gibraltar taken from the Spaniards by Admiral Rook.

The battle of Blenheim, won by the duke of Marlborough and allies, against the French, the same year. The Court of Exchequer was instituted in England the same year.

1706 The treaty of Union betwixt England and Scotland, signed July 22.

The battle of Ramilies, won by Marlborough and the allies (same year.)

1707 The first British Parliament.

1708 The battle of Oudenarde, won by Marlborough and the allies.

Sardinia erected into a kingdom, and given to the duke of Savoy the same year.

1710 Queen Anne changes the Whig ministry.

The cathedral church of St. Paul, London, rebuilt by Sir Christopher Wren, in 37 years, at one million expense, by a duty on coals, (same year.)

1713 The peace of Utretcht.

1714 Queen Anne dies at the age of fifty, and is succeeded by George I.

Interest reduced to five per cent.

1715 Lewis XIV dies, and is succeeded by his great grandson, Lewis XV.

The rebellion in Scotland begins in September, under the earl of Mar, in favor of the Pretender. The action of Sheriff-muir, and the surrender of Preston, both in November, when the rebels dispersed, (same year.)

1716 The Pretender married to the princess Sobieski, grand daughter of John Sobieski, late king of Poland.

The act passed for septennial parliaments, (the same year.)

1719 The Mississippi scheme at its height in France.

The South Sea scheme in England begun April 7; was at its height at the end of June; and quite sunk about September 29, (the same year.).

1727 King George I. dies, in the 68th year of his age, and is succeeded by his only son, George II.

Inoculation first tried on criminals, with success, (the same year.

1732 Kouli Khan usurped the Persian throne, conquers the Mogul empire, and returns with two hundred and thirty-one millions sterling.

Westminster bridge, consisting of fifteen arches, begun 1738; finished in 1750, at the expense of £389,000, defrayed by parliament.

1739 Letters of marque issued out in Britain, against Spain, July 21, and war declared October 23.

1743 The battle of Dettingen won by the English and allies, in favor of the queen of Hungary.

1744 War declared against France.

Commodore Anson returns from his voyage round the world the same year.

1745 The allies lose the battle of Fontenoy.

1746 The rebellion breaks out in Scotland, 1745; and the Pretender's army defeated by the duke of Cumberland, at Culloden, April 16.

1748 The peace of Aix-la-Chapelle, by which a restitution of all places, taken during the war, was to be made on all sides.

1751 Frederic, Prince of Wales, father to George III., died.

1752 The new style introduced into Great Britain, the 3d of September, being counted the 14th.

1753 The British Museum erected at Montagu-house.

1755 Lisbon destroyed by an earthquake.

1756 146 Englishmen are confined in the black hole at Calcutta, in the East Indies, by order of the Nabob, and 123 found dead next morning.

1757 Damien attempted to assassinate the King of France.

1759 General Wolfe is killed in the battle of Quebec, which is gained by the English.

King George II. dies October 25, 1760, in the 77th year of his age, and is succeeded by his grandson, George III., who, 22d of September, 1761, married the princess Charlotte, of Mecklenburgh Strelitz. Black Friar's bridge, consisting of nine arches, began in 1760; and finished 1770, at the expense of £52,140, to be discharged by a toll. Toll taken off in 1785.

1762 War declared against Spain.

Peter III., emperor of Russia, is desposed, imprisoned and murdered, (same year.)

George Augustus Frederic, prince of Wales, born August 12, (same year.)

1763 The definitive treaty of peace between Great Britain, France, Spain and Portugal, concluded at Paris, February 10, which confirms to Great Britain the extensive provinces of Canada, East and West Florida, and part of Louisiana, in North America; also the islands of Granada, St. Vincent, Dominica, and Tobago, in the West Indies.

1764 The parliament granted £10,000 to Mr. Harrison, for his discovery of the longitude by his time-piece.

1765 An act past annexing the sovereignty of the island of Man to the crown of Great Britain.

1766 A spot or macula of the sun, more than thrice the bigness of our earth, passed the sun's centre April 21.

1771 Dr. Solander and Mr. Banks, in his majesty's ship, the Endeavor, lieutenant Cook, returned from a voyage round the world, having made several important discoveries in the South Seas.

1772 The king of Sweden changes the constitution of that kingdom.

1773 Captain Phipps is sent to explore the North Pole, but, having made eighty-one degrees, is in danger of being locked up by the ice, and his attempt to discover a passage in that quarter proves fruitless.

The Jesuits expelled from the Pope's dominions, (the same year.

The British parliament, having passed an act laying a duty of three pence per pound upon all teas imported into America, the colonies, considering this as a grievance, deny the right of the British parliament to tax them, (the same year.)

Deputies from the several American colonies met at Philadelphia, at the first General Congress, Sept. 5, (the same year.)

First Petition of Congress to the King, November, (the same year.)

1775 The first action happened in America between the king's troops and the provincials at Lexington, April 19.

Articles of confederation and perpetual union between the American provinces, May 20. George Washington appointed a General and Commander in Chief of the American armies June 15. A bloody action at Bunker's Hill, between the royal troops and Americans, June 17.

1776 The town of Boston evacuated by the king's troops March 17.

The Congress declare the American colonies free and independent states July 4. The Americans are driven from Long Island, New York, in August, with great loss; and the city of New York is afterwards taken possession of by the king's troops, (the same year.)

1777 General Howe takes possession of Philadelphia. Lieutenant-general Burgoyne is obliged to surrender his army at Saratoga, New York, by convention, to the American army, under the command of generals Gates and Arnold, October 17.

1778 A treaty of alliance, concluded at Paris, between the French king and the thirteen united American colonies. The earl of Carlisle, William Eden, Esq., and George Johnstone, Esq., arrived at Philadelphia the beginning of June, as commissioners, for restoring peace between Great Britain and America. Philadelphia evacuated by the king's troops June 18. The Congress refuse to treat with the British commissioners, unless the independence of the American colonies were first acknowledged, or the king's fleets and armies withdrawn from America. An engagement was fought off Brest, between the English fleet under the command of admiral Keppel, and the French fleet, under the command of count d'Orvilliers, July 27. St. Lucia taken from the French December 28.

1779 St. Vincent taken from the French. Granada taken by the French July 3.

1780 Admiral Rodney takes twenty-two sail of Spanish ships, January 8. The same admiral also engages a Spanish fleet, under the command of Don Juan de Langara, near Cape St. Vincent, and takes five ships of the line, one more being driven on shore, and another blown up January 16. Charleston, South Carolina, is surrendered to Sir Henry Clinton, May 4. Pensacola, and the whole province of West Florida, surrender to the arms of the king of Spain May 9. The Protestant Association, to the number of 50,000, go up to the House of Commons, with their petition for the repeal of an act passed in favor of the Papists, June 2. That event followed by the most daring riots in the city of London, and in Southwark, for several successive days, in which some Popish chapels were destroyed, together with the prisons of Newgate, the King's Bench, the Fleet, several private houses, &c. These alarming riots were at length suppressed by the interposition of the military, and many of the rioters tried and executed for felony. Five English East Indiamen and fifty English merchant ships, bound for the West Indies, taken by the combined fleets of France and Spain, August 8. Major Andre, adjutant-general to the British army, hanged as a spy, at Tappan, in the province of New York, October 2. A declaration of hostilities were published against Holland Dec. 20.

1781 The Dutch island of St. Eustatia was taken by admiral Rodney and general Vaughan Feb. 3. Retaken by the French Nov. 27. A bloody engagement was fought between an English squadron, under the command of admiral Parker, and a Dutch squadron under the command of admiral Zoutman, off the Dogger Bank, Aug. 5. Earl Cornwallis, with a considerable British army, surrendered prisoners of War to the American and French troops, under the command of General Washington, and count Rochambeau, at Yorktown, in Virginia, Oct. 19.

1782 Trincomalee, on the island of Ceylon, was taken by admiral Hughes, Jan. 11. The island of St. Christopher was taken by the French Feb. 12 — St. Nevis 14 — and Montserat 22. The House of Commons addressed the king against any further prosecution of offensive war on the continent of North America, March 4. Admiral Rodney obtains a signal victory over the French fleet, under the command of count de Grasse, near Dominica, in the West Indies, April 12. The French took and destroyed the forts and settlements in Hudson's Bay, August 24. The Spaniards defeated in their grand attack on Gibraltar, Sept. 13. Treaty concluded betwixt the republic of Holland and the United States of America, Oct. 8. Provisional articles of peace signed at Paris, between the British and the American commissioners, by which the Thirteen United American colonies are acknowledged by his Britannic majesty to be free, sovereign and independent states, Nov. 30.

1783 Preliminary articles of peace between his Britannic majesty and the kings of France and Spain, signed at Varsailles, Jan 20. The order of St. Patrick instituted Feb. 5. Three earthquakes in Calabria Ulterior and Sicily, destroying a great number of towns and inhabitants, Feb. 5th, 7th, and 28th. Armistice betwixt Great Britain and Holland, Feb. 10. Ratification of the definitive treaty of peace between Great Britain, France, Spain and the United States of America, Sept. 3.

1784 The great seal stolen from the lord chancellor's house, Great Ormond Street, March 24. The definitive treaty of peace between Great Britain and Holland, May 24. The memory of Handel was commemorated by a grand jubilee at Westminster Abbey, May 26, (continued annually for decayed musicians, &c.) Mr. Lunardi ascended in a balloon from the Artillery ground, Moorfields, the first attempt of the kind in England, September 15.

1786 Commercial treaty signed between England and France, Sept. 26. £471,000 of 3 per cent. stock transferred to the landgrave of Hesse, for Hessian soldiers lost in the American war, at £30 a man, November 21.

1787 Mr. Burke, at the Bar of the house of lords, in the name of all the commons of Great Britain, impeached Warren Hastings, late governor-general of Bengal, of high crimes and misdemeanors, May 21.

1788 In the early part of October, the first symptoms appeared, of a severe disorder, which affected the reason of George 4th. On the 6th of November they were very alarming, and on the 13th a form of prayer for his recovery was ordered by the privy council.

1789 His majesty was pronounced to be in a state of convalescence, Feb. 17, and on the 26th to be free from complaint. A general thanksgiving for the king's recovery, who attended the service at St. Paul's, with a great procession, April 23. General George Washington proclaimed first President of the United States of America, April 30. Revolution in France — capture of the Bastile — execution of the governor, &c., July 14.

1790 Grand French confederation in the Champ de Mars, July 14.

1791 Dreadful riots in Birmingham, in consequence of some gentlemen meeting to commemorate the French revolution, July 14. Marriage of the duke of York to the princess of Prussia, Sept. 29; remarried in England, Nov. 23. Insurrection in St. Domingo, in November.

CHAPTER XIV.

ST. DOMINGO OR HAYTI.

THE island of HAYTI, a colored republic, formerly called HISPANIOLA, or ST. DOMINGO, lies at the entrance of the Gulph of Mexico, between 17 and 21 degrees north latitude, and between 1 and 8 degrees east longitude; 450 miles long, and 150 broad. The face of the country presents an agreeable variety of hills, vallies, woods, and rivers. It is extremely fertile, producing sugar, coffee, rice, cotton, indigo, tobacco, maize and cassava root. The European cattle are so multiplied here, that they run wild in the woods. The two great chains of mountains, which extend from east to west, and their numerous spurs, give rise to innumerable rivers — repel the violence of the winds — vary the temperature of the air, and multiply the resources of human industry. They abound with excellent timber, and mines of iron, lead, copper, silver, gold, some precious stones, and mercury.

Hispaniola was the cradle of European power in the new world. Columbus landed on it the 6th of December, 1492. The natives called it *Hayti*, signifying high or mountainous land ; it was also called Quisquya, that is, great country, or mother of countries. Others say it had the name of *Bohio*, which means a country full of habitations and villages. Columbus called it Hispaniola, or Little Spain, which name the Spaniards still retain, though *St. Domingo* is the name commonly used by other nations; so called from St. Domingo, the capitol, which was thus named by Columbus, in honor of his father. When the Spaniards discovered the island, there were on it, at least, a million of happy inhabitants, who were reduced to sixty thousand in the short space of fifteen years! It formed five kingdoms, each governed by caciques. The names of these kingdoms were Magua, Marien, Higuay, Maguana and Xaraguay. The Spaniards had possession of the whole island for 120 years, when they were compelled to share it with the French.

The population in the year 1788, whites 27,717 —free people of color 21,808 — slaves 405,528. About the year 1793, a war broke out, after repeated acts of oppression on the part of the whites, which severed the blacks from the French empire. Here opened the first scene of the great drama. This most horrid war has terminated in the expulsion of the whites from all parts of the island, and the establishment of an independent government, administered by a *colored* people. Dessalines, a chief, was proclaimed Emperor of Hayti, under whose virtue, talents, and bravery, the people of this government succeeded in the arduous struggle for liberty.

The events of this period are singularly important, as connected with the establishment and progress of civil and religious liberty and free institutions.

PORT AU PRINCE (except in time of war, when the Governor-General was directed to remove to Cape Francois) was considered as the metropolis of the colony. In 1790 it consisted of about 600 houses, and contained 2,754 white inhabitants. The situation is low and marshy, and the climate, in consequence, very unhealthy. It is surrounded moreover by hills, which command both the town and the harbor; but both the hills and the vallies are abundantly fertile. To the east is situated the noble plain of Cul de Sac, extending from thirty to forty miles in length, by nine in breadth, and it contained one hundred and fifty sugar plantations, most of which were capable of being watered in times of drought, by canals admirably contrived and disposed for that purpose. The circumjacent mountains were at the same time clothed with plantations of coffee, which extended quite to the Spanish settlements.

The population and state of agriculture in the Western Province was as follow: white inhabitants of all ages 12,793, blacks in a state of slavery 192,962; plantations of clayed sugar 135, of muscovado 222. Plantations of coffee 894, of cotton 489, of indigo 1,952, besides 343 smaller settlements.

The Southern Province, extending upwards of sixty leagues from Cape Tiburon, along the southern coast of the island to L'Ance a Pitre, contained twelve parishes, and three chief towns—Les Cayes, Jeremie and Jacmel. It possesses no safe harbors, and its roads are dangerous. The shipping that load at Les Cayes take refuge, during the hurricane season, at La Baye de Flamands.

The population in this department was composed of 6,037 whites, and 76,812 slaves. Its establishments consisted of 38 plantations of white sugar, and 110 of muscovado; 214 coffee plantations, 234 of cotton, 765 of indigo, and 119 smaller settlements.

The quantity of land in cultivation throughout all the parishes was 793,923 carreaux, equal to 2,289,480 English acres, of which about two-thirds were situated in the mountains; and that the reader may have a state of the agriculture at one view, I shall subjoin a summary of the preceding accounts, from whence it will appear that the French colony contained, the beginning of 1790, 431 plantations of clayed sugar, 362 of muscovado, total, 793 plantations of sugar; 2,117 of coffee, 789 of cotton, 3160 of indigo, 54 of cacao or chocolate, 523 smaller settlements, chiefly for raising grain, yams, and other vegetable food; making 8,536 establishments of all kinds throughout the colony.

The population in 1790, on a like summary, appears to have been 30,831 whites of both sexes and all ages, (exclusive of European troops and sea faring people,) and 434,429 slaves. In this account, however, the domestic slaves, and colored mechanics employed in the several towns, are not comprehended. They amounted to about 46,000 which made the number of slaves throughowt the colony 480,000

Of the free people of color, no very accurate account was obtained. Mons. Marbois, the intendant reported them, in 1787, at about 20,000. In 1790, the general opinion fixed them at 24,000.

The exterior appearance of the colony, as I have observed in another place, every where demonstrated great and increasing prosperity. Cultivation was making rapid advances over the country. The towns abound in

warehouses, which were filled with the richest commodi-
ties and productions of Europe, and the harbors were
crowded with shipping. There were freighted in 1787,
for Europe alone, 470 ships, containing 112,253 tons,
and navigated by 11,220 seamen. Many of them were
vessels of very large burden; and the following is an accurate account, from the intendant's return of the general
exports, on an average of the years 1787, 1788 and
1789, viz.

Average Exports, from the French part of St. Domingo,
before the French Revolution.

			Livres.
Clayed sugar	lbs.	58,642,214	41,049,549
Muscovado sugar	"	86,549,829	34,619,912
Coffee	"	71,663,187	71,663,187
Cotton	"	6,698,858	12,397,716
Indigo	hhds.	952,607	8,564,563
Molasses	"	23,061	2,767,320
An inferior sort of rum, called taffia	"	2,600	312,000
Raw hides		6,500	52,000
Tanned ditto.		7,900	118,500

The total value at the ports of shipping, in livres of St. Domingo, was　　171,544,666

being equal to £4,956,780 sterling money of Great Britain; and if all the smuggled articles were added, together with the value of mahogany and other woods, the
whole amount would probably exceed five millions of
pounds sterling.

If this statement be compared by the rule of proportion with the exports from Jamaica, the result will be considerably in favor of St. Domingo, i. e., it will be found
that the planters of Jamaica receive smaller returns from
the labors of their slaves, in proportion to their numbers, than the planters of St. Domingo have received
from theirs. For this difference various causes have
been assigned, and advantages allowed, and qualities ascribed to the French planters, which, in all probability, on full inquiry, had no existence. The true
cause arose, undoubtedly from the superior fertility of

the soil, and the prodigious benefit which resulted to the
French planters from the system of watering their sugar
lands in extreme dry weather. This is an advantage
which nature has denied to the lands in Jamaica, except
in a very few places; but has freely bestowed on many
parts of St. Domingo, and the planters there availed
themselves of it with the happiest success. And such,
in the days of its prosperity, was the French colony of
St. Domingo.

BRIEF SKETCH OF THE LATE AND PASSING REVOLUTION IN HAYTI.

The following account of the recent revolution in the
political state of Hayti is from the letter of JOHN CAND-
LER to the editor of the Anti-Slavery Reporter, dated
" York, (Eng.) 1st of 9th month, 1843." Its compara-
tively peaceful character reflects much credit on the often
calumniated people of that land:—

" It has been long known in Europe that, owing to certain acts of despotic power on the part of General Boyer
the late President of Hayti, a feeling of dissatisfaction
with his government had become very prevalent throughout the republic. The towns of Cayes, and Jeremie and
Jacmel, situate in the south-west of the island, and distant
more than a hundred miles from the capital, had been distinguished throughout the revolutionary and civil war for
a spirit of fierceness and insubordination, which the actors
who lived in these towns, and who took part in favor of
public liberty, denominated patriotism. At Cayes, in particular, there always resided a number of well-educated
individuals, most of them mulattoes, who are ardent in the
cause of their country's freedom. In this town, the acts
of the late Government were likely to be criticised with
unsparing severity, and its arbitrary sway resisted. As
General Boyer increased his attacks on constitutional liberty, instead of growing milder by the check he received,
the citizens of Cayes, in self-defence, and for the sake of
their fellow-countrymen, formed themselves into a political
union, and strove secretly to thwart and oppose his gov-

ernment. Towards the end of last year (1842) they considered themselves strong enough to bid defiance to the ruling powers, and proceeded to publish a manifesto of the wrongs of the nation. These wrongs, as stated by themselves, may be thus enumerated:—

"1st. The neglect under which agriculture was suffering, owing to the oppressive provisions of the rural code. 2d. The almost total neglect by the Government of elementary education. 3d. The imposition of taxes bearing with unequal weight on the laboring classes. 4th. The annihilation of the liberty of the press, the overthrow of the trial by jury and corrupt judges. 5th. The deteriorated state of the currency. 6th. The election of senators by the President's fiat. 7th. The expulsion of deputies from the House of Representatives at the point of the bayonet, and their banishment from Hayti. On all these and sundry other complaints and grievances, the manifesto enlarges with angry eloquence, and calls on the Haytiens as one man to resist the power of the tyrant, and to overthrow his domination.

"The President is charged with the crime of high treason against the republic, a new provincial Government is organized, and General Herard is declared the 'Executive Chief.' A new civil war seemed now inevitable; the patriots had touched a chord which vibrated in almost every heart of the people; they had raised the standard, they had passed the rubicon, and were now resolved that nothing but obstacles evidently insurmountable should stop their onward march to freedom.

"The President became alarmed; he put on a show of determination and vigor, but acted a hurried part; he felt that with all the soldiers of Port au Prince at his back, and his body-guards around him, his position was insecure. He sent for General Inginac, his Secretary of State, and despatched him to Petite Goave, a town on the borders of the disturbed district, with orders to facilitate the expedition of the regular troops, which he was about to send through that town to put down the insurrection. 'I entered on my office,' says General Inginac, 'on the 4th of February, and exerted myself to the utmost; but soon found that all my efforts were useless. I returned to the capital, but before I reached its gates I was met by an order to place myself at the head of a column to arrest the

progress of the insurrection, by opposing force to force.
I might, in advancing, have caused the slaughter of my
fellow-citizens, but I found that even this alternative would
have left me without success. And proceeding some way
on my march, I thought it my duty to fall back upon Gres-
sier, to avoid a sanguinary conflict.' Other commanders
in the interest of Boyer were, however, not so wise; several skirmishes took place between them and the insurgents, and some lives were lost. Three slight battles were
fought. 'The first of them,' says the *Proces Verbal*,
'took place near Pestel on the 21st of February. We
had to deplore the loss of twenty men on both sides. The
second was fought about a league from Jeremie on the 25th
of the same month, and was the most disastrous; the result of the engagement, which lasted two hours and a half,
were twenty men killed on our side, and a hundred and
upwards of the other army, and about an equal number
wounded. The last battle was fought at the gates of Leo-
gane, on the 12th of March. The enemy, in losing fifty
of their own men, did us no harm. The loss of life, trifling as it appears, compared with the dreadful blood-shed-
ding to which the Haytiens had been accustomed in former days, is deeply to be lamented; but the clemency of
the victorious party, and the moderation they evinced, is
much to their honor, and serve clearly to show that Hayti
has an improved and improving people, on whom the les-
sons of the past have not been thrown away. As the insurgents, now patriots, advanced in their career, the troops
sent to oppose them gave way; regiment after regiment
joined their standard; the revolution became successful.
The news of their triumph having reached Port au Prince,
the capital, Boyer, left alone and defenceless, took refuge
in an English vessel which lay in the harbor, and fled to
Jamaica. Gen. Herard, his opponent, took possession of
the city. 'On this day,' says the *Proces Verbal*, 'the
4th of April, 1843, the year 40 of the Independence of
Hayti, and the first of its regeneration, at eight o'clock in
the morning, the Executive Chief chosen by the will of the
sovereign people, Charles Herard the elder, repaired to the
Government house to instal the members of the Provisional
Government.' The Chief, after pronouncing a discourse in
which he recalls to the recollection of his hearers the leading events of Boyer's administration and misgovernment,

and relates the history of the last few months, passed in opposition to his rule, addresses four of his fellow-citizens and calls them to his councils. 'I never consider myself,' says the speaker, 'as any other than a servant of the people, and the instrument of its will. I have but one thought, but one object, the overthrow of tyranny and the regeneration of my country. The destructive part is accomplished; the regenerative part is now to be commenced. Citizens Imbert, Voltaire, Guerrier, and Segretier, in the name of the sovereign people, and in virtue of the power conferred upon me by the act of the 21st of November, 1842, I proclaim you members of the Provisional Government.' The Chief having thus surrendered his power into the hands of the people, the latter re-elected him unanimously to a seat at the Board of Government, and constituted him the colleague of those whom he had just called to office. A salute of a hundred and one guns was fired in honor of the new appointments; a *Te Deum* was chanted with great pomp, and the multitudes who had assembled to witness the ceremony, dispersed. Let us now review the acts, orders and decrees that have emanated from the new Government since its installation, and see how far the people of Hayti are qualified for the task on which they have entered, of regenerating the Commonwealth.

" 1st. The ex-President Boyer is declared guilty of high treason, and all his real and personal estate forfeited to the republic.

" 2d. All the estate, real and personal, of parties accused, (their names are mentioned, including those of General Inginac, Senator Ardouin, and two or three public functionaries,) are sequestered provisionally, subject to the decision of a jury. The farms and sugar-works to be let by auction for a given term, and the money to be paid to the Minister of Finance, out of which, and out of the proceeds of sales, if hereafter such sales should be ordered by a jury, the claim of creditors and those parties are to be satisfied. Sums of money to be immediately allowed for the support of the wives of the accused, and the bringing up of their families.

" 3d. Several new ports are opened to foreign commerce, and all restrictions of commerce hitherto existing between Hayti and the British West India islands are removed, and certain duties on the importation of foreign goods are temporarily reduced.

"4th. The popular committees or clubs of the different communes are directed to send in lists of persons whom they consider to be best qualified to serve the Republic in the various offices of judge, justice of the peace, curate, vicar, church warden, school-master, and prison-keeper, with a view to the selection by the new Government of all public functionaries in different departments of the State.

"5th. The national guard, or militia, under officers of their own choice, to come into the field for drill, twice every week, without receiving pay, till further orders are issued.

"6th. The executive chief is directed forthwith to make a military law of the island, to bring all the inhabitants to acknowledge the provisional government.

"7th. The communes are directed to meet in primary assemblies to choose an electional body of 620 members, which 620 members, when they have verified their powers, are to elect one-fifth of their number to constitute a national assembly, to which shall be entrusted the power of forming a new constitution for Hayti. Every industrious man, of the age of twenty-one years, to be entitled to vote in the primary assemblies.

"The members of the national assembly are appointed by a special decree to meet at Port au Prince, 15th September, to exercise all their high functions of the delegated office. Thus far the Provisional Government has proceeded on its course with great moderation; life is held sacred, property is respected, the liberty of the subject is preserved inviolate. The great questions of reform, such as those which relate to the education of the people, the reduction or annihilation of the standing army, the regulation of import and export duties, and the jurisprudence of the country are left to be determined and acted upon by the Executive Government that may be chosen by the national assembly. It is delightful, however, to observe that the individuals now in power hold sound and enlightened opinions on some of these important topics, and especially on the momentous one of national education. Elementary instruction, they tell us, ' The vehicle of mor-

ality and happiness, the vital principle of nations, is almost
unknown in Hayti; it is there deprived of all support; it
there has no encouragement;' and they call on the people
to remember that, ' it is this absence of education, above
all other causes, that has served to depress Hayti, and to
keep her stationary. Are not our young people the hope
of their country? Is not this the class that must transmit
to posterity the precious deposit, that our predecessors
have confided to us? Brute force never leads to anything
good; we must listen to reason's voice; we must light the
torch of civilization by educating the people.'

"The late contention, though of short duration, has
brought much misery on the country, and has plunged the
new Government into deep financial difficulties. The
fields and provision grounds in the south of the island have
been ransacked by the army for subsistence, and owing to
the absence of the owners, who had left their homes to
join the insurrectionary party, their renewed cultivation
had been neglected; there is, therefore, at this moment, a
great dearth of exportable produce. The trade of the
towns has been paralyzed. Added to these disastrous consequences, arising out of the recent movements, are the
melancholy results of the great earthquake, and of a fire
that occurred soon after in Port au Prince, which, together, have destroyed property to an awful extent. The
Haytiens, however, are not discouraged; they are resolved to exert themselves, and to cultivate the arts of peace;
they believe themselves to be on the way to surmount all
their difficulties; they write and speak like men who have
learned a great deal; they have full reliance on their qual-
ifications for self-government. We trust that the experi-
ment about to be made of forming a new constitution, and
of framing laws suited to the present and future exigencies
of society, may be entered upon with prudence, and carried
through with wisdom. Hayti will then become what her
situation in the Western Archipelago, and her natural ca-
pabilities fit and intend her for, a fruitful land with a prosperous people."

For those who question the industry of the Haytiens,
we subjoin the following tables, showing the exports
from the island of late years. No better proof can be
given of the general industry of a people, than the

amount of their productions, and the record of the custom house is one of the readiest evidences of this, though of course but an approach to a just estimate. It enables, us, however, to compare one nation with another.

It will be remembered that the population of the island is rated from 800,000 to 900,000.

From Essays on the Colonies, &c., by Judge Jeremie.

Exports in 1832 from Hayti.

Coffee,	50,000,000 lbs., valued at $4,400,000	
Cotton,	1,500,000	
Tobacco,	500,000	
Cocoa,	500,000	
Dye Wood,	5,000,000	
Tortoise Shell,	12,000	
Mahogany,	6,000,000 feet.	
Hides,	80,000	

From the American Almanac.

	U. S. Imports from Hayti.	U. S. Exports to Hayti.	Ex. from England to Hayti.	France, in 1833, exported to Hayti, $701,729 Import. from Hayti.
1829	$1,799,809	$ 975,158	Av. annual	
1830	1,507,140	823,178	ex. from	
1831	1,580,578	1,318,375	1830–35,	
1832	2,053,386	1,669,003	$1,759,216	$905,432
1833	1,740,058	1,427,963		
1834	2,113,717	1,436,952		
1835	2,347,556	1,815,812		
1836	1,828,019	1,240,039		
1837	1,440,856	1,011,981		
1838	1,275,762	910,255		
1839	1,377,989	1,122,559		
1840	1,252,824	1,027,214		
1841	1,809,684	1,155,557		

The trade with Germany is considerable, but we have not been able to obtain any statistics of it.—See M'Culloch's Dictionary, Art., Port au Prince.

If we estimate the value of Haytien exports at $6,000,000 annually, as the first table would authorize, it would be $7 per head for the population — which is the ratio in the United States. When we take into account our superior advantages of accumulated capital, education, &c. &c., this result is very honorable to Hayti.

EXTRACTS

From the Translation of the Letter of Abbe Gregoire, Bishop of the Department of Loire and Cher, Deputy of the National Assembly, to the Citizens of Color in the French West Indies, concerning the Decree of the 15th of May, 1791.

'FRIENDS, — You were men; you are now citizens. Reinstated in the fulness of your rights, you will, in future, participate of the sovereignty of the people. The decree which the national assembly has just published respecting you, is not *a favor;* for a favor is *a privilege:* and a privilege to one class of people is an injury to all the rest. They are words which will no longer disgrace the laws of the French.

'In securing to you the exercise of your political rights, we have acquitted ourselves of a debt: not to have paid it, would have been a crime on our part, and a disgrace to the constitution. The legislators of a free nation certainly could not do less for you than our ancient despots have done.

'It is now above a century ago that Louis XIV solemnly acknowledged and proclaimed your rights; but of this sacred inheritance you have been defrauded by pride and avarice, which have gradually increased your burthens, and embittered your existence.

'The regeneration of the French empire opened your hearts to hope, whose cheering influence has alleviated the weight of your miseries: miseries of which the people of Europe had no idea. While the white planters resident among us were loud in their complaints against *ministerial* tyranny, they took especial care to be silent *as to their own.* Not a hint was suggested concerning the complaints of the unhappy people of mixed blood; who, notwithstanding, are their own children. It is *we*, who, at the distance of two thousand leagues from you, have been constrained to protect those children against the neglect, the contempt, the unnatural cruelty of their fathers!

'Citizens, raise once more your humiliated countenances, and, to the dignity of men, associate the courage and nobleness of a free people. The 15th of May, the day in which you recovered your rights, ought to be for ever memorable to you and to your children. This epoch will periodically awaken in you sentiments of gratitude towards the Supreme Being; and may your accents ascend to the vault of heaven, towards which your grateful hands will be extended! At length you have a country. Hereafter you will see nothing above you but the law; while the opportunity of concurring in the framing it, will assure to you that indefeasible right of all mankind, the right of obeying yourselves only.

'You have a country, and it will no longer be a land of exile, where you meet none but tyrants on the one hand, and companions in misfortune on the other; the former distributing, and the latter receiving contempt and outrage. The groans of your afflictions were punished as the clamors of rebellion; and situated between the uplifted poniard and certain death, those unhappy countries were often moistened with your tears, and sometimes stained with your blood.

'You have a country, and happiness will shine on the seat of your nativity. You will now enjoy in peace the fruits of the fields which you have cultivated without compulsion. Then will be filled up that interval, which, placing at an immense distance from each other, the children of the same father, has suppressed the voice of nature, and broke the bands of fraternity asunder. Then will the chaste enjoyments of conjugal union take place of those vile sallies of debauchery, by which the majesty of moral sentiment has been insulted. By what strange perversion of reason can it be deemed disgraceful in a white man to marry a black or mulatto woman, when it is not thought dishonorable in him to be connected with her in the most licentious familiarity!

'You are accused of treating your slaves much worse than the whites: but, alas! so various have been the detractions with which you have been aspersed, that it would be weakness in us to credit the charge. If, however, there be any foundation for what has been advanced on this head, so conduct yourselves in future as to prove it will be a shameful calumny hereafter.

'Your oppressors have heretofore endeavored to hide from their slaves the light of Christianity, because the religion of mildness, equality and liberty, suits not with

such blood thirsty men. May *your* conduct be the reverse
of *theirs*. Universal love is the language of the gospel;
your pastors will make it heard among you. Open your
hearts to receive this divine system of morality. We
have mitigated *your* misfortunes; alleviate, on your part,
those of the unhappy victims of avarice, who moisten
your fields with their sweat, and often with their tears.
Let the existence of your slaves be no longer their tor-
ment; but by your kind treatment of them, expiate the
crimes of Europe!

'Strictly obedient to the laws, teach your children to
respect them. By a careful education, instruct them in
all the duties of morality; so shall you prepare for the
succeeding generation, virtuous citizens, honorable men,
enlightened patriots, and defenders of their country!

'How will their hearts be affected, when, conducting
them to your shores, you direct their looks towards
France, telling them, "Beyond those seas is your parent
country; it is from thence we have received justice, protection, happiness and liberty. There dwell our fellow
citizens, our brethren, and our friends: to them we have
sworn an eternal friendship. Heirs of our sentiments,
and of our affections, may your hearts and your lips repeat our oaths! Live to love them; and, if necessary,
die to defend them."'

THE THREE COLORED REPUBLICS OF GUIANA.

The republics which have been formed many years;
viz., the republic of the Oukas, along the Upper Maroni;
that of the Seramicas, on the Upper Seramica; and that
of the Cotticas, on the Upper Cottica.

These interesting communities are in the interior of
the Dutch province of Surinam, about midway between
the rivers Amazon and Oronoco. These are *maroons*,
[from *cimarron*, a Spanish word, signifying *wild*,] or African slaves who have fled into the woods, and have attained to an acknowledgement of their independence by
the colonists. The two former of these republics have
existed ever since the year 1766; that of the Cotticas

commenced in 1772. A treaty concluded in 1809 by the colonists with these African states, confirmed their independence. From that time, relations of amity and commerce have been established between them and the Hollanders. Africans, who had forcibly emancipated themselves, [as stated in Stedman's History,] triumphed, hand to hand in the fiercest battles. Reinforcements were sent from Holland to the assistance of the colony; but the European troops wasted rapidly away, under a burning sun, led from forest to forest by the valiant and hardy heroes who constantly eluded their pursuit, or gave them battle on the most disadvantageous grounds. The colony was, at times, reduced to the utmost confusion and distress, and after a long and very severe contest, commissioners were sent to treat with these intrepid Africans. They were introduced to a handsome chief named Araby, who received them politely. Taking them by the hand, he desired them to sit down upon the greensward, on each side of him; assuring them that since they came in so good a cause, none dared or wished to molest them. A treaty of peace was agreed upon, on condition that a quantity of fire-arms, ammunition, and various other articles, should be delivered to the African chiefs at the ratification of the treaty, and every year thereafter.

The commissioners received, in return, some very good advice.

Mr. Abercrombie, one of the commissioners, asked for some of the principal officers, as hostages. Araby replied, it would be time enough for that, when the treaty was finally concluded: if they pleased, they might then have his youngest son to be educated in the colony; he would not give the Christians the slightest trouble about his subsistence—he would himself provide for that.

The treaty was ratified, and the stipulated articles sent, with an escort of six hundred men. The commander, who was deemed something of a coward, was in such haste to withdraw, that he delivered the presents without remembering to demand the hostages. But this made no difference with Araby; he did as he had pledged his word; and sent several of his officers to Paramaribo.

The heroes took a solemn oath to observe the treaty,

and required the same of the white commissioners; but they insisted upon having it taken in their own form; alleging that the Christian oath had been so often broken, that they placed no value upon it.

This took place in 1761; and in the same year a treaty was concluded with the Seramicas.

Cotticas, being a third division of Africans, rose and commenced their struggle for liberty and independence; which was definitely acknowledged, as we must infer from Mr. Balbi's excellent geography, in 1809. [D. L. Child.]

The Scale of Complexion; the Color of the Skin.

Between Black and White is a Mulatto:

Between Mulatto and White is a Quaderoon.

Between Quaderoon and White is a Mestizo. (After this the color becomes imperceptible to us.)

Between Mulatto and Black is a Sambo.

Between a Sambo and Black is a Mangroon.

Between a Mangroon and Black the white hue is lost.

The complexion of the Indian tribes :—Reddish, Copper, Brown, Black, and a white mixed hue.

We are all one, and oppressed in this land of boasted Liberty and Freedom. "But wo unto them by whom it cometh."